1936

THE HAUNTED CASTLE

PLATE I

THE CASTLE OF OTRANTO

(From the Italian edition)

THE HAUNTED CASTLE

A STUDY OF THE ELEMENTS
OF ENGLISH ROMANTICISM

BY

EINO RAILO

LONDON
GEORGE ROUTLEDGE & SONS, LTD.
NEW YORK: E. P. DUTTON & CO.
1927

PRINTED IN GREAT BRITAIN BY
THE EDINBURGH PRESS, 9 AND 11 YOUNG STREET, EDINBURGH

TO THE READER

*D*URING *some thirty years, beginning in* 1740 *with Pamela and ending in* 1770 *with Humphrey Clinker, the production of the great English eighteenth-century realists, Richardson, Fielding, and Smollett, flourished and gave to the literary activity of those years their definite atmosphere. In* 1763 *appeared the last collection of Ossian's Songs, in* 1765 *Percy's ballads; in* 1770 *Chatterton and Akenside died, in* 1771 *Gray and in* 1774 *Goldsmith. During the following decades Burns kept the flag of poetry flying, but owing to the dialect form of his diction, did not, at the time, achieve fame; Bowles wrote his sonnets, Cowper his verses and Crabbe attained fame as a poet. Though poetical values were thus created, the decades in question were obviously a time of seeking, marked, indeed, by attempts to escape from the bonds of classicism, without, however, attaining to the full notes of a new harmony —it was a time that may be likened to the trough of a wave that was to endure to the turn of the century, when the greater romantic movement was to begin. This period of literary groping, to be exact, the last four decades of the eighteenth century, is the incubation period of the larger movement; during its course we find, side by side with better-known names, numerous modest writers collecting material for the larger movement, refining it for the use of those to come.*

When, owing to the friendly advice of Professor Yrjö Hirn of the Helsinki University, I was induced to study a typical writer of this period, M. G. Lewis, my attention was drawn in increasing degree not so much to the literary personalities of the period as to the literary material out of which they constructed their works. As authors they seemed unsubstantial beside the material that each of them in his own way collected and refined, eventually for the service of more famous successors. Romanticism is, in general, a field of literature where attention is in great measure directed to the material round which an author weaves his fabric, as it is from this that romantic literature derives a considerable part of its

v

TO THE READER

peculiar character. It is only natural that this observation should apply particularly to the preliminary phases of a romantic movement, when the material in question is being gathered and sifted. An additional reason for interest in this period was the small appreciation usually accorded it in the history of the romantic movement.

The purpose of the present work is consequently to serve as a guide to English horror-romanticism, and by presenting the chief materials used by it and grouping them according to the various themes employed, to show how the main romantic movement that began at the turn of the century and is represented in all shorter expositions of the subject as a suddenly bursting wave, as a kind of spontaneous revolution, is in all essentials the outcome of an organic development with widely spread roots that penetrate deep into the past. It is intended to show how the romanticism that permeates the latter decades of English eighteenth-century literature, referred to above as horror-romanticism, together with the materials round which it is built, derives from and centres around certain definite mental images which in noticeable degree influence the work of the latter movement and continue to exist as influences even after their original form has been forgotten. The book thus resolves itself into a synthesis of the material that gives to English romantic literature its particular individuality, beginning from the earliest practical starting-point.

In this synthesis the first question that arises concerns the stage on which the Romanticists grouped their characters and built up their incidents and emotional atmosphere. From its earliest beginnings English romantic literature displays a rare affection for Nature and the feelings awakened by it; when to this are added the yearnings of the Romanticists for the historical past, a conception is evolved of a romantic stage to which I have given the generic name of The Haunted Castle, and which, in my opinion, forms a synthesis of horror-romantic material. This stage is built up of manifold materials and is thus able to produce the emotions aimed at by romanticist writers. The primary object of this book is to show how and from what sources this conception arose, how it becomes in decisive degree a controlling framework for romantic creative vision, and how, altering and developing with the times, it keeps its significance through all the different phases of the romantic revival and forms even to-day an important constituent in the neo-romantic movement. Within this conception are to be found the other materials of the Romanticists, grouped in their essential features according to origin and nature, beside and around certain leading images.

As a starting-point I have taken Horace Walpole, horror-romanticism conscious of its mission having begun in England with him. The termination of my inquiries has to a great extent been left open and examples have been freely plucked from quite recent authors, as the various themes chosen for study will often be found to point far into the future, and such examples—in no way to be regarded as exhaustive—can cast a good deal of light over the development and significance of the themes affected. It would in any case have been an artificial proceeding to attempt to draw a strict boundary within which eventual conclusions would have to be found, as in reality no such boundary exists. In this way the circumscription of the subject-matter of this book has proved easier in length than in breadth. I must point out that I have not regarded it my duty to deal with every author of the period under discussion; so soon as my purpose, the illumination of material, has in my own view been sufficiently effected, I have ceased to accumulate examples. Any other method would have resulted in un-wieldiness and have given to the book a catalogue-like character from which even in its present state I fear it is not wholly free.

From the general plan of the work I have permitted myself one apparent digression: the biography of Lewis. This was done partly because of the nature of his literary production, and his position as the central author of the horrors-school; partly because of the opportunity which it affords for descriptive glimpses into the time when these authors worked upon the sensibilities of the public. By this step I have hoped to furnish my exposition with something of the background of real life, success in which could hardly fail to endow it with depth and actuality. As a matter of fact I know at present of no biography of Lewis containing the latest facts about his life. And as, finally, its inclusion affords a good opportunity for a closer treatment of contemporary melodrama and German literary influences, it completes in this respect one important side of my exposition.

As regards quotations, mention is not made everywhere of the pages in the original works where they occur; the great number of extracts would have made the addition of figures cumbrous.

CONTENTS

I

THE HAUNTED CASTLE

SECT.   PAGE

1. *The Castle of Otranto* — Horace Walpole, his life and pursuits — Strawberry Hill — *The Mysterious Mother* **1**

2. Clara Reeve, *The Old English Baron* — Ann Radcliffe, *The Castles of Athlin and Dunbayne* — *The Sicilian Romance* — *The Romance of the Forest* — *The Mysteries of Udolpho* **4**

3. Outward circumstances attending the birth of *The Castle of Otranto* : " W. Marshall, Gent." and " Onuphrio Muralto " . . .   **5**

4. Stage setting of the romanticism of terror in the works of Walpole, Reeve and Radcliffe — The Castle of Otranto and its subterranean vaults — The haunted empty house of Reeve — Silhouettes and position of Radcliffe's castles — Their atmosphere of ruins and desolation and romantic twilight — Furniture and the bell — Doors, secret passages and trap-doors — Romantic moonlight, wind and storm — The surrounding landscape and mood expressed by it **7**

5. Time-relation between stage setting and events and " historical " colour — Spenser's fairy castle — Shakespeare's castles and their bells — Actual ancient castles of England **14**

6. Mrs. Radcliffe's atmosphere of desolation — The hermitage of Spenser and Milton — The " mossy tower " — Landscape poets and the followers of Milton — " Crepuscular romanticism " and its materials — Graveyard-poetry — Beauty of mountains — James Beattie's atmosphere of sublimity — Ossian — Radcliffe's landscapes — Salvator Rosa — The idyll created by the landscape poets and Milton — Share of Walpole, Reeve and Radcliffe in the creation of the Haunted Castle — William Beckford's *Vathek* . . .   **19**

7. Tyrants of the Haunted Castle — Manfred, Montoni, etc. — The historical Otranto — Shakespeare's tyrant-types. Relation of Otranto to Hamlet and the sequence Hamlet-Manfred-Montoni — John Moore's *Zeluco* — Richardson's Lovelace — *Vathek* . .   **28**

8. The young hero of romance — Theodore in Otranto, etc. — Secret birth and the mysterious birth-mark — Melancholy — Outward appearance of the romantic hero — Shakespeare's young heroes and mysterious marks of identity **38**

9. The persecuted maiden — Isabella and Matilda — The flight along subterranean vaults and the extinguished lamp — Mrs. Radcliffe's young heroines, their outward appearance and education — Richardson's persecuted maiden — Shakespeare's adventurous maiden — Part played by the maiden's flight in the plot . .   **40**

10. Romantic love — Loves of the young hero and the tyrant — Modes of address and ideas of propriety — Rococo and pastoral coquetry — Relation to plot **44**

11. Mrs. Radcliffe's sentimentality — How much of it was Nature — Emotional poetry and moonlight — Inheritance from " crepuscular romanticism " — Shakespeare's sense of Nature — Melancholy — Shakespeare and Milton — Collins and the followers of Milton .   **46**

ix

CONTENTS

SECT.

PAGE

12. The devout wedded partner—The pious type of monk—Monks in Shakespeare—A sequence of hermits—The monks in *The Mysterious Mother*—Twin-brother of the tyrant-type—Other characters—The old trusted servitor of the Haunted Castle and his relation to the plot—The violent and ambitious woman—Supernumeraries in the landscape 49

13. Minor themes of the romantic movement—Music and musical instruments—Songs and boating—Religious devotion awakened by music—Miniatures, portraits and old manuscripts and their relation to the plot—Old letters—The lamp and the proximity of the ghost 53

14. The sense of excitement—Supernatural events in the Castle of Otranto—Walpole's purpose in making use of these—Clara Reeve's methods—Mrs. Radcliffe's means of raising excitement . 55

15. Renascence of wonder in English literature — Comparison with Shakespearean material, witches, supernatural beings and ghosts—Ghosts in English literature—Richardson, Fielding and Smollett—Percy's *Reliques*—Johnson and the belief in ghosts—Addison and Steele on ghosts—Advent of the miracle in romanticism the renewal of an old motive—Source of Walpole's miracles—Sense of excitement in Radcliffe 63

16. Horrific character of the novel—Methods of Walpole and Clara Reeve in dealing with the supernatural; lack of suggestive power—Mrs. Radcliffe's power of suggestion—Incest—Relation of authors to their own romanticism—Walpole's conception of his work—Degree of romanticism of Radcliffe and Reeve—Refined general stamp of their work—Effect of horror-romanticism on contemporary readers—Gray—Chateaubriand and description of the Castle of Combourg—Altered direction of literary taste 71

17. Public success of horror-romanticism—Satire awakened by it—Jane Austen, Maria Edgeworth, Sarah Green and E. S. Barrett . 76

II

MATTHEW GREGORY LEWIS

1. A survey of English writers in 1794—Matthew Gregory Lewis . . 81

2. His parents and the literary and musical interests of his mother—Childhood and school-days—A ghostly romantic memory from his childhood 82

3. Lewis's relations with his mother—Studies at Oxford and first literary attempts—Sojourn in Paris in 1791 and the theatre of the Revolution—*Le Souterrain*—*Les Victimes Cloîtrées*—Back in Oxford—Literary interests—Studies—Sojourn in Weimar, 1792-93—Description of German society—Literary interests—Return home in 1793 and departure for The Hague in 1794 . . 84

4. Life at The Hague—Lewis's conception of the Dutch and French—Visit to the army—Effect of *The Mysteries of Udolpho* on Lewis—Birth of his *Ambrosio*—Speed of his literary work—His play *The Twins*—Home from The Hague in November, 1794—Appearance of *Ambrosio : or The Monk*, in 1795—Reasons for its vitality and contents of the novel—Ambrosio's tale, Raymond and Agnes and the Bleeding Nun, Lorenzo and Antonia—The motto of the novel—Sources of the novel 88

5. Criticisms of *The Monk*—*The Pursuits of Literature* of Thos. J. Mathias and his sentence—Reaction—A parody of *The Monk*—Seizure of third edition—Lewis eliminates the offending portions—Views of Scott, Byron and Moore—Lewis's nickname . . . 92

CONTENTS

SECT.   PAGE

6. Social position of Lewis after the appearance of the book and his reputation—Complaint by his father—Outward appearance of Lewis—Description of Lewis by Scott and Byron—Byron's *English Bards and Scotch Reviewers*—Company kept by Lewis—He becomes a Member of Parliament—Lewis falls in love—Crazy Jane—*The Bugle* 96

7. Lewis devotes himself to writing—He founds a home—His play *The Castle Spectre* and R. B. Sheridan—Great stage success and its reasons—Good and bad art—*The Castle Spectre* and Drury Lane—Contemporary recollections of the play—Its sources and Lewis's prologue—The lifeguard blacks and Walter Scott—Criticism in one of the reviews 100

8. Translations by Lewis — Schiller's *The Minister*—Kotzebue's *Rolla : or the Peruvian Hero*—Thirteenth Satire of Juvenal—Method of Lewis in translating Schiller's play—*The East Indian*—Lewis's account of his sources and the actual truth—Performance at Drury Lane—Its prologue and epilogue 103

9. Lewis's collection of ballads and Walter Scott—Lewis as the teacher of Scott—The historical significance of their meetings and collaboration—Scott's translations from the German—Friendship between Scott and Lewis 106

10. *Tales of Terror* ballads 1799—*Tales of Wonder*, 1800—Joint edition as *Tales of Wonder* in 1801—The introductory dialogue of the collection—List of Lewis's romantic themes—Unfavourable reception of the book—Moral tone of the ballads 108

11. Lewis as a poetical extemporizer—The play *Adelmorn : or, the Outlaw*, 1801 — Contents and performance — The play *Alfonso, King of Castile*, 1802—Contents, performance and reception—Lewis's own opinion of the play—Parting of Sheridan and Lewis—Relations with the Covent Garden Theatre—His monologue *The Captive*, its performance and reception, 1803—Lewis mistakes his field—His sense of opposition 110

12. Lewis's home at Barnes—His aristocratic social circle—Relations with Moore—With Byron—Byron, Shelley and Lewis at Diodati in 1816—Conversation on ghosts—Shelley's position with regard to the production of Lewis—Frankenstein—Historic significance of the meeting of three Romanticists—Lewis's mother attempts to become an author—Disturbed relations between Lewis and his father—Death of Lewis's father—Inherited wealth . . 114

13. Zschokke's *Abällino—The Bravo of Venice—Rugantino*—Motive of dual personality—Position of Lewis with regard to his German sources —The play *Adelgitha* (1806), its fundamental idea and stage directions—*Feudal Tyrants*, 1806—Benedicte Naubert's novel—*German Horrors*—Popular hawked literature—*Romantic Tales* . 119

14. The play *The Wood Dæmon — One o'Clock*, 1811—Contents and stage directions—Value as a melodrama—The play *Venoni*, its sources, contents and performance—Plays with horses on the stage—Lewis's *Timour*—Its nature of a costume play and great success—*Rich and Poor* 123

15. Lewis's opinion of slavery—What Johnson thought of slavery—Lewis and Wilberforce—First journey to Jamaica, 1815-16—His journal and Coleridge's opinion of it—*Nancy-tales* of the niggers—*The Isle of Devils*—Lewis's work for the benefit of his negroes—His last will and codicil added in Diodati in 1816—Journey to Italy, 1816-17—Second journey to Jamaica, 1817-18—The death of Lewis and his posthumous reputation . . . 127

16. English authors at the time of Lewis's death 132

CONTENTS

III

LATER DEVELOPMENTS OF THE PICTURE OF THE HAUNTED CASTLE

SECT PAGE

1. Refinement of Walpole's style—Lewis's horror-romantic realism—Disintegration of the Walpole-Radcliffe stage setting and the ensuing greater liberty—Development of the Haunted Castle along new paths 135

2. The Haunted Castle as described by Lewis—Above-ground part of the monastery at Madrid—Lindenberg Castle—Stage setting for *The Castle Spectre*—The Haunted Castle in the plays and ballads of Lewis—Subterranean portion of the Madrid monastery—The German *Burgverliess*—Atmosphere of dungeon and graveyards—Nature-setting in Lewis's work—The bell 136

3. Walter Scott and the Haunted Castle—*Lay of the Last Minstrel*—*Marmion—Woodstock—Ivanhoe*—Part played by the Haunted Castle in the historical novel 141

4. The Haunted Castle in the works of S. T. Coleridge—*Christabel, Remorse* and *Zapolja*—Relation of Byron to the horror-romanticist stage—*Hours of Idleness, Lara, The Prisoner of Chillon* and *Mazeppa*—His Oriental romanticism and sense of Nature 147

5. The Haunted Castle in the early works of Shelley—Poems—*Zastrozzi* and *St. Irvyne*, and the influence of Lewis and Radcliffe in these—Shelley's sense of Nature 151

6. C. R. Maturin's stage of horrors—*The Fatal Revenge*—*The Milesian Chief—Bertram—Manuel— Fredolfo—Melmoth the Wanderer*—William Godwin's *Caleb Williams* and *Leon*—Mary Shelley's *Frankenstein* 155

7. Idyllic landscape attached to the Haunted Castle—Robert Southey—*Joan of Arc—Thalaba the Destroyer—Madoc—The Curse of Kehama—Roderick*—Southey and the Haunted Castle—The epilogue to *Joan of Arc*—Odes and Ballads—*Thalaba* and *Madoc*—Southey's Orientalism, a Gothic trait—The bell—Southey's roots in horror-romanticism—Coleridge's sense of Nature and his idyllic landscapes—Horror-romanticism in the early work of Wordsworth—His sense of Nature and progress to real Nature—Traits from the sphere of horror-romanticism in Thomas Moore—*Ballads* and *Lalla Rookh* 157

8. Continuance of the picture of the Haunted Castle in later literature—Lytton's *Zanoni* and Hawthorne's *The Marble Faun*—Poe's *William Wilson, Ligeia, The Assignation, The Oval Portrait, The Masque of Red Death* and *The Fall of the House of Usher* . 167

9. Significance of the Haunted Castle for later literature—The historical novel—Scenes of terror in neo-romantic literature—New machinery for its transformation—The chief themes proceeding from its circle 171

IV

THE CRIMINAL MONK

1. Ambrosio derived from France—The monks of Walpole and Mrs. Radcliffe—Merits of Lewis in making known the type of criminal monk—Monks in German romantic literature—Ambrosio a conglomerate of Laurent in *Les Victimes Cloîtrées* and Montoni in *Udolpho*—Belongs outwardly to the line of Manfred—His station in life and fall, and the effect on the reader of his fate—Fault in the method of temptation 173

CONTENTS

SECT. PAGE

2. Attitude of the reader towards *The Monk*—Later figures who spring up around Ambrosio—Mrs. Radcliffe's *The Italian* (Schedoni)   .   176

3. Other descendants — Maturin's *The Fatal Revenge* (Schemoli) — Morosini in *The Milesian Chief*—Scott's *Ivanhoe* (Brian de Bois-Guilbert)—Landor's trilogy *Andrea of Hungary* (Fra Rupert)   .   180

4. Double life led by Ambrosio and the followers attracted by it— E. T. A. Hoffmann's *Elixir of the Devil* (Medardus)—Victor Hugo's *Notre Dame de Paris* (Claude Frollo)—E. T. A. Hoffmann's *Fräulein von Scudery* (the goldsmith Cardillac)—R. L. Stevenson's *Strange Case of Doctor Jekyll and Mr. Hyde*—*Markheim*—Oscar Wilde's *Picture of Dorian Gray*   183

5. Direct descendants of Ambrosio — Double personality — Poe's *William Wilson* and the *Man of the Crowd*—Double personality and the theory of heredity—Tannhäuser and Medardus   .   .   188

V

THE WANDERING JEW AND THE PROBLEM OF NEVER-ENDING LIFE

1. Chronicles of Roger of Wendover and Matthew of Paris—Biblical foundation of the legend—Connection with Buddha—Connection of the legend of Malkus with that of St. John—Influence of the story of Cain—The names Cartaphilus and Johannes Buttadeus—Book on Ahasuerus from the year 1602—The name Ahasuerus—French variants of the work   191

2. Ahasuerus in seventeenth and eighteenth century literature—Goethe and the Ahasuerus legend — Chr. D. Fr. Schubart's poem *The Wandering Jew*—Schiller's *Geisterseher*—Percy's ballad   .   .   194

3. Ahasuerus in *The Monk*—Agreement with Schubart's conception—His melancholy and outward appearance which links him to the line of Manfred—His glance—Development of the romantic glance   .   197

4. The story of Faust and Ambrosio's bargain for his soul—The story of Theophilus—The story of St. Barsisa—Augustin Calmet's work—*Michel Lovis* and Urban Grandier's bargain for their souls—The Wandering Jew and the tale of Faust—The Philosopher's Stone and the Elixir of Life—Eternal youth and health   .   .   199

5. Godwin's *St. Leon*—*Hermippus Redivivus*—Skill of St. Leon at alchemy. Shelley and the Ahasuerus motive—Queen Mab—The ballads and fragments of a poem on the Wandering Jew—St. Irvyne and Ginotti—Hellas   201

6. Southey's *Curse of Kehama*—Maturin's *Melmoth the Wanderer* .   .   207

7. Lytton's *Zanoni* — The Rosicrucian Brotherhood — Contents of *Zanoni* — The Rosicrucians Zanoni and Mejnour—Zanoni's glance—Mejnour's laboratory—Lytton's tale, *The Haunted House*—Rider Haggard—Pierre Benoit   209

8. The various groups of themes in literature derived from the story of Ahasuerus—Its adaptability to many purposes   215

CONTENTS

VI

THE BYRONIC HERO

SECT.   PAGE

1. The line of Manfred—Hamlet, Eblis, Satan—Lovelace and Zeluco, etc.—Oswald in Wordsworth's play *The Borderers*—Coleridge's Ordonio (in the play *Remorse*)—Schiller's *Karl Moor*—Godwin's Bethlem Gabor—The French development of *Weltschmerz*—English origin of the Byronic hero 219

2. Part of Walter Scott in the creation of the Byronic hero—*Lay of the Last Minstrel*—*Marmion*—*Lady of the Lake*—*Rokeby*—*Lord of the Isles*—*Harold the Dauntless* 222

3. The part of Byron—*The Giaour*—*The Bride of Abydos*—*The Corsair*—*Lara*—*The Siege of Corinth*—*Parisina*—*The Prisoner of Chillon*—*Mazeppa*—*The Island* 232

4. Poems of Byron's youth—*Childe Harold*—*Don Juan*—Byron endows the dark hero with a definite form and character . . . 238

VII

GHOSTS AND DEMONIAC BEINGS

1. Use of ghosts an old-established practice in literature—Belief in ghosts one of the commonest traits in folk-lore—First stage of their use—Moral reason for their introduction—The ghost a *deus ex machina*—Appearance of the ghost as an important factor in romantic circumstances—A new chapter in the history of ghosts—The ghosts of Margaret and Sweet William—Significance of Percy's ghost-ballads—Bürger's *Lenore*—*Alonzo the Brave and Fair Imogene* . 243

2. Sources of the ballad of *Alonzo*—Percy's *Margaret and William*—Bürger's *Lenardo und Blandine* and *Lenore*—Schiller's *Geisterseher*—The highest point of terror in *Alonzo*—The tale of the Bleeding Nun in *The Monk*—Its fundamental motive and highest achievement of terror—Ghost of Antonia's mother—Condition of effectivity in use of ghosts—Part played by Lewis in spook-romanticism 246

3. Traces of Lewis's ghosts—Scott's *Marmion, Lay of the Last Minstrel, Bride of Lammermoor, The Tapestried Chamber, The Betrothed, The Monastery* and *The Abbot*—Spook-romanticism in Scott—Byron's *Oscar of Alva* and *Lara*—Shelley's ballads—*Ghasta, A Ballad* and *The Spectral Horseman* 252

4. Coleridge's *Ancient Mariner*—kinship with ghost-scene introduced at the height of a festival—Relation of Southey to spook-romanticism 255

5. Traces of the ghost-scene in Poe's works—*The Masque of Red Death* and the *Shadow*—Emily Brontë's *Wuthering Heights* . . . 257

6. Lucifer in Lewis's novel—Lucifer's outward appearance at the encounter with Antonia—His beauty—His melancholy—Interest of the Romanticists in the Devil—Materialistic depictments—Mefisto—Examples of use of the Devil 258

7. The assistant of Lucifer, Matilda—Cazotte's *Le Diable Amoureux*—Carathis in *Vathek*—Ambrosio's temptation by a picture—The picture in Schiller's *Geisterseher*—Other dæmons and spirits in Lewis's works 260

8. Coleridge's *Geraldine*—The "Dweller of the Threshold" in Lytton's *Zanoni* and *The Haunted and the Haunters*—Conception of the eyes as a source of terror 262

9. Scott's *Lay of the Last Minstrel*—Southey's part in demoniac witch-women—Poe's *Ligeia* and *Morella*—Villiers de L'Isle-Adam—Hawthorne's *The Marble Faun* 265

CONTENTS

VIII

INCEST AND ROMANTIC EROTICISM

SECT.   PAGE

1. Antiquity of the incest-motive and examples—The Old Testament and the Mosaic Law—Prevalence of incest in folk-poesy—The Kullervo group of runes   267

2. Incest in Shakespeare—Hamlet and the psycho-analytical method—Elizabethan dramatists—Walpole's *Mysterious Mother* and psycho-analysis—Incest a typical romantic theme—Walpole's part in its appearance in his own romantic circle 269

3. Mrs. Radcliffe and the incest-motive—Share of Lewis therein—Incest-motive as a touchstone of the author's character—Scott, Southey and Wordsworth—Walpole, Coleridge, Lewis, Byron and Shelley—*Astarte* or the question of Byron and Mrs. Leigh—Byron's defiant character and love of mystery—*The Bride of Abydos—Cain—Manfred* 272

4. Relation of Shelley to the incest-motive—His parallel loves—Vision of *Alastor—Epipsychidion—Rosalind and Helen—Revolt of Islam—The Cenci* 276

5. The important part played by the incest-motive in English romanticism—Various phases of romantic love—Persecution of young women an erotic trait—Scenes of eroticism and horror painted in solitude psychical symptoms of neurasthenia—Fundamental unhealthiness of romantic eroticism 279

IX

THE YOUNG HERO AND HEROINE AND OTHER CHARACTERS

1. The tyrant the chief hero of romanticism—Importance notwithstanding of the young hero and heroine 283

2. Young heroes of Walpole, Reeve and Radcliffe—Weakness of Lewis's young heroes—Landor's *Gebir* and its high idealism—Southey's young heroes as the representatives of a bright heroic ideal—Southey's character and his view of life—His battle on behalf of his ideal of the young hero— *Vision of Judgment* of Southey and Byron 284

3. Walter Scott's young heroes—Dark and blond type and examples . 286

4. Byron's young hero melts into the Byronic hero—Shelley as the poet of the blond idealistic hero—Outward appearance of his hero—Idealistic, positive and optimistic principles—Spirit of battle—Freedom from self-imposed sense of guilt—Symbolic of a philosophy dreaming of happiness for mankind—Place among Landor's and Southey's young heroes 288

5. The young heroine of Walpole, Reeve and Radcliffe—Radcliffe's dark and blonde type—Lewis's Antonia and Virginia—After Lewis the young heroine becomes a parallel type to the young hero—Landor, Southey and Shelley—Rossetti's *Blessed Damozel*. 290

6. Walter Scott's young heroines—Division into Radcliffe's two types and examples—The real young heroine of Scott—Jeanie Deans in *The Heart of Midlothian*—Development of the young heroine through Scott to a character of actual life 292

7. Byron's young heroines—Love their only idealism—Their poetically described exterior—Romantic sorrow part of their fate—The young heroine an essential factor in Byron's poetry . . . 295

CONTENTS

SECT.   PAGE

8. Great significance of the young hero and heroine—The old butler
   and example of the type—The talkative chambermaid an effective
   foil to the high-flying heroine—Note on the significance of the
   central themes of horror-romanticism for later romanticism   .   296

X

OTHER THEMES

1. Sense of oppression and of innocence in danger—Perpetual flight—
   The creation of an atmosphere of excitement a special aim of
   the horror-romanticists—Crime, and criminals as persecutors of
   innocence—With a redistribution of parts the chief factors ready
   for detective and criminological fiction—Godwin's *Caleb Williams*
   and its significance in the development of the detective story—
   Charles Brockden Brown and his production—Poe's share in
   the detective story—*The Gold Bug* and *The Murders in the Rue
   Morgue*—Conan Doyle an imitator of Poe   299

2. Typical themes for a seafaring nation—Defoe and Swift and their
   nautical romanticism—Smollett as a depicter of sea-life—Coleridge's
   Ancient Mariner the key to exotic tales of sufferings at sea—
   Wordsworth, Scott and Byron as depicters of adventures at sea—
   Poe's *Narrative of Arthur Gordon Pym* and *The Gold Bug*—Stevenson's *Treasure Island*—Lasting favour accorded to nautical
   romanticism   303

3. The romantic portrait in Walpole, Radcliffe and Lewis—Portrait of
   Melmoth—Poe's *Oval Portrait*—Rossetti's *Hand and Soul*,
   Saint Agnes of Intercession and *The Portrait*—Lytton's miniature
   invested with evil powers—Oscar Wilde's *Portrait of Dorian Gray* .   304

4. The young hero's love of solitude—Melancholy, longing for love and
   emotional affinity with nature—Loneliness of the Byronic hero a
   matter of morals, of withdrawal beyond good and evil—Madness
   as a theme of the romantics—Walpole, Radcliffe and Lewis—
   Maturin's *Melmoth*—Shelley's *Julian and Maddalo*—Scott's gently
   insane characters   307

5. The Black Art in horror-romanticism—Its significance in the creation
   of mystery—*Manfred* and *Frankenstein*. The Jung-Stilling theory
   of the three components of the human being—Poe's *Mesmeric
   Revelation* and *The Case of Mr. Waldemar*—The vampire-motive—
   Byron—Somnambulism—Hypnotism and the transmigration of
   souls as literary themes—Poe's *Tale of the Ragged Mountains* .   309

6. Mary Shelley's *Frankenstein* and its political contents—Godwin's
   Enquiry concerning Political Justice—Poverty of principles in
   romanticism before the French Revolution—Effect of revolutionary
   ideals on the mutual groupings of English Romanticists and
   relation of these groups to each other—Short character-sketches of
   the chief authors of English romanticism   311

7. Exoticism—Predilection for the Middle Ages—Distance, a condition
   of romance—The Roman Catholic Faith and the Inquisition—
   Byron's Orientalism—Hellenism of Landor and Shelley — Exoticism denotes in general liberation from the boundaries set by
   familiar surroundings   314

8. Style of *The Castle of Otranto*—Narrative form used by Reeve and
   Radcliffe—Modernity of Lewis's method—Godwin and Maturin as
   narrators and depicters—*Gebir* and the revival of the fantastic
   epos—The romantic drama and melodrama—The ballad and its
   significance as a means of spreading the romantic movement—
   Significance of romanticism as a stage of transit into the new
   century   316

CONTENTS

XI

SUSPENSE AND TERROR

SECT.   PAGE

1. " The romanticism of terror," a name justified by the facts—Its aim —Terror awakening beauty—Preliminary stage of terror—Nature of the state of terror—The creation of suspense a method to achieve terror 319

2. Suspense in various works of the school and its various natures— Outward excitement and that created by suggestion—The latter a condition for the achievement of terror 319

3. Suggestion an essential factor in the creation of an atmosphere of terror—Different horror-romanticist works from the standpoint of suggestion—Suggestive realistic treatment of horrors by Lewis— Other examples—Dim consciousness of the great value of suggestion in earlier work of the same class 321

4. The submersion in an atmosphere of horrors of a mind tuned up by suggestion, effected with the aid of the supernatural and un- natural—Different methods of the horror-romanticists in aiming at an atmosphere of horrors—Later horror-romanticists . . . 323

5. Difference between literary horrors and those of the arena—Primary and secondary colours in literary horrors—Romantic atmosphere, longing, nocturnal Nature inclining the mind to sensitiveness— Harmony of daytime Nature and the idyllic—Stormy night scenes, sublime mountainous landscape and solitude—Suffering and criminality—Tragedy—Terror-awakening beauty . . 325

NOTES 329

LIST OF ILLUSTRATIONS

PLATE   PAGE

I. The Castle of Otranto .   .   .   .   *Frontispiece*

II. The Lone Enthusiast   24

III. A Typical Romantic Landscape by Salvator Rosa   .   26

IV. Theodore and Isabella in the Subterranean Vaults .   40

V. Matthew Gregory Lewis   96

VI. The Temptation of Ambrosio   176

VII. The Wandering Jew   194

VIII. The Spectre of the Slain   244

I

THE HAUNTED CASTLE

I

THE student of English literature is fairly certain at one time or another, as he arrives at the dawning romanticism of the latter half of the eighteenth century, to come across a small and unassuming booklet entitled *The Castle of Otranto*, with the subtitle *A Gothic Story*. The book consists of some hundred and fifty pages and has as frontispiece a fine steel engraving of an elderly man with a wide-awake expression dressed in eighteenth-century costume; underneath is the magnificent name: HORACE WALPOLE, EARL OF ORFORD. Acquaintance with the book in question, which appeared in 1764, is apt to awaken a varied series of visions of romantic authors and of the materials and history of romanticism, for scarcely a handbook of English literature exists in which some kind of mention is not made of it and of its noble author.[1]

Horace Walpole, born in 1717, was the third son of Robert Walpole, the all-powerful minister of George II. After the usual education at Eton and Cambridge, he was despatched on the Grand Tour to France and Italy, in the company of an Eton schoolmate of like age, the poet Thomas Gray. Their travels lasted two years, after which the friends fell out [2] and returned to England. Walpole was now entrusted with certain lucrative posts and for twenty-six years continued a Member of Parliament. At no time had he any particular reputation in political circles, and when his father's career closed in 1742, his private interests began gradually to gain the upper hand. In 1747 he purchased the property called Strawberry Hill, on the Thames, near Windsor, and there he spent the remainder of his life, wholly absorbed in antiquarian, artistic and literary interests. He inherited the title of Earl of Orford in 1791 and in 1797 he died.

We may regard Walpole as a typical upper-class dilettante who, living in comfortable circumstances and lacking a definite aim in life, is tempted to devote his time to congenial minor occupations. Feeling himself attracted by the past, by the " Gothic Era," [3] he commenced to study the period with all the spasmodic enthusiasm of the amateur. The antiquarian spirit has ever been strong in England, and in the middle of the eighteenth century, when the bonds of classicism were beginning to break and attention was concentrating upon those things which seemed to bear the ennobling and inspiring marks of time, it broke out in a laborious studying, describing and collecting of old coins, buildings and ruins, ancient poetry, etc. While better-equipped men were patiently creating a scientific basis for such study, devoted and enthusiastic laymen of the type of Walpole appeared; men of a class whose ludicrous side has been perpetuated by Scott in the person of Mr. Oldbuck, who provided the model for Dickens' immortal chairman of the Pickwick Club. To be sure, the satire hardly applies to Walpole, who was in his way a learned man, and whose keen intelligence and refined, even if sometimes mistaken, feeling for art awaken respect; nevertheless, the " Gothic " rubbish collected at his country-house recalls irresistibly certain of the best and most stupendous finds of Messrs. Oldbuck and Pickwick.[4]

The memory of Walpole as a collector of antiquities has been preserved chiefly through his whim of transforming Strawberry Hill into a kind of Gothic castle. The elements and basic outlines of Gothic architecture had not at that time been fully investigated, and the necessity for a thorough reconstruction on the basis of style remaining unperceived, the methods adopted were simple enough. In the measure permitted by the previous structure of Strawberry Hill and the disposition of its rooms, a round tower was added here, a chapel thrown out there, stained glass placed in the windows, old armour and weapons distributed in suitable spots, a mantelpiece made out of an altar, and so on, the result being fondly imagined to constitute a Gothic castle. Thus twenty years were occupied in these reconstructions and the collection of material, during which time Strawberry Hill acquired fame and became a resort for hosts of the curious. The proprietor and creator of the establishment was apparently well satisfied with the result, for he published an illustrated account of the place.[5]

Though Walpole had thus revealed his imperfect acquaintance with the Gothic style, Strawberry Hill helped considerably in bringing about renewed knowledge and appreciation of the period. It is permissible for us to smile at Walpole's building, but it has its own special significance as an expression of the conception which, despite the many well-preserved real medieval relics in England, Walpole and the majority of his contemporaries had formed for themselves of that almost legendary building, " the haunted castle," the notion of which he attempted to delineate in his new romanticism. The knowledge that this famous stage-setting of the "terror-romanticists" actually existed in two separate versions before its introduction into literature is not without interest.

This is not to be taken as implying that Walpole's Gothic building activities at Strawberry Hill were the sole generators of his desire to experiment with the Gothic spirit in literature. The attention of those days was in general, and in a manner expressly calculated to inspire authors, directed towards the Gothic. Edmund Burke had, in 1756, published his study of our ideas of the sublime and beautiful, thereby formulating the theory which the whole school of terror followed in practice. And in 1762, two years before the appearance of *The Castle of Otranto*, Bishop Hurd (1720-1808) had published those *Letters on Chivalry and Romance*, which furnished powerful support to the brothers Warton in their delight and interest in antiquities. Hurd appears as an enthusiastic advocate of the "Gothic Era," propounding the question whether Gothic romance might not contain something peculiarly suited to the views of a genius and to the ends of poetry, and whether the philosophically inclined people of his own day had not gone too far in making of it a perpetual source of ridicule and contempt. He avers that if Homer had known it, he would have preferred it to the manners of his own times, as he would have found in it more "gallantry" and "superior solemnity of superstitions." The influence of such views and of Hurd's book in drawing attention to Gothicism cannot be overestimated. Among those in whom a desire was born to attempt practical results in this field was Walpole. His knowledge of medieval conditions was, however, fragmentary and inexact. He had his own conception of its architecture, but he knew nothing of its literature, with the exception, perhaps, of a few popular ballads. When speaking of Gothicism in the prologues and epilogues to the *Castle of Otranto* and to his play *The Mysterious Mother*, he instinctively appeals to Shakespeare who was, as we shall see later, an important guide for the author in matters and conceptions connected with Gothicism.

Walpole was a busy letter-writer, his correspondents including the poet Gray and Madame du Deffand, whom he had met in Paris in 1765. As a composer of lively and witty letters he was among the foremost writers of his day. Of the rest of his productions I have mentioned only his play *The Mysterious Mother*, written in 1768, that being the only work except *The Castle of Otranto*, which falls within the sphere of this study.[6]

2

At this point I would like to bring in two women authors who make their appearance in the field opened up by Walpole, for in view of the material used in building up their books they are best dealt with side by side with him.

Clara Reeve (1729-1807) was the daughter of a clergyman and lived a great part of her life at Ipswich. She appears to have belonged to the type of silent literary worker whose days pass in study and the planning of works, but who are unable to discover that special field which would bring them unqualified success. She must be regarded as a learned woman, for she was capable of translating into English *Argenis*, the famous Latin romance of the Scotch writer John Barclay ; her translation was published (the original appeared in 1621) in 1772 as *The Phœnix*. She had thus already reached the age of forty-three when her first work appeared. About the same time her attention was attracted by *The Castle of Otranto*, and in 1777 she published a book, written according to a literary programme of her own, called *The Champion of Virtue : A Gothic Story*. The following year a new edition appeared with the title of *The Old English Baron*, by which name it is now generally known. Since then many further editions have appeared of this work which, among all her rich production, is the only one falling, either in respect of subject or general importance, within the limits of the present study.

The other author in question is Ann Radcliffe, *née* Ward (1764-1823). She is reported to have received a good education and to have possessed opportunities of meeting many well-known people at the home of her relatives. In intellect and outward appearance, indeed, in her whole being, she was a notable and fascinating figure. At the age of twenty-three she married William Radcliffe, editor and proprietor of the

English Chronicle. Ann Radcliffe was born in the July preceding that December which saw the appearance of *The Castle of Otranto.* At twenty-five she set out to continue the literary tradition inaugurated at her birth with *The Castles of Athlin and Dunbayne,* which was published in 1789. Henceforward the number of her works increases rapidly : *The Sicilian Romance* appeared in 1790 and *The Romance of the Forest* in the following year. Her most famous book, *The Mysteries of Udolpho,* was published in 1794. This interval of three years was no long time, remembering the unusual length of the book. *The Italian,* also a lengthy work, appeared in 1797, when the authoress had reached the age of thirty-three. These novels constitute the bulk of her production and will be dealt with in these pages.

In 1795 she published an account of her travels on the Rhine and in the Lake District (*A Journey through Holland,* etc.). After the publication of *The Italian* she remained altogether silent, partly, no doubt, because she had exhausted her own particular field of work. After her death a romance, *Gaston de Blondeville,* saw the light (1826) ; her poems, many of which are contained in her romances, appeared in a separate collection in 1816.⁷

3

During his constant endeavours to provide his " Gothic " castle with relics of medieval days, the idea seems to have occurred to Walpole that it might be worth while trying to affix and to present to others, in the form of fiction, some of the Gothic fancies with which his own brain was teeming. As to the manner in which this idea was realized, he himself has left us, in a letter to a friend, the following original account : " Shall I even confess to you, what was the origin of this romance ? I waked one morning in the beginning of last June from a dream, of which all I could recover was, that I had thought myself in an ancient castle (a very natural dream for a head filled, like mine, with Gothic story) and that, on the uppermost banister of a great staircase, I saw a gigantic hand in armor. In the evening I sat down and began to write, without knowing in the least what I intended to say or relate. The work grew on my hands, and I grew fond of it. Add, that I was very glad to think of anything rather than politics. In short, I was so engrossed with my tale, which I completed in less than two months, that one evening I wrote from the time

I had drank my tea, about six o'clock, till half an hour after one in the morning, when my hands and fingers were so weary, that I could not hold the pen to finish the sentence, but left Matilda and Isabella talking in the middle of a paragraph." [8]

We observe the author's satisfaction with his work and that he was no longer afraid to disclose himself as its writer. In this he was affected by the reception accorded to the book, as until he was assured of its success he had attempted to hide his paternity. The first edition of *The Castle of Otranto*, printed at his own printing-press at Strawberry Hill, had been given out as a translation by " W. Marshall, Gent.," from the Italian manuscript of a certain " Onuphrio Muralto." To mislead the public Walpole had written in his preface : " The following work was found in the library of an ancient Catholic family in the north of England. It was printed at Naples, in the black letter, in the year 1529. How much sooner it was written does not appear. The principal incidents are such as were believed in the darkest ages of christianity ; but the language and conduct have nothing that savours of barbarism. The style is the purest Italian. If the story was written near the time when it is supposed to have happened, it must have been 1095, the era of the first crusade, and 1243, the date of the last, or not long afterwards." . . . The author had obviously been afraid that the strangeness of his book might well, at a time when his father's enemy, Doctor Johnson, and the school of taste represented by him still wielded an unshaken and formidable power over the reading public, expose him to ridicule, and had therefore deemed it prudent to hide for the time being behind a pseudonym and the artifice of a literary hoax. But critics and the public are not so easily misled. Was not the book printed at Strawberry Hill, whose owner's Gothic interests were widely known ? Even the name " Onuphrio Muralto " carried a faint oral suggestion of " Horace Walpole." The preface, too, contained unmistakable hints that the author had had some actual castle in his mind, which could be 'none other than Strawberry Hill. Therefore, when the book was favourably received, Walpole emerged from his hiding-place, in the next edition defending his tactics by explaining that he had mistrusted his own abilities and the novelty of the attempt. He had " resigned his performance to the impartial judgment of the public, determined to let it perish in obscurity, if disapproved ; nor meaning to avow such a trifle, unless better judges should pronounce that he might own it without a blush."[9]

The stage-setting with which before long the student of horror-romanticism is inevitably confronted is a species of old " Gothic " castle, the scene of innumerable horrors, capable of touching the imagination each time we see it, as when the curtain rises on ramparts and towers bathed in the spectral moonlight of *Hamlet*. The reader quickly observes that this " haunted castle " plays an exceedingly important part in these romances ; so important, indeed, that were it eliminated the whole fabric of romance would be bereft of its foundation and would lose its predominant atmosphere. The entire stock-in-trade of horror-romanticism in its oldest and purest form consists, as will be shown in the following pages, chiefly of the properties and staff of this haunted castle, and, as we proceed farther in time, of motives based in the first instance upon these, so that to my mind acquaintance with the materials of horror-romanticism is best begun with this central stage and its appurtenances. Let us start, therefore, with a visit to the ancient vaults of Otranto Castle.[10]

Of the castle's outward appearance no actual description is given, nor does the rapidity of the narrator's style permit him to linger over a calm and detailed picture of his setting. Nevertheless, the reader's imagination is soon aware of a concentration on the limited sphere of what seems to be a medieval castle. We are taken into the castle-yard and the chapel, where a marriage is taking place, and into various rooms, of which one contains the collection of ancestral portraits indispensable to such an edifice. The underground portion is full of bewildering vaulted passages, one of which leads through a secret door to a cave beyond the castle confines, another to the church of St. Nicholas. An awesome silence reigns in these subterranean vaults, a silence broken only by the creak of rusty hinges as a breath of air somewhere sets an old door moving. In their gloomy shade the maiden, flying from the lord of the castle, can at first hardly make out the faintly gleaming object in some hiding-place, and then only with difficulty does she perceive it to be the key to the complicated lock of a secret trap-door. The banqueting-hall is fitted with galleries whence the young heroine can, unseen, regard her lover and where she can fall into the inevitable swoon when the tyrant sentences him to death or lifelong confinement in the deepest dungeon of the darkest tower. Over the gate hangs a brazen horn which one cannot fail to notice, especially as the reason for its being there is hard to understand.

With some few such strokes Walpole conjures up his castle before the reader, avoiding overmuch detail, but continually stimulating the imagination. It must be admitted, too, that he has succeeded, for some hint of strangeness and austere majesty is undoubtedly left in the mind.[11] A good example of what his fantasy of a Gothic castle betokened to him in importance and atmosphere is provided by the opening lines of *The Mysterious Mother*, into which he has effectively condensed the whole of Gothic horror :

> What awful silence !   How these antique towers
> And vacant courts chill the suspended soul,
> Till expectation wears the cast of fear ;
> And fear, half-ready to become devotion,
> Mumbles a kind of mental orison,
> It knows not wherefore.

Clara Reeve did little to develop this side of romanticism, nor does Walpole's manner of introducing the chief setting of his book seem to have appealed to her. One invention, however, she did make, which was to become an essential ingredient of all tales of horror in which the stage is an old castle, or for that matter, any other ruined building. In *The Old English Baron* we find, for the first time, deliberate use of an empty suite of rooms supposed to be haunted. The castle of the deceased Lord Lovel, now occupied by a usurper, Baron Fitz-Owen, is little more than an ordinary country house, reminiscent rather of her own time than of the Middle Ages, yet it has the peculiarity that certain rooms, for some secret reason cautiously hinted at, have long been closed. We are finally informed that it was in these rooms that the castle's rightful owner, Sir Walter Lovel, was murdered and his body hidden. We understand also that it was fear of his ghost which gave them the reputation of being haunted. An old suit of armour is still preserved there, the breastplate of which is stained with blood ; the murdered man's bones are under the floor. The furniture is decayed and falling to pieces ; the fabrics moth-eaten. The portraits of the rightful owners are turned towards the wall, and everywhere we find mournful reminders of past happiness, love and passion. Into the framework supplied by Walpole, Clara Reeve thus pours the first leavening of female sensitivity. Little else of import—no subterranean passages, secret doors or similar contrivances—is to be found in her work.[12]

8

If, as we have seen, Walpole gave us the first features of the haunted castle with the all-important inventions of secret passages and trap-doors, and Clara Reeve added the ghost-ridden suite, it was Ann Radcliffe who developed this series of imaginary pictures to the full. With powerful imagination and inventiveness and a melancholy poetry she enriches the outlines derived from her predecessors to such an extent that in this field there was little else to add.

To begin with, she gives the castle's silhouette in clear, strong lines. It can be situated, for instance, on the coast, on the highest peak of a steep mountain, where wild romantic tempests freely rage. The slopes of the mountain are abrupt and dangerous. The castle is built with Gothic magnificence, its high towers seeming in their proud inaccessible majesty to frown defiance on the whole world ; the entire edifice bears witness to the power of its past owners. These outward traits, which in themselves possess an effectivity not to be denied, continue to expand in the writer's imagination, forming a solemn background for her scenes and plot. Everything in the castle, its towers, vaulted portals, drawbridge, moat, bear the stern impress of ancient might and splendour. As we approach the castle of Udolpho at sunset, in the fading light its stout towers, ramparts and breastworks stand threatening and cruel on the brink of a giddy precipice ; it looms there silent and lonely and sublime, monarch of the whole scene, defying all who dare to penetrate its mysteries.[13]

But as we approach closer, sadness fills our minds. In the magnificent yards the marble is shattered and weatherworn, and around the tall, broken windows grass has grown which now " waves to the lonely gale." Ivy has sprouted from the collapsing ramparts, bearing witness to the decline of former power. Above the gigantic gate, guarded of old by two strong towers, weeds and tall grass have replaced the waving flags, seeming to sigh in the wind over the surrounding desolation. A crenellated wall once joined together the towers, and below them was a stout breastwork ; the walls stretched formerly along the edge of the precipice. Mrs. Radcliffe loves castles which are falling into ruin ; ruins are, to her mind, more romantic than a sound building.[14]

She is not yet, however, satisfied, but brings into the circle of the haunted castle the old abbey and monastery. The broken arches and solitary towers of these rise gloomily impressive among the twilit trees, producing an eerie atmosphere tinged with devotion. A monastery of this description can be a big group of Gothic buildings, whose dismal towers and fear-awakening walls rise proudly, lonely and uncrushed amidst the surrounding dark shadows. The old building in a romantic forest can also be a former monastery, the past magnificence of which awakens in the spectator a respectful, timid feeling of devoutness.

In these descriptions of Mrs. Radcliffe's, all specially long and detailed, the dominant feeling is one of a deep and penetrative romanticism, deliberately adapted to suit every circumstance of the story, all of which serves to show how dear this particular atmosphere was to the author and how prominent a place it occupied in her emotional life. Thus, the site of the monastery is sometimes a kind of natural meadow shadowed by tall, dense trees, as old perhaps as the building itself, which cast over the scene " a romantic gloom." Thick ivy covers the walls, and owls lodge in the deserted towers. Stones and fragments of the walls lie around in the grass, which gently waves in the wind. To describe the melancholy sense of desolation which broods there, the writer has recourse to Ossian's phrase : " The thistle shakes its lonely head, the moss whistles to the wind." [15]

The halls are paved with marble, the rooms are large and high. In some the gloom is enhanced by the panelling, which is almost as dark as darkness itself. In solemn mood we pace the rooms and corridors, whose long perspectives display a simple nobility of line and breathe " a holy calm." The windows are high and arched, furnished with stained glass and often shadowed by ivy ; into the spacious and gloomy chambers they emit a solemn twilight, capable of affecting the heart to the extremity of terror. A melancholy silence dwells in these deserted rooms, the tall arches of which are upborne on pillars of black marble." [16]

The embellishments include portraits and hangings. The castle bell or clock has its own peculiar significance, either as a proclaimer of the time or as the bearer of a message. It is, in a fashion, a personal being that closely follows the fate of the castle and its inhabitants. It is the " great clock " of the castle, the " ancient monitor of the hall below." " Ay, there is the old clock . . . there he is still; the cannons have not silenced him ! . . . There he was roaring out in the hottest fire I have seen this many a day." To the prisoner under sentence of death who in the silence of the night hears it strike One, it is like an echo of the death-chimes. It awakens the persecuted maiden from her dreams, to remind her that hope is vain and that all that is left for her is to sink under her anguish. She hears it strike every quarter, but when it finally strikes One, its note sounds ominous and fatal to her last hope. On her arrival at the castle she had heard the bell and listened to it with a tremulous foreboding in her heart as its voice was borne to her on the wind. Chime followed chime, fading away in " sullen murmur " far behind the mountains, and in her heart the feeling was born that it tolled in the beginning of a fateful period.[17]

An exceedingly important part is played in Mrs. Radcliffe's books by the castle doors and passages, which are extremely numerous, winding and narrow, so that they form a veritable labyrinth. There is a constant moving along dark and winding passages to remote parts of the castle, reached usually through a small, iron-bound door. On our escape from the dungeons we have the luck to find in the thick dust a trap-door—our foot having previously caught in its ring—and summoning all our strength we are enabled at the last moment, as the steps of our pursuers echo nearer, to slip through into the castle vaults. Here we are uncertain at first what direction to take, until again our luck discloses a heavy door in the opposite wall. This leads to a new system of vaulted passages which stretches beyond the castle walls and contains a tunnel leading to a hidden cave somewhere in a forest. A tapestry often hides the little secret door to an inner room; at the other end of this there may be large double doors embellished with heavy carvings. A merciful ray of moonlight, piercing in some marvellous way through a chink in the wall of this vaulted labyrinth, often helps us at critical moments to find such secret roads to salvation.[18]

To this romantic building of the trio Walpole—Reeve—Radcliffe belong important properties, atmospheric and otherwise, well adapted to heighten the desired impression. Walpole uses moonlight. At the very moment when the tyrant is engaged in blackest night on some deed of darkness, the moon emerges from behind a cloud, revealing a ghastly scene that alarms him and prevents the crime from being committed. Through the coloured windows of great churches it shines dim and mysterious, illumining to the tyrant's view the glassy eyes of his dead heir, a witness to the violent and tragic end of his line. The moon is intended to awaken a nocturnal atmosphere fraught with mystery and tinged with fantasy, fear and sadness. It lends an indistinct and weird shape to each feature; it is a theatrical searchlight cast from the wings at suitable moments to reveal to the terror-stricken audience visions and scenes of fear.[19]

We have already mentioned the wind which causes doors to creak on their old rusted hinges. As the draught that wanders through subterranean passages, the wind has a special duty assigned to it by Walpole; it has to sweep through the vaults in sudden gusts and, meeting the persecuted heroine just when her flight is at its climax, to extinguish, to the reader's terror, the lantern or candle in her hand, leaving her in awful, pitch-black darkness. When it whines in the night outside the despairing and trembling maiden's window, the loquacious chamber-maid takes it for a sighing ghost. Lightning is the mighty ally of wind and storm: at a critical moment there comes a sudden burst of thunder that shakes the foundations of the haunted castle, hinting at the existence of avenging, eternal powers.[20]

With regard to the surrounding landscape Walpole, who writes economically, has little to say, but in its way this little is very descriptive. Near to the castle there is a forest and behind this mountains which contain caves running down to the sea. These have formerly been tenanted by hermits, but are now regarded as the haunts of evil spirits. Clara Reeve, too, is sparing of such details. In her book there is hardly any moonlight or thunder, but there, likewise, a busy gust of wind does its duty. When the young hero attempts to open the door of the haunted chamber the wind immediately extinguishes his lamp, leaving him in darkness. And when the rightful heir arrives at the castle of his forefathers, a considerate squall seems to roar out a welcome to him.[21]

Much more frequently does Mrs. Radcliffe use such aids. Her castles and monasteries are set in beautiful, often majestic surroundings. She is fond of guiding her readers through districts devoid of signs of human habitation. Only the roar of distant torrents and the cries of birds of prey break the awesome and oppressive silence. The valleys are surrounded by steep mountain ridges, along the slopes of which waterfalls dash at furious speed, only to calm down at their feet to placid lakes. The dismal twilight of the woods, the soft calm of evening and the tranquil peace and solemnity of the landscape lull the soul to a pleasant sense of oblivion. We fare, to take an example, along a valley, on each side of which are steep mountains. The sublime silence of the scene is disturbed only by the noise of distant waters and the cry of a bird high in the air. Emerging from this austere neighbourhood, an idyllic landscape, in effective contrast to the former, opens out before us. Its hills and valleys are bedecked with fields, vineyards and orchards. The shaded valleys are frequently adorned by a gently meandering stream, or tiny dwellings half-hidden among foliage. Between the trees gleams the tower of a monastery, and a little lake mirrors on its clear surface the surrounding beauty. The green woods and fields, the flowering meadows, the musical tinkle of the translucent brook, the contented humming of insects—all seem to refresh the soul and to make of life a blessing. The rising sun has his part well rehearsed ; over the horizon appears first an inexpressibly glowing line, which swiftly broadens until the sun has emerged in all his majesty, revealing the whole face of nature, brightening every tint of the landscape and scattering glittering beams over the dewy surface of the land. A kind of " sweet romanticism," to use the author's own words, breathes from these landscape paintings executed with so much feeling.[22]

The hum of the wind in empty vaults, in forests, in the grass growing over ruins ; the storm that shrieks around the castle set on a high mountain, and the ghastly moonlight— of all these Mrs. Radcliffe makes exceedingly rich use. Cold autumnal winds howl dismally ; in mighty gusts they play an accompaniment to the lonely hours of night ; in sudden squalls they tear over the waste of sea, dashing the foaming waves with unspeakable force against the rocks. When a deathly silence reigns in the castle halls one can hear an eddy of wind creep, as it were mysteriously, through the corridors. As a low and mournful murmur it comes from the mountains, speeding " hollowly " over the earth, bringing in its train mists and coldness. It extinguishes the heroine's lamp as though trying to crush in her the last beam of hope, until finally every sound is swallowed up in the mighty rumbling of thunder. Bleak clouds, dank and tattered, fly swiftly across the face of the moon, which intermittently casts its pale light between them, revealing a mournful and depressing scene. Sometimes, however, its rays fall with a gentler, more poetic radiance on the waves softly dying on a delightful sandy beach ; sometimes they seem to linger over a dewy landscape in the solemn hush of midnight, and then of the moonlight, the waves and the night a " scene of tranquil beauty " is born.[23]

5

Despite its brevity, the above account will have given an idea of that horror-romanticist stage-setting, the haunted castle, and of a number of closely related features, as they appear in the works of the authors in question. We have seen that Walpole preferred a fairly contemporaneous setting with his action ; in all essentials this applies also to Clara Reeve, though she adds, in the form of the haunted suite, a little of the past history of her castle. As regards the unity of time in these novels, we note their attempts at historical colouring. In the preface to the first edition of his book, Walpole gravely informs us that the story is considered to take place at the time of the Crusades and that he has faithfully tried to depict the customs of those days. In his foreword to a later edition of the same work, Sir Walter Scott goes so far as to state his belief that Walpole's purpose was to create a picture of the domestic life and habits of feudal times such as one can suppose them to have been in reality.[24] However this may be, the historical colouring is so vague and the presence of any real understructure of manners and customs of the period so doubtful, that it is difficult to agree with this critic. In so far as a mere statement that the story belongs to the period in question and the mention of knights, hermits, saints and miracles can be said to provide a " historical " background, we are ready to admit the fact.

In like manner *The Old English Baron* has pretensions to historical colouring. The book tells us, indeed, how the young knights of the Fitz-Owen family departed for France, there to take part in a war in King Henry the Sixth's time, where each of them reaped honour and fame. Mention is even made of a combat in the lists. Yet all the while the characters speak and act pretty much as people did in the eighteenth century, with the same polite expressions and conversational style, so that the period of Henry VI fades far into the background.

In this respect Mrs. Radcliffe has a freer hand, for in her books the Middle Ages are necessary only for the creation of the setting. The action in *The Castles of Athlin and Dunbayne* takes part, it is true, in medieval times, and possibly it was the author's intention to present to us a picture of the Scottish feudal lords and their relations with one another, but *The Sicilian Romance* is laid in the sixteenth century. *The Romance of the Forest* is concerned with the adventures of a French aristocrat in the seventeenth century ; *The Mysteries of*

Udolpho with Italian sixteenth-century *condottieri ;* and the story of *The Italian* is laid in the eighteenth century. As already mentioned, the characters are contemporaneous with their castles only in the first of the above romances, in the others they act amidst the ruins of castles and monasteries. Even of these later periods, however, Mrs. Radcliffe had no great knowledge, and one would be unwilling to admit that her romances have any significance as historical fictions. On the contrary, her characters speak and act fairly alike, whether they are of the Middle Ages or of the eighteenth century. And yet, despite this weakness of " historical " colouring there is reason for us to remember its existence, for, such as it is, it is of considerable importance as a feeler in the direction taken by much future work.

To return to the materials of romanticism, I would point out that of the three authors dealt with, only Mrs. Radcliffe seems to be perfectly clear as to what constitutes the romantic. In every one of her books the setting is some castle, monastery or old building of the type described earlier, which with its antiquity—the frosts of time—awakens in the characters (chiefly the women) who belong to a later age, a series of the most varied " romantic " moods, thus providing the author with plentiful opportunities for depicting such moods and, incidentally, of enjoying them herself. What in Walpole's compact book are merely hints, which Clara Reeve did not appreciably develop further, are expanded in Mrs. Radcliffe's work to a breadth and variety which seem to exhaust the subject, a fact of extreme interest to the student of literary material.

But before continuing with this side of the subject, let us pause to deal with a question that naturally crops up at this point. Was the haunted castle, as depicted by Walpole and his followers, an original invention ? As I shall frequently have cause to refer to parallel passages in Elizabethan romantic literature, Shakespeare in particular, I must here point out that the object of these passages is rather to provide analogies and historical perspective than to make it appear that Shakespeare is the actual *source* of Walpole's inventions in each separate case. For the latter argument there are no proofs ; yet that does not alter the fact that it is natural and legitimate to compare the materials used by the two and, from the point of view of historical development, illuminating.

Looking backward, therefore, to Elizabethan times, to the romanticism of Spenser and Shakespeare, one observes that while Spenser depicted in his *Faerie Queene* that epic brimming with wandering knights, enchanted castles and caves of terror, in a word, with the whole boundless wealth of the spirit of adventure and faerie—magic castles in keeping with his species of poetry, Shakespeare brings on to the stage the haunted castle in approximately the same shape and under the same illumination as the later romanticists. Spenser's castle is

> A stately Pallace built of squared bricke,
> Which cunningly was without morter laid,
> Whose wals were high, but nothing strong nor thick
> And golden foile all over them displaid,
> That purest skye with brightnesse they dismaid :
> High lifted up were many loftie towres,
> And goodly galleries far over laid,
> Full of faire windowes and delightful bowres :
> And on the top a Diall told the timely houres.

Thus he describes the allegorical dwelling that could perhaps be interpreted as representing the abode of earthly lusts and sin. When Arthur, after taking the wandering Una under his protection, sets out to seek the Red Cross Knight, they arrive finally " nigh to a castle builded strong and hye," at the gates of which he blows that famous blast on the " horne of the bugle small " (that still echoes in every romantic tale of chivalry), defiantly demanding admission. After his victory, when he searches the castle for the imprisoned knight, he can find no one ; not a voice answers to his shout, " there raignd a solemne silence over all." The rooms gleamed with gold, but the floors were besmirched with innocent blood ; Christians had been sacrificed on the altar, whose blessed souls were constantly crying to the Lord for revenge. From his dungeon the Red Cross Knight answers to Arthur's call in " an hollow, dreary, murmuring voyce." Breaking open the door, Arthur feels no floor beneath his feet, only a deep chasm " as darke as hell," where the victim is kept. The gloomiest scenes of terror in the robbers' castles of the romanticists cannot excel in realism these paintings of Spenser's glowing imagination, of which a fine example is also the description of a cave of terror :

> Ere long they come where that same wicked wight
> His dwelling has, low in an hollow cave,
> For underneath a craggy cliff ypight,
> Darke, dolefull, dreary, like a greedy grave,
> That still for carrion carcases doth crave :
> On top whereof ay dwelt the ghastly Owle,
> Shrieking his balefull note, which ever drave
> Far from that haunt all other chearefull fowle ;
> And all about it wandring ghostes did wayle and howle.[25]

Despite the allegorical nature of Spenser's poetry, the romantic materials contained in it are thus, both in substance and in general hue, so like those of later romanticism that *The Faerie Queene* can be regarded as an important source of such material. When, in addition, we remember the honour shown him even in the strictest classical times, his special position as a favourite of the elfs of poetry, one whose fairy epic could be admired and looked upon as an astounding pheno-menon, and also that one of the most significant symptoms of the dawn of romanticism was a revival of interest in Spenser's poetry, it becomes obvious that a clear and natural connection exists between his fairy castles and the similar conceptions of the later romanticists.[26]

Shakespeare's castles are more directly related to the haunted castles of the later period, although, appearing as they do in stage plays, they demand more of the reader's intuition and imagination than the direct pictures of romances. Northam Castle, in which Prince Arthur is kept a prisoner, awakens a dreary impression. With regard to the Tower we learn that it is " Julius Cæsar's ill-erected tower " and has a " flint bosom."[27] In the spectator's imagination the Tower becomes a well of evil deeds and the source of the gloomy prison atmosphere accompanying them ; it is there that the Duke of Gloucester has the two children murdered, having previously himself murdered Henry VI. The dismal castle of Pomfret is likewise the scene of cruel murder. Macbeth's castle, where he murders Duncan and where Lady Macbeth, walking in her sleep, washes away the blood from her hands, is just the place to awaken in the mind a powerful vision of an ancient abode of horrors with its related deeds of darkness. The Castle of Elsinore is already a haunted building in full accordance with all the demands of horror-romanticism ; its ramparts reflected in the moonlight and the wandering ghost seeking revenge, together with the romantic belief in the supernatural which, like an accompaniment and confirmation, creeps in with the conversation between the watchers, form a picture of the haunted castle which has perhaps struck deeper and more permanently into the public mind than any other setting of this nature.[28] It seems natural that Shakespeare, especially after the revival of romanticism had brought about increased interest in him, and his plays began to be made public in their original form, should play an important part in the spread of the conception that a medieval castle of the descrip-tion implied, with all the memories of terror clinging to it, was a powerful aid towards awakening that atmosphere people had learned to call romantic.

The influence of Shakespeare is also apparent in a trifling detail often appearing in these romances, viz., the castle bell, or as it may be, timepiece, already remarked upon. In the plays of Shakespeare it has its own special duty, which at times produces a mystic, fateful impression of voicing the pitilessness and insensibility of Time. The chime of a bell is mentioned in *The Merry Wives of Windsor*. In the *Comedy of Errors*

> The capon burns, the pig falls from the spit,
> The clock hath strucken twelve upon the bell.

In *Twelfth Night* " The clock upbraids me with the waste of time." In *King John* mention is made of " Old Time the clock-setter," of " bell, book and candle," of " the midnight bell with his iron tongue and brazen mouth." While awaiting his fate in Pomfret Castle, Richard II hears the clock strike and in an access of terror believes himself to be a clock.[29] In *King Richard III* a bell is heard whose chime at the beginning of the battle of Bosworth sounds in some way fateful. In *Julius Cæsar* the bell breaks up the meeting of the conspirators with its chime, proclaiming the hour for the fateful excursion. When about to visit the Senate, Cæsar chances to ask Brutus the hour, information which from the lips of Brutus has an ominous sound. Portia, thinking of her forebodings and of Brutus, asks a passing sibyl the time ; at the beginning of the decisive stage of the battle of Philippi, Brutus remembers to ask the hour. Thus in all these mighty tragedies of fate this little trait, the constant noting of time, makes of the clock or bell the Fate which mercilessly reckons the lives of men in fleeting moments. Before his death, Banquo asks his son how far the night has progressed and is told : " The moon is down, I have not heard the clock." Lady Macbeth soothes her restless conscience by imagining : " It was the owl that shriek'd, the fatal bellman, which gives the stern'st good night." The chiming of a clock marks a climax of fearful excitement when it informs Macbeth that the hour for the murder has struck. In *Othello* the chiming of a bell interrupts the struggle which ushers in the misfortunes brought upon Cassio by Iago ; the bell rings with such insistence that even Othello's nerves give way and he orders the dreadful bell to be silenced. From these passages it will be seen that in Shakespeare's case the bell or clock was of importance as a herald of fateful moments and the emotional scenes induced by these. The fact was noted by later writers, who intensify, as we shall see further on, the significance of this ally to majestic proportions.

A third source from which the haunted castle has borrowed some of its features, and without which it would indeed lack all analogies in historical reality, is the actual atmosphere created by medieval buildings, castles, churches, etc., and by their real history and the legends connected with them. As soon as the budding interest in antiquities had brought such buildings to the fore and the romantic state of mind had begun to develop, it was merely a question of time before poetry would be written under the influence of the moods induced by them. This was actually what happened in Walpole's case, whose keenness for Gothic relics and local studies of such material eventually caused him to attempt to build a counterpart to his inner vision, which was then transferred by him into the realms of poetry.

From such distance and from so many sources, therefore, are the stones of the haunted castle taken. The merit of Walpole and his school is that they brought the haunted castle from the background into the foreground, making of it a decisive factor in the romanticism of their works.

6

As already pointed out, Mrs. Radcliffe added to the imaginary buildings of her forerunners an atmosphere of ruin, with the " feeling of desolation " that is its inevitable complement. She placed her buildings now in a sternly beautiful, wild landscape, now in a smiling, sweetly poetical idyll. At the same time, expanding what was only hinted at by the others, she made skilful use of atmospherical factors, storms, wind and thunder, and other such aids to poetical atmosphere as, for instance, moonlight. Here too the question presents itself as to whether even these features were new inventions or whether analogies could be found in the past. By way of answer I append the following greatly condensed notes.

With regard to the atmosphere of ruin, one can hardly help thinking of the hermit's hut that frequently appears in Spenser, to which seems to cling an air of romantic age :

THE HAUNTED CASTLE

A litle lowly Hermitage it was,
Downe in a dale, hard by a forests side,
Far from resort of people that did pas
In traveill to and froe : a litle wyde
There was an holy chappell edifyde,
Wherein the Hermite dewly wont to say
His holy thinges each morne and eventyde :
Thereby a christall streame did gently play,
Which from a sacred fountaine welled forth alway.

The picture evoked here provides the first sketch of that mossy hermitage which finally becomes an essential completing touch to all romantic descriptions of forests.[30] The same hermitage is found in Milton, who, in *Il Penseroso*, expresses the hope that

. . . may at last my weary age
Find out the peaceful hermitage,
The hairy gown and mossy cell,
Where I may sit and rightly spell
Of every star that heaven doth shew. . . .

In the same poem, in which purely romantic moods are frequently invoked, he interprets his desire

To walk the studious cloisters pale,
And love the high embowèd roof,
With antique pillars massy-proof,
And storied windows richly dight,
Casting a dim religious light.

The imaginative picture thus created found great favour during the dawn of the romantic period, and from then onwards the hermit and hermitage became to poets the oracle and symbol of true, calm and experienced wisdom.

Parallel with this conception a type of ruin appears that might be termed the " mouldering turret " or the " mossy tower." " The high lonely tower " appears already in *Il Penseroso :*

Or let my lamp, at midnight hour,
Be seen in some high lonely tower. . . .

As soon as James Thomson, William Shenstone, Mark Akenside and John Dyer began to deal in their poetry—and also, in the case of Shenstone, in practice—with untrammelled nature in contrast to nature forced into classical, *i.e.*, geometrical forms, the mossy tower appears as an unfailing focus to their landscape vistas, rising to equal rank with the hermitage,

as the sacred chapel does in Spenser. In *The Seasons* (1730),
Thomson writes with feeling of a

> . . . valley sunk and unfrequented, where
> At fall of eve the fairy people throng . . .
>
> . . . . . .
>
> Of him whom his ungentle fortune urged
> Against his own sad breast to lift the hand
> of impious violence. The lonely tower
> Is also shunned, whose mournful chambers hold,
> So night-struck fancy dreams, the yelling ghost.

Shenstone caused to be built in his famous garden a kind of
" ruinated priory," a cave and a hermitage, and in his elegies
developed around ruins seen in the twilight, with their silently
flitting night-moths, bats and owls, a romantically poetic
evening atmosphere that trembles on the brink of the lachrymose. Dyer is particularly worth noting for his affection for
high mountains and ruins. In his *Grongar Hill* (1727) he
compares the temporal character of human life with a ruined
tower ; and even the title of another of his poems, which
appeared in 1740, is *The Ruins of Rome*. One of his lines deals
with " the dead hour of night," during which the hermit often
hears while praying " Aghast the voice of Time disparting
towers." William Julius Mickle waxes poetical in his *Syr
Martyr* (1767) over " Desmond's mouldering turrets," upon
which quiver " The trembling rye-grass and the harebell blue."
Akenside published his *Pleasures of Imagination* in 1744 and a
collection of Odes in 1745, both of which gave rise to a series of
Odes and *Pleasures* written in the strain of elegaic romanticism
peculiar to these landscape poets.[31]

Thus the lonely tower and the atmosphere of the past
came down in inheritance, partly direct from Milton, partly
through the landscape poets, to that contemporary group of
poets whose leading spirits were Doctor Johnson's friends
Joseph and Thomas Warton, William Collins and Thomas
Gray. All of these were masters of the ode, that form so
characteristic of English poetry, and worked in the spirit of
Milton's minor poems. Thomas Warton's *Pleasures of Melancholy* (1747) contains the following poetical prayer :

> O lead me, queen sublime, to solemn glooms
> Congenial with my soul ; to cheerless shades,
> To ruined seats, to twilight cells and bowers,
> Where thoughtful Melancholy loves to muse
> Her favorite midnight haunts. . . .
> Beneath yon ruined abbey's moss-grown piles

Oft let me sit, at twilight hour of eve,
When through some western window the pale moon
Pours her long-levelled rule of streaming light :
While sullen sacred silence reigns around,
Save the lone screech-owl's note, who builds his bower
Amid the moldering caverns dark and damp ;
Or the calm breeze, that rustles in the leaves
Of flaunting ivy, that with mantle green
Invests some wasted tower. . . .

In his ode *To Evening* Collins seems to gather into one work all the romantic material inherited and developed along the lines referred to above. " The weak-eyed bat," " the beetle winding his small but sullen horn," " the twilight path," " the darkening vale," " pensive pleasures sweet," the ruin, " Whose walls more awful nod by thy religious gleams," the hut " that from the mountain's side views wild and swelling floods," " dim-discovered spires and their simple bell," " the gradual dusky veil,"—these materials give to the poem its somewhat mournfully meditative effect as of one gazing at a quiet evening landscape. A similar list of materials characteristic of twilight-romanticism could also be drawn up from Gray's *Elegy, Written in a Country Churchyard*, in which the poet is moved by the sight of lonely and forgotten graves in the twilight to eulogies of unassuming, faithful labour. " The curfew tolls the knell of parting day," " and all the air a solemn stillness holds," " the beetle wheels his droning flight,"

From yonder ivy-mantled tower
The moping owl does to the moon complain
Of such as, wandering near her secret bower,
Molest her ancient solitary reign.

Parallel with the above, a powerful influence in the direction of graves, the fleetingness of life, and ruins, was exerted by the graveyard poetry which gives such a special stamp to eighteenth-century English poetry. Its originator was, in a way, Thomas Parnell (reviver in *The Hermit*, 1710, of the hermit-motive), whose *Night-piece on Death* (1722) is the first graveyard-romanticist phenomenon since the days of Shakespeare. He was followed by Edward Young, author of the famous *Night Thoughts* (1742-1743) and Robert Blair, author of *The Grave* (1743). Other followers include James Hervey, the first part of whose *Meditations and Contemplations* (1745-1746) is entitled " Meditations among the Tombs," and Nathaniel Cotton in his *Night-piece* (1751), which brings us already to the Wartons, Collins and Gray. Young was a night-prowler; of daylit landscape he sees practically nothing; but with the fall of night vision comes to him as to an owl, and in darkness and moonlight he glides among graves and other emblems of mortality, wrapped in a fine and romantically pleasurable despair. With solemn elocution he writes:

> Night, sable goddess! from her ebon throne,
> In rayless majesty, now stretches forth
> Her leaden sceptre o'er a slumb'ring world.

"Silence and darkness" are to him "solemn sisters," "twins." Blair's expressed purpose was "to paint the dismal horrors of the grave." In these descriptions of mortality one senses echoes from Milton, Shakespeare (*Hamlet* in particular) and the Bible, especially the Book of Job.[32]

Of mountainous beauty the English ever had appreciation. Thomson depicts mountains which are "horrid, vast, sublime" (*The Autumn*, line 711), mountain torrents and floods. The mind of Thomas Gray was romantically open to Alpine beauty, as witness his *French Diary* (1739): "The road runs over a Mountain, which gives you the first taste of the Alps, in it's magnificent rudeness, and steep precipices. . . . You here met with all the beauties so savage and horrid a place can present you with; Rocks of various and uncouth figures, Cascades pouring down from an immense height of hanging Groves of Pine Trees, and the solemn sound of the stream, that roars below, all concur to form one of the most poetical scenes imaginable." The same comprehension of mountainous beauty appears in his *Lake Diary* (1769).

Admiration for the sublime appears early also in French literature. *Les Mémoires de Miledi B*** (1760, before Rousseau's *La Nouvelle Héloïse*), to take an instance, describes how her father, overcome by melancholy, fled to dream in solitude, where he could view the unbanded powers of nature in all their glory—high mountains whose peaks seemed to fade into the clouds, gloomy forests into which no ray of sunlight ever penetrated, the savage cries of birds of prey and the howls of wild beasts as they fled into their lairs. In *La Nouvelle Héloïse*, in the letters of Saint-Preux to Julie and especially in the famous chapters in which he speaks of La Meillerie, Rousseau depicts the beauty of the Alps: he tells how he desired to relapse into his dreams and how the majestic features of the surrounding nature prevented him—the high rocks hanging over his head like ruins, the roaring cataracts dashing down from the heights and the brawling streams in the deep chasms. Contrasted with such scenes we often find that Rousseau's favourite landscape is a peaceful idyll of cultivated land, quite as in Mrs. Radcliffe. It is not impossible that Mrs. Radcliffe derived impulses from Rousseau's descriptions of Alpine beauty, seeing that *La Nouvelle Héloïse* was a well-known and much-read book in England in her youth.[33]

These examples, to which I have no desire to add, show that the way had led along the lines traced above to just those moods which are most characteristic of Mrs. Radcliffe's work. A step farther towards the creation of a romantic and austere, even, one might say, of a wild atmosphere of solitude and desolation, was made by James Beattie in *The Minstrel, or the Progress of Genius* (1771-1774)[34], a work that attracted considerable attention in its day. The hero of the poem, the youth Edwin, is fond of wandering " at large the lonely mountain's head," of roving, wrapt in wonder, " beneath the precipice o'erhung with pine," where " from cliff to cliff the foaming torrents shine." He enjoys " each gentle and each dreadful scene," finds delight " in darkness and in storm," " in balmy gloom," " in the mournful howl of the storm," " in the owl's terrific song," etc. :

> . . . . Whate'er of beautiful, or new,
> Sublime, or dreadful, in earth, sea, or sky,
>   By chance, or search, was offer'd to his view,
> He scan'd with curious and romantic eye.

He is an " enthusiast " of solitude, who delights in walking long distances to the shore of a foaming sea, to watch and to listen " with pleasing dread to the deep roar of the wide-weltering waves." He wanders in districts where rock is piled on rock, with here and there a solitary tree and moss-grown boulders, and where the cry of a lonely eagle is heard ; the voices of the forest and river lull his soul to rest and open out to him romantic visions.—All this is extremely familiar to readers of Mrs. Radcliffe.

Finally, as one of the chief founts of beauty in austerity, there is yet to be mentioned, in connection with the atmosphere of desolation in Mrs. Radcliffe's books, James Macpherson's *Ossian*, which appeared complete in 1763. The gloomy and tragic sadness of this work casts its shadow far and wide over the poetry of the ensuing period. The feeling of desolation, night, storm and sorrow in *Ossian* is deep and impressive. The sun shines rarely, and then only through " a silent shower " ; " thou comest forth in thy awful beauty." The gates of the

PLATE II

Listening with pleasing dread to the deep roar
Of the wide-weltering waves. ———

THE LONE ENTHUSIAST

(From Beattie's *The Minstrel*)

[*face p.* 24

castle lie open and dark and the wind whines in the deserted yards; over the threshold the trees strew their dead leaves, and "night's whisper is present." The wind has its own attributes; it is "the breeze of the valley" and "the breeze of the desert," "the light-winged gale"; it howls in empty court and whistles round the half-worn shield. It blows in "sudden squalls" or dashes "cold and frosty" over foaming seas; it sighs in the grass growing on a grave "where I often sit in the mournful shade." "Mossy stones," "mossy towers" and "grass murmuring in the wind" are frequent poetical images in *Ossian*. A special bleak, sadly-poetical part is played by the thistle, that old emblem of Ossian's race. "Thou bender of the thistle of Lora," the poem apostrophizes the wind, which "drives the thistle in autumn's dusky vale"; "the lonely blast of ocean pursues the thistle's beard"; "the thistle shook there its lonely head, the moss whistled to the wind," sings the poet, overcome by the melancholy of solitude, unaware that he was creating a phrase that owing to its poignancy was to adhere to the memory of posterity, so that Mrs. Radcliffe, for instance, writing in a similar mood, could use it word for word as her own. The moon in *Ossian* rises "broad"; its rays glitter on the rocks as it looks down through the clouds on to a mournful plain, or when, "cold and pale," it "sinks in the western wave." The poet of *Ossian* loved roaring torrents and landscapes with winding rivers, whose "distant roar," or "dismal roaring" can be heard. The clouds are "dark-rolling" and the thunder rolls on the hill. "Autumn is dark on the mountains; grey mist rest on the hills. The whirlwind is heard on the heath. Dark rolls the river through the narrow plain. A tree stands alone on the hill. . . ." The low minor chords of Ossian's organ are richly represented and have sounded clearly in Mrs. Radcliffe's ear.[35]

If, however, we were to conclude from the foregoing that Mrs. Radcliffe formed her images and descriptions entirely from old material, we should be doing her a great wrong. Actually, Mrs. Radcliffe was a rarely independent writer, not to be classed summarily as a mere borrower from the sources enumerated. Raleigh says that in her books there is nothing she herself has not created.[36] My purpose in dealing with the development of various images is to describe the original and varied path, uninfluenced by the rest of European literature, which was taken also in this respect by English romanticism from the very beginning.

Before proceeding to other matters, a few words must still be added on the exterior composition of Mrs. Radcliffe's landscapes, within which she sounded the moods described above. The scenes of her books are mostly laid in France and Italy, whose landscapes are described in connection with the journeys undertaken by the characters. The author possessed no first-hand knowledge of these countries; even her journey along the Rhine was not made until all her romances had been published. She was thus unable to describe from experience, she had to feed her imagination on other writings and pictures. In *The Mysteries of Udolpho* she states outright, in connection with a certain landscape, that it was one Salvator Rosa would have chosen for a canvas had he lived at the time. The opinion indeed seems general that the models of the landscapes she constructs are to be sought in Salvator Rosa's pictures, an explanation well-founded in some respects but not in all.

The austere side of her landscapes has been subjected to so much analysis that we are compelled to admit that she has imbibed something of the romantic austerity of nature elsewhere than in a mere collection of pictures. The landscapes of Beattie, imbued with the *Ossian* atmosphere, form in themselves sufficient sources of inspiration. As regards her idyllic scenes, one can well doubt whether they would have seen the light if her predecessors had not included the school of nature poets which, following the example set by Milton, turned its attention to the natural, quiet, summery, idyllic beauty of the English country-side, to

> Russet lawns, and fallows gray,
> Where the nibbling flocks do stray;
> Mountains, on whose barren breast
> The labouring clouds do often rest;
> Meadows trim with daisies pied,
> Shallow brooks and rivers wide;
> Towers and battlements it sees
> Bosom'd high in tufted trees . . .

as Milton writes in *L'Allegro*. This English landscape, for which Milton provides an elaborately worked model of great poetical beauty, is the inexhaustible centre of English nature-poetry, and after it had been virtually revived by James Thomson, appears in ever-new forms, attuned to every key. Although Mrs. Radcliffe sometimes adds " copses of mulberry-bushes " and other details unconnected with English landscape, to give her pictures a French or Italian touch, behind it all we descry this English idyll of poetry, which had evidently

PLATE III

A TYPICAL ROMANTIC LANDSCAPE BY SALVATOR ROSA

(By courtesy of the Trustees of the National Gallery)

[face p. 26

left a deep impression on the nature-loving soul of the author.[37]

All that I have written concerning the origins of the haunted castle might tempt the reader to conclude that I denied all individual part in its creation to the Walpole-Reeve-Radcliffe trio. To abolish any such misunderstanding I should point out that the details leading to the final emergence of the haunted castle were, in the case of the earlier writers, only secondary details, swift flashes of pictures accompanying the main action ; no one had as yet either discovered their possibilities or desired to make of them other than an accompaniment. With the trio this accompaniment becomes the central feature ; in their works the haunted castle achieves a position of independence, becoming almost the action by means of which they develop their romantic visions. Herein lies their special and original invention, and thanks to it they are entitled to appear as a definite, original school.

In connection with the haunted castle we have yet to consider William Beckford, a fabulously rich dilettante whose place is beside Walpole. Here was another romanticist who sought the aid of the builder to give concrete form to his romantic visions. In Wiltshire he built Fonthill Abbey, that marvellous tower of Babel, in the plan and mysterious chambers of which he tried to express his overwhelming romantic imagination. Like Walpole, he transferred some portion of his vision into literature, publishing in 1787 a story in French entitled *Vathek, an Arabian Tale*. His book had been anticipated, however, in the previous year by an unauthorized English translation done from his manuscript. Although Beckford's little book can be regarded, on the whole, as an expression of the interest awakened by Antoine Galland's French version of the *Arabian Nights*, which had appeared at the beginning of the century (1704-1717)—among others, Voltaire made use of the Oriental world thus opened up, clothing many of his satires and short stories in quasi-oriental dress—Beckford's work is to be looked upon as an example of English romanticism ; for, despite its Oriental setting, it contains all the materials of this school. It is worth while keeping in memory as the first expression of that love for Oriental attire which is such a feature of English romanticism. One of the aims of the book was to evoke terror, though the means employed differ from those used by Walpole. In the castle of Eblis, a species of Oriental Lucifer, one feels the striving towards a purely Gothic atmosphere of austere majesty. " The Caliph and Nouronihar beheld each other with amazement at finding themselves in a place which, though roofed with a vaulted ceiling, was so spacious and lofty that at first they took it for an immeasurable plain. But their eyes at length growing familiar to the grandeur of the objects at hand, they extended their view to those at a distance, and discovered rows of columns and arcades, which gradually diminished till they terminated in a point, radiant as the sun when he darts his last beams athwart the ocean." [38] The gigantic proportions of Eblis's castle show the dimensions to which a mysterious building of this nature could be expanded by a romantic imagination.

7

X The chief character in *The Castle of Otranto* is its master Manfred, of whom a dark and forbidding picture is given. He is not the rightful heir to Otranto, but a descendant of the usurping family, and in consequence his mind is ceaselessly oppressed by the prophecy of Saint Nicholas that " the Castle and Lordship of Otranto should pass from the present family whenever the real owner should be grown too large to inhabit it." [39]

The story begins at a point when the fulfilment of this prophecy is nigh ; at a time, therefore, when according to the wish of Saint Nicholas the mastership of Otranto is about to pass to the rightful heir of Alfonso, whom Manfred's grandfather Ricardo had murdered. By these means Manfred is made to appear from the beginning as a character struggling against an inevitable fate. When his only son dies in consequence of a supernatural incident, he wishes to leave his wife, who can no longer be expected to provide him with an heir, and to wed the betrothed of his son. But divine and mortal powers are arrayed against him, and soon the rightful heir comes on the scene in the guise of a young peasant called Theodore. Theodore falls in love with Manfred's daughter Matilda, but as Alfonso's blood cannot mix with that of the murderer's family, the marriage is impossible. The wedding is prevented by Manfred's murdering his own daughter; the prophecy being then fulfilled by the disclosure of Theodore's birth. Manfred abdicates and with his wife enters a monastery. Such, in brief, is the plot of the book.

The interest centres chiefly around Manfred, for one reason, because he seems familiar. He is possessed by a single idea, the realization of which is a matter of life and death with him, viz., the retention of the family power. The prophecy and his knowledge of his grandfather's crime combine, however, in making him uncertain and illogical, and in exposing him to fierce, spiritual conflicts. He is transformed into a being inhuman, savage and passionate, occasionally capable of some slight show of feeling, though taciturn and gloomily silent. When he sees Theodore for the first time he flies into a rage because of the youth's resemblance to the picture of Alfonso. It is expressly stated that Manfred was not the type of tyrant who practises cruelty for his pleasure, and that only fate had made his character, which was otherwise humane, so stern and unbending, and that his virtues were ever awake when passion had not befogged his brain. His heart was sensitive to outside influences, but his pride forbade him to show it. Those who were ignorant of the cause of his secret agony could not understand his temper ; in their eyes he was scarcely sane, deliberately ill-treated his daughter and was a gloomy and lonely man, oppressed by the consciousness of a coming unhappy fate. He is the luckless hero of a tragedy of destiny, for whom we can feel sympathy.[40]

Compared with him, Clara Reeve's tyrant, Lord Walter Lovel, is on a much lower plane, hardly more than a common criminal. The goal of all his strivings is to amass riches and honours, and it is for this that he has recourse to crime. Only in the obstinacy with which he denies his guilt to the last does he show any firmness of character.

On the whole, Mrs. Radcliffe's tyrants revert to the type of Manfred, though the motives behind their deeds are often more insignificant in nature. The predominant passion is love of power and riches. As men of fierce and morose nature they are entirely in the grip of their passions, slaves to anger, the lust for revenge and pride ; men from whom no good can be expected. We are told that in their moments of fury and revenge, their imagination is unable to conceive methods of torture to equal their desires. No gentler feeling or mode of thinking alleviates their tyrannic sense of power or guides them to good deeds ; their every act is one of boundless oppression and unscrupulousness. Only the desire for revenge can restrain their cupidity. The hidden cause for their harshness is often, as in Manfred's case, a dark crime perpetrated either by the tyrant himself or by his family. It hardens the heart, leads to new crimes and is not confessed until on death-bed, from which all honest men naturally draw back in horror.

Others, again, die proud and unrepentant. With such tyrants love is nothing but passion ; one sight of the heroine is sufficient to inflame them, and their unbridled nature refuses to admit of any obstacle. Outwardly they are often handsome and stalwart. Thus we are given to understand that Montoni, the darkly-glancing lord of Udolpho, is a man of " an uncommonly handsome person," whose features are expressive and manly. They indicate a commanding and quick-tempered nature, but the chief impression they awaken is one of gloomy taciturnity and a meditativeness bordering on melancholy.[41]

Of all Mrs. Radcliffe's characters Montoni is the one best adapted to awaken interest and the one for whom the author herself, despite her attitude of horror, has the greatest affection. The model for Montoni is to be sought in Manfred, but while in the latter we have a fairly uncomplicated character, whose aims and deeds are easy of comprehension, the silent and gloomy Montoni has something enigmatical about his person. The crimes of Manfred and his family are known to us, but whether Montoni or his family have anything on their consciences remains uncertain to the end. A strange, suspicious atmosphere is created around Montoni which causes us to believe anything of him without proof or reason. As he wanders through the passages of his dilapidated castle, silent and darkly defiant, brooding over some secret thought, yet noble and beautiful in appearance, or sits cold and mocking amongst his accomplices, gambling or drinking, he achieves in some way an effect of romantically majestic proportions which attracts our interest owing to its novelty. Curiosity inclines us to ask who and what he really is and what his thoughts are ; what the reason for his return to the deserted castle of Udolpho and what his plans there ; but the questions remain unanswered. Montoni remains to the end an enigma. The reader is left with the suspicion that the author had indeed been capable of constructing a romantic, enigmatical type, but that her talent had proved insufficient to provide this type with a tragic fate based on a true mission in life. He is married to a French noblewoman, Madame Cheron, whom he takes with her niece to Italy, to the castle of Udolpho. There he attempts to gain possession of his wife's entire fortune and failing in this, ill-treats her until she dies. In the end he is imprisoned by the Venetian government for political reasons and dies a mysterious death in prison, unrepentant, secretive in death as in life.

Mrs. Radcliffe's other tyrants are depicted in a feebler, more summary style. Malcolm, master of Dunbayne, is

" proud, oppressive, revengeful," " mighty in injustice and cruel in power." He has seized his brother's lands, murdered him and cast his son out into the world ; having murdered the Lord of Athlin he tries to murder the latter's son Osbert, and even attempts to compel the daughter Mary to become his mistress. He fails, however, in these schemes and meets his death. On his death-bed he repents : " I have understood virtue, but I have loved vice. I do not now lament that I am punished, but that I have deserved punishment."

The actual death of a tyrant of this description is something out of the ordinary : he invariably expires " with a strong sigh." The Marquis of Mazzini holds his wife confined in lifelong imprisonment in the dungeons of his castle and intends marrying off his daughter Julia against her will ; but he falls by the hand of his second wife Maria de Vellorno. He too repents on his deathbed : " The retribution of heaven is upon me. My punishment is the immediate consequence of my guilt." Such is the main story of *The Sicilian Romance*.

In *The Romance of the Forest* the Marquis de Montalt has murdered his brother and believes he has murdered his niece Adeline. She has, however, escaped with her life to be cast on the mercy of her uncle, who tries to seduce her. This proves to be the last of his crimes ; he is imprisoned, takes poison and dies, tortured by the remembrance of his crimes. A more interesting figure is a secondary tyrant, a nobleman called de la Motte, in whose castle hidden away in the forest Adeline comes to dwell. De la Motte is a weak character who does not scruple to improve his position by common highway robbery, and for this reason falls into dangerous dependence on the Marquis de Montalt. Because of his poverty he is bitter and envious, without moral backbone and even cowardly, scorn tempered by pity being awakened in us by his craven spirit. Yet in these surroundings he is a new type whom we shall meet again in the future. Finally, I mention the impressive Jesuit Schedoni, of the long romance *The Italian*, whose tall apparition and fanatic glance, coupled with the terrors of the Inquisition, provide the essence of the work in question.

Such are the tyrants of these romances. Of all the masters of haunted castles to whom so many hundreds of pages have been devoted, the type most likely to adhere to the memory is that represented by Manfred-Montoni, the lonely, stalwart, saturnine and black-browed man of beautiful countenance, whose spiritual life is in the grip of some secret influence and who, by reason of his intelligence and strength of will and the volcanic nature of his passions, stands out from his surroundings as an independent individual. In this respect Mrs. Radcliffe, in particular, has had a vision of something superhuman, of a superman with uncommon qualities, whose soul and actions are dominated by passions unknown to the ordinary mortal, passions verging on the demoniac. This is reason enough for us to seek the origin of the Manfred-Montoni type.

The title of *The Castle of Otranto* would naturally lead us to suppose that the theme of Walpole's book was connected with the real Otranto in South Italy, in the thirteenth century ruled over by Manfred, a natural son of Frederick II. He, like Walpole's Manfred, was a usurper ; his nephew's name was Conrad. The historical Manfred seized his territory from Frederick II. Walpole's Manfred believes Frederick of Vicenza to be the rightful owner of Otranto. Both Frederick II and Frederick of Vicenza are believed to have died in Palestine. The builder of the real castle of Otranto was Alfonso of Aragon. Although, when shown a picture of the real Otranto, Walpole professed to have known nothing of the existence of such a place while writing his book, declaring that he had chanced upon it while searching the map for a South Italian name, it seems certain that the actual history of Otranto did to some extent guide his pen. A second theory can be broached which supports and amplifies the above assumption as to his sources. We have already dealt with the haunted castle of Shakespeare, and a glance at the preface to the second edition of *The Castle of Otranto* makes it clear that in our search for Walpole's models we must not forget to examine the plays of that author. In his argument with certain French critics regarding Shakespeare's method of introducing comic relief into tragedies, Walpole points out that the contrast between the sublime and the naïve thus brought about " sets the pathetic of the former in a stronger light." For this reason he too introduced into his story the lively and chattering Bianca, claiming the protection of " the brightest genius this country, at least, has produced " for his temerity. Having thus, according to his own account, inaugurated a new species of romance, he continues : " But I should be more proud of having imitated, however faintly, weakly, and at a distance, so masterly a pattern, than to enjoy the entire merit of invention." It is my opinion that this statement should be taken in a fairly literal sense and the conclusion formed that Shakespeare was Walpole's model in other matters than in the juxtaposition of the sublime and the naïve.[42]

Leontes of *The Winter's Tale*, suspicious, cruel in his passion, is obviously a related type to the romantic tyrant ; a parallel type completing the picture is Hubert of the dark complexion and criminal air in *King John*. Belonging to the same series of passionate strong men is the Duke of York in the Second Part of *Henry VI*. In *Julius Cæsar* the description of Cassius recalls to mind the proud, brooding hero of the romanticists :

> He thinks too much : such men are dangerous.
>
> .   .   .   .
>
>   He reads much ;
> He is a great observer, and he looks
> Quite through the deeds of men ; he loves no plays,
> . . . he hears no music ;
> Seldom he smiles, and smiles in such a sort
> As if he mock'd himself, and scorn'd his spirit
> That could be mov'd to smile at anything.
> Such men as he be never at heart's ease
> Whiles they behold a greater than themselves,
> And therefore are they very dangerous.

The same gloomy mood is revealed in Brutus's phrase :

> Between the acting of a dreadful thing
> And the first motion, all the interim is
> Like a phantasma, or a hideous dream.

Lady Percy (in the First Part of *Henry IV*) asks of that passion-ridden strong nature her husband :

> Why dost thou bend thine eyes upon the earth,
> And start so often when thou sitt'st alone ?
> Why hast thou lost the fresh blood in thy cheeks,
> And given my treasures and my rights of thee
> To thick-eyed musing and curst melancholy ?

In Hamlet we find the same type with dark passions, conflicting emotions and pale melancholy still further developed. Wrapt in the dark meditations occasioned by the murder of his father, his mother's marriage, the appearance of his father's ghost and the duty of vengeance, Hamlet appears not only in a spiritual, but likewise in a physical sense as the embodiment of black melancholy, unhealthily brooding over dismal thoughts ; a type over whom " clouds hang," who wears " the colour of night," " inky cloak," " solemn black " ; " there is something in his soul o'er which his melancholy sits on brood." He reflects on suicide, and refrains only because religion forbids it, finding meanwhile the tasks of life " weary, stale, flat and unprofitable." This melancholy cannot, however, extinguish the passion which is part and parcel of his nature and which is revealed to us in sudden, mighty flashes. Even at the end Hamlet remains veiled to us in impenetrable mystery which prevents our seeing clearly the true problems of his inner nature; in this respect he has ever been and still is foremost amongst the mysterious heroes of romance.

Shakespeare obviously thought much over this enigmatical character and from it created the variations enumerated above (to which we may add the young Pericles, who, disappointed in love, sinks into a Hamlet-like mood with " the sad companion, the dull-ey'd melancholy," and, developed to unscrupulous cynical criminality, Richard III) in lack of which the hero of the romanticists might have remained uninvented or at least become much tamer in colour. Even now a kind of synthesis of the characters mentioned is liable to form of its own accord in the mind of the reader of Shakespeare, a conception of a sombre, lonely, in some way noble personality which adheres to the memory. This is probably what happened in Walpole's case. Inspired by this unconscious memory he gave life to a name discovered perhaps by chance on the map of Italy.

Another circumstance which connects these romances with Shakespeare is the construction of the plots, to which a word or two may here be devoted. As we have seen, the underlying action in most of them is dictated in some form or other by an act of usurpation and fraternal hate and the unravelling of the consequences of these, a basis extremely characteristic of the construction of Shakespeare's plays. In *The Tempest*, for instance, Prospero's brother has banished him and usurped his throne; in *As You Like It* the young duke banishes the old and usurps his power. King John orders the murder of his nephew Arthur, whose right to the crown is greater than his own. King John is poisoned. In the historical plays the question is throughout of usurpation. The cause of the catastrophe in *Romeo and Juliet* is a family feud which forbids the love of the young people for each other. The plot of *Macbeth* rests on usurpation by means of murder. In *Hamlet* one brother has killed another and laid hands on his wife and his power. In *King Lear* Edmund usurps his foster-brother's inheritance and position. In *Cymbeline* the rightful heirs are kidnapped and brought up in hiding. In this respect Shakespeare may be called the father of the romantic plot, and watching over its cradle, bequeathing to the infant now one, now the other gift from his endless treasure.[43]

THE HAUNTED CASTLE

With regard particularly to *The Castle of Otranto*, the story, the basis of which is an act of usurpation, often more resembles a drama than descriptive and narrative work. As we have seen, it contains exceedingly little descriptive matter in the way of landscape and nature. For the greater part it consists of short matter-of-fact observations, rapid and lively conversation in brief sentences, and changing scenes of dramatic suddenness and effectivity. All the events move swiftly towards the final catastrophe. The need for dramatic action has absorbed the author's mind to an extent that has left him no time for a calmer, more epic narrative style with descriptions. Walpole informs us that in his story he has followed closely the laws of drama. It cannot, therefore, be considered far-fetched if we declare that not only Shakespeare in general, but especially *Hamlet* and perhaps, to some extent, *The Winter's Tale* formed the inner point of departure for *The Castle of Otranto*. In detail the assumption is founded on the following observations.

With both authors the starting-point of the plot is a previous murder and usurpation, and its purpose is to bring about the downfall of the present ruler. In each case the struggle against the usurper is led by a supernatural power, the visible antagonist being the rightful heir. The heir has been absent up to the opening of the story and does not arrive until the programme drawn up by fate for vengeance has been set in action by a supernatural agent. A portrait of the murdered head of the family appears, likewise a ghost, which materializes in order to warn the heir. Ophelia and Matilda are in love with their respective young heroes and both meet with a tragic end. In *Hamlet* the ghost is introduced almost at the beginning ; in *The Castle of Otranto* a miracle occurs. The former " bodes some strange eruption " to the State, the latter the fulfilment of a prophecy with a like intention.

Supernatural matters are treated by both authors with naïve directness and are fully believed in. Finally, in Manfred himself, in his sombreness and his struggle against fate, there is something of Hamlet, though in relation to the plot Manfred would of course correspond to Hamlet's stepfather and Theodore to Hamlet. An oracular prophecy similar to that in *The Castle of Otranto* appears in *The Winter's Tale*, to the effect that " King Leontes shall not have an heir till his lost child be found." Just as Leontes is defying this prophecy, word is brought to him that his son has died. Manfred, too, is informed of the sudden demise of his son in similar circumstances. Hermione and Hippolita, as suffering and noble wives, have also much in common. When we recollect that mysterious prophecies of the nature indicated are not infrequent in Shakespeare, we may assume that Walpole founded his on the models thus provided.

Taking all this into account, we cannot reasonably deny a certain justification for the assumption mentioned, though, of course, there can be no question of mathematical certainty. At the head of the family tree showing the lineage of Manfred-Montoni, *i.e.*, the gloomy hero of the early romanticists, we can place the famous Prince of Denmark. By this step we shall have traced back the dark hero of romance who has graced so many pages of later fiction to that source which, with its superabundant wealth, provides the natural basis for work of this description, even, one might say, the conditions for its development—to Shakespeare. To my mind, this is in no way in conflict with the assertion that later romanticism completed and gave depth to the picture of its hero with details derived from another early line of development, viz., with the defiance and titanic qualities of Milton's Satan. Hamlet and Satan are related souls, night-dark brooders over deep mysterious thoughts, whose likenesses, having hitherto journeyed apart, combine in the Byronic hero.

In completion of the above I may remark that Montoni can boast of a parallel who helps to establish his lineage ; a person who, although not actually a member of the romantic family, has nevertheless proved capable of endowing many of its children with certain easily recognizable features— an obvious proof of hidden relationship. In 1786, three years before the appearance of Mrs. Radcliffe's first book, the Scotch physician John Moore published a novel entitled *Zeluco, Various Views of Human Nature, Taken from Life and Manners Foreign and Domestic.* The chief character in the book, Zeluco, is a coldly selfish and cruel nature who reveals these traits in childhood. He is the descendant of a noble Sicilian family and as a soldier of Spain lives the life of a rake. His path leads from pleasure to pleasure, especially in affairs of love, women being merely the playthings of his sensuality. His reward is an increasing sense of emptiness, a spiritual unrest, a constantly gnawing conscience, and thus his days are spent in inner agony and the perpetration of ever new crimes. In his person we recognize the villain of the picaresque authors, Ferdinand Fathom, but in addition we descry in him a romantic gloom and grandeur that reminds us of Montoni.

If his character and deeds had been clothed in Montoni-like mystery, whetting the reader's fear and curiosity, he would have been a typically romantic apparition. Even now he takes his place, thanks to many of his characteristics, in the line Hamlet-Manfred-Montoni, and projects his shadow far into the future.[44]

And now we come to the question as to whether Richardson's type of noble rake, Lovelace, who, as an embodiment of views and habits inherited from the gay days of the Stuarts, crops up in coarser or finer form in Fielding and Smollett, played any part in the origin of the romantic tyrant. In *Clarissa Harlowe* Richardson gives the following description of Lovelace: " That he was a generous landlord ; that he spared nothing for solid and lasting improvements upon his estate, and that he looked into his own affairs, and understood them ; that he had been very expensive when abroad, and contracted a large debt (for he made no secret of his affairs). He was a sad gentleman to women. If his tenants had pretty daughters, they choose to keep them out of his sight. He was never known to be disguised with liquor, but was a great plotter and a great writer ; that he lived a wild life in town. He was good-humoured."

Clarissa's fate weighs on his conscience and he falls in a duel. The type is obviously lacking in the trappings of romance, above all in mystery and gloom. His defiance is the pride and tenacity of a gentleman careful of his honour, and not the deeper feeling of revolt against fate. For this reason it is difficult to perceive any organic connection between him and the romantic tyrant. Zeluco was, perhaps, based on him, for both are seducers and roués, and in this particular he may have furnished material for the picture of Don Juan. By later writers he has been regarded as a totally different type from the gloomy tyrant of romance. Thus, for instance, in *Peveril of the Peak*, Sir Walter Scott depicts him (vide Buckingham—noble, handsome, courtier-like, generous, well-attired, good-humoured, brave and witty, but as regards women a complete Lovelace) without the qualities of defiance, gloom or mystery. And as such he exists in Dickens, in the person of David Copperfield's friend Steerforth.

Before leaving the tyrant, let us return once more to the Caliph Vathek, Beckford's Oriental tyrant. We are told quite at the beginning that " When he was angry one of his eyes became so terrible that no person could bear to behold it, and the wretch upon whom it was fixed instantly fell backward, and sometimes expired." The conception expressed here of the power inherent in the human eye is worth remembering.

8

A contrast to the tyrant's uncontrollable temper and gloom is furnished by the sunny humanity and joyous outlook, coupled with outward beauty, embodied in the young hero of these romances. On his brow there sits no stigma of crime and bad conscience; it shines clear, and he regards the world with open and candid gaze. The hero of Walpole's story, the peasant Theodore, rises to increasing importance. He falls in love with Manfred's daughter and saves Isabella from insult; Manfred sentences him to death, but at the very moment of his execution a birth-mark, a bloody arrow, is seen on his shoulder, and at the sight the pious Father Jerome is moved to cry out: "Gracious heaven, what do I see! It is my child! my Theodore!" Jerome, formerly Count Falconara, was once married to Alfonso's daughter, and his lost child is thus the rightful heir to Otranto. The gentleness of his birth has already been revealed in his manners, which display an aristocratic charm and a pleasing humility; he is ready to sacrifice his life in the service of the oppressed and fears no one when the persecuted maiden seeks his protection. It is expressly stated that his sins are no more numerous than can be expected of one of his age. When in love, he delights to wander in shady places, as these harmonize best with the pleasant melancholy that fills his soul—quite in the manner of Valentine in *Two Gentlemen of Verona*, who sighs amidst his love-sorrows:

> Here can I sit alone, unseen of any,
> And to the nightingale's complaining notes
> Tune my distresses and record my woes,

or of the lovelorn Orlando in *As You Like It*, who in the romantic forest of Arden will

> . . . carve on every tree
> The fair, the chaste, and unexpressive she . . .,

or of Romeo, whose love-sickness the poet depicts in the following lines:

> —underneath the grove of sycamore
> So early walking did I see your son:
> With tears augmenting the fresh morning's dew,
> Adding to clouds more clouds with his deep sighes.

On the death of his beloved Matilda he marries her friend Isabella, the betrothed of Manfred's dead son—not because he loves her as well, but because, as the bosom friend of the departed, she can assist with her memories in keeping alight the eternal melancholy which now pervades his soul. In appearance he resembles the portrait of his ancestor Alfonso, which depicts " a lovely prince, with large black eyes, a smooth white forehead and manly curling locks like jet." With this description the outward appearance of the romantic hero was established once and for all.[45]

Clara Reeve's hero, Edmund, appears in similar circumstances to those of Theodore. He too is of unknown birth ; his mother has disappeared and he grows up a poor farmer. But his great gifts, his manly and open nature and unfaltering love of truth distinguish him from the crowd and procure him a better education and honours. Finally, in a marvellous manner, he too regains the titles and property of his ancestors. In his case, the clue to his identity is a necklace left him by his mother.

On the whole Mrs. Radcliffe's young heroes resemble those described above, but are still more romantic, braver and more " refined." Osbert, the young lord of Athlin, is especially prominent in military exercises, for as the son of a noble he has inherited qualities. His lively and warm imagination make him a lover of poetry, inclined to day-dreaming ; his favourite pastime is to wander in the stern, romantic mountains of Scotland, much as Beattie's Edwin. The fearsome and sublime attract him more than the gentle and harmonious. " Wrapt in the bright visions of fancy " he often loses himself " in awful solitudes." In outward appearance he is tall and majestic, his behaviour and manners are tinged with nobility, while in his countenance manliness and dignity are combined. This earlier type of Mrs. Radcliffe's undergoes development in that it is later completed, as in the case of Valancourt in *The Mysteries of Udolpho*, by the addition of a rococo elegance of deportment, while in his manners, even in his speech, one discerns a touch of pastoral sensitivity which often degenerates into tearful sentimentality. Many of these heroes have familiar tasks assigned to them—their duty is to rise on the strength of their legal rights from insignificance to an influential position and great happiness. The mysterious birthmark is not lacking : " It is my Philip. That strawberry on his arm confirms the decision." [46]

As a general rule the type appears in these romances as

the protector and future husband of the persecuted heroine.

The mysterious birth-mark or the object left with the child on its desertion, which serves to identify the young hero, is an old feature of popular legends about kings and is used by Shakespeare, though in his case it cannot be regarded as in any way typical. The lost princes in *Cymbeline*, Gniderius and Arviragus, are recognized by a birth-mark resembling a star of blood on the throat of one of them. Rings play in Shakespeare the part of tokens of identity. As for Shakespeare's young heroes, they possess, in my opinion, all the characteristics of romanticism. Orlando in *As You Like It* is manly, gentle, strong and brave. Prince Arthur in *King John* impresses the reader as a refined and noble, beautiful youth. The prophecy relating to the young Earl of Richmond (Part III of *King Henry VI*) gives a clear description of the romanticist's ideal of a pure youth :

> His looks are full of peaceful majesty,
> His head by nature fram'd to wear a crown,
> His hand to wield a sceptre, and himself
> Likely in time to bless a regal throne.

Beside fiery Romeo one might mention the fine and romantic Paris, who is an obvious Valancourt-type. And with regard to Cymbeline's sons one might declare that despite their lowly station, their deportment and deeds betray noble birth. In accordance with such models the young hero of romance was doubtlessly created. It is characteristic of the type that in spite of all the authors' efforts to raise these heroes to the position of chief character in their works, a striving we can follow, for instance, in Mrs. Radcliffe's books, they are nowhere successful. The youths are too pure and move too much in the light to be truly romantic. It is for this reason that the hero's future is less assured than that of his dark-complexioned enemy, to whom he is finally driven to secede some of the most significant traits of his outward appearance.

9

Let us now improve our acquaintance with Walpole's persecuted maiden, with the virtuous Isabella. When, with evil purpose, Manfred seizes her hand, terror renders her half-dead ; she screams and flees from him. Whither ? Where

PLATE IV

THEODORE AND ISABELLA IN THE SUBTERRANEAN VAULTS

(From the Italian edition of *The Castle of Otranto*)

[*face p. 40*

find a shelter from the tyrant's clutch? In the castle's mysterious vaults, of course. Thither she hastens, but there new terrors assail her. Every little noise and breath of air fills her heart with dread. She walks on tiptoe and as slowly as her impatience will allow, stopping frequently to listen for pursuers. Suddenly she seems to hear a mysterious sigh. Trembling with fear she retreats a pace or two. Then it seems to her that someone approaches ; her blood curdles, for she believes herself about to fall again into Manfred's power. All the horrors the imagination can call up rise before her mind, and at that very moment a gust of wind extinguishes her lamp (with which, despite the suddenness of her flight, she is provided) and she is left helpless in pitch darkness. At this critical moment the author skilfully guides to her side the young hero, who leads her through secret caves and passages to shelter. Even at such a moment as this, however, the maiden does not forget her womanly dignity and good reputation : " Alas ! what mean you, sir ? " said she. " Though all your actions are noble, though your sentiments speak the purity of your soul, is it fitting that I should accompany you alone into these perplexed retreats? Should we be found together, what would a censorious world think of my conduct? " [47]

In spite of her many vicissitudes, Isabella finds happiness in the end. Otherwise is it with Manfred's daughter Matilda. Although she is of surpassing beauty and only eighteen, her father fails to show any interest in her. At the death of her brother she tries to restrain her own sorrow, the better to be able to console her despairing parents. A quiet timidity is part of her nature ; she feels that her vocation is to become a nun. Hearing the sentence pronounced by Manfred, that Theodore's head is to fall " this very instant," she sinks into a swoon. And when she opens the door of Theodore's prison to set him free, it is with the remark : " Young man, though filial duty and womanly modesty condemn the step I am taking, yet holy charity, surmounting all other ties, justifies this act." She will not blame her father for her death, but forgives everything, like the " emanation of divinity " she is said to be. [48]

Clara Reeve's Emma has nothing particularly romantic about her. She is an ordinary gentle and beautiful girl without even any remarkable adventures. After a happy childhood she marries the hero, presenting him, in the quickest possible time, with five sons and a daughter, all of which is carefully recorded by the author. The " persecuted female " in this romance is Edmund's mother.

In Mrs. Radcliffe's mind there was an especially clear picture of what a romantic maiden ought to be, which she presents with the gesture of one showing off an ideal. ¡ The type in question is about twenty, of medium height, slenderly built, but extremely well-proportioned. Her face is half-hidden by the dark hair which falls in plaits over her bosom. Her beauty is enhanced by the " soft and pensive melancholy " which lends to her blue eyes such an interesting air. ǀ Where the question is of two sisters, one of them, Emily, for instance, is of harmonious and feminine build and has a beautiful face, fair hair and a " sweet expression " in her dark-blue eyes, while Julia is airier and livelier, with dark and flashing eyes and dark auburn hair which curls in beautiful profusion upon her neck. An attempt is sometimes made to describe the heroine by relating how she tried to hide her face in her robe, and how, notwithstanding, the long auburn tresses which flowed in " beautiful luxuriance " over her throat and bosom revealed an inkling of her " glowing beauty." In danger or anguish her face takes on an expression of " captivating sweetness." Almost every one of Mrs. Radcliffe's maidens are described in this manner. " In person Emily resembled her mother, having the same elegant symmetry of form, the same delicacy of features, and the same blue eyes, full of tender sweetness." A brunette beauty is described thus : " Dark brown hair played carelessly along the open forehead ; the nose was rather inclined to aquiline ; the lips spoke in smile, but it was a melancholy one ; the eyes were blue, and were directed upwards, with an expression of peculiar meekness ; while the soft cloud of the brow spoke the fine sensibility of the temper."

ǀ We are even given a little information regarding their education. Nearly all are skilful in drawing and cannot look upon a " sublime landscape " without attempting to immortalize it with their pencil. Embroidery is another of their accomplishments, and they are exceedingly skilled in music. " Laura was particularly fond of the lute, which she touched with exquisite sensibility." The lute is the favourite instrument of persecuted maidens, for its sad tinkle when fingered in the twilight or in the pale moonlight under the influence of melancholy or grief or unhappy love accords well with their emotions and the melting tunes they are wont to hum.[49]

Such is approximately the maiden of these romances. In Walpole's story she is still at the Ophelia-Imogen stage, but in Mrs. Radcliffe's works she becomes the realization of her own ideal of maidenhood, reflecting the qualities demanded in those days of a really refined young maiden. To the type attaches something of the mincing virtue, coyness and capacity for blushing at the right moment found in the heroines of pastoral poems and in rococo womanhood, all with good manners as their ultimate aim. The romantic maiden of impetuous and passionate type whom we might have expected to find, the maiden who loves rashly, is still unknown ; though in Mrs. Radcliffe's habit of dividing her heroines into fair and dark types there is some indication of future developments in this quarter. Some amount of influence seems ultimately to have been exerted by a model from the immediately preceding period—by Samuel Richardson's type of young woman. If we divest Isabella of her medieval costume, listen to her conversation and take note of her fortunes, we soon discover " the virtuous maiden in distress." Both types are young and unusually beautiful, noble in their thoughts and exceedingly jealous of their virtue, which tyrants and wicked lords do their best to threaten. Their chastity is constantly in the greatest danger, but each time Pamela seems on the point of ruin, she manages to escape unharmed, exactly as Marina in *Pericles*. Both preserve their mental balance in the most delicate situations, until, mostly after countless tears, blushes, and moral sermons, they end up with a happy marriage. Richardson defines Clarissa Harlowe in the following terms : " A young Lady of great Delicacy, Mistress of all the Accomplishments, natural and acquired, that adorn the Sex, having the strictest Notions of filial Duty." [50]

This existence of endless persecution was now laid by the Walpole-Reeve-Radcliffe trio in romantic surroundings, and given greater effectivity by real adventures, the chief feature of which is a perpetual flight from persecutors in circumstances of great romanticism and terror. The maiden with adventures is familiar from Shakespeare, but in his case the type is, so to speak, commonly active, and not, like the maiden of early romanticism, a passive figure. What makes the persecution and hairbreadth escapes of the romantic maiden interesting to the student of literature is that, as a factor of excitement added to the plot, they point the way to the novel of excitement, and can for this reason be regarded as constituting a practically new invention of great vitality.

10

After all this discussion concerning the young hero and maiden of romance, it seems fitting that we should now permit them to achieve their most secret desire, that is, permit them in all privacy to confess their love. It might not be amiss to begin with a few words as to the nature of this elemental passion in the romances in question.

Love is one of the chief concerns of these books. The story of Matilda and Theodore is truly romantic, for is not one the daughter of a prince and the other, at least for the moment, a mere peasant ? The lovers need only see each other a few times before the flame of love burns so intensely that it can no longer be extinguished. Theodore refers to his beloved in such terms as " blessed saint," " divine protectress," " emanation of divinity," " charming maid," etc.; in his laments at her death-bed he used " every expression that despairing love could dictate." The virtuous and modest Matilda is more restrained, addressing her admirer only in terms like " young man," " noble youth," and letting herself be kissed only on her lily hand.[51] Their love is irritatingly platonic and moves within the strictest conventional limits. Still more prosaic and matter-of-fact is Manfred, who declares that his sole reason for contemplating marriage is the hope of a heir ; and equally so Isabella, in whom one can discern faint symptoms of jealousy. In Clara Reeve's work love is extremely everyday in quality, but in this respect Mrs. Radcliffe is better than her forerunners.

She, too, depicts the tyrant's love as undiluted passion or as a coldly calculating desire to safeguard his interests by marriage, but the love of the hero and heroine is so noble and pure that it is difficult to gauge its strength and the amount of fire under the superficial ashes. Here, too, love awakens at the first glance, on which occasion the youth regards the maiden " earnestly and mournfully " or " with mournful tenderness."

The maiden's behaviour awakens in the hero's heart " a mixed delight of hope and fear," of a kind never before experienced by him, and he cannot dispel her image from his mind. One of the preliminary ways of confessing love is the serenade : in the silence of the night the maiden hears, after a melancholy prelude, " a voice of more than magic expression swelled into an air so pathetic and tender, that it seemed to breathe the very soul of love." These mournful and tender

44

glances, serenades and sighs continue for hundreds of pages without getting any further. Finally the young hero sums up all his courage and puts the decisive question, not however with the impetuosity born of romantic passion, but in strict conformance with the finicking code of manners known to us from the laws of love according to pastoral guides, a code which apparently satisfies the author's own conception of the right procedure in such delicate matters. " Suffer me," he says in a tremulous voice, kneeling elegantly before his beloved, " to disclose to you the sentiments which you have inspired, and to offer you the effusions of a heart filled only with love and admiration." And when the maiden has given the coyest of coy signs that the conversation meets with her approval, the hero is so moved that he can scarcely do more than " weep his thanks over her hand," which he nevertheless now dares to hold in his own. When Valancourt is to propose to Emily— an event ripening through several hundred pages without yet coming to a conclusion—the situation becomes downright awkward. The hero feels it is now or never, but cannot proceed. They talk over journeys made in common and in the hero's voice is " a tremulous tenderness," but only after numerous detours does he finally venture to express the admiration he feels for Emily's " kindness." He receives no answer for the simple reason that Emily is in such a whirl of emotion that she cannot speak. He is afraid she is about to faint and tries to assist her, but at that Emily naturally re-covers sufficiently to " a sense of her situation." She is indeed in love with Valancourt, but is afraid of awakening his passion for the reason that she is not yet certain as to his suitability as a husband. In the end, the young hero has to be satisfied with her assurance that " she must think herself honoured by the good opinion of any person her father had esteemed," and that " you do both yourself and me injustice when you say I think you unworthy of my esteem : I will acknowledge that you have long possessed it, and—and——" (Here Emily faints in earnest, so that Valancourt is left after all without the historical definite answer he craved, which, as a matter of fact, he does not receive until quite at the end of the book. Re-covering, Emily says : " Can you excuse this weakness ? ") [52]

This over-elaborate style in matters of love is altogether alien to Shakespeare, whose full-blooded maidens care little in general for such circumspect ways and, where love is in question, do not conceal their desires. It is alien likewise to Richardson, whose Pamela would, without doubt, honestly and straightforwardly have given her consent, if only the noble lord had openly proposed marriage. But it is familiar from the world of rococo and pastoral idylls, whose conventions still carried weight among the devout and genteel bourgeoisie of eighteenth-century England, of whose virtues and culture Mrs. Radcliffe was herself a good representative.

It is illuminative to note that despite all their attempts in this direction, these authors are unable to lift love to the position of the chief material of their books. As depicted by them love is bloodless and dispassionate, conventionally insipid. This is due to their other aims, chief amongst which, as I have already stated, is the evocation by various materials and artifices of a romantic atmosphere of terror and suspense.

II

This dissertation on love brings us to another emotional factor in these romances, which is descriptive particularly of Mrs. Radcliffe's characters—sentimentality. In Walpole's book there are not many words of it ; instead, though not in any great degree, we find the " pale melancholy " frequently commented upon. Clara Reeve's work also yields in this, as in so many other respects, a scanty harvest, but in Mrs. Radcliffe's books it is all-pervading and takes an important place among her materials. There the eyes are filled " with tears of mingled joy and sorrow " ; " moving " scenes are enacted by the characters, emotions express themselves for the most in " tears and cries," and Heaven is thanked with clasped hands. The hearts of Mrs. Radcliffe's young women are susceptible to the gentlest ripples of the tender passion ; they are especially sensitive to all beauty, before all to that of nature. They, too, love to wander in majestic mountain scenes, where the lofty solitude and the sublime views that open out to them awaken a " holy fear " in their hearts. The beauty of landscapes, the soothing murmur of tall trees and the gentle plashing of waves lulls their minds to a delightful peace. Often, at such moments, they touch the strings of their lutes and as it were unconsciously, and with astonishing prosodical skill, arrange their thoughts in correct sonnet form, or still more frequently in an ode, the fashionable form of poetry of those days. The result is one of Mrs. Radcliffe's poetical interludes, "To Autumn," "To the Sunset," "To a Bat," "To a Nightingale," "To the Wind," "Song to an Evening Hour," etc. Extremely

characteristic of these is the song " To Melancholy," of which I
quote the following verses :

> Spirit of love and sorrow—hail !
> Thy solemn voice from far I hear,
> Mingling with evening's dying gale :
> Hail, with this sadly pleasing tear.
>
> O ! at this still, this lonely hour,
> Thine own sweet hour of closing day,
> Awake thy lute, whose charmful power
> Shall call up fancy to obey ;
>
> To paint the wild romantic dream,
> That meets the poet's musing eye,
> As on the banks of shadowy stream,
> He breathes to her the fervid sigh.[53]

We walk in romantic woods in the moonlight ; dim rays of
light, like a rain of enchantment, percolate through the over-
arching branches ; the heart is moved, old memories awaken
and our emotion dissolves in tears. To add to the effect we
hear at this moment a love-sick baritone sing on the bank of a
purling stream the eternal sadness of life and the torture of
love. All present fall to weeping and the tears flow in such
abundance that the very pages seem moist. Excessive emotion
is one of the main characteristics of Mrs. Radcliffe's work.

As to the origins of this sentimentality and melancholy,
she herself provides the key. The mottoes to her chapters
are quotations from Shakespeare, Milton, Thomson, Warton,
Gray, Collins, Mason, etc., which show the sources whence
this sentimentality, like the atmosphere of ruins analyzed
earlier, is derived.[54] The breezy and fresh sense of nature
in Shakespeare's works included materials that could well
be turned into sentimentality. In *Two Gentlemen of Verona*
Proteus advises Thurio to

> Visit by night your lady's chamber-window
> With some sweet consort to their instruments
> Tune a deploring dump ; the night's dead silence
> Will well become such sweet-complaining grievance.

Sylvia swears by " the pale queen of night." *The Merchant of
Venice* gives considerable scope to romantic moonlight. " The
moon shines bright," says Lorenzo to Jessica, continuing :

> . . . in such a night as this,
> When the sweet wind did gently kiss the trees
> And they did make no noise, in such a night
> Troilus methinks mounted the Troyan walls,
> And sigh'd his soul toward the Grecian tents,
> Where Cressid lay that night.

In the duet that ensues both enumerate their highest examples of great love, fondly imagining their climax to have occurred on " just such a night as this." Lorenzo declaims :

> How sweet the moonlight sleeps upon this bank !
> Here will we sit, and let the sounds of music
> Creep in our ears : soft stillness and the night
> Become the touches of sweet harmony.

The garden-scene in *Romeo and Juliet* takes place in the bewitching light of a southern moon, to the accompaniment of a nightingale. These and the other examples given earlier show why Mrs. Radcliffe could place him at the head of a series which ends in her own lachrymose and sighing sentimentality.

The emotional material and crepuscular melancholy inherited by her from the rest of the poets enumerated has already been referred to ; all that need be said is that none of them can compare with her in tearfulness. What were, so to speak, auxiliary factors in their case, became her chief ingredients, which she cultivated with so much assiduity and skill that, as we have seen, she was able to compress into twelve lines most of the verbal coinage of sentimental romanticism.

As regards the state of " melancholy," this, too, is not unknown to Shakespeare. He is not, however, to blame for its excessive cultivation in later times ; the responsibility in this respect is much more Milton's, of whose youthful moods it is the outcome. He begins *L'Allegro* on a defiant note :

> Hence, loathéd Melancholy,
>   Of Cerberus and blackest Midnight born
> In Stygian cave forlorn
>   'Mongst horrid shapes, and shrieks, and sights unholy !
> Find out some uncouth cell
> Where brooding Darkness spreads his jealous wings
> And the night-raven sings ;
>   There under ebon shades, and low-brow'd rocks
> As ragged as thy locks,
>   In dark Cimmerian desert ever dwell.

But in *Il Penseroso* we find him renouncing " vain, deluding joys," which are " the brood of Folly without father bred !", and turning to welcome what he had erstwhile cast out :

> But hail, thou goddess sage and holy,
> Hail divinest Melancholy !
> Whose saintly visage is too bright
> To hit the sense of human sight,

And therefore to our weaker view
O'erlaid with black, staid Wisdom's hue . . .

· · · · · ·

Come, pensive Nun, devout and pure,
Sober, steadfast, and demure,
All in a robe of darkest grain
Flowing with majestic train. . . .

Thus Milton flung his melancholy, with other materials of romance, to ring over a classical century, to echo with new accumulated features in the poetry of a whole school that bears his stamp. Collins, for instance, in *The Passions ; An Ode for Music*, sings :

With eyes up-raised, as one inspired,
Pale Melancholy sat retired ;
And from her wild sequester'd seat,
In notes by distance made more sweet,
Pour'd through the mellow horn her pensive soul :
    And dashing soft from rocks around
    Bubbling runnels join'd the sound ;
Through glades and glooms the mingled measure stole,
Or, o'er some haunted stream, with fond delay,
    Round an holy calm diffusing,
    Love of peace, and lonely musing,
In hollow murmurs died away.

A little more, a touch of deeper sadness and tears, and Mrs. Radcliffe's gamut of emotions is complete.

12

Let us now return to deal with the other characters in these romances. To begin with, let us take Manfred's pious and suffering wife Hippolita, who is no less than a saint, and whose descendants are found in every later romance in which an unhappy mother and child is needed. One cannot deny that the hard fate of Hippolita and her son Conrad reminds us of the noble Hermione and young Mamillius in *The Winter's Tale*, whose relationship to Leontes is in many respects similar to that of Hippolita to Manfred.

A more interesting figure is the worthy old monk of Otranto, Father Jerome, whose duty it is to preach peace and harmony, to adjust quarrels, to exhort to repentance and to teach people how to control their evil passions. In such form the man of the Church appears in all the romances now in question—a further example being Clara Reeve's Father Oswald—and is, in my opinion, a derivation of the hermit-motive dealt with earlier. In his present guise, owing to his excessive virtue and piousness, the monk is lacking in real romantic fascination, and must therefore be transformed into a " wolf in sheep's clothing " before the romanticists could succeed in making of him that embodiment of human crime which is to be his chief part in the future. Shakespeare provides a beautiful rendering of a good and gentle monk in Father Laurence (*Romeo and Juliet*), but in his works the opposite type is commoner. The suspicion is voiced that King John " is poison'd by a monk " :

> A monk, I tell you ; a resolved villain
> Whose bowels suddenly burst out. . . .

Cardinal Beaufort in the Second Part of *King Henry VI* is an ambitious and violent Prince of the Church, who dies in terrible fashion of poison with the added agony of a guilty conscience :

> For suddenly a grievous sickness took him,
> That makes him gasp and stare, and catch the air,
> Blaspheming God, and cursing men on earth.
> Sometime he talks as if Duke Humphrey's ghost
> Were by his side ; sometime he calls the king,
> And whispers to his pillow, as to him,
> The secrets of his overcharged soul. . . .

This kind of death is typical of the criminal monk as depicted by Protestant authors. Walpole himself enriches the gallery of such portraits in *The Mysterious Mother*, a play in which there are two criminal monks. Benedict is ready to perpetrate any deed of horror for the benefit of the Church, the only law recognized by him being the welfare of the Church. Walpole's Benedict becomes thus the prototype for such characters of the terror-romanticists. (I would here point out that my reason for not dealing with Mrs. Radcliffe's Schedoni in this connection is that he is more suitably included in a later chapter.) It is not without interest to follow how these monk-types, which originally bore the devout and naïvely innocent physiognomy of the hermit, gradually become transformed—in England as though in response to an outbreak of the Puritan spirit and in France to the anticlerical revolutionary spirit— into the kind of representative of vileness and popery the Protestant world fain would have seen in all such servants of the Roman Catholic Church. They become at the same time twin-brothers to the tyrant-type and even assimilate certain of the general outward characteristics of that sombre hero of romanticism. As we shall perceive later, the motive of the criminal monk was to prove extremely fruitful in the hands of terror-romanticist authors.

Passing by with a brief mention Walpole's loquacious and merry chamber-maid Bianca, whose task was, by her lively and witty chatter, " to set the pathetic in a stronger light," and for whom a model both as to name and character is to be found in *Othello*, and Clara Reeve's Sir Philip Harclay, Edmund's helper and friend, who is a kind of Sir Charles Grandison— compassionate, humane, kind to every one, of firm principles, unassuming, brave, etc.,—we arrive at Clara Reeve's old butler Joseph, the trusted servant of the Lovels. After the haunted suite, he is her second important innovation. This old man fulfils his duties faithfully, sighing and mourning over the fate of his former master and the latter's heir. It is clear that he knows something of weight bearing on the matter, but only after much persuasion does he relate what he knows. In the end he becomes the helper of the young rightful heir and a witness in his favour, being among the first to recognize and accept him. He it is who glides about the castle in these romances like a brownie, now and again letting fall some strange hint, a remark, or an enigmatic exclamation, gradually creating an atmosphere of suspense and mysterious fear which some- times brings the other servants, who are invariably super- stitious by nature, to the verge of panic. After this he becomes an important adjunct to haunted castles and romantic family histories. In Mrs. Radcliffe's works, the type is richly re- presented in a highly developed form. A corresponding character is to be found in Shakespeare : such are the old faithful servant Adam in *As You Like It* and Imogen's servant Pisanio in *Cymbeline*. The contrasting figure, the ever- ready criminal tool of the tyrant, met with also in these romances, is similarly to be found in Shakespeare : Goneril's servant Oswald begins the series of such villains.

Mention must be made of a certain female type in Mrs. Rad- cliffe's books who reveals possibilities of further development. This scheming and criminal-minded ambitious woman is seen in Mazzini's wife, Maria de Vellorno, who plays the part of a passionate and vicious high-born lady, not averse to committing any crime for the slightest personal advantage. The type is common in Shakespeare ; examples include the Duchess of Gloucester (*Henry VI*), and Margaret, the famous " She-wolf of France " ; Tamora in *Titus Andronicus ;* Lady Macbeth ; Regan and Goneril in *King Lear ;* the Queen in *Cymbeline*

—the cruel stepmother of fairy-tale—and Dionyza in *Pericles*. Belonging to the same class of woman on the Oriental side is Vathek's sorceress-mother Carathis.

Finally mention must be accorded the figures with which Mrs. Radcliffe peoples her landscapes ; these include travellers, gipsies, robbers and soldiers on the march. Her idyllic village scenes are enlivened by the presence of peasants, venerable elders and disporting young people. The curses of her robbers are heard even above the crash of the thunder : " Amid the peals of thunder, the oaths and execrations of the combattants added terror to the scene." These robbers live in caves or old disused buildings and are recognizable by their costume and the wild look in their eyes. A common sight is one where robbers are conveying the heroine towards an awful cave, the mouth of which is hidden behind pine-branches : " Her dreadful screams, her tears, her supplications, were ineffectual."

In *Two Gentlemen of Verona* we have robbers of whom one swears by " the bare scalp of Robin Hood's fat friar." In this case the thieves are outlawed gentry who conduct their profession on " noble principles." The forest scene where Valentine appears as a robber chieftain is made typically romantic by the fact that his own beloved, whom he is seeking, is brought before him captive. In *As You Like It* a romantic cave in the Forest of Ardennes provides a dwelling. The famous coast-scene, too, in *The Winter's Tale*, where Perdita is left in the desolate wilds, is gloomily romantic, a contrast being supplied by Florizel and Perdita's pastoral idyll. Hired assassins appear frequently in Shakespeare's plays. In *Titus Andronicus* we find mention of a chasm hidden away in the forest into which the corpse is flung :

> . . . What subtle hole is this,
> Whose mouth is cover'd with rude-growing briers,
> Upon whose leaves are drops of new-shed blood . . .

The witches in *Macbeth* appear on a deserted heath and in a cave, calculated with the accompanying noise of thunder and the lightning to give an impression of sombre nature. Such long-familiar materials as these came down in inheritance to the school of romanticism both directly and apparently also through the so-called picaresque school, an example being the works of Tobias Smollett, in which robber and cave-scenes of this description abound, particularly in connection with journeys.[55]

Before proceeding to deal with those features which gained

for the romances their reputation of being ghost-stories, there is reason to refer briefly to a few secondary details exploited freely and skilfully by romantic writers to obtain the atmosphere desired at a given point.

13

Even in details Mrs. Radcliffe shows a fine taste in her choice of what is specifically romantic. I shall deal first with music, which, as we have seen, plays an important part in the accomplishments of her young ladies. Almost all of Mrs. Radcliffe's characters are musical. Peculiarly romantic instruments appear to be the lute, guitar, French horn and oboe, the last-mentioned appearing frequently in Shakespeare also. Wandering in the forest, we are regaled with " a mournful strain, played with exquisite expression, from a distant horn," while the " delight which the scenery inspires, is heightened by the tones of a French horn." A traveller sometimes awakens every fair echo in the forest with " the tender accents of his oboe." Where the question is of a complete band or orchestra, the romanticist is unwilling that it shall be seen, preferring himself to listen to music at a distance, for greater softness of tone. " The musicians were placed in the most obscure and embowered spots, so as to elude the eye and strike the imagination." The music rendered is full of sentiment, soothing to sorrow and productive of tranquillity and peace and the strength to bear one's fate without repining. " He was on the point of resigning his virtue . . . when the soft notes of a lute surprised his attention. It was accompanied by a voice so enchantingly tender and melodious, that its sounds fell on the heart of Osbert . . . and he dissolved in kind tears of pity and contrition." The heroine is awakened from her dreams by soft melodies, so sweet and entrancing that they wipe away sorrow and grant the soul a tender and pensive pleasure. Especially romantic are those situations where the music accompanies the beat of oars on a moonlit sea. When Montoni is in Venice we are taken for a boating excursion in the moonlight through the lagoons and hear a formal competition of song and music between the signors and signorinas. On another page we are told: " The sound of the oars ceased, and a solemn strain of harmony (such as fancy wafts from the abodes of the blessed) stole upon the silence of the night. A chorus of voices now swelled upon the air, and died away at a distance. In the strain

Julia recollected the midnight hymn to the Virgin, and holy enthusiasm filled her heart." These are portions of *The Sicilian Romance* where Mrs. Radcliffe gives herself up to Catholic mysticism and the devotion born of its religious ceremonies, experiences which cause certain passages of her narrative to breathe the air of a world unknown to Protestant countries.[56]

Typically romantic are also the miniatures and the old manuscripts which relate of marvellous, fateful and terrible secrets. A miniature portrait is usually valued for the reason that it is the only remaining picture of some dearly-beloved person who has passed away ; it awakens old memories and provides an object beside which one can weep beautiful and legitimate tears in the silent watches of the night. Ever since the portrait of Hamlet's father and that of Ricardo saw the light, pictures of long-departed friends or relatives have in general played an important part in romantic stories. In the heated brains of the romanticists, the old conception of a picture awakening to life which happens when Walpole makes Ricardo's picture step out of its frame, gradually acquired new substance and with the passage of time accumulated new details.[57]

The old manuscript discovered in some secret hiding-place naturally contains a thrilling and terrible confession which has a decisive effect on the story ; the reading of it at night-time, when the wind howls without, is a good way of keeping up the excitement, even of increasing it, if the perusal is interrupted at its most interesting point. Very often the whole book is supposed to be based upon the discovery of just such an old manuscript. Did not "W. Marshall, Gent." declare *The Castle of Otranto* itself to be the translation of an Italian manuscript by Onuphrio Muralto, discovered in the north of England ? The whole of Clara Reeve's story is founded on an old manuscript accidentally discovered, and the same applies to Mrs. Radcliffe's *The Sicilian Romance*. In *The Romance of the Forest* Adeline finds in a forest castle a manuscript : " It was a small roll of paper, tied with a string and covered with dust " ; to her horror she recognizes her father's handwriting and learns that he has been murdered by his brother, the Marquis de Montalt, the man who is even then trying to encompass her ruin. Such was the entry into literature of the mysterious, forgotten, long-lost document—often discovered between the pages of a book, frequently couched in cipher, and disclosing either a will, a confession, a map or something of the kind—round which so many romantic tales have been written.[58]

Romantic also are the old letters, the time-yellowed papers found in the secret drawer of some recently deceased relative. Around them hovers a breath of past happiness and of sorrows now ended. Before setting out on a journey, St. Aubert shows his daughter Emily a little casket containing a few old letters and other papers; in the event of his death she is to burn them unread. We shall see later to what use the author could put this invention; meanwhile we note that the romanticism of old letters tied together with faded ribbon has been discovered.

The lamp which is extinguished at the most thrilling or dangerous moment by a breath of air or a gust of wind has already been mentioned. We need only refer to one of its most remarkable properties; whenever the heroine, or for that matter a whole company, is seized by a secret and unfathomable supernatural terror they believe themselves to see the lamp burn with a strange bluish flame. "Holy St. Peter!" cries Annette, Emily's loquacious chamber-maid, "look at that lamp, see how blue it burns!" What causes such a change is the propinquity of the ghost.[59]

14

Assuming that I have succeeded in providing some idea of the stage-setting of these romances, of the events occurring in them, of their character and materials, I shall now proceed to those marvels, horrors and tricks of construction on which their reputation as ghost-stories is based, and which are responsible for the thrills they awaken. These thrills, these feelings of suspense, are characteristic of the books in question, and form one of the reasons for my dealing with this species of literature as a class apart.

Really marvellous things occur in *The Castle of Otranto*. While Manfred's son Conrad is on his way to church for his wedding, a helmet of enormous size falls on him from the air without warning and crushes him to death. This casque, which is a hundred times larger than any helmet ever made for mortal man and furnished with a proportionately large black plume, is discovered to emanate from the statue of Alfonso. It goes on to work further miracles. When Theodore is thrust into captivity beneath it, it presses its edge through the stone paving, making a hole through which the prisoner reaches the castle vaults; and when Manfred is about to do violence to

Isabella, this remarkable helmet rises on a level with the windows, its plume waving as though in a storm, while a hollow clanking is heard. The plume moves violently again when the retinue of the Marquis Vicenza approaches the castle, nodding three times as though some invisible wearer had bowed.

In the castle hall there is a portrait of Manfred's grand-father, the original usurper of Otranto. Suddenly, Manfred sees the picture expand its chest, sigh deeply, leave the frame and step down, motioning to the grandson to follow. Manfred obeys, but just as he is about to follow the phantom into a certain room, an invisible hand quickly closes the door. Later on the servants relate that they had seen the foot and part of the leg of a ghost, corresponding in size to the dimensions of the helmet. The brazen horn mentioned earlier blows two blasts, as though to welcome an approaching procession, which includes a hundred knights who bear a gigantic sword, so heavy that they droop under their burden. As they come abreast of the helmet, the enormous sword of its own volition flies out of their hands towards the helmet and remains there immovable. This sword has been found by the Marquis Vicenza far away in Palestine, where a dying hermit had informed him of its existence ; from the hermit he learned also that his daughter Isabella was in danger. As the Marquis, however, does not seem to carry out the wish of Saint Nicholas with due exactitude, this wish having for its object the down-fall of Manfred, the hermit's ghost appears to him in the castle chapel. Thunderstruck, the Marquis suddenly sees the former hermit before him, under his cowl the fleshless jaws and empty eye-sockets of a skeleton.

A statue of Alfonso, the former rightful owner of the castle, stands in the chapel ; the conversation turning on the marriage between Conrad and Isabella, three drops of blood fall from the statue's nose, signifying that the blood of the usurper and murderer may not mix with innocent blood. The chamber-maid Bianca sees on the top banisters of the main staircase a hand in armour, so big, so big—— Bianca does not, it is true, say how big it was, but we can conclude it to have accorded in size with the sword, helmet and foot. A last miracle is pro-vided by the final catastrophe : the walls of the castle are thrown down with a mighty force and the form of Alfonso, dilated to an immense magnitude, appears in the centre of the ruins. It is heard to utter : " Behold in Theodore the true heir of Alfonso," and, accompanied by a clap of thunder, ascends solemnly towards heaven. The clouds disperse, Saint

Nicholas appears to receive Alfonso, after which both vanish " in a blaze of glory " and are lost to mortal sight.[60]

The legend-like naïvity with which these marvellous happenings are cast before the reader from the very first page, with no attempt at explaining their nature, is at first undoubtedly apt to evoke amazement ; but this soon fades, for one is quickly aware that this side of the story is intended to be read in the light of a medieval legend overflowing with miracles, in which the marvels of fairy-tales are presented with a solemn air, as though natural to the surroundings in which the story moves. Was it not Walpole's purpose to combine the two species of romance, the old and the modern ? In the preface to the second edition he expressly points out that in the former variety all was imagination and improbability, while the latter attempts to imitate nature ; he has tried, therefore, in his own book to give full scope to his imagination, at the same time guiding the actions of his mortals in full conformity with the laws of nature and common logic. He regarded the method as quite natural in a story of this type (witness the preface to the first edition), dealing as it does with a time when belief in all kinds of miracles prevailed to an extent that made any description of the life of those days inconceivable without them. Walpole stuck to his programme faithfully, for the weird miracles seem indeed to have little connection with the motives underlying the actions of his characters, except of course where they intrude violently into the life of some particular individual. If the characters had been really influenced by them and the result had been something truly medieval, reflecting the atmosphere of a world dominated by miracles and strange beliefs, Walpole's book might have had a value beyond that of a mere terror-romanticist curiosity. As it is, it is vain to seek any deeper purpose in the miracles of Otranto ; they were inserted by Walpole in conformity with his theory, with the intention of producing the kind of work promised in his preface. With these artifices of his it was hardly possible for Walpole to build up any true atmosphere of suspense ; what there is springs from the constant danger to which Isabella is exposed.

Clara Reeve's method is essentially different. She admits outright in her preface that her book is the literary offspring of *The Castle of Otranto*, written " upon the same plan " and being " an attempt to blend together the most attractive and interesting circumstances of the ancient romance and modern novel." To achieve this purpose the necessary interest was to be awakened by " a sufficient degree of the marvellous, to excite the attention, enough of the manners of real life, to give an air of probability to the work ; and enough of the pathetic, to engage the heart in its behalf." As regards *The Castle of Otranto*, " it palls upon the mind. . . . The reason is obvious; the machinery is so violent that it destroys the effect it is intended to excite. Had the story been kept within the utmost *verge* of probability, the effect had been preserved." This, then, is the programme followed by Clara Reeve in writing her romance.

The difference between it and Walpole's book is at once apparent in the fact that Clara Reeve does not include more of the supernatural than we are ordinarily accustomed to in the form of old tales and our general superstitiousness. Thus the murdered Lord Lovel appears to his friend Philip Harclay in a dream, bidding him welcome to the castle. The servants are convinced that the ghosts of Lord and Lady Lovel have often been seen in the haunted suite. Strange noises and apparitions frighten those who have the temerity to enter these rooms. A noise is heard there as of someone moving through a narrow passage. In his sleep the young hero sees his parents, who give him their solemn blessing. He seems to hear from the room below a great din, the clashing of swords and the sound of something falling with a loud crash. A grisly, hollow sigh is heard three times, all the doors fly open, a pale glittering light appears at the door and a man clad cap-à-pie enters the room. On the arrival of the rightful heir the gates and double doors of the castle fly open untouched by human hand. At the moment of his entrance into the lower hall, the doors of all the rooms open.[61]

As we can see, these materials contain nothing particularly new or even startling, as they are already known from tales and traditions of superstition. As the author herself does not seem inclined to overestimate their importance, but of set purpose leaves us uncertain as to whether her characters really believe in them, and as to whether they were actually experienced or merely dreamed, she succeeds in creating at the most a cosy atmosphere of ghost-stories told by the fireside. Some faint thrill of secret dread and horror is naturally included, especially as the author adds to the interest and suspense by certain small artifices which Mrs. Radcliffe was to use later with such effect. These include the suspense reflected in the young hero's alarm when, after hearing those dreadful sighs, his fear is increased by hearing a knocking at

the door. Without doubt he—and the reader with him—
expects some gruesome phantom to appear, but in answer to
his exhortation the door is opened by—the old seneschal of
the castle. Here we have one of the first examples of a situation of terror and suspense being ended ludicrously.

Mrs. Radcliffe was not satisfied with either method of
using the supernatural. Walpole gave only the naïve miracles
of legend, Clara Reeve an ordinary ghost-story atmosphere;
what Mrs. Radcliffe wanted—without any explanatory pre-
faces—was to abolish such stratagems but yet create a much
stronger and deeper atmosphere of secret suspense. To
achieve this she set to work in the following manner.

She arranged her plot and action so that the chief impression is a sense of the young heroine's incessant danger;
her life is a perpetual flight from one peril to another. This
and the manner of her numerous escapes provide the main
story. " The public were," says Sir Walter Scott, " chiefly
aroused, or rather fascinated, by the wonderful conduct of a
story in which the author so successfully called out the feelings
of mystery and of awe, while chapter after chapter, and
incident after incident, maintained the thrilling attraction of
awakened curiosity and suspended interest." [62]

An example is the following passage. Already on the fifth
page of *The Sicilian Romance* we are told of a light seen one
evening in the unused wing of the castle, which is naturally
haunted. Suddenly this light disappears, and we are given no
solution to the mystery. This uncertainty, which increases
the reader's suspense the longer it can be maintained, continues until at last, following a reappearance of the light, a
quite ordinary man emerges from a door in the castle tower
with a lantern in his hand. To a great extent the suspense
created by our expectancy of something special, perhaps even
of something supernatural, now collapses, leaving us somewhat discomfited; then, without warning, the thread is
taken up again. What was this mysterious man doing in the
uninhabited tower? The owner makes light of the matter
and with his servants searches the whole building. In vain,
for no explanation is discovered. Finally, the rumour that the
castle is after all haunted gains more and more credence,
especially after the unknown man has once again flickered into
view with his lantern.

Curiosity is then awakened by strange and fearsome wails,
heard in the silence of the night. These sounds are " sullen,"
" hollow," " dreadful," and the awe created by them is con-

siderable. " One night, as he lay ruminating on the past, in melancholy dejection, the stillness of the place was suddenly interrupted by a low and dismal sound. It returned at intervals in hollow sighings, and seemed to come from some person in deep distress." A groan, longer and more dreadful, was repeated. He asks his father what these sounds can mean and is given the explanation that a certain della Campo had been murdered in the castle in his grandfather's time ; perchance it is the murdered man's spirit that wails because he had not been given Christian burial. The laments meanwhile continue, becoming increasingly exciting and nerve-racking.[63]

Thus the flashing of the mysterious lantern and the wailing continue through hundreds of pages, almost to the end of the book, at which point the reader's suspense and devouring curiosity is ended in a manner apt to disconcert and irritate : the sighing ghost turns out to be no della Campo, but the living wife of the castle's cruel master, whom the monster has given out as dead, after having hidden her in a secret dungeon in the castle vaults. The lantern-bearer is her servant, employed to carry food to her. It was this poor captive who at night-time sighed and lamented her fate, wholly unaware that her voice carried to her children's ears. And to give the last fine touch to her narrative, the author permits the discovery to be made by the captive's daughter, just as she herself is in flight from her own threatening fate. Yet, despite this undoubtedly thrilling and dreadful crime, the reader feels that he has been fooled ; his curiosity has been excited to such a pitch that he cannot be satisfied with this extremely " natural " *dénouement.*

The Romance of the Forest does not rise to such heights. The reader is alarmed by strange voices in corridors, by rumours that the ghost of a murdered man walks at night amidst the ruins, and even by an occasional hollow sigh in the silent darkness. But all this is deprived of any effect by being described as the ordinary superstitiousness of the servants ; and once, when the heroine believes herself to see a real ghost, the reader is all too soon made aware that it is a freak of the frightened girl's imagination. Listening in her lonely chamber to the murmur of the wind, Adeline thinks she hears a sigh. " Her imagination refused any longer the control of reason, and turning her eyes a figure, whose exact form she could not distinguish, appeared to pass along an obscure part of the chamber." To this exalted state had she been brought by a perusal of the manuscripts referred to earlier.[64]

There is no denying that *The Mysteries of Udolpho* are exceedingly mysterious at times. By forbidding Emily to read the letters in his casket, St. Aubert whets both her curiosity and that of the reader ; but she—in contrast to the reader—is willing to curb hers. On her father's death she burns them without so much as a glance. The effect of this literary artifice is to leave a half-resentful curiosity germinating in the reader's mind, causing him to imagine all manner of mysteries, a curiosity that increases during the hundreds of pages where nothing is done to satisfy it. At the very end of the book it turns out that there was nothing of particular import in the letters : they referred to the love affairs of the dead man, which have little to do with the main story. They have thus been used solely as an artifice to keep the reader's interest and curiosity alive.

In the convent where St. Aubert dies, wonderful guitar-music is frequently heard at night. No one appears to know who the musician is and no one has seen him. Sometimes the music is accompanied by a voice so sad and sweet that it really seems supernatural. The music often pauses after a few solemn chords, rises again to " pensive delight " and ceases in a final melody that seems to " waft the hearer's soul to Heaven." This miracle, too, has its natural explanation ; the musician is a half-crazy nun, Signora Laurentini, who is the legal owner of Udolpho. It was her mysterious disappearance that created the rumour that Montoni had murdered her ; the cryptic, knowing utterances of the old seneschal and a certain dreadful painting hidden behind a black cloth all help to bear out this suspicion.

Once, while walking idly through the deserted halls and corridors of the castle, Emily chances to see in one of the rooms a picture with a black silk curtain before it. Her curiosity is awakened and she wants to lift the veil, but does not dare. The prattling maid Annette, who has arrived on the scene, exclaims : " Holy Virgin ! what can this mean ? This is surely the picture they told me of at Venice." By this time the reader, too, has had his curiosity excited and page by page he awaits a solution to this mystery. The birth of this mystery is aptly described by Jane Austen in her *Northanger Abbey*. Isabella asks Catherine :

" Have you gone on with Udolpho ? "

" Yes, I have been reading it ever since I woke, and I am got to the black veil."

" Are you, indeed ? How delightful ! Oh ! I would not

tell you what is behind the black veil for the world ! Are not you wild to know ? "

" Oh ! yes, quite ; what can it be ? But do not tell me : I would not be told upon any account. I know it must be a skeleton ; I am sure it is Laurentina's skeleton. Oh ! I am delighted with the book ! I should like to spend my whole life in reading it, I assure you ; if it had not been to meet you, I would not have come away from it for all the world."

At last, one evening, Emily calls up all her courage and lifts the cloth, only to let it fall again in terror and to flee. What it was that frightened her is even now left untold. Not until the plot is finally unravelled do we learn that the veil did not conceal a painting but a niche in the wall containing the waxen effigy of a corpse wrapped in a winding-sheet. Its face is partly decomposed and eaten by worms, which are to be seen on the face and hands. The Udolpho family had been compelled to procure this emblem of mortality as a punishment for some sin committed against the Church. Such is the entire history of this awesome hidden picture, whose sole mission in the book is to create an atmosphere of suspense and mystery apart from the actual plot.

Here are a few more examples of Mrs. Radcliffe's methods. Montoni intends to tell his friends what he knows concerning the disappearance of Signora Laurentini, and begins, " ' But as there are some singular and mysterious circumstances attending that event, I shall repeat them.' ' Repeat them,' said a voice." The company is startled, but Montoni retains his composure and tries to continue : " 'Listen, then, what I am going to say.' ' Listen,' said a voice." Whereupon the company breaks up in alarm and even the reader hardly knows what to think. He has been led by the expressions of the old seneschal to suspect Montoni of having murdered Signora Laurentini, the castle's rightful owner, and now he believes that the story Montoni was about to relate, until Laurentini's ghost took a hand in the matter, was merely intended to dispel any suspicions attaching to him. The voice may also have been an echo, or only the whispering of Montoni's own conscience. As it turns out, there is nothing supernatural in the occurrence, the owner of the voice being an escaped prisoner who, in his strayings through the castle, had chanced upon a secret passage behind the wall where the company were gathered ; to frighten the tyrant he had repeated his words in a ghostly voice. Montoni has played absolutely no part in Signora Laurentini's disappearance, whatever other crimes he may have on his conscience. Mrs. Radcliffe had learned this artifice from Walpole's *Mysterious Mother*, in which a strange echo of quite natural origin startles the plotting monks.

An awesome being is wont to appear at night on the walls of Udolpho. The soldiers have seen it but have not accosted it. It is spoken of in such whispers that the reader's imagination, ever ready to be fired by the weird and the supernatural, is led on to the most erratic fancies. But here again, there is nothing extraordinary, only an ordinary prisoner who, with the permission of his gaoler, steals out at night for a breath of air.

It must be said of Mrs. Radcliffe's books that they really succeed in awakening an atmosphere of suspense, so that the reader is more afraid of what might happen than of what does happen. The real events are of a nature calculated to dissatisfy the expectations previously awakened, and therefore the final impression they make is feeble. She, too, thus failed to invent a uniformly effective and successful technique.

15

How, we may ask, did these writers come to light upon the supernatural as literary material, to occasion this " renascence of wonder " [65] in English literature ? In seeking the answer to this question let us not forget the literary programmes published by Walpole and Clara Reeve, in which they state their intention of combining ancient and modern traits in their works, thus hinting at their sources. The " ancient " denoted their conceptions and memories of older Elizabethan romanticism, of the literature of the time when Spenser revived in his *Faerie Queene* the chevaleresque romanticism of Arthurian legends with their Excaliburs and corresponding huge helmets, and when Shakespeare, as we have so often been reminded, cultivated romantic material in a spirit that was to prove decisive for later romanticists. To my mind the most obvious and influential source is Shakespeare, of whose machinery of the supernatural a brief summary may be given.

Witches, evil spirits and supernatural beings appear more frequently in Shakespeare's plays than in any later literature. Take Ariel, spirit of air, who can raise winds and " burn in many places " in the eyes of frightened sailors ; or the witch Sycorax, who for various evil deeds and fearful witchcraft has been banished from her home, and who recalls to our minds the vampires of romance and fairy-tale; or her son Caliban, half-beast, a loathsome personification of animal nature in man as conceived in the terribly penetrative vision of the poet. Unsurpassed in its romantic half-light and its finely poetical intuitive joy of life is the fairy kingdom in *A Midsummer Night's Dream*, King Oberon and his dream court.[66] In the first part of *Henry VI* Joan la Pucelle is depicted as allied with supernatural beings which appear at her incantations. The second part of the same play provides the sorcery scene in Gloucester's garden, when the sorcerers Jourdain, Bolingbroke and Southwell raise a spirit called Asmath, with the intention of putting to it several momentous questions. The true hour for witchcraft is the

> Deep night, dark night, the silent of the night,
> The time of night when Troy was set on fire ;
> The time when screech-owls cry, and ban-dogs howl,
> And spirits walk, and ghosts break up their graves. . . .

The fearsome witches in *Macbeth* first appear weaving their weird spells on a romantic deserted heath, amid the crashing of thunder and the flashing of lightning ; they are next seen in a typical witches' cave, cooking " deeds without a name " in the black slime of their cauldron. In this scene, the romantic atmosphere of black magic is as perfectly rendered as one could wish, and is intensified by the wild and dismal nocturnal illumination. The description of the apothecary's shop in *Romeo and Juliet* brings to mind the magician's laboratories of the romanticists :

> And in his needy shop a tortoise hung,
> An alligator stuff'd, and other skins
> Of ill-shap'd fishes. . . .

The list of accessories for the witches in *Macbeth* is peerless.

Materials of this description do not, it is true, appear in the works with which we are at present concerned, but in later romantic works they are of importance for the furnishing of fear-inspiring interiors. With regard to ghosts, which do enter into the present analysis, Shakespeare is an obvious master in their application and in his knowledge of ghost-lore. In the *Merry Wives of Windsor* we are informed that the correct time for spirits to walk is in the night between twelve and one o'clock. From *Measure for Measure* we recollect " the dead midnight," while the awesome atmosphere is enhanced by the talk of executions and the appearance of the executioner and his assistant. In *Richard III* the ghosts of all those whom he has murdered appear to the sleeping king, foretelling his defeat in the approaching battle. Awakening from an agonized sleep he laments :

> O coward conscience, how dost thou afflict me !
> The lights burn blue. It is now dead midnight.
> Cold fearful drops stand on my trembling flesh. . . .

The ghost of Julius Cæsar appears to Brutus on the eve of a decisive battle. Macbeth personifies the dread visions of his troubled conscience in the ghost of Banquo, addressing it at the height of the festival :

> Avaunt ! and quit my sight ! Let the earth hide thee !
> Thy bones are marrowless, thy blood is cold ;
> Thou hast no speculation in those eyes
> Which thou dost glare with.

And what is Lady Macbeth as, carrying a candle, she walks in her sleep and apostrophizes the blood-stains on her hands, but the phantom of the criminal white woman of the haunted castle who walks the scene of her bloody deeds. A typical terror-romanticist scene is the castle of Elsinore in the moonlight, with its armour-clad sentinels who are afraid of ghosts and seized by a feeling of dread, come to the famous conclusion that there is more between heaven and earth than Horatio dreamed of in his philosophy. When " the dead vast and middle of the night " arrives, when the clock strikes one and the ghost of Hamlet's father appears, the scene of horror is complete. We are told that a ghost is like air, invulnerable, and that when the cock crows for the first time it disappears like " a guilty thing upon a fearful summons." We learn, further, that the herald of morning, the cock, wakens with its song the god of Day, when supernatural beings vanish. On Christmas Eve the cock crows the night through, and then no ghost can walk. For this reason Christmas Eve is a healthy time ; the planets exert no evil influence, no charm can work and witches are without power. Hamlet's comrades forbid him to follow the ghost, fearing that it might entice him into a place of danger, there to alter its shape and to destroy him. A ghost seeks revenge because it has been violently snatched from this life in the flower of its sins, unrepentant. It can appear at will to some members of a company and remain invisible to others, as witness Banquo's ghost ; only the accomplice, Lady Macbeth, can understand her husband's terror.

It will be seen from these examples that the ghost had attained a truly important position in the plays of Shakespeare and had thus at an early date become a familiar and tolerated object in English literature. An alien, noting the part played in English literature and legends by ghosts and related superstitions might be excused for concluding that a leavening of the blood-inheritance of weird and awful, neolithic visions of terror left by the ancient Celts was still at work. It is illuminating to descry signs of this leavening even in literary periods consciously based on the intellect and a desire for reality, periods when Fancy, the adored chief muse of the romanticists, was shut up closely in a cage, hardly daring to emit a warble, with stern Doctor Johnson keeping guard outside like an angry watch-dog.[67] Thus, for instance, Richardson, who desired above all else to depict reality and to keep his imagination in check, makes Pamela fly from Mrs. Jewkes in the night, fixing, according to established custom, the hour of her flight at midnight, when the night was dark and foggy.[68] It is the same eerie hour as the terror-romanticists use for sending their young heroines into the night to escape from some threatening danger.

The great realist Fielding, who in a general aspect is a quite modern narrator, refers in mocking tone to matters supernatural, yet he too can be caught napping. Thus we read that in Mr. Allworthy's Gothic house there was " an air of grandeur that struck you with awe." The hour of midnight often seems to him " dreadful and ghostly." He takes pleasure in scenes where someone is dressed in white blood-stained garments, has his face whitened and a sword put into his right hand and a candle into his left ; Fielding is sure that even in a churchyard one would hardly find a more gruesome object. Ghosts interest him to such an extent that he writes " a wonderful long chapter concerning the marvellous," in which he attempts to show which supernatural beings can fittingly be used by a modern author. He admits that " the only supernatural agents which can in any manner be allowed to us moderns, are ghosts, but of these I would advise an author to be extremely sparing." For moonlight he has a truly romantic eye : " The solemn gloom which the moon casts on all objects, is beyond expression beautiful, especially to an imagination which is desirous of cultivating melancholy ideas." He tells the story of a ghost that beat its own still living friend ; describes a scene where a persecuted woman is saved from robbers in a forest ; and waxes sentimental on hearing an owl at midnight, to which he gives the poetic appellation of " shrill chorister of the night." [69]

May it be granted, however, in Fielding's case that his standpoint towards these matters—as towards so many others—was airily and merrily satirical. By Tobias Smollett, that fine picaresque writer, they are treated with greater gravity; his books bear frequent witness to an awakening interest in romantic materials. Thus Strap and Roderick Random are alarmed at midnight by the intrusion of a raven, which, need it be stated, is the pet of the Devil and of witches. Captain Trunnion is so scared by a ghost fashioned by these two young scamps that a cold sweat bedecks his limbs, his knees rattle together and his hair stands on end. Ferdinand, Count Fathom, spends the night in a forest where the inky darkness and the silence and solitude of the spot awaken strange visions in his soul. The lightning begins to flash, the thunder to roll and the storm breaks in a deluge of rain. Rinaldo, hearing that his beloved Monimia has died and been buried in a certain lonely church, decides to visit her grave at night-time. Of course the night turns out unusually dark. Arrived at the church and walking in its deserted vaults he hears a clock strike midnight echoed by the cry of an owl from some adjacent ruins. He regards his companions with bloodshot eyes, begs them to leave him, and casts himself on his sweetheart's grave, where he remains until morning. The following night he repeats his pilgrimage and falls into a trance. Organ melodies played by an invisible hand awaken him and the whole church is suddenly illuminated. Staring around he sees a woman in white attire who cries " Rinaldo " in Monimia's voice. He is struck dumb with terror, his hair bristles and cold tremors shake him. But to his delight, and the reader's disappointment, the white being turns out to be Monimia herself, who, to escape from the clutches of Count Fathom, has feigned death and allowed her effigy to be buried.[70] James Beattie's young Edwin would

> Dream of graves, and corses pale;
> And ghosts, that to the charnel-dungeon throng,
> And drag a length of clanking chain, and wail,
> Till silenc'd by the owl's terrific song,
> Or blast that shrieks by fits the shuddering isles along.

An account of the use of romantic ghost-material in earlier [71] and contemporary literature would swell to impracticable dimensions. I would particularly mention that the romantic treatment of ghosts in folk-poetry, introduced into literature about this time by Percy's ballads with considerable effect, if not precisely on the authors now under discussion, is dealt with further on, in direct connection with the influence it exerted. To show, however, how characteristic of this period and that immediately preceding it the subject of ghosts really was, I will only add that Doctor Johnson devoted considerable thought to it. It sounds almost incredible that while reading Shakespeare at Oxford he should have been afraid of the ghost in *Hamlet*, even as Gray admits to having experienced fear the first time he read *The Castle of Otranto*. Descriptive in this respect are the conversations with Boswell at The Mitre :

"We talked of belief in ghosts. He said, 'Sir, I make a distinction between what a man may experience by the mere strength of his imagination, and what imagination cannot possibly produce. Thus, suppose I should think that I saw a form, and heard a voice cry, Johnson, you are a very wicked fellow, and unless you repent you will certainly be punished, my own unworthiness is so deeply impressed upon my mind, that I might *imagine* I thus saw and heard, and therefore I should not believe that an external communication had been made to me. But if a form should appear, and a voice should tell me that a particular man had died at a particular place, and a particular hour, a fact which I had no apprehension of, nor any means of knowing, and this fact, with all its circumstances, should afterwards be unquestionably proved, I should, in that case, be persuaded that I had supernatural intelligence imparted to me '."

In 1762 came the sensation of the Cock Lane ghost, which Johnson was said to have believed in, though according to Boswell this was not the case, Johnson being one of those who helped to expose the trickery practised in this affair. At all events, Johnson and Boswell conversed several times in all gravity on the subject of ghosts and the reasons for their materialization, sometimes even in company ; "speaking of ghosts," "the conversation turning on ghosts" and other similar openings to paragraphs in Boswell's work, prove that the supernatural was common subject of conversation in those days.[72]

The possibilities of utilizing ghosts in plays and in literature in general were also theoretically discussed in the eighteenth century—both Addison and Steele wrote on the subject in *The Tatler* (1709), *The Spectator* (1711-13) and *The Guardian* (1713). Fun is made of scenic ghosts. Addison declared that nothing pleased and alarmed a British public more than a ghost, especially if it appeared in a bloody shirt. A play was often saved by its ghost, even though it did no more than walk

across the stage or rise from a trap-door and without a single
word sink out of sight again (*Spectator*, No. 44). Steele opines
that the Grub Street publishers purposely frighten their superstitious countrymen with tales of murder, ghosts, wonders and
demons. He himself was wont to conjure up his spirits on
the approach of winter and to keep his ghosts ready for the
long, dark evenings (*Guardian*, No. 58). Addison too is of the
opinion that there should be a special season for these various
terrors, and that when they are used solely as poetical aids, one
cannot only endure but even approve them. The ghost in
Hamlet is a masterpiece of its kind, executed with all the artifices
necessary to either interest or fear (*Spectator*, No. 44). With
regard to ghost scenes he declares that they awaken in the reader
a pleasant species of terror. They recall memories of childhood's
tales and touch the springs of secret fear in each of us. On the
whole, he remarks, we are convinced that the world contains
other intelligent beings than ourselves and that there are
several categories of spirits obeying different laws from those
to which mankind is subjected. Therefore when any of these
is presented to us in credible form, we cannot regard the
presentment as wholly preposterous. Among writers addicted
to the use of the supernatural, the English—says Addison—
are the best, and best among these is Shakespeare. This is,
however, due to his genius (*Spectator*, No. 141). Within these
bounds Addison thus tolerated ghosts—presented credibly
and with genius.

Finally, I would point out that the appearance of ghosts
and, generally speaking, of scenes of terror in romantic literature
denoted thus a revived use of material found in older literature
and among the everyday surroundings of the authors, with the
difference, as regards literature, that it was now given greater
prominence and could even form the chief interest. Before
proceeding to deal with the achievements of Walpole and his
followers in this field, I must first add a word or two regarding
their sources.

The origin of Walpole's miracles is obscure, nor have I
anything definite to say on the subject. Alfonso's grave and
the statue from whose nose dripped blood, recall the grave
and the statue that awoke to life in the story of Don Juan.[73]
Even the name Isabella appears in the same story. Also the
living statue in *The Winter's Tale*, Hermione, may more
directly have affected the author's conception. Walpole's
enormous sword that had been discovered in Asia Minor and
the procession needed to carry it carry one back to the time of

the Crusades, at which period the action is supposed to occur. At Antioch a marvellous discovery is said to have been made at that time, nothing less than the spear of Longinus having been excavated, at a depth of six feet, in the moment of greatest danger. This spear was carried in a long procession through the streets of Antioch. It is worth noting that Walpole's sword was also discovered at a depth of six feet. Consciously or not, Walpole was perhaps led, in his search for some miraculous Oriental object, to imitate the legend of the spear ; remembering King Arthur's Excalibur and the correspondingly large crested helmet, he altered the spear to a sword. The trifling detail of the six feet had meanwhile fastened in his memory and slipped into his description, to give rise later to the suspicion that what he is really talking about is the spear of Longinus. I give the idea for what it is worth. Walpole may also have been thinking of the depth of an ordinary grave when he wrote his six feet ; the matter is a small one. Gulliver's sword, too, was a gigantic one when borne by the pygmies.

It is equally difficult to draw positive conclusions with regard to the origin of the enormous helmet—apart from the fact that it originally belonged to Alfonso's statue. Its size may have been a logical consequence of the dimensions of the sword, for the bearer of such a weapon would naturally be proportionately equipped throughout. The author's imagination may also have been touched by the many famous helmets of which stories go back to antique days. Pallas Athene was depicted as wearing a helmet with a large waving plume ; King Arthur's helmet has already been mentioned ; and in no case may we forget the helmet of Mambrinus, famed in tales of chivalry, which so excited Don Quixote's admiration. What Don Quixote took to be the helmet was only the brass disk of a village barber, but to him it was the wonder of wonders, fashioned in pagan days for the fabulously big-headed hero. Such magnifying of facts in an author's imagination is by no means rare. Let us leave therefore Walpole's helmet in peace, while impressing on our minds its waving plume, for that is to prove to be of great vitality.[74]

The materials used by Clara Reeve and Mrs. Radcliffe and the origin of these have already been sifted. All that is left to be dealt with is Mrs. Radcliffe's great invention, the creation of an atmosphere of suspense, which in greater degree than the evocation of actual terror is the special characteristic of these romances. Models for Mrs. Radcliffe's methods exist in older literature, especially in Shakespeare. A good example is the scene in *Macbeth*, immediately after the murder, where a loud continuous knocking is heard at the castle gate. The spectator can hardly refrain from connecting with this noise a sense of the existence of some retributory power, and in increasing suspense listens to the knocking. It makes a deep impression on all concerned, one proof of which is that Lady Macbeth remembers it when walking in her sleep. But just as suspense is at its height, a ludicrous effect is attained by the entry of the knocker, a perfectly normal human being. The artifice is the same as that used by Mrs. Radcliffe. Here we find an instance of the terror of melodrama and of melodramatic methods being adapted for use in the new type of romance.[75]

16

It may now be as well to point out that the romances with which we are dealing are not " ghost-stories " in the general acceptance of the term. The ghosts in them are, after all, but secondary characters. Walpole's chief aim was to present a series of medieval miracles grafted on to everyday life ; Clara Reeve's the creation of an atmosphere of ruins and legends ; Mrs. Radcliffe's the creation of a dramatic feeling of suspense running parallel with her copious outbursts of sentimentality. This feeling of suspense is nevertheless raised sometimes to such a pitch that the passage from suspense to actual terror is achieved.[76]

As we have previously noted, the literary programme followed by Walpole and after him by Clara Reeve, was to combine the ancient and the modern. Besides placing their action in the past, they strove to achieve an " ancient " effect by the use of supernatural material. This brings us to the question, first of their success in dealing with the supernatural, and secondly of the extent and form in which such material can be used in literature.

To my mind, Walpole and Clara Reeve were on the right track, in that when they did chance to make use of the supernatural they did not seek to weaken and possibly to efface the effect by any pseudo-natural explanations. My own view is that the supernatural is a perfectly legitimate subject for imaginative works of art, with the proviso, however, that by his power of suggestion, the author succeeds in subjecting the reader's imagination to his own, in other words, succeeds in lulling the reader's logical faculties and hypnotizing him into the charmed circle of the writer's own imagination. It is therefore necessary for the author to be equipped with strong suggestive powers, and to achieve his aim he must also have acquired considerable skill in construction. It is this lack of power of suggestion and technique that renders ineffective Walpole's and Clara Reeve's use of the supernatural. Their marvels are unrelated to the psychic life of their characters, and thus fail to affect the reader even indirectly. Lack of suggestion is likewise responsible for the final non-appearance of a psychic state of horror, for this, too, demands a relaxing of the logical faculties and a psychic stiffening into a hypnotic attitude of fear. It would have been an additional error if they had attempted to invent some natural explanation for their supernatural agencies, for it would have effaced even the slight effect their miracles unquestionably do achieve by their suddenness and dimensions.

Mrs. Radcliffe's skilfully built atmosphere of suspense and her technical deftness show that she understood the importance of suggestion and made frequent and conscious use of it. Her mistake is that she uses her power solely for suggestion's sake, without considering what possibility she had of satisfying the expectations it awakened. As her imagination fails to supply what the reader has been led to await, and most of her enigmas are explained away as insignificant auxiliary details capable of perfectly natural solutions, the final state of the reader is one of irritation and chagrin. Once the power of suggestion is used to awaken an earnest expectation of anything, in the present case of something supernatural, this expectation must be fulfilled, if only for the reason that the reader demands it. On the other hand, Mrs. Radcliffe's power of suggestion is great enough to induce a certain measure of terror, so that her books can be regarded as to some extent earning the epithet of " romances of terror." I conclude, therefore, that none of these writers succeeded in discovering a definitely effective method of using the supernatural, although they certainly did make some inventions of value in this sphere, the most important being the use of suggestion.

Mention of methods of inducing terror brings up another motive, lacking in these romances, but present in Walpole's play. I refer to incest. A wife who has loved her deceased husband too well takes, in all secrecy, the place of her son's mistress, because of the young man's resemblance to his father. She bears him a daughter, whom she brings up as an adopted child. But when father and daughter, unaware of their consanguinity, fall in love and are about to wed, the mother is compelled to reveal her terrible secret. Such was the manner in which Walpole cast before the world this unnatural theme, which was so often to fascinate later romanticists. I shall deal, however, with this motive in detail further on, in connection with a greater mass of material than can be given here.

* * *

Reading these books constructed of materials so strange and so remote from normal life, one often wonders what the inner relation of the authors to their romanticism can have been. Were they themselves in the grip of the enchantment they sought to cast over others, or were they merely skilful stage-managers, who, retaining their own calm, made conscious use of various artifices to awaken the emotions of their readers ? Walpole's life and interests teach us that the romance which breathes of the medieval past fascinated him, and that he could make great sacrifices for the pleasure of building himself a miniature world which would recreate its atmosphere. Though as an aristocrat he affected to despise the trade of a common author, he was nevertheless unable to hide the fact that *The Castle of Otranto* was extremely dear to him. Apparently he had expended more care over this little book than he liked to admit, and unfriendly criticisms hurt him very much. He has called it the only one of his works that pleased him, and informed us that while writing it he gave free rein to his imagination until he was as though a-fire with visions and fancies. He planned it—according to his own words—in defiance of all rules, critics, and philosophies, and for this very reason believed he had succeeded better. He was confident that after a while his poor castle would have admirers enough.[77] After all this we cannot but believe that there was one corner in the soul of this famous dandy and aristocrat in which dwelt love of romance, of weird and mysterious beauty. With regard to Clara Reeve it must be admitted that owing to the fact that she began her book with the intention of demonstrating a theoretical programme, bent on producing a work superior to Walpole's, her motives cannot have been solely inspired by romantic feeling and inclination ; proof of this is the lack of colour that characterizes her book, and her subsequent silence as a writer of romances. Mrs. Radcliffe, again, despite her somewhat cheap artifices of suspense and terror, was a truly romantic soul, who filled her quiet and secluded life with the delightful fancies of nature-mysticism. In her books she is often obviously confessing her own deepest feelings and emotions. " I remember," she writes on one occasion, " that in my youth this gloom used to call forth to my fancy a thousand fairy visions and romantic images. I can linger, with solemn steps, under the deep shades, send forward a transforming eye into the distant obscurity, and listen with thrilling delight to the mystic murmuring of the woods. . . ." " ' These scenes,' said Valancourt, ' soften the heart like the notes of sweet music, and inspire that delicious melancholy which no person, who had felt it once, would resign for the gayest pleasures.' " [78]

To my mind these are the confessions of a really romantic soul, which open out to the reader the heart and spiritual atmosphere of a person who cultivates this side of the emotions. The old Muses have been banished and in their stead two new ones reign : Melancholy and that beloved Fancy who is made responsible for all the outpourings of the romanticists, from their mistiest " evening sentiments."

In connection with the above may I add the general criticism that ripens in the reader's mind as he makes the acquaintance of these romances : their tone and the taste displayed in them is cultured, even refined, bearing witness to the authors' devoted strivings to produce something of literary value and to find expression for the strange and mysterious beauty that nature and the past reflected in their souls. They were not swayed by thoughts of what the financial results of their work might be—although in Mrs. Radcliffe's case, taking into consideration the period, they were considerable—not, at least, to any degree that might have tempted them to produce mercenary efforts at awakening excitement and horror, and consequently they were able to maintain the standards of highly-cultured persons, which were a good deal higher than that of the mass-production which was shortly to be witnessed in this field. Thus for the student and for posterity they have been able to retain their reputations as interesting, perhaps somewhat peculiar, literary personalities.[79]

After reading *The Castle of Otranto* the poet Gray wrote to Walpole that it " made him cry a little." It is obvious that the effect of these books on contemporaries was different from and much deeper than that made on us, who can indeed laugh heartily over *The Castle of Otranto*, but hardly weep. Let us recollect that Doctor Johnson, too, was afraid of the ghost of Hamlet's father when reading Shakespeare at Oxford. And while dwelling on their effect on contemporaries I cannot refrain from remarking on the experiences related to us from his childhood in the castle of Combourg in Brittany by the great French romanticist Chateaubriand. In his *Mémoires d'Outre-Tombe* (Edmond Biré ed., I, pp. 70-72, 134-139), he describes his castle home. On arrival there the façade showed gloomy and forbidding between the trees. Its gates were stoutly built, large and old-fashioned, its walls crenellated, its towers pointed. Here and there were numerous secret passages and staircases, galleries and labyrinths, and everywhere was silence, gloom, and stone-faced enigma. The evenings at Combourg were oppressive. Old Chateaubriand would walk backward and forward in the big, dark drawing-room, where the only illumination came from the fireplace, wearing a white cloak and cap, long and lean as a ghost, coming into the firelight and passing again into the shadows, saying not a word, while the children whispered by the fire. His mother and sister Lucile slept at one end of the castle, his father at the other, and the boy in his own lonely room in one of the towers. With the approach of evening, all the old tales of Combourg's robbers and murderers would awaken to live in the imaginations of his mother and sister, together with memories of the wooden-legged ghost of that early master of Combourg who sometimes appeared in the castle corridors, accompanied by a black cat. In his solitary chamber the boy heard all the mysterious, nocturnal noises of the old castle. At times the wind seemed to be creeping through the passages, then it sighed plaintively; suddenly his door would be violently shaken and from the subterranean parts of the building a murmuring would be heard. Then everything would be still, only to break out again in noises. On her sleepless nights his sister Lucile, a romantic, visionary nature, sat out on the staircase, a lamp by her side, listening to the voices of the night and the great castle clock. When the clock struck twelve, ushering in the hour of ghosts and crime, Lucile would strain her ears and conjure up visions of terror, gloomy deeds in the far past, perhaps of death personified, whom she sometimes believed that she saw in person. Chateaubriand remarks that in Scotland Sir Walter Scott would have regarded Lucile as *une femme céleste* blessed with the gift of inner vision.

Combourg was doubtlessly the kind of place that Chateaubriand describes in the above; but if one recollects that prior to this account, written in manhood, he had dwelt a considerable time in England, in those very years when the romanticism of the haunted castle flourished most—he had made the acquaintance, among others, of M. G. Lewis, and regarded

The Monk and *Caleb Williams* as the only romances likely to survive out of half a century's production (*Mémoires*, II, p. 195) —the tone of his description and the materials found therein give rise to the idea that he had included in his account a little of the literary haunted-castle atmosphere which he could hardly have failed to find in England, and which dominated the romantic imagination of the period.

The Castle of Otranto appeared in 1764, *The Mysteries of Udolpho* thirty years later. During the interval much terror-romanticist literature had been written, so that the materials of which it was composed had become known; the decade of its highest flourishing was nigh. It began to be clear which phases of it were capable of further development, which were exhausted and stale. Signs of the change in literary taste had been clearly visible both in England and on the Continent; the proofs included, during the decade in question, besides those referred to in this chapter, such works as Chatterton's *Rowley Poems* (1777), Goethe's *Götz von Berlichingen* (1773), Bürger's *Lenore* (1774), and Cazotte's *Le Diable Amoureux* (1772). Even a counter-movement, satire, was already in course of formation in England.

17

It will already have emerged from the foregoing that terror-romanticism had found huge public favour. The years following the publication of *The Mysteries of Udolpho* were the heyday of this type of literature, a time finally crowned by the appearance of such works as *The Italian* and Lewis's *The Monk*. But there were persons, even among authors, whose clear intellect and logical, penetrative mode of thought forbade them to accept the new school. In mentioning *Northanger Abbey* I have already presented one such author to the reader, namely, Jane Austen; another was Maria Edgeworth. The first is naturally of most consequence and more directly responsible for the satire cast on the terror-romanticists, of which a brief account may be not without interest.

It is strange to think that the most effective satire in this respect, that which apparently did most to restrain Mrs. Radcliffe's activity as an author and caused her to postpone the publication of her *Gaston de Blondeville* from year to year, was from the pen of a woman. While Mrs. Radcliffe and the others, mostly women-writers, were developing terror-romanticism to its ultimate pitch, gaining thereby the unanimous approval of male publishers and readers, the daughter of a rural clergyman sat at her tiny writing-desk in the family living-room, amidst its daily bustle, writing—and no one can say how she found time for her task—such masterpieces as *Northanger Abbey* (not published until 1817), *Sense and Sensibility* (1811), *Pride and Prejudice* (1813), *Mansfield Park* (1814), *Emma* (1816) and *Persuasion* (1817). These six works, which still hold an honoured position in the best English fiction, were written between the years 1796 and 1810, but failed to find a publisher before 1811 ; and even then the best of them, the first to be written, did not appear until after the author's death, together with *Persuasion*. As early as 1797 Jane Austen had offered *Northanger Abbey* to a publisher in Bath, who bought it for ten pounds. But probably the purchaser regarded it as an imperfect piece of work and the enterprise of publishing it as foolhardy, for he locked it up in his desk and forgot it there for long years, until the author redeemed it from him. Better proof of the extent to which bad literature had affected the public taste and depraved it would be difficult to find.

Jane Austen's literary quality is a kind of bright and sunny lightness of touch which hides an unerring sound sense. With fine touches her deft brush conjures up before us the figures of her contemporaries, especially of all those whose pilgrimage had in it anything humorous or ludicrous. English literature would be poorer in spirited and apt character-drawing if Jane Austen had failed to enrich it with such gems as the gossipy gatherings at Bath and the foolish women and lords of that aristocratic health-resort. Parallel with this side of her art, her sound literary sense, so free from all romanticism, flashes forth in deftly-aimed satire against the terror-romantic orgies of her day. For any one who has read *The Mysteries of Udolpho* and fallen a little under its spell, it would be difficult to find a better antidote to its unreal scenes of terror than *Northanger Abbey :* all fear of ghosts and suspense born of musty secret passages in tyrants' castles dissolve like vapour in sunshine, leaving only a healthy, somewhat shamefaced smile at such puerilities. Catherine and Isabella continue the conversation already quoted, in the course of which Isabella remarks that she has drawn up for her friend a list of ten such works, viz., *Castle of Wolfenbach*, *Clermont*, *Mysterious Warnings*, *Necromancer of the Black Forest*, *Midnight Bell*, *Orphan of the Rhine* and *Horrid Mysteries*. " ' Those will last us some time,' she concludes. To which Catherine answers : ' Yes ; pretty well ; but are they all horrid ? Are you sure they are all horrid ? ' ' Yes, quite sure ; for a particular friend of mine, a Miss Andrews, a sweet girl, one of the sweetest creatures in the world, has read every one of them. I wish you knew Miss Andrews, you would be delighted with her. She is netting herself the sweetest cloak you can conceive. I think her as beautiful as an angel, and I am so vexed with the men for not admiring her ! I scold them amazingly about it.' "

After remarking that he has not read *Udolpho*, Mr. Thorpe declares : " ' Novels are all so full of nonsense and stuff ! There has not been a tolerably decent one come out since *Tom Jones*, except the *Monk* ; I read that t'other day. . . . No, if I read any it shall be Mrs. Radcliffe's ; her novels are amusing enough ; they are worth reading ; some fun and nature in *them*.'

" ' Udolpho was written by Mrs. Radcliffe,' said Catherine."

With such light touches does Jane Austen stamp the whole of this species of literature as the favourite reading of foolish girls and of stupid persons, people who have not the faintest idea of what literature, rightly understood, denotes.

Miss Edgeworth, too, mocked at the romanticism of her times in her story " Angelina or L'Amie Inconnue," *Moral Tales* (1801), in which Angelina, after a sentimental correspondence with a certain Araminta, leaves her home and seeks shelter with her friend in distant idyllic Wales. The outcome is trouble on the journey and disagreeable experiences at her destination : the idyllic cottage in Wales turns out to be a dirty hovel and the romantic Araminta an uncultured person.

Among those who poured ridicule on the terror-romanticists mention may be made of Sarah Green (*Romance Readers and Romance Writers*, 1810) and E. S. Barrett (*The Heroine, or, the Adventures of a Fair Romance Reader*, 1813), in whose works romanticism is developed in practice and the light of everyday experience is brought to extravagant conclusions.[80] Unlike Jane Austen, whose works have retained their value owing to their own positive qualities, Barrett went so far in his satire that the fate of his book was irrevocably bound up with this aspect of his talent. He built up his book wholly as a satire against terror-romanticism, and is consequently dependent, as an author, on whether the object of his satire is known. During his own day, when the romances he aims at were widely known, his book found great favour, but once terror-romanticism was forgotten the point of his satire was lost. For those who have occasion to read the books in question, Barrett's work is still enjoyable and the ridicule cast by it apt ; its author deserves to be rescued from oblivion.

Let us now return, however, to a point in time somewhere near the year that first saw the appearance of *The Mysteries of Udolpho* for a detailed consideration of the author who was soon to crown the achievements of terror-romanticism with what is in many respects its highest and perhaps most widely-appreciated work.

II

MATTHEW GREGORY LEWIS

I

WE have now arrived, if we leave out of account *The Italian*, which appeared somewhat later, to about the year 1794. Pausing a while to glance at the literary landscape, we are met by an interesting view. Samuel Johnson has been dead these ten years ; Robert Burns has only two more years to live ; Horace Walpole is an old man of seventy-seven ; Clara Reeve is sixty-five and Ann Radcliffe thirty, though the latter is already at the height of her production and approaching its swift decline. Walter Scott is twenty-three and engaged in legal work ; it is ten years since he made the acquaintance of Percy's ballads and by now he is well-versed in the folk-poetry, antiquities and history of his country. Samuel Taylor Coleridge returns this year to Cambridge, having successfully negotiated his release from the dragoon regiment to which an unlucky love affair and pecuniary misfortunes had driven him ; at Oxford he meets Robert Southey and dreams with him of a pantisocratic community to be founded on the banks of the Susquehanna. He publishes his first work this year. William Wordsworth is twenty-four and has been imbibing revolutionary ideas in France, whence he succeeds in escaping a little before the heads of his Girondist friends begin to fall ; his first works have already been published and he is considering a life altogether devoted to his muse. Thomas Moore is fifteen and is planning his translations of *Anacreon*, while with his friend Emmet he surrenders himself heart and soul to the idea of Irish liberty. Thomas de Quincey has reached the age of nine and is just beginning the life of a spiritually-orphan and lonely schoolboy. Charles Lamb, aged nineteen, works in an office. Walter Savage Landor has achieved the same age and is known at Oxford as the " Mad Jacobin." Ch. R. Maturin is twelve.

William Godwin publishes this year his *Caleb Williams*. Byron is six, Shelley two and Keats' birth is close at hand. The time is thus an eventful one in the history of English literature; behind it the sun of classicism has definitely set and before it lie decades rich in hopes, promise and results of a new trend in literature, of new aims in poetry, of high ideals and freedom.

This same year the staff of the British Embassy at The Hague included a young gentleman who probably attracted a good deal of attention there. He was below the average in height and short-sighted; his eyes, bulging like those of a crab, gave him an unusual appearance; he was extremely talkative and merry, fond of playing the clavier and of writing poems to which he himself would compose melodies. He took part in social life, but was above all interested in literature, especially in his own prospects of becoming an author. This young man was Matthew Gregory Lewis, or "Monk-Lewis," as he was later called. As a great part of the continuation of the present work centres around his production, particularly that part of it comprised in *The Monk* (1795), it will be as well to become acquainted with his life.[81]

2

Matthew Gregory Lewis was born in London, on July the 9th, 1775. His father, Matthew Lewis, was Deputy-Secretary for War and his mother, Frances Maria Sewell, the youngest daughter of another high official, Thomas Sewell. The father appears to have been purposeful and strict, but a good and noble man; the mother, who was much younger than her husband, was merry, beautiful and slender, musical, dwelling in another spiritual world than that of her husband.[82] Before her marriage she was one of the most celebrated beauties at Court, much admired for her dancing and musical talent. As a married woman she was in the habit of holding musical soirées, to which she invited the foremost musicians of the day. She seems to have been interested in literature; at least there is evidence of her having read Joseph Glanville's *Saducismus Triumphatus* (1681), a work abounding in descriptions of witches and visions.[83] Without attaching too much importance to this book (which, in the lack of other information, invariably crops up in all biographies of Lewis), for it can hardly have been Mrs. Lewis's favourite reading, one must still allow it a certain significance for the reason that the curious copperplates contained in it, including one in which the Devil is seen beating a drum over Mr. Mompesson's house, may well have amused a lively little boy and given a certain trend to his imagination at a very early age. Mrs. Lewis was also religiously inclined, the emotional side of her nature finding satisfaction in the mysticism of religious ceremonies. Such in brief was the home in which Matthew grew up as the eldest of four children, in comfortable circumstances, surrounded by the social, pleasure-seeking, literary and artistic circles of London.[84]

Mat, as he was called, was a precocious child, small and delicate in build. As the spoiled playmate of his mother he early learned to display a naïvely grave interest in the affairs of his elders, calling his mother "Fanny" and acting as her arbiter in matters of taste. The affectionate relations between mother and son never altered. Mat was in general an obedient and dutiful child. After a preliminary course at a private school, he entered Westminster School on June 19, 1783, and stayed there until 1790. Among his schoolmates was Robert Southey, who joined the school in 1788 and left in 1792. During his schooldays Lewis is said to have distinguished himself as an amateur actor, and indeed the staging of plays seems to have been one of the chief delights of his childhood.[85] Also his musical gifts appeared early.

Among the memories of those early years, one of a ghost-romantic nature is perhaps worth relating. As a child he frequently stayed in the country with one of his father's relatives living at Stanstead Hall, whose main building was extremely old. One part had long been closed, so that in conformity with the national tendency, it was looked upon as haunted. The servants, in particular, maintained this belief, and there was one room, richly furnished in an old-fashioned style, past whose large folding doors little Mat was led to his bedroom each evening, which had such a reputation that no reward could have induced them to enter it after dark. Each time—so Lewis himself later related—he was taken past this gloomy chamber, he would cast a fearful glance at it, as though expecting its high, curiously-carved doors to open and some dreadful being to appear.[86]

3

While Lewis was still at school, the marriage of his parents was dissolved, and Mrs. Lewis proceeded, as a first step, to Paris. Her husband made her a liberal allowance, but she was chronically short of money. As she could no longer approach her former husband for help, Matthew had to do the best he could to assist her out of his pocket-money and any extra sum he could beg from his father. These transactions are woven throughout the comrade-like correspondence which now began between mother and son, in which Matthew acts as a medium for the transmission of news between his mother and the rest of the family, a duty which he performed with undeniable tact and wit. Another special motive for corresponding frequently was provided by Matthew's literary attempts, begun according to his own explanation in the hope of procuring by this means additional help for his mother. These first excursions into literature filled most of his leisure at Christ Church, Oxford, whither he repaired in the autumn of 1790 to complete his studies. The visible result (definitely finished at Paris) was a play, now lost, called the *Epistolary Intrigue*. His mother was entrusted with the task of offering it to Drury Lane Theatre, the chief part having been written for Mrs. Jordan, but the play was refused. The mortification of the fifteen-year-old author over this check is clearly reflected in a letter of this period.[87] The preface to a later play, *Rivers, or the East Indian*, contains a statement that it was written when the author was fifteen, from which we can safely conclude that it was based on the *Epistolary Intrigue*. While at Oxford he tried his hand at a prose story as well, also revised at Paris ; it was never published, but we know it to have been a humorously satirical depictment of the outpourings of young women entitled *The Effusions of Sensibility*. To judge from the extracts published posthumously it appears to have been a parody of Richardson written in Fielding's style.[88]

Matthew was intended for a diplomatic career and hence we find him at Paris in the summer of 1791 ; though even without that motive the customary amount of travel for a young man of his class would probably have fallen to his share. He was too young, however, to understand what was happening at the time in Paris ; at least in his letters to his mother we find no indication in that direction. They contain chiefly advice in regard to a scenic adaptation his mother was engaged in. What does become plain is that he studied the theatre of the Revolution with enthusiasm, writing to his mother that he knew "at least twenty French operas, which, if translated, would undoubtedly succeed; but after Kemble's refusing Bluebeard, the most interesting production of that kind, I quite despair. There is an opera, called 'Le Souterrain,' where a woman is hid in a cavern in her jealous husband's house; and afterwards, by accident, her child is shut up there also, without food, and they are not released till they are perishing with hunger. The situations of the characters, the tragic of the principal characters, the gaiety of the under parts, and the romantic turn of the story, make it one of the prettiest and most affecting things I ever saw. . . . 'Les Victimes Cloitrées' is another which would undoubtedly succeed." We learn from this that romanticism of *The Sicilian Romance* type was already in favour in France and that even in Paris Lewis was in contact with the branch of literature which later was to become peculiarly his own. No such spiritual influence as worked upon Wordsworth appears to have affected him during his stay in Paris. His chief concern seems to have been the attainment of a literary reputation.[89]

In March 1792, we find him again in Oxford, ill and depressed by literary disappointments. He has done some translating, completing a version of a play entitled *Felix*[90] and "two or three other things to try the fortune with." He writes irritatedly to his mother that "it does not merely consist in writing an opera, which will succeed when acted, but the difficulty lies in *getting* it acted." Like all other beginners he is loath to believe that the fault lies in his own work, but prefers to condemn those who refuse to accept it. He requests his mother to try Drury Lane with *Felix*. About the same time he began work on a book in the style of *The Castle of Otranto*; but neither was this ever published, even if it was finished. Yet it was an important preliminary study for his famous play *The Castle Spectre*. With regard to his work at Oxford we have no exact information. Latin and Greek were universally studied, so that his version of Juvenal is probably an inheritance from this period. He also kept pleasant company and made an occasional incursion into gambling. However, a diplomatic career necessitated some knowledge of German, and it was to acquire this that Lewis set out for Weimar in the summer of 1792.[91]

He arrived at Weimar on July 27th. Conditions in the

town were then unsettled owing to the war; the Duke was with the army at Coblenz, whither Goethe, too, repaired on August 8th, and most of the people prominent in society were away. Nevertheless, Lewis made a few acquaintances and on July 30th could write to his mother: "The few people who are still here are extremely polite, and I doubt not when I know a little of the language, I shall find the place extremely agreeable. Among other people to whom I have been introduced, are the sister of Schweter, the composer, and M. de Goëthe, the celebrated author of Werter; so that you must not be surprised if I should shoot myself one of these fine mornings."

The Sufferings of Young Werther had appeared in English in 1779, and seems to have been known to Lewis. He studied German assiduously, taking lessons every day, and reported good progress. His social circle satisfied him. "I must tell you that my situation is very pleasant here," he wrote to his mother, adding: "Nothing can be more polite than the people belonging to the court. The two duchesses are extremely affable and condescending; and we have nothing but balls, suppers, and concerts. Thank God, I weary myself to death: but it is always some comfort to think I am wearied with the best company; and I really believe the fault is in myself, and not in other people." After a visit to Berlin he gives the following account of life there in aristocratic circles: "There are some things, to be sure, which are not quite so elegant and well ordered as in England: for instance, the knives and forks are never changed, even at the duke's table; and the ladies hawk and spit about the room in a manner the most disgusting. . . . I was perfectly astonished at the crowds of princes and princesses, dukes and duchesses, which were poured upon me from every quarter. It put me in mind of Foote's observation upon France, that every mangy dog he met was either duke or marquis." [92]

Even while in Germany he did not neglect his literary work but continued to strive eagerly towards the goal he had set himself. At first he wrought upon the book that was to be in the style of *Otranto*, only to meet with failure again: "I write and write, and yet do not find I have got a bit further, in my original plan. . . . I have got hold of an infernal dying man, who plagues my very heart out. He has talked for half a volume already, and seems likely to talk for half a volume more; and I cannot manage to kill him out of the way for the life of me." Indeed he never did succeed in this, for in *The Castle Spectre* the dying man definitely revives.) Having learned the language he studied German poetry and proceeded to translate from it into English; in February 1793, he has a collection of poems ready, partly translations, partly original, and is extremely hopeful. He believes himself to have succeeded with his translations, for he has read them to the authors of the originals and received nothing but friendly opinions. Notwithstanding this, the collection never saw the light, though some of the pieces are probably to be found in his later *Tales of Terror and Wonder*. While at Weimar he began to remodel his *Epistolary Intrigue*, which now became a play called *The East Indian*. This was offered through his mother and Mrs. Jordan to the theatres, but without success.

Although the visible results of his labours while in Germany were thus small—serious work was, indeed, not to be expected from so young a man—he learned the language and became acquainted to some extent with German literature, preparing himself in this wise for his later position as the introducer of German romanticism into English literature. Byron's story of Lewis freely translating from *Faust* to him at the Villa Diodati, in the autumn of 1816, may be taken as an indication that Lewis was regarded as an expert in German literature. Such proficiency in a foreign language is nothing extraordinary now, but was rare enough in England at the time of which we are speaking.[93]

Early in the spring of 1793 Lewis returned home. For about a year he took up nothing in earnest, but spent his time in amusements and in visiting friends at their country seats. He stayed, nevertheless, at Oxford and began there a translation of Schiller's play *Kabale und Liebe*. Except for a few newspaper articles he does not appear to have attempted any serious original work. As regards these newspaper articles, they serve to reveal his burning desire to be looked upon as an author, for in connection with them he writes : " I should not even scruple paying a guinea and a half, but no more, if the editor will not put them in for nothing." His mother still bore his manuscripts to their destination, while he continued to act as go-between for his parents, an office that often proved disagreeable. At length, his father secured him a post at the British Embassy at The Hague, whither he proceeded in May 1794, arriving on the evening of the 15th. Here he was ultimately to accomplish a work that would satisfy his burning desire for literary fame.

4

Lewis arrived in Holland with a hopeful conception of the intellectual attainments of the Dutch, but soon changing his opinion, he turned his back on the Mynheers, being certain "that the devil *ennui* has made The Hague his favourite abode." Now he associated solely with the French *émigrants*, of whom there were many at The Hague in those days. Every alternate evening he was a guest in Madame de Matignon's salon, where " a very agreeable coterie " of French aristocrats was wont to gather. " After such a society the Dutch assemblies must be dreadful," he wrote to his mother. Later in the summer he spent a week with the army, dined at the Duke of York's table, and was even presented to a royal personage—all events worthy of being related to his mother. During his visit to the British Headquarters he was likewise able to note the disorder prevailing among the troops and the dissatisfaction of the officers ; venturing almost within the battle-zone, he saw the army in action, and his kind heart was deeply touched by the horrors of war. For cruelty, irrespective of which side committed it, he had the same condemnation, writing to his mother : " The French are adored wherever they go, while the allied forces are execrated and detested. In truth, I am sorry to confess that no ravages more wanton and unjustifiable were ever committed in the annals of war, than have been perpetrated by all the combined army, and more particularly by the English." Throughout his whole life Lewis was to show himself exceptionally gentle-hearted and humane.

In the spring before he sailed for The Hague, Mrs. Radcliffe's *Mysteries of Udolpho* had been published and had found a grateful reader also in Lewis ; he regarded it as " one of the most interesting books that has ever been published." He obviously read the book with the greatest eagerness and seems to have been specially fascinated by Montoni's flashing eyes, dark countenance and sombre nature. The fashionable *Weltschmerz* and melancholy that tinged at times even Lewis's otherwise joyous soul, now took on Montoni's apparition and brought our author to such fancied depths of despair that he imagined himself to be possessed by a spleen as gloomy as that of Montoni. In all gravity he asks his mother whether she has ever observed any likeness between Montoni's nature and his own.

Noting with a comprehending smile this spiritual attitude,

we are not surprised to learn that *The Mysteries of Udolpho* inspired Lewis to take up again his story in the style of *Otranto*, as hopeful as ever. Yet it came no nearer to completion, for seized by a new idea, in working out which he probably made as much use of his *Otranto*-motive as his new construction allowed, Lewis put it aside. On Sept. 23rd, 1794, he wrote to his mother: " What do you think of my having written, in the space of ten weeks, a romance of between three and four hundred pages octavo ? I have even written out half of it fair. It is called *The Monk*, and I am myself so much pleased with it that, if the booksellers will not buy it, I shall publish it myself." In his last letter from The Hague, dated Nov. 22nd, he mentions the size of his book as 420 pages, and remarks that " there is a great deal of poetry inserted." [94]

Such masterpieces of romance often seem to have been written with suspicious rapidity. Walpole wrote his book in less than two months, Beckford wrote his in six weeks and now comes Lewis with his in ten.[95] These figures speak more for the imagination of the authors than indicate the actual time of writing, for it is difficult to believe that a youth of eighteen could manage to complete, in the intervals of his office and his amusements, the manuscript of a romance of 400 pages, and even write a clean copy of one-half of his book. Probably Lewis had begun to collect themes of terror from French and German sources when he was at Paris and Weimar, and was continuing this work when the definite idea for his plot came to him at The Hague. He must have had some of his material prepared beforehand, if only for the reason that *The Monk* was not the only work to be completed there, another being the little play called *The Twins, or, Is It He or His Brother*— a comedy of errors on an old motive, which was performed a single time.[96] In addition, he had tried assiduously, during the whole period of his stay, to find a publisher for his poems and to get his play accepted, though he succeeded in neither. Somewhat boastingly he wrote to his mother: " You see I am horribly bit by the rage of writing." At the end of November he returned to London and the following year saw the publication of his first book *Ambrosio, or The Monk*, which brought him immediate fame.

The fate of this novel shows how a book with few merits from an artistic point of view can yet, by reason of its other qualities, achieve fame, and even inspire ideas that in the hands of more skilful artists may form the foundation for admitted works of art. The secret lies in the capacity possessed by literary phenomena of this description for hiding in a poor and distorted form far-reaching ideas, which are instinctively recognized as such and which exert their own influence. At the same time there may be connected with them something akin to the literary strivings of their day, making them of its essence, and thus lending them a certain significance as historical documents. By such reasoning can the vitality of Lewis's romance be explained. Its substance is briefly as follows :

Ambrosio is an abbot of the Capuchin monastery at Madrid, young, about thirty, and famed for his devoutness. As a child he had been found on the monastery steps and accepted by the monks as a gift from the Virgin. Observing his piousness and model character, the Devil decides to encompass his ruin. To this end he causes a woman far advanced in cabbalistic wisdom, Matilda de Villanegas, to fall in love with the handsome abbot. She succeeds in interesting him in her portrait, and then, attiring herself as a novice and penetrating into the monastery, she proceeds to fascinate him with her person. Owing to his inexperience and the overwhelming temptation to which he is subjected, Ambrosio falls victim to Matilda's charms on the first suitable occasion. Satisfaction brings with it remorse, but Matilda's sophistries and the memory of the pleasures he had enjoyed soon drown the voice of conscience. Then follows an extension of his passions and a feeling of surfeit towards Matilda, who has meanwhile sold her soul to the Devil and become a species of female demon. Unmoved by the monk's coldness, she uses her magic to turn his lust towards Antonia, the daughter of a poor widow. When the widow, whose name is Elvira and who is in reality Ambrosio's mother, chances to defeat his evil intentions in time, she is murdered by the monk. Helped by Matilda he then gains possession of Antonia and after violating her murders her likewise, becoming thus unwittingly the destroyer of both his mother and his sister. Ambrosio and Matilda are then seized by the Inquisition and under torture are compelled to confess their crimes. In her capacity of demon, it is easy for Matilda to liberate herself from her bonds and to teach Ambrosio how to conjure up the Devil so that he too may sell his soul and escape. In mortal fear Ambrosio follows her advice and sells his soul, whereupon he is taken away by the Devil and murdered elsewhere.

This is the chief theme of *The Monk*, but parallel with it Lewis develops two other threads which work very loosely into the main plot. A great part of the romance is taken up by the love-story of Don Raymond and Agnes. The only connection between this and the plot is that Agnes has once, while a nun in the convent of St. Clara at Madrid, accidentally revealed to Ambrosio her love for Don Raymond, and for this has been severely punished : she is given out as dead, but is in reality condemned to lifelong imprisonment in the convent catacombs, where she is discovered after the arrest of Ambrosio. The scene of Raymond's story is laid, for the most part, in Germany, in a castle haunted by the ghost of the Bleeding Nun. Here Ahasverus once appears as Raymond's helper. Again, Agnes's brother Lorenzo is in love with Antonia, who acts thus as a link with the main narrative. In the final catastrophe all these threads are gathered together in the death of Antonia, the discovery of Agnes and the arrest of Ambrosio. The period is indefinite, but the reader calls up in imagination the time of the Inquisition and Philip II as a suitable background for the story.

Of its actual materials of terror, which will be dealt with in another connection, Lewis gives an idea in the lines from Horace chosen as a motto :

> Somnia, terrores magicos, miracula, sagas,
> Nocturnos lemures, portentaque.

As regards his sources, Lewis himself gives the following account of them in a foreword :

" The first idea of this romance was suggested by the story of the *Santon Barsisa*, related in the *Guardian*.—The Bleeding Nun is a tradition still credited in many parts of Germany ; and I have been told that the ruins of the castle of Lauenstein, which she is supposed to haunt, may yet be seen upon the borders of Thuringia. *The Water King*, from the third to the twelfth stanza, is the fragment of an original Danish ballad ; and *Belerma and Durandarte* is translated from some stanzas to be found in a collection of old Spanish poetry which contains also the popular song of *Gayferos and Melesindra*, mentioned in *Don Quixote*. I have now made a full avowal of all the plagiarisms of which I am aware myself, but I doubt not many more may be found of which I am at present totally unconscious."

The vagueness of this account lays it open to suspicion, and literary workers, chiefly German, have expended much labour in elucidating Lewis's real sources. To say the least, it must be admitted that as the work of so young and inexperienced a writer, *The Monk* is a singularly ripe achievement. Doubts concerning its originality have been increased by the fact that Lewis never again attempted anything original in the larger prose forms, but contented himself with poems, plays or adaptations. Nevertheless, the truth of the matter is that on the whole Lewis was right in his statement : he had found the themes for his work chiefly in French and German romanticism, but in fields that we are right in regarding as common property and fair game for any writer. As these sources have been exhaustively dealt with elsewhere, it is only necessary here to refer the reader to the Notes,[97] especially as the matter will be more than once touched upon in connection with the various themes.

5

As soon as *The Monk* began to be known, it became the object of heated controversy. Offence was taken at the puppyish sapiency that led Lewis to lecture on the unsuitability of the Bible as reading for the young, and at the sensuality of the book, which is considerable but hardly more pronounced, even if more unnatural, than certain passages in the works of Smollett and Fielding. But everything in Lewis's book was liable to oppress its readers by a kind of new and strange, unabashed realism that irritated and angered the pharisaical portion of the public. In the course of its notice *The Critical Review*[98] remarked : "The horrible and the preternatural have usually seized on the popular taste, at the rise and decline of the literature. . . . The same phenomenon, therefore, which we hail as a favourable omen in the belleslettres of Germany, impresses a degree of gloom in the compositions of our countrymen. We trust however, that satiety will banish what good sense should have prevented ; and that, wearied with fiends, incomprehensible characters, with shrieks, murders and subterraneous dungeons, the public will learn, by the multitude of the manufacturers, with how little expense of thought or imagination this species of composition is manufactured. . . ." The reviewer calls the legend of the Bleeding Nun " truly terrific," the flaming cross on the forehead of the Wandering Jew " a bold and happy conception," and Matilda " the author's masterpiece." " The whole work is distinguished by the variety and impressiveness of its incidents and the author everywhere discovers an imagination rich, powerful and fervid. The sufferings which he describes are so frightful and intolerable, that we break with abruptness from the delusion and indignantly suspect the man of a species of brutality, who could find a pleasure in wantonly imagining them, and the abominations . . . are such as no observation of character can justify, because no good man would willingly suffer them to pass, however transiently, through his own mind. . . . Figures that shock the imagination and narratives that mangle the feelings, rarely discover genius, and always betray a low and vulgar taste. . . . we declare it to be our opinion, that the Monk is a romance, which if a parent saw in the hands of a son or daughter, he might reasonably turn pale. . . . though the tale is indeed a tale of horror, yet the most painful impression which the work left on our minds was that of great acquirements and splendid genius employed to furnish a mormo for children, a poison for youth and a provocative for the debauchee."

This review reflects fairly accurately the general opinion regarding the book. *The Analytical Review* [99] finds fault with the author's parallel plots and the two catastrophes, which, by dividing the interest, always make a poor effect; the language and customs were not " Gothic " enough to fit in with the superstitious life of the period. *The Monthly Review* [100] was of the opinion that the whole narrative was pervaded by " a vein of obscenity " which, from a moral point of view, would destroy for ever the fine reputation the author's skill would otherwise have secured him. *The European Magazine* [101] wrote that this " singular composition," which had neither originality, morality, nor even probability to commend it, had awakened the public curiosity and kept it alive because " such is the irresistible energy of genius." The reviewer in *The Monthly Mirror* [102] had read the book a second time and derived " if possible, more gratification, than on the first." The character of Ambrosio he regards as a masterpiece. *The Scot's Magazine* [103] regretted that youth should be exposed to the evil influence of such books, which the circulating libraries were indefatigable in spreading. The year 1798 brought from Thos. J. Mathias, in an annotated satirical " poem " in dialogue form entitled *The Pursuits of Literature*, a fierce attack on Lewis, the prologue of the concluding dialogue being devoted to *The Monk*. The passage is so descriptive of the literary style and the ideas of those days that I take the liberty of quoting from it at some length.[104]

" But there is one publication of the time," says stern Mr.

Mathias, " too peculiar and too important to be passed over in a general reprehension. There is nothing with which it may be compared. A Legislator in our own parliament (Lewis had in the meantime become M.P.), a member of the House of Commons of Great Britain, an elected guardian and defender of the laws, the religion, and the good manners of the country, has neither scrupled nor blushed to depict and to publish to the world, the arts of lewd and systematic seduction, and to thrust upon the nation the most open and unqualified blasphemy against the very code and volume of our religion : and all this with his name, style and title prefixed to the novel or romance called ' The Monk.' Nay, even one of our public theatres has allured the public attention still more to this novel, by a scenic representation of an episode in it.

" *O Proceres Censore opus est, an Haruspice nobis !* I consider this as a new species of legislative or state-parricide.

" What is it to the kingdom at large, or what is it to all those whose office it is to maintain truth, and to instruct the rising abilities and the hope of England, that the author of *The Monk* is *a very young man ?* That forsooth he is a man of genius and of fancy? So much the worse. That there are very poetical descriptions of castles and abbies in this novel ? So much the worse again, the novel is more alluring on that account. Is this a time to poison the waters of our land in their springs and fountains? Are we to add incitement to incitement, and corruption to corruption, till there neither is, nor can be, a return to virtuous action and to regulated life? Who knows *the age* of this author? I presume very few. *Who does not know,* that he is a Member of Parliament? He has told us all so himself.

" I pretend not to know, whether this be an object of parliamentary animadversion ; but we can feel that it is an object of moral and of national reprehension, when a Senator openly and daringly violates his first duty to his country. There are wounds, and obstructions and diseases in the political, as well as in the natural, body, for which the removal of the part affected is alone efficacious. At an hour like this, are we to stand in consultation on the remedy, when not only the disease is ascertained, but the very stage of the disease, and its specific symptoms? Are we to spare the sharpest instruments of authority and of censure when public establishments are gangrened in the life-organs?

" There is surely something peculiar in these days ; something wholly unknown to our ancestors. But men, however dignified in their political station, however gifted with genius, or with fortune, or with accomplishments, may at least be made ashamed, or alarmed or be convicted, before the tribunal of public opinion. Before that tribunal, and to the law of reputation, and to every binding and powerful sanction by which that law is enforced, is *Mr. Lewis* this day called to answer."

One might have thought that this stern judge would have been contented with these rhetorical weapons borrowed from Cicero, but such was not the case. He goes on to say that he could hardly believe his own eyes at the sight of the magic letters " M.P." on the title-page of *The Monk* and hastened to the publisher for corroboration. The answer decided him. The seventh chapter of the second part of the book was " indictable at Common Law." To illumine the matter by historical examples he states that during the reign of George II an unhappy author called Edmund Curl had been placed in the stocks at the instance of the Public Prosecutor for publishing a couple of immoral works, and that a certain John Cleland had been prosecuted for issuing a book entitled *Memoirs of a Woman of Pleasure*. In certain statements concerning the Bible Lewis had added blasphemy to his other offences.[105]

The savageness of these attacks caused a reaction to set in. Partisans were not lacking also for Lewis. In the same year in which Mathias's work appeared, an answer to it was published called *Impartial Strictures on the Poem called ' The Pursuits of Literature,'* etc., which mockingly called attention to the exaggerated fierceness and bombast of the attacks in relation to their object. An *Epistle in Rhyme to M. G. Lewis*, etc., which appeared in 1798, is a satire on the attacking advocates of virtue and public morality, attempting in rhyme and prose to defend Lewis's cause. The best proof of the interest attracted by *The Monk* was finally the publication by a certain " R. S. Esq." of a parody in three parts entitled *The New Monk* (1798), a book which was coldly received.

Nevertheless, the attackers succeeded in setting the Society for the Suppression of Vice in movement. The third edition of Lewis's book was seized by the authorities and in the ensuing lawsuit Lewis was ordered to eliminate the pages dealing with the Bible and a number of highly sensual passages, these alterations being effected in the fourth edition. Nowadays the book has been re-issued in its unexpurgated form without causing an outcry or awakening moral indignation.[106]

Sir Walter Scott was far from despising the book, remarking

once, in connection with Lewis's later production, that the latter had never written anything to equal *The Monk*.[107] Byron, who also belonged to Lewis's circle of friends, noted in his diary some years later that the writer of the descriptions in *The Monk* might well have been Tiberius at Capri. Failing to understand how a youth of twenty could have written such a book he had taken it up to see what there was in it that could have given rise to such a tumult. In Thomas Moore's opinion *The Monk* was a " libidinous and impious " story.[108] As we have already remarked, the book brought Lewis the nickname of " Monk," by which he was usually thereafter called.

6

" Monk-Lewis " was now the lion of the day in literary circles and sunned his dwarfish person in the light of fame. He accepted the name without demur, and even tolerated it on his letters. Indeed, it became so familiar with use that many were unaware that he had any other name. What was worse, those unacquainted with the man believed him to be a vicious person, because, forsooth, no one not immoral could have written such a book. Thus Lewis, decent, according to all evidence, well-conducted, good-tempered and kind-hearted, became something of a notorious character with a blasted reputation. He probably cared little on his own account, but it occasioned him some worry owing to his father's resentment against the implication cast upon his son. Lewis Senior sent him a chiding intimation of his regret ; he received in reply a letter of apology of which the following is an extract :

" Though certain that the clamours against *The Monk* cannot have given you the smallest doubt of the rectitude of my intentions, or the purity of my principles, yet I am conscious that it must have grieved you to find any doubts on the subject existing in the minds of other people. To express my sorrow for having given you pain, is my motive for now addressing you ; and also to assure you that you shall not feel that pain a second time on my account. . . . it never struck me, that the exhibition of vice, in her temporary triumph, might possibly do as much harm as her final exposure and punishment would do good. . . . It was, then, with infinite surprise that I heard the outcry raised against the book, and found that a few ill-judged and unguarded passages totally obscured its general

PLATE V

MATTHEW GREGORY LEWIS

(From the portrait by H. W. Pickersgill, R.A., by courtesy of the Trustees of the National Portrait Gallery)

[face p. 96

tendency . . . I need . . . request your pardon for the uneasiness which this business has given you. . . ." [109]

All who had read *The Monk* admitted it to be a remarkable, even an astonishing work; their wonder was increased on making the acquaintance of the writer, who was in many respects as remarkable as his book. Sir Walter Scott, for instance, whom Lewis chanced to meet about this time, says : [110] " Mat had queerish eyes—they projected like those of some insects, and were flattish on the orbit. His person was extremely small and boyish—he was indeed the least man I ever saw, to be strictly well and neatly made. I remember a picture of him by Saunders being handed round at Dalkeith House. The artist had ingeniously flung a dark folding-mantle around the form, under which was half-hid a dagger, a dark lantern, or some such cut-throat appurtenance ; with all this the features were preserved and ennobled. It passed from hand to hand into that of Henry, Duke of Buccleuch, who, hearing the general voice affirm that it was very like, said aloud, ' Like Mat Lewis ! Why that picture's like a *Man !* ' He looked, and lo ! Mat Lewis's head was at his elbow. This boyishness went through life with him. He was a child and a spoiled child, but a child of high imagination ; and so he wasted himself on ghost-stories and German romances."

Another subsequent friend, Byron, regarded him as a kind and good-tempered person, but " pestilently prolix and paradoxical and *personal*. If he would but talk half, and reduce his visits to an hour, he would add to his popularity. As an author he is very good, and his vanity is *ouverte*, like Erskine's, and yet not offending." [111] On another occasion Byron calls him " really a good man, an excellent man . . . very good fellow," whose company was " pleasing," which did not, however, prevent the great poet from protesting that " Lewis was too great a bore ever to lie . . . a good man, a clever man, but a bore." When Byron became bored with Lewis's visits, he revenged himself by inviting a third equally lively person (at Diodati Madame de Staël) for the pleasure of hearing the two shout each other down. Again, Byron says : " He was a jewel of a man, had he been better set, I don't mean *personally*, but less *tiresome*, for he was tedious, as well as contradictory to everything and everybody. Being short-sighted, when we used to ride out together near the Brenta in the twilight in summer, he made me go before, to pilot him : I am absent at times, especially towards evening, and the consequence of this pilotage was some narrow escapes to the M. on horseback.

Once I led him into a ditch over which I had passed as usual, forgetting to warn my convoy, once I led him nearly into the river, instead of on the moveable bridge which incommodes passengers; and twice did we both run against the Diligence which, being heavy and slow, did communicate less damage than it received in its leaders, who were *terrafied* by the charge; thrice did I lose him in the grey of the gloaming, and was obliged to bring-to to his distant signals of distance and distress;—all the time he went on talking without intermission, for he was a man of many words." [112] The faults in Lewis's character are revealed by Sir Walter Scott when he observes that " Lewis was fonder of great people than he ought to have been, either as a man of talent or as a man of fashion. He had always dukes and duchesses in his mouth, and was pathetically fond of anyone that had a title. You would have sworn he had been a parvenu of yesterday, yet he had lived all his life in good society." It is to be noted that the above accounts are by friends, so they can scarcely be regarded as exaggerations. Byron finally immortalized Lewis in amusing fashion in *English Bards and Scotch Reviewers*, addressing him as follows :

> Oh ! wonder-working Lewis ! monk or bard,
> Who fain wouldst make Parnassus a church-yard !
> Lo ! wreaths of yew, not laurel, bind thy brow,
> Thy muse a sprite, Apollo's sexton thou !
> Whether on ancient tombs thou tak'st thy stand,
> By gibb'ring spectres hail'd, thy kindred band ;
> Or tracest chaste descriptions on thy page,
> To please the females of our modest age ;
> All hail, M. P. ! from whose infernal brain
> Thin-sheeted phantoms glide, a grisly train :
> At whose command " grim women " throng in crowds,
> And kings of fire, of water, and of clouds,
> With " small gray men," " wild yagers," and what not,
> To crown with honour thee and Walter Scott ;
> Again all hail ! if tales like thine may please,
> St. Luke alone can vanquish the disease ;
> Even Satan's self with thee might dread to dwell,
> And in thy skull discern a deeper hell.

After he had become a literary celebrity, the reception accorded in the salons of London to this short-sighted, kind-hearted, shrill-voiced, argumentative little man left nothing to be desired. During the years following the appearance of his book he moved chiefly in the highest circles, visiting, among other places, Inverary Castle and Dalkeith House, where he was known of old. He was also presented at Court.

In 1796 he was " elected " Member of Parliament for Hindon Wilts. (in succession to William Beckford)—probably at the instigation of his family—and the appearance of the letters M.P. on his visiting-cards naturally served to enhance the authority of their bearer. On his introduction to the House, he was welcomed as a famous author by no less a person than Charles James Fox—a manœuvre mainly intended, in all probability, to irritate those conservative circles in which moral indignation ran high. A few particulars regarding the social side of his life may fittingly be given here.

In the life of every man—and especially of every poet— a woman appears. No ghost, but a noble-born maiden, Lady Charlotta Campbell, daughter of the Duke of Argyll, claimed Lewis's love. The summer of 1797 seems to have been devoted to this new interest. The attachment was undeniably romantic : an untitled youth and a duke's daughter, and in those days such an affair was hopeless. Still, in a poetic sense, it did its duty by stimulating the lover's lyrical vein to a swifter flow. The fruits of this inspiration, an indefinite number of love-songs, have remained hidden for the most from the eyes of the world, yet to judge from a few surviving verses, Lewis's love—it is uncertain whether it was returned— contained the usual measure of

> Stolen sweetness of those evening walks,
> When pansied turf was air to winged feet,
> And circling forests by ethereal touch
> Enchanted, wore the livery of the sky.

No other significance or result appears to attach to his love-story.

During their summer rambles at Inverary, Lewis and Lady Charlotta are said to have encountered an insane girl, commonly known as " Crazy Jane." This was an excellent theme for a poem, and soon Lewis had completed, in four verses, the lament of a betrayed maiden, sentimental in tone and with a moral bias. Knowledge of the poem spread and it became a prime favourite of the great public, set to music by many composers and sung by famous singers. Further proof of the favour it achieved is that the milliners soon began to provide their clients with special " Crazy Jane " hats. While at Inverary, Lewis used also to compile a handwritten weekly called *The Bugle*, in which even the illustrations were his own, filling its pages with prose and poetry, sentiment and humour and hints regarding the alleged relations between various members of the merry party gathered at the castle. He was also a tireless arranger of amateur theatricals ; one of the plays presented by the guests at Inverary in the summer of 1797 was *Barbarossa*, to which Lewis wrote an epilogue.[113]

7

The success that had crowned his romance made Lewis decide to devote himself entirely to literature. He withdrew from diplomacy and later even relinquished his seat in Parliament. His father does not appear to have opposed this decision, as he settled an annual allowance of one thousand pounds on his son, a sum which enabled Lewis to lead an independent and carefree existence. He now established his own bachelor quarters at Barnes, and took his place in Society.

After the appearance of his romance his aim was to write a play. Returning to his often-begun and as often abandoned *Otranto*-theme, he formed it into a play called *The Castle Spectre, A Dramatic Romance*, produced for the first time at Drury Lane on December 14th, 1797.[114] The object of greatest interest in this play was the ghost, the inclusion of which had been vainly opposed by the manager and proprietor of the theatre, R. B. Sheridan. In the preface to the printed book Lewis remarks that it had been said that if Sheridan had not advised him to be content with one ghost, he would have marched a whole regiment of them on to the stage ; affecting to take the matter seriously, he informs his readers that the story is untrue. " Never," he says, " was any poor soul so ill-used as Evelina's, previous to presenting herself before the audience. The friends to whom I read my drama, the managers to whom I presented it, and the actors who were to perform it, all combined to persecute my spectre, and requested me to confine my ghost to the green-room. Aware that, without her, my catastrophe would closely resemble that of *The Grecian Daughter*, I resolved upon retaining her. The event justified my obstinacy. The spectre was as well treated before the curtain as she had been ill-used behind it ; and as she continues to make her appearance nightly, with increased applause, I think myself under great obligations to her and her representative."

If public success were any measure of the value of a play, *The Castle Spectre* would be one of the most noteworthy dramatic works of its period, for it was performed no less than forty-seven times in succession and revived on several occasions. For this success it had to thank its terror-romantic element, its gloomy, medieval atmosphere of castles, murder and ghosts, which, confined hitherto to prose romances, in its new melodramatic form now captured the theatre and increasingly large circles of the public.) Even the printed edition achieved a wide circulation, for that printed in 1803 is already the eleventh. For the moment the material with which it dealt was that desired by the public. Friends and connoisseurs of real art stamped the new school of taste as dangerous and inferior, but they were unable to wean the sensation-loving public from its latest toy. The problem of how best to induce the ordinary man to support good art instead of bad seems to have been as acute then as now. The actor Cooke, for instance, is reported to have said : " I hope it will not be hereafter believed, that the C. Sp. could attract crowded houses, when the most sublime productions of the immortal Shakespeare would be played to empty benches." Sheridan is said to have replied to an offer by Lewis to wager the whole of the receipts of *The Castle Spectre*, that he would not wager such large sums, but willingly what the play was worth. And once when he was asked how he could bring himself to pollute the stage with such an abortion as *The Castle Spectre*, his ready reply was : " Abortion, my dear friend, look at the treasury. I have long entertained the idea of converting *Romeo and Juliet* into a comic opera ; despatching the fiery Tybalt with the bravura ' The soldier tired ' ; Mercutio to the lively air of ' Over the Hills and far away,' and winding up with a grand scene in the graveyard, with the shades of the Capulets dancing among the tombstones to the solemn dirge of ' Where are you going, my pretty maid? I am going a-milking, sir, she said.' Won't it be capital? Lewis's success ensures my own." [115]

So far as the theatre pay-box is concerned, the anecdote is true enough. Drury Lane Theatre was at the time in great financial difficulties, and Lewis's play was a " lucky hit " which night after night filled the theatre coffers and helped to improve its position. Lewis had thus done the theatre a good service with his play, though he himself received almost nothing for it ; at least Sir Walter Scott said, when asked how much Lewis had benefited thereby, " Little of that, in fact to its author absolutely nothing, and yet its merits ought to have brought something handsome to poor Mat. But Sheridan, the manager, generally paid jokes instead of cash." [116]

Michael Kelly, who wrote the music for the play, relates

in his *Reminiscences* [117] that it had " a prodigious run." The cast included John Kemble, Mrs. Jordan and Mrs. Powell, the latter " a splendid spectre." " The sinking of the ghost in a flame of fire, and the beauty of the whole scene had a most sublime effect." Mrs. Siddons wrote to a friend that the " appearance of the ghost at the end of the fourth and fifth acts had as great an effect upon the audience as anything I ever saw, producing a tumult of applause." Shelley's friend, Thomas Love Peacock, who was thirteen when the play was produced, makes one of the characters of his *Gryll Grange* (1860) [118] say that ghosts were in such high favour in his youth that the first question regarding a new book was whether it contained a ghost, and that *The Castle Spectre* was responsible for the fashion.

In his preface Lewis acknowledges his sources and the assistance he had received in his work. He has imitated scenes in Walpole's romance and Schiller's play *The Robbers;* the fact is that his plot is built on the lines of *The Castle of Otranto*. We can also add that the all-important ghost is obviously a gentler version of the Bleeding Nun, now conceived in the spirit of a protective ancestress. The play further provides a marginal note by Lewis to the effect that a certain passage is not to be taken as pointing a moral ; he is afraid that without such a caution it might be averred that the whole play was intended to inculcate the " doctrine of fatality " ; he has had good opportunities of discovering the marvellous faculty possessed by some people of misrepresenting the thoughts of others. In other ways, too, Lewis displayed caution ; before it was presented he gave the manuscript to his sister Maria to read, in order that she might strike out anything that savoured in the slightest of immorality. But even that did not entirely save him from reproach. He had allowed his epicurean monk to say on one occasion : " Now my late patroness, the baroness of O'Drench—Ah to hear the catalogue of her crimes was quite a pleasure, for she always confessed them over a sirloin of beef, and instead of telling a bead swallowed a bumper." This provoked a later critic [119] to ask how " any person not destitute of sense could write such stuff, " and to answer his own question with the remark that " Lewis's mind was strangely warped where a friar was concerned." The lines concerned seem however to be fairly natural in the mouth of this particular character. The same writer regarded the two black bodyguards in Lewis's play as an anachronism. When a like objection was made against Brian de Bois-Guilbert's Saracen slaves, Sir Walter Scott [120] referred to what Lewis had said : " Mat treated the objection with great contempt, and averred in reply, that he made the slaves black, in order to obtain a striking effect of contrast, and that, could he have derived a similar advantage from making his heroine blue, blue she should have been." Scott then defends his historical right to such a proceeding.

A review in one of the magazines [121] seems to give the secret of *The Castle Spectre*'s success with the public : " The extraordinary popularity of this play has been attributed, and we think not without justice, to the happy management the author has exhibited in the paraphernalia of his spectre, and to the air of romance he has given to the principal situations. In the characters there is nothing strikingly new, or remarkably powerful ; and the incidents are such as have been found in most of our serious novels, from The Old English Baron down to the author's own Monk. Notwithstanding . . . Mr. Lewis has put the whole together with so much art, that even those scenes with which we have been the most familiar in the closet, have frequently the effect of novelty now that they appear in a dramatic shape."

With *The Castle Spectre* Lewis had thus revived the terror-romantic melodrama on the English stage.

8

During a visit to Scotland in the summer of 1793, Lewis had translated Schiller's play *Kabale und Liebe*, which, in 1797, he published as *The Minister*. A second edition appeared the following year, but it was not performed until 1803, when it was given at the Covent Garden Theatre as *The Harper's Daughter*. Another work of this period is *Rolla, or the Peruvian Hero*, which appeared in 1799 and is a translation of Kotzebue's play *Spanier in Peru oder Rolla's Tod*.[122] It was never produced, for the reason that in his *Pizarro*, Sheridan had built up a better play from the same source. Readers, however, were not lacking, for even this book achieved a second edition. The same year saw the publication of a translation of Juvenal's Thirteenth Satire under the title of *Love of Gain*, a fruit, probably, of Lewis's Latin studies at Oxford.

The Minister is a graphic example of the treatment to which Lewis could subject the work of a foreign author ; the " translation " is really an adaptation, begun arbitrarily and in conformity with Lewis's own peculiar taste in regard to names. Miller becomes Münster, his daughter Luise, Julia; von Kalb, Ingelheim; Ferdinand, Casimir Rosenberg; and Lady Milford, Fredericia von Ostheim. Especially characteristic is the alteration of the scene of the play to Brunswick and the period to 1580; Lewis obviously intended to dress up Schiller's bourgeois tragedy into something in better accord with the "romantic" taste of his own public. He was not in the least daunted by the resulting grave anachronisms, as for instance when Fredericia refuses to accept jewels purchased with blood-money obtained from the sale of a sovereign's subjects; he extricates himself from this dilemma with the remark that a reviewer in one of the magazines (he believed it was *The Critical Review*) had with full reason criticized the glaring anachronism in this passage, but as he (Lewis) himself was capable of similar lapses, he could all the easier forgive Schiller them. This high-handed proceeding of first giving a poor rendering of another author's notable work, and then allowing the blame for errors due to the tasteless and unsuccessful adaptation to fall on the original author, does not speak well for Lewis's conscientiousness and artistic taste or for his critical sense; the callousness thus displayed for the rights of others can meanwhile be explained as springing partly from the schoolboyish superficiality of Lewis's character, partly from the vague conceptions then entertained of the rights of an author in respect of his work. The criticism of *The Monk* in the *Monthly Review* contains a passage reflecting contemporary ideas on literary borrowings and adaptations: "The great art of writing consists in selecting what is most stimulant from the works of our predecessors, and in uniting the gathered beauties in a new whole, more interesting than the tributary models. This is the essential process of the imagination, and excellence is no otherwise attained. All invention is but new combination. To invent well is to combine the impressive."

It is not strange that Lewis's contemporaries saw little that was blameworthy in his methods. After he had once again remodelled his *East Indian*, he wrote for the printed version, which appeared in 1800 (the stage version in 1799), a preface in which, with a great appearance of candour, he gives a few crumbs of truth, while hiding in effect the whole truth. Thus with regard to his sources he states: "The Plot of this Comedy, as far as regards Rivers's visits to Modish and Mrs. Ormond, was taken from the *Novel of Sidney Biddulph*; Mr. Sheridan has already borrowed the same incident from the same source, and employed it (though in a different manner) in the *School for Scandal*." What catches our attention in this statement is its inaccuracy ; there is no such thing as a *Novel of Sidney Biddulph*, though there certainly does exist a story called *The Memoirs of Miss Sidney Biddulph* (1761) by Mrs. Frances Sheridan, mother of R. B. Sheridan, which would thus according to Lewis have furnished the theme for *The School for Scandal*.[123] Is it possible that Lewis, working at his play before he was sixteen, as he himself points out, could have developed this theme independently, without succumbing to the temptation to imitate the existing famous play on the same subject, which he had doubtlessly seen ? It seems improbable, and a comparison between the two plays shows clearly enough that the *East Indian* was modelled on *The School for Scandal*. It is a similar picture of a gossiping, scandal-hungry society, with corresponding characters, letters and tricks of construction ; its only addition is a dash of the precociously successful amours of a young woman and of tearful, oppressed, honourable poverty. The plot is ultimately unravelled by the wealthy East Indian, Rivers (Sheridan's Oliver Surface).[124]

After protracted negotiations Lewis succeeded in getting his play produced ; it was performed for the first time at the Drury Lane Theatre on April 22nd, 1799 (Mrs. Jordan's benefit night), with Kemble in the part of Rivers and Mrs. Jordan as the heroine Zorayda, Rivers's daughter. We learn from Lewis's preface that the acting was superb throughout ; Kemble in particular distinguished himself. It was only performed twice in that season, but was included in the repertory the next December. Its reception by the public was at first favourable, but (says Lewis) as soon as Sheridan took the stage " mounted on his great tragic war-horse Pizarro," he quickly blocked the way for Lewis, " trampling his humble pad-nag of a Comedy under foot without the least compunction." Lewis had furnished his play with a prologue and an epilogue. In the former, which was delivered by H. Kemble, he depicts the enthusiasm with which he had worked on the play, in his early youth, and how, having completed it, he said to himself : " It isn't perfect, but it's vastly well ! " Since then divers tribulations had sharpened the author's critical sense, which now pounced with all severity on every hidden fault and revealed the imperfections of its fancied beauties. The epilogue is characteristic of its author ; amidst the rumble of thunder and flashing of lightning the ghost of Queen Bess comes on to the stage, informing the public that she had been granted leave by Pluto to visit London; if the new play at the Drury Lane proved successful she could stay on in London— so Pluto had decreed—for the duration of its run, but if it failed to attract the public she was to return immediately, taking the author with her.

9

We have not yet exhausted Lewis's literary labours during the years following the appearance of *The Monk*. Reference has been made earlier to the translations, apparently of ballads and folk-songs, undertaken in Germany. As the ballads scattered throughout *The Monk* had been well received, the idea occurred to the author of compiling a collection of ballads, in which he could utilize these renderings from the German and which might become a parallel work to and a continuation of Percy's *Reliques*. In the spring of 1798, Scott's friend William Erskine happened to meet Lewis in London[125] just as the latter was preparing his collection and looking out for further contributions. Erskine showed him Scott's translations of Bürger's *Lenore* and *Der wilde Jäger*, remarking that Scott had more of the same sort. The delighted Lewis decided to ask for his collaboration; and thus were the two authors brought together. Proof that Scott regarded his introduction to Lewis as an important event is provided by Thomas Moore's entry in his diary[126] when he records that Scott stated that the first person to induce him to try his poetical gifts was Mat Lewis. Scott's biographer, J. G. Lockhart, relates that the brilliant, though meteoric, fame of *The Monk* had made a dazzling impression on the literary aspirants of Edinburgh, and that Scott, who was perhaps always inclined to regard public favour as a proof of literary merit, and throughout his life exaggerated everybody's talents but his own, regarded Lewis's invitation to collaborate as a flattering mark of attention. He immediately answered Lewis's letter and placed all his translations and adaptations at the latter's disposal. In his answer, Lewis thanks him not only for his permission, but also for " the handsome manner in which that permission was granted," and continues : " The plan I have proposed to myself, is to collect all the marvellous ballads which I can lay hands upon. Ancient as well as modern will be comprised in my design. . . . But as a ghost or a witch is a sine-qua-non ingredient in all the dishes of which I mean to compose my hobgoblin-repast," he could not use all

Scott's material. Nor did he approve altogether of the translations, but made alterations, eliminating Scotticisms and improving the rhythm.[127] Scott accepted this teaching with gratitude, and said afterwards of Lewis's technical equipment that " he had the finest ear for rhythm I ever met with—finer than Byron's." Lewis appears to have opened Scott's eyes to the practical demands of poetry as regards diction, rhythm and rhyme, so that his " severe lectures, " as Scott later termed these criticisms, proved of considerable service to his pupil.

On a visit to Scotland Lewis met Scott for the first time at Inverary, where the adored Lady Charlotta Campbell is said to have been the leader of a joyous, social life. Back in Edinburgh again, Lewis invited Scott to dinner ; years afterwards, Scott still remembered the elation awakened in him by this invitation. He had been sixteen when he met Burns and since then he had not met anyone with an established reputation as a poet ; now a poet, whose romance had attracted the widest attention and whose ballads *Alonzo the Brave* and *Durandarte* had inspired him with a passionate desire to try his own hand at poetry, who was further known in the highest circles of London society, and was one of the lions of Mayfair, had shown him the attention of not only inviting his collaboration, but of asking him to dinner ! One understands how encouraging all this must have been to the young Scottish lawyer, for whom a literary reputation was still a distant dream.

It may seem a strange coincidence that Scott's virile muse should have been schooled by Lewis's spectral nymph, and it is undeniably one of the minor wonders of literary history ; nevertheless, it has its own clear logic. Lewis and Scott had the same hobby, the interpretation and introduction into English of German romanticism, and this would at once bring them into perfect harmony ; secondly, their relations reflect the historical fact that the romantic school founded by Scott, Byron, Shelley, etc., was in point of fact based on the earlier school of Lewis and his predecessors, *i.e.*, on a romanticism now comparatively unknown, which yet, despite the modesty of its artistic achievements, represents an extensive preliminary labour of digestion and preparation, providing in many respects the vital basis for features that later attained brilliance and fame.

At that time Scott had on hand a translation of *Götz von Berlichingen*, the inspiring influence of the chevaleresque romance of this work having penetrated thus far. Of course he showed this translation to his new friend, who, ever helpful, began seeking a publisher for it. He approached his own publisher, J. Bell, who had sponsored *The Monk*, and succeeded in arranging an agreement according to which Scott was to receive twenty-five guineas for the first edition and as much for a second should it be called for. The book appeared on the basis of this contract in February 1799. A second edition was not demanded until long afterwards. Lewis wrote to Scott informing him that the remuneration was small, because the book was a first literary work; thus ignoring, or perhaps he " did not take in earnest," the translations of *Lenore* and *Der wilde Jäger* which Scott had published in 1796, as though they had only been manuscripts offered for his collection of ballads. It is not impossible, though, that they were shown to him in manuscript form, for Scott may have worked on them subsequently to their appearance in print.[128]

The friendship between Lewis and Scott was never disturbed. In 1814 Lewis returned to him a number of books borrowed " sixty years since," remarking in his letter : " I must mention, that hearing *Waverley* ascribed to you, I bought it, and read it with all impatience. I am now told it is not yours, but William Erskine's. If this is so, pray tell him from me that I think it excellent in every respect, and that I believe every word of it. . . ."

10

The first part of Lewis's collection of ballads, the *Tales of Terror*, was published at Kelso, in 1799. The following year he published in the same town the second part under the title *Tales of Wonder* ; in 1801 both appeared in London, with several new " tales " added, as *Tales of Wonder*. For this edition he wrote an introductory dialogue, a conversation in verse between the author and " a friend," in which he elucidates his own romantic principles. To his friend's chidings for writing such tales, whose sole reward will only be " a nursery's praise, " and to uttered hopes that " these scribblers soon shall mourn their useless pains and weep the short-lived product of their brains, " he answers by admitting that the day of his ghostly muse was on the wane, declaring at the same time that he was indifferent to public opinion and tasteless fashion. Fashion, he declares, is a terrible force, before which both " sense and judgment " yield, whether " she

loves to hear an untaught savage speak moral axioms in his
wilderness, or bids the bard, by leaden rules confined, to
freeze the bosom and confuse the mind, while feeling stagnates
in the drawler's veins, and fancy is fettered in didactic chains ;
or rouses the dull German's gloomy soul, and pity leaves for
horror's wild control, pouring warm tears for visionary crimes "
—Lewis would have none of it, his taste was still his own.
" His mind unaltered views, with fixed delight, the wreck of
learning snatched from Gothic night" ; his soul knows
" Grecian fire " and " Roman grace," yet marks with pleasure
how the flame of ancient days blazes with triumphant brightness in Britain. Obeying the law of variety in pleasure, the
heart turns willingly from classic brightness to Gothic gloom,
which breathes awe and rapture ;

> How throbs the breast with terror and delight,
> Filled with rude scenes of Europe's barbarous night !

Lewis then recounts the objects which inspire him with
romantic pleasure ; these include the groaning of forests and
the roar of nocturnal storms over blasted heaths, which set the
darkest powers of the imagination in motion, restless war and
papal craft, which shut each softening ray from lost mankind ;
the days when only the fatal light of error shone, when Science
was unknown and the active energies of the soul were fettered
and benumbed at the foot of the tower of Superstition (Lewis's
favourite word) ; the pale-eyed maid suffering her penance
and the votary praying at the sainted shrine ; the wizard who
awakens the slumbering grave ; the war's glittering front, the
trophied field, the hallowed banner, and the red-cross shield ;
knightly tournaments, the crimes of feudal barons and the
proud grandeur of feudal days ; the martial soil of Scandinavia,
Morven's mountains and the snows of Lapland ; barbarian
chiefs falling in fierce battles and partaking in Odin's bloody
feasts ; the harp of Ossian acclaiming heroic deeds to listening
grey old soldiers proud of their scars ; the ghost wandering at
the dread hour of midnight and lamenting its woes to the
silent moon ; Danish pirates on forays and a Saxon baron,
proud and sullen in his fierce anger ; the ivy-clad walls of a
solitary convent ; the loud cry of the night-owl, the dim
lamp of dungeon, the midnight cloister, a vanishing procession,
flaming tapers, and the chanted rite—according to Lewis all these

> Rouse, in the trembling breast, delightful dreams,
> And steep each feeling in romance's streams !
> Streams, which afar in restless grandeur roll,
> And burst tremendous on the wond'ring soul !

Now gliding smooth, now lashed by magic storms,
Lifting to light a thousand shapeless forms ;
A vaporous glory floats each wave around,
The dashing waters breathe a mournful sound,
Pale Terror trembling guards the fountain's head,
And rouses Fancy on her wakeful bed ;
" From realms of viewless spirits tears the veil,
And half reveals the unutterable tale ! "

This remarkable poetical catalogue of terror-romantic material is obviously Lewis's confession of faith. Recalling what has been written in the previous chapter, it is difficult to find in it anything not mentioned there. It shows that the terror-romanticists really had their own carefully-compiled array of subjects to inspire their creative work.[129]

The book met with disfavour. Lewis was said to have called his work *Tales of Wonder*, when what he had actually published were " Tales of Plunder." Only Scott's contribution escaped criticism, and even brought him some acknowledgment from the reviewers ; Lewis's own reward was a satirical poem by Geo. Watson Taylor entitled *The Old Hag in a Red Cloak, dedicated to the writer of the " Grim White Woman."* This poem was directed against the prevailing bad taste in literature, as represented in Lewis's work. Another satirical poem by an anonymous writer, *More Wonders*, sought to defend the literary rights of other authors against Lewis's arbitrary adaptations.

A trifling circumstance serves to illumine the naïvity of Lewis's nature. Grown wiser since the lesson of *The Monk*, he tried to instil even into these tales of terror some moral or didactic lesson. Many of them ended in a comically serious, moral exhortation directed to young girls. He informs us that his *King of the Clouds* was written to prove to damsels that it might profit them to know a little grammar ; the heroine of this particular story would assuredly have fallen a victim to demons if she had not been lucky enough to know the difference between the comparative and the superlative. Comment on such an attitude of mind is needless.

II

Lewis was in the habit of amusing his company by fixing some fleeting impression in a little poem. Often, too, he would compose a melody to these poems. He was especially fond of writing poems with accompanying melodies for his sister Sofia to sing, and his skill was so much admired that writers of farces and tableaux often sought his assistance in the poetical side of their work. Lewis's song " No, my Love, no," set to music by Kelly, which is contained in Dibdin's scenic adaptation (after Kotzebue) *Of Age To-morrow*, became one of the favourite melodies of the day, was found on every music-stand and heard in every street. Kelly relates that after being requested by the Prince of Wales to compose a simple English ballad, he begged his friend Lewis to write the words for him. The ballad was called " To-morrow," and, according to Kelly, was greatly liked.

But Lewis had also other irons in the fire during these years. The success of *The Castle Spectre* spurred him on to renewed attempts in the field of drama, and he wrote a new play of chivalry and superstition on the lines of *The Robber*, entitled *Adelmorn, the Outlaw*, which was produced at Drury Lane on May 4th, 1801. Its plot is briefly as follows : Baron Ulric has committed a murder and accusing the innocent Adelmorn of the crime, succeeds in procuring his banishment and in inheriting the wealth of his victim ; he does not confess until the ghost of the murdered man comes down from Heaven, surrounded by cherubim, to bring him to account. Adelmorn, who, as the innocent victim of oppression, has meanwhile had excellent opportunities for delivering flaming lines *à la* Karl Moor, is now restored to his former station and honours. He, too, experiences a miracle, for in a supernatural vision he learns the identity of the real murderer. A wicked monk plays the part of an accomplice. Influences of Kotzebue's *Menschenhass und Reue* and of Mrs. Radcliffe's *Romance of the Forest* and *The Italian* are discernible in the play. It can hardly be said to demonstrate successfully, in a dramatic sense, Lewis's actual purpose, which was to show that when the criminal's heart is at its hardest, conscience brings him to confess. After the first performance Lewis had to strike out a few lines to which exception had been taken, and to tone down his ghost scene. The play only survived some ten performances, being given for the last time on March 7th, 1802, by when it had been cut down from three acts to two.

Although the reception of this " noble outlaw " had been so chilly, Lewis was not disheartened. He had ready in his pocket a new play, a polished tragedy called *Alfonso, King of Castile*, regarding the writing of which he informed his mother that he had " begun a tragedy in blank verse, but I stick in the third act, at a reconciliation between a king and a princess—the two stupidest people I ever met with." He managed however to clear this reef, and his new play was completed to prove that he had other grand effects up his sleeve as well as ghosts. The faithful chieftain Orsino, wrongly suspected of treason, lives in the most secret and romantic banishment in a forest-cave. His son, the wild Cæsario, a kind of primitive Byron-Werner-Ulric type, plans revenge on the king, although he is married to the king's daughter Amelrosa, which again does not prevent him from making love to Ottilia, a species of female hyena. The gunpowder mine laid by Cæsario explodes, as it was intended to do, at one o'clock, but the king is saved. When Cæsario thereupon tries to murder his sovereign, Orsino comes on the scene in time to step between them, and in a passion of loyalty kills his own son. A second grand effect, a burst of thunder, brings the conspirators to their knees, to beg and to receive a noble and regal pardon. No wonder a certain critic wrote: "This tragedy delights in explosions. Alfonso's empire is destroyed by a blast of gunpowder, and restored by a clap of thunder. After the deaths of Cæsario and a short exhortation to that purpose by Orsino, all the conspirators fall down in a thunder-clap, ask pardon of the king and are forgiven. This mixture of physical and moral power is beautiful ! " [130]

Alfonso appeared in book-form before its production on January 15th, 1802 ; the only occasion, however, when the last act was performed as originally written was at the Haymarket Theatre on February 28th, 1803. Altogether about ten performances were given of the play. The public received it not unfavourably, although the numerous murders gave rise to some protests. On the whole, as a work of Lewis's, *Alfonso* had one merit in the eyes of his contemporaries that had hitherto been lacking : it could by no means be called immoral. Lewis had indeed become extremely cautious in this respect, as is seen from his answer [131] to a review in which his play had been termed stupid. Lewis says : " To the assertion that my play is stupid, I have nothing to object ; if it be found so, even let it so be said. But if, as was most falsely asserted of *Adelmorn*, any anonymous writer should advance that my tragedy is immoral, I expect him to prove his assertions, by quoting the objectionable passages. This I demand as an act of justice."

Lewis himself attached great value to this play and was as happy over its moderate public success as he was disconcerted at the mocking and biting criticisms. " In writing it," he states, " I have spared no pains—it has gone to the public not as a good play, but as the best I can produce. Very possibly, nobody could write a worse tragedy ; but it is a melancholy truth, that I cannot write a better." [132]

The true motive in *Alfonso*, unflinching loyalty to the king and the great principle of faithfulness in general, had not been perceived by Lewis and presented with due poetical force and conviction, but had been suffered to become lost amid theatrical effects and a striving after scenic excitement.

Alfonso was produced at Covent Garden and not, like his former plays, at Drury Lane, for Sheridan's venomous criticisms and satire had ended by driving Lewis elsewhere. Harris, the manager of the Covent Garden Theatre, received him with the utmost flattery, which can only be regarded as proof that Lewis's plays were on the whole financially successful. " Mr. Harris has taken," relates Lewis,[133] " all of a sudden, a fancy for everything that I do. . . . 'Anything that you choose to be brought forward, shall be produced immediately.' He seems to think he cannot have enough of my writing. How this happens I am ignorant : but the fact is, that he is as full of civility, and compliments, and fine speeches, as he can cram."

It was a pleasant situation for a dramatic author. Lewis took advantage of it to show that ghosts and powder-mines had not yet exhausted his themes of terror. In 1803 he produced a monologue entitled *The Captive*, which had the most agitating effect on the audience. *The Captive* is the despairing monologue of a mother confined in a madhouse, and mirrors her gradual lapse into insanity, ending with her sudden restoration to health. The setting is a cell fitted with an iron grating, in which the captive declaims her part to the accompaniment of music. As this monologue, unpleasant enough when read, was delivered with the utmost realism by a famous actress of those days, Mrs. Litchfield, it affected the nerves of the audience to such an extent that two persons fell into hysterics during the performance and two afterwards. Even the actress was near to fainting and Lewis himself con-fessed to feeling uncomfortable ; [134] he had hoped that pity would move the audience to weep, instead, it was overcome by terror. The presentment of insanity on the stage—an experiment characteristic of the terror-romanticists—had thus either failed, or had succeeded too well.

In following Lewis's literary career from *The Monk* to *Alfonso*, one searches in vain for what might truly denote a development in a literary sense. The success of *The Castle*

Spectre caused Lewis to mistake his own gifts and to leave the prose narrative form that would have been his real sphere; thus he was set adrift on the tide of the light and superficial taste of his day. His works are not the expressions of spiritual experiences; they are surface compositions of materials culled here and there. His knowledge of German led him merely to the German plays and tales of chivalry, and not to the high spirit of art that flourished at the time. The reader will doubtlessly have perceived by now that his literary production merits no attention from an artistic point of view; it is his central position as a typical terror-romanticist that compels us to linger in his company.

Lewis possessed the spirit of opposition and his ideas really clashed with contemporary thought in England. He was possessed by a desire to present matters in a different light from that prescribed by convention, but lacked the courage for the task. In all his writings after *The Monk* he was exceedingly careful not to say anything that might be construed as immoral or irreligious, and it is possible that this caution stifled what might otherwise have crept into his work of personal interpretation of life. He was no Byron to defy his surroundings, yet he was kin with Byron. Before proceeding to his later work let us glance once more at his private life, his social circle and his friends.

12

The bachelor quarters at Barnes to which we have already referred were Lewis's favourite home. The drawing-room was decorated with numerous mirrors, pictures, vases and shields bearing poetical adages of his own composition. He was a keen collector of valuable bijoux and curiosities, and was specially interested in old seals. His library included a considerable amount of German literature.

Here he was often visited by his friends, among them persons of high degree, such as Frederica, Duchess of York, whose special favourite he seems to have been. Mention has already been made of his weakness for titles; Lewis himself would not admit it, but averred that he was wholly free from prejudice in this respect. " I care nothing about rank in life," he once wrote to his mother, " nothing about what other people may think or say; and have always, both in my public writings and private life, shown (what Mr. Pitt pleased to call) a pleasure in spitting in the face of public opinion. I live as much with actors, and musicians, and painters, as with princes and politicians, and am as well satisfied, and better indeed, with the society of the first, as with that of the latter. But I absolutely require that people should possess some quality or other to amuse me, or I had rather be by myself."

Despite this assurance of Lewis's, Scott's testimony is probably trustworthy and is borne out by the following extract from one of Lewis's letters:[135] "I have my rehearsals to attend, which last to four o'clock. I am also now going to pass some days with Lord Holland, who, on Monday last, lost his uncle, General Fox, and can only see few people. After that, I have some thoughts of accepting young Lambton's offer of conveying me down in his barouche to the Brighton Races, and thence to Worthing, to see Lady C. Campbell, and then to bring me back again with his horses. After this expedition, I shall probably go to Oakend, and stay some time there, and at Lord Carrington's; then to my sister's, if she can receive me, and thence probably to Lord Melbourne's. . . . The Princess of Wales chose to send for me into her box at the Argyle Rooms, made me sup with her, asked me to dinner, and kept me till three o'clock in the morning. . . . To-day I dine at York House, and then sup with the Princess of Wales at the Admiralty. . . . I received a command from the Duke of Clarence to dine with him at Bushy. . . ." A life of such wide social and gastronomic duties is probably a wearing one.

Lewis kept, however, still better company. He made the acquaintance of Thomas Moore comparatively early, presumably soon after Moore's arrival in London (1799). From one point of view at least the encounter must have been amusing to them both: Moore was, as Scott relates[136] " a little, very little man. Less, I think, than Lewis, and somewhat like him in person. God knows, not in conversation, for Mat, though a clever fellow, was a bore of the first description." Moore's experience of the literary criticism and reading public of those years had been like that of Lewis: the same accusations of immorality and corruption of youth had been levelled at him for his renderings of *Anacreon* as at Lewis for *The Monk*. For the humbly-situated Irishman, Lewis, who was the senior by four years, was with his assured social position and his nimbus as a favourite of the theatre-going public a " great friend," through whom one might profit. Thus Lewis became the patron of Moore as he had been the patron of Scott. In the autumn of 1802, for example, Moore appears to have begged some favour of Lewis and appealed to his influence, as in his reply [137] Lewis promises to do all in his power; he fears however that he can accomplish little for Moore, not being one of the latter's " great friends," but on the contrary, a " little one in every sense," as he humorously styles himself. Moore recommends him to a certain writer as a man well acquainted with the theatre,[138] who knows the inside of a theatre better than anyone else. Lewis appears on his part to have read some of Moore's proofs in 1803, and acted thus as a kind of literary adviser. [139] For all that, their relations were apparently never especially intimate, nor did they admire each other's work. Byron relates [140] that Lewis failed to appreciate the beauties of *Lalla Rookh*, and in accordance with his own tastes liked Ch. R. Maturin's *Manuel* better.

The friendship between Lewis and Byron, of which we have already spoken, seems to have begun after the latter's first journey abroad. In the autumn of 1813 they were, according to Byron's diary, on terms of great friendship. Byron was then at the height of his fame in England, admired by all, the pale and beautiful hero of women and drawing-rooms, whose keen perceptions, genius and boldness were feared, and who was known to think as others would have wished to think had they but had the courage. Lewis, too, fell into his wake. From Byron's remarks, it appears that in spite of the poet's smiles at the eccentricities of his friend and his opinion that he was an idle chatterer, he nevertheless respected him and gave heed to his advice. Thus, in the preface to *Marino Faliero*, he tells us that Lewis had furnished him with good advice during a conversation at Venice in 1817 touching on the plan of his play. " If you make him jealous," Lewis said, " recollect that you have to contend with established writers, to say nothing of Shakespeare, and on exhausted subject;—stick to the old fiery Doge's natural character, which will bear you out, if properly drawn; and make your plot as regular as you can."

Lewis showed more discernment in his criticisms of the works of others than in planning his own. One of Lewis's visits to Byron occurred on August 18th, 1816, when he met Shelley, who made a note of the encounter in his diary.[141] " We talk of ghosts; neither Lord Byron nor Monk G. Lewis seem to believe in them, and they both agree, in the very face of reason, that none could believe in ghosts without also believing in God. I do not think that all the persons who profess to discredit those visitations really discredit them, or if they do in the daylight, are not admonished by the approach of loneliness and midnight to think more respectfully of the world of shadows." Shelley was acquainted with Lewis's production. His romantic imagination, ever inclined to meditation over mystic problems, had found nourishment in his youth in Lewis's *Tales of Terror*,[142] and in his list of books read with his wife during 1814, he has included *The Monk* (we will later on see from the romances written in his youth, that he had read it before). So, in meeting Lewis at Byron's, he well knew whose acquaintance he was making.

The preface which Mary Godwin later appended to her *Frankenstein* shows that ghosts and ghost-lore were a frequent subject of conversation with Byron, Shelley and their circle of friends in Switzerland in 1816. After reading a German ghost-story, Byron proposed that the four of them (Byron, Shelley, Mary Godwin and the physician Polidori) should each write a ghost story. From this proposal sprang *Frankenstein*.[143]

In the meeting of these three romanticists there is to my mind something symbolical of literary history. First Lewis, representative of the primitive stage of romance, of spadework, unhewn material and groping purpose ; of the romanticism of ghosts, robbers and knights in the popular form assumed by it in England, France and Germany at the end of the eighteenth century ; secondly Byron, who, basing his material in many respects on the elementary matter represented by Lewis, sensed in it the striving towards opposition and liberty, and refining it in the fire of his genius, beat from it the armour for his great spirit, raising romanticism to the position of a factor of attack and battle, and arrogating unto it, under its mantle of rhetorical enthusiasm, the whole of human life ; thirdly Shelley, who, setting out likewise from primitive romance, had soon, true to his swift, anticipatory spirit, crystallized into misty, fragile pictures of supernatural beauty all that in human life seemed truly desirable to him, rising above terrestrial life into the exalted cool region of the stars. Three different stages of literary development converged thus at Diodati, embodied in three writers of one and the same period.

As for the rest of Lewis's private life, a special feature in it is formed by his relations with his mother. This little woman who had separated from her husband lived with her children in turns, always returning with special affection to shelter with her son, who was indeed her actual support. On occasion, however, even these two could differ, as once when Lewis heard that his mother was intending to launch out as an author. He begged her on no account to do so, not even under a pseudonym, for the secret would inevitably transpire. " I cannot express to you in language sufficiently strong, how disagreeable and painful my sensations would be, were you to publish any work of any kind, and thus hold yourself out as an object of newspaper animadversion and impertinence. I am sure every such paragraph would be like the stab of a dagger to my father's heart. It would do a material injury to Sophia ; and although Maria has found an asylum from the world's malevolence,[144] her mother's turning novel-writer would not only severely hurt her feelings, but raise the greatest prejudice against her in her husband's family. As for myself, I really think I should go to the continent immediately upon your taking such a step." Lewis then assures his mother that an author's trade is not to be coveted, as it brings its adherents " envy, slander and malignity." He finally expresses his opinion that it is not a woman's " business to be a public character and that in proportion as she acquires notoriety she loses delicacy "—a sign of the times that indicates the value set on women authors in some circles, a disparagement not altogether unvisited on male writers too. Mrs. Lewis's dreams withered after this, but Lewis had a hard task to conciliate his offended mother.

A new character who appears on the stage of his life about this time is a certain Mrs. R., who had found favour with Lewis Senior and whose relations with him were no secret. Matthew's sisters Maria and Sophia, both married, soon submitted to necessity, but not so Matthew, who obstinately refused to kiss the hand of Mrs. R. A ponderous correspondence followed, stern and dictatorial on the father's side, humble and polite, but in its essence consistently adamant, on the part of the son. His father reduced his allowance ; the quarrel extended to the whole family, but Mat declined to surrender and so fled to Scotland in the summer of 1804. Not until the following spring would he consent to a formal reconciliation ; but father and son met only rarely afterwards.

Lewis's father regarded him, as the words spoken on his deathbed imply, as a " foolish boy." In November 1811, the older man had fallen seriously ill, whereat Matthew, who as a child had veritably adored his father and later respected at least his iron will and proud inflexibility, began to beg for a real reconciliation ; whether or no he was induced to do this, besides by his truly kind heart, by the fear that his father might disinherit him, is not for us to say. Not daring to visit his parent without permission, towards the end of March 1812, he wrote begging to be allowed to come. The father was disinclined, however, to open the letter immediately and delayed reading it. As Matthew thus received no answer, he approached a friend of his father and requested his services in procuring an interview. He succeeded in gaining his object, but by that time Lewis Senior was dying and Matthew had perforce to be content with the three words of reconciliation : " God bless you ! " His father died on May 17th, 1812, leaving the whole of his considerable fortune to " his beloved son." He is reflected in the life of Lewis as a kind of Dombey ; an inflexible, proud and purposeful Englishman of " Doctor Johnson's days," firm and narrow in his principles, a man whom one is compelled to regard with greater respect than many of the characters that flash past during the author's career.

Inherited wealth made little change in Lewis's private life. During his father's lifetime he had, in addition to his place at Barnes, maintained a second establishment at the Albany, and at these two homes he continued to live. He now bought his mother a house near Leatherhead, in Surrey. It was christened The White Cottage, and thither Mrs. Lewis moved with her cat, her dog and her canary, to an existence varied by the visits of her children, books, music and Bible-readings. In many other ways Lewis showed his love for her and for his relatives in general, dispersing, meanwhile, in silence, considerable sums for charitable purposes.[145]

13

After the literary labours already described came a pause in Lewis's production, to be attributed probably to the unfavourable reviews of his recent plays. He read Gibbon and Voltaire and made the acquaintance of *Corinne*, but with characteristic juvenility declared that he could remember nothing of their contents.[146] We find him ultimately forsaking serious literature and immersing himself again in German robber-romanticism. He set to work on an adaptation of J. H. D. Zschokke's famous romance *Aballino, der grosse Bandit*, which had appeared in 1794, and while at Inverary in the summer of 1804 finished a corresponding English robber-story which he called *The Bravo of Venice*. For his own rendering the studied also Zschokke's scenic adaptation of his romance, his work gaining thereby in dramatic verve; the Rosamunde of his model, a Schiller-like, exalted, idealistic heroine, becomes in Lewis's version Rosabella, who is, in conformity with the trend of English romance, a gentler, more feminine and lovable maiden; the rough Aballino turns into the more polished Flodoardo; the *dénouement* has been freely rewritten with the intention of increasing the dramatic effect. The book appeared in 1805 and attained a wide circulation. The following year Lewis prepared his own scenic adaptation, *Rugantino*, which was successfully presented at Covent Garden; the final scene, in which the dreaded robber stands revealed as a noble-minded peer, the benefactor of Venice and the worthy wooer of the Doge's daughter, had been formed by Lewis into a huge pantomime, in which the gods of Olympus appeared and Rosabella and Flodoardo made their exit in a sea-shell drawn by dolphins.

For the student of literary material a particular significance attaches to this play, owing to its inclusion of a new theme in English literature, *viz.*, the idea, in its most primitive form, of a double existence. As will be shown, its origins can be discerned already in Lewis's earlier works and *Aballino* gave only its most superficial and elementary outlines—a noble character becoming a robber for the purpose of defeating a robber-band with its own weapons—nevertheless, perhaps because of the garish nakedness with which the idea was expressed, it was peculiarly adapted to arouse the attention of the romanticists and to provide them with food for thought.

As the only mention Lewis makes of his sources in these adaptations is an intimation that they were taken from the German, the praise of the reading public was directed to him alone; on suitable occasions he would, however, make vague attempts to evade this admiration by referring in general terms to his German sources. Knowing the wide circulation and the favour achieved by Zschokke's works in Germany, one cannot but remark on the indifference or ignorance displayed by English reviewers in their apparently vague knowledge of Lewis's sources; for more than ten years he was allowed to construct his works on German models and to publish them as his own in practically undisturbed peace, without even an attempt by anyone to show authoritatively and in detail the true source of his inspiration. The explanation is to be sought partly in the Napoleonic wars, and partly perhaps in the fact that the reviewers did not consider Lewis's work worth the labour and the publicity such a course would have entailed.

We must remember, too, that literary borrowings were not viewed with any particular disfavour in those days.[147]

We come finally, with the year 1806, to the last of Lewis's large plays—*Adelgitha, or the Fruits of a Single Error*. In his preface he tells us that before he began to seek some niche in history in which to place his lady and gentleman, he had previously constructed his plot and decided on his characters. As his chief character seemed to resemble Robert Guiscard, he named his hero accordingly, whereby the play was given historical colouring, although as a matter of fact it was not a historical play. It is a moralizing work which attempts to show how it is in our power to refrain from sinning, but an overwhelming task to cease once we have begun. This moral is demonstrated by Adelgitha, the wife of Robert Guiscard, who, despite all her struggles, is driven by the force of circumstances to ruin because of a false step before her marriage.

More than to the declamatory lines of the play, interest attaches nowadays to the stage directions, which clearly reveal Lewis's " Gothic " taste. The first scene takes place in a grove flanked by the chapel of St. Hilda, where candles are burning, a convent being visible in the background. A bell rings and a procession of nuns appears. The second setting is a " Gothic " room ; the third a garden with the towers of a castle showing over the trees in the background ; the fourth act provides first a " Gothic " room with burning candles, then a kind of gallery hewn in rock, and finally a series of caves opening towards a moonlit mountain and adorned with steps hewn into the rock, ivy and other plants, a cross and a skull and cross-bones ; the fifth, Adelgitha's room, followed by a " splendidly illuminated Gothic hall," in which, besides Robert Guiscard and his knights, " an ancient Minstrel with his harp and four younger Minstrels ranged behind him " appear and sing " a martial ballad." The refrain " we swear that we'll conquer, or perish " (for king and country) is taken up by the knights, each brandishing a drawn sword in one hand and a goblet in the other—a scene that has later become extremely common in romantic patriotic dramas, and was obviously intended by Lewis to stir the feelings of his countrymen in the great struggle with France. One is compelled to admit that in *Adelgitha* Lewis has attempted to delineate individual character with some success ; his play is less schematic in this respect than most of the dramas of those days.

Another work of Lewis's, to appear in 1806, was his *Feudal*

Tyrants, or the Counts of Carlsheim and Sargans. This is a romance in four parts, taken from the German, as Lewis (on the title-page of the second edition, at least) vaguely informs us. He might have added that it was a fairly faithful translation of Benedicte Naubert's romance *Elisabeth, Erbin von Toggenburg, oder Geschichte der Frauen von Sargans in der Schweiz,* published at Leipzig in 1789. When it was noticed in *The Critical Review* as an original work founded on German romance-themes, Lewis held his peace. This translation reveals in a graphic manner the source whose products Lewis was attempting to foist upon the English reading-public—the cheap German pedlar-romance, a species of literature that had swollen to unique dimensions. With the spread of the school of taste represented by Lewis, this type of literature, the " German horrors " of English literary history, had begun to reach England in the form of translations. Parallel with these " horrors " and influenced chiefly by the works of Mrs. Radcliffe and Lewis, an original, purely English school of such work had likewise begun to flourish, and together the two were responsible, at the turn of the nineteenth century, for an extraordinarily large mass of pedlar-literature that laid under its thrall the uneducated public and even threatened, as we have seen, to oust all better work from the theatre. Only the combined influence of Jane Austen's trenchant irony, the general feeling of surfeit and finally Sir Walter Scott's narrative art, which while satisfying all classes retained a high literary standard, helped at last to stem this destructive flood of bad literature, or at least to lead it into subordinate channels.[148]

Lewis probably earned a good deal of money by his books, as in 1808 he published a new work in the style of its predecessors, *Romantic Tales*, a collection of prose stories and poems in four volumes. In his preface he remarks that it is as unpleasant to him to accept admiration that is not his due as it is for him to deprive those who are entitled to it of their due meed of praise ; notwithstanding, he finds it difficult to define how much of the book is his own work and how much borrowed from others, for even in the parts least his own he has made such thorough alterations that he could with less labour have produced original work. He solves the problem by begging the reader to lay everything that fails to please to his account and everything that pleases to the account of others.[149]

The *Romantic Tales* complete in prose form his earlier *Tales of Wonder*. In spite of their many shortcomings, the picture they give of the author's gifts of selection is not entirely unfavourable.

14

We have anticipated somewhat and have neglected to mention the little play in two acts called *The Wood Dæmon, or the Clock has Struck*, which helped to fill the bill at the Drury Lane Theatre on April 1st, 1807. The theme is taken from the ballad of the " Grim White Woman." Before long, Lewis had enlarged it to a whole-evening play in three acts, which was performed with great success over thirty times in 1808. In 1811 it was again rewritten, this time as *One o'Clock, or, the Knight and the Wood Dæmon;* it was now a " grand musical romance," with music by M. B. King and M. Kelly, and was produced at the Lyceum Opera on August 1st. The libretto, which was published somewhat later, is dedicated to the Prince of Wales. The Wood Dæmon has rendered the knight Hardyknute invulnerable and given him eternal youth and the power to win all female hearts, but in exchange he stipulates for human blood each seventh day of August. Should he fail to receive this sacrifice before a certain enchanted clock strikes one, Hardyknute is to become his slave for all eternity. The stage directions provide the clearest idea of the legendary, terror-romantic nature of the play. One sees, to begin with, a romantic forest, a tiny cottage and a mountainous background, all in the moonlight, with groups of wood-spirits here and there. These increase in number, the moonlight becomes transformed into a ruddy glare and a storm begins to rage ; the witch Sangrida enters to celebrate her festival of storm. The cock crows. Later, when Hardyknute arrives before his castle at the head of a triumphant procession, his romantic daughter releases the captured knights and ladies from their fetters ; the captive giant Haako lends by contrast a touch of fairy-tale to the scene. Then comes a " Gothic " hall with a big stained-glass window in the rear wall ; marble steps lead to a raised door. The Four Seasons and their satellites execute a ballet. The music dies away and beside a table we see a woman in black who takes Hardyknute through the door in the wall. A loud burst of thunder is heard and all becomes dark. Hardyknute rushes on the stage with drawn sword. A new burst of thunder is heard. The big window opens and Sangrida appears in a chariot drawn by dragons, vanishing finally in a rain of fire. The closing scene takes place in a necromancer's cave in which a lamp is burning. The background displays an open, iron-barred door and a flight of steps. In the centre is an altar, which bears several candlesticks; around it two enormous snakes are coiled. On one side is a high stand and on this the effigy of a kneeling giant who points with his right hand to the clock on his left shoulder. The other side is taken up by the rock and an iron-barred door, fastened with a huge padlock. Hardyknute attires himself in his magic cap and cloak, takes a magic wand and proceeds to weave spells. A stream of blue fire issues from the serpents' mouths and from the centre of the altar rises a gigantic golden head. Before Hardyknute has had time to murder the victim who is to help him pay his debt of blood, a third person advances the clock, which strikes one. At that Sangrida enters and kills Hardyknute. He falls into the arms of four devils who appear from behind the altar and is deposited by them on the altar. The snakes coil themselves round him and the whole altar sinks into the earth. The cave vanishes and when the stage is again illumined we are in a " Gothic " hall. Grand Chorus.

As regards scenic construction and the constant rise in the action and excitement, one must admit that the play fulfils fairly large demands. Everything has been calculated with a view to holding the spectator in an uninterrupted state of suspense, in which only the music and songs provide respite and rest. As a romantic melodrama the play can be called a success. The source of its plot is, according to Lewis, a drama called *The Three Brothers* by Pickersgill, produced at Drury Lane in 1807 ; some of the songs are adapted from the German and French. One can discern, however, in the characters and scenes, more alien influences than Lewis saw fit to admit.[150]

His production now nears its end. On December 1st, 1808, *Venoni, or the Novice of St. Mark's,* was presented at Drury Lane, adapted, as already mentioned, from de Monvel's play *Les Victimes Cloitrées.* The subject-matter of this play casts a certain illumination over the materials that went to the making of *The Monk* and deserves to be studied. The scene is in Messina. A youth of noble birth, Venoni (the Dorval of the original) intends to wed Josepha (Eugenie), but his mother, who is entirely under the influence of her treacherous confessor, the abbot Cœlestino (Laurent), succeeds in postponing the wedding and in getting Josepha transferred to the convent of St. Ursula at Naples. There the report is spread that

Josepha has died, which causes the sorrow-struck Venoni to enter a monastery. When the play begins his novitiate is approaching its end and he is about to take the vow, but owing to the exhortations of his friends still hesitates. But Cœlestino, who aims at making Josepha his mistress and at securing Venoni's great inheritance for the monastery, succeeds in prevailing on him to adhere to his purpose. The monastery stands wall to wall with the convent of St. Ursula, a secret passage connecting the two buildings. When Venoni finally becomes aware of the abbot's intentions, he is immured in a subterranean dungeon. A certain Ludovico has already been imprisoned there for twenty years; to pass his time he has made an opening between his cell and the one to which Venoni is brought. The muscular Venoni succeeds in breaking his way into the secret passage leading to the convent. We now learn that Josepha is not dead but a prisoner in the convent, where Cœlestino tries with the help of the abbess Veronica to seduce her, until Venoni forces his way to her rescue. In all this we are obviously being regaled with the chief features of the monastery and convent in *The Monk*, as well as with a primitive version of Ambrosio and the cruel abbess; further, the play deals exhaustively in the kind of romanticism attaching to secret tunnels and attempts at flight from prisons.[151]

The above is taken from the revised version of the play. In its original form the third act showed two prison cells, divided from one another by an enormously thick wall. In the one was Venoni and in the other Josepha, both unaware of the other's proximity. Even in these circumstances they had the politeness not to interrupt each other. Not until one had finished his outburst of fury did the other commence her laments, and when this had gone on for some twenty monologues, the audience could no longer restrain its giggling. The first night was thus an unqualified fiasco. Lewis then recast his third act in a single night; it was hastily rehearsed and in this new form the play proved a great success. It had already reached its eighteenth performance when the theatre was burned down.

This success failed to satisfy Lewis. In the preface to *Venoni* he affirms that " this will probably be the last of my dramatic attempts. The act of composing has ceased to amuse me; I feel that I am not likely to write better than I have done already; and though the Public have received my plays certainly with an indulgence quite equal to their merits, those merits even to myself appear so trifling, that it cannot be worth my while to make any further efforts at the attainment of dramatic fame." He did not however adhere to this decision. In February 1811, a great pantomime, *Bluebeard*, was produced at Drury Lane, in which, to the exceeding joy of the public of the time, horses were included in the cast. Its success inspired the competing Covent Garden Theatre to launch out in the same line, and consequently Lewis wrote by request *Timour, the Tartar*. He tells us that Harris had expressly begged for a play in which horses would appear on the stage, but he himself, doubtful as to the talent of this new class of actor, had restricted their use within extremely narrow limits.

The play has no claim to be regarded as dramatic art, but is simply a circus piece, ranking among the spectacles which great variety theatres sometimes offer their audiences. For such a purpose *Timour* was very well suited, for in addition to possessing an exciting plot—a series of hairbreadth escapes—it is a fine costume play. Timour enters clad in a yellow satin shirt, red trousers, green boots, a dagger inlaid with gold at his belt, a gleaming turban on his head and a gold chain round his neck; the pretty head of the heroine Zorilda was covered by a helmet, her breast by a silver corslet, while her dress was white satin petticoat, richly ornamented, long crimson train; her boots were yellow.[152] When she rode on to the stage perched on a magnificent stallion, the audience was completely won over. *Timour* was given forty-four times in succession and was revived as late as 1831, on that occasion at Drury Lane.

It filled the second half of a bill on April 29th, 1811, and began its career as a whole evening's entertainment on May 1st. Strangely enough, while waiting for the curtain to rise, there was a good deal of hissing among the first-night audience, who had heard that it was to be an equestrian play, mingled with protests against the inclusion of horses. The protesters quickly found themselves however in a small minority and equestrian plays were soon all the rage. Those were indeed years of degradation for the English stage.[153]

About this time, too, Lewis formed the play of his youth, *The East Indian*, into an opera, which as *Rich and Poor*, with music by Horn, was presented at the English Opera-house in June 1812. One of the songs was the still familiar " Banks of Allan Water." [154]

15

As a liberal, imbued with the spirit of opposition, and a member of Sheridan's world, Lewis supported the Whigs in politics, being already inclined by ties of friendship to enrol himself amongst the admirers of Charles James Fox, for the nephew of that politician, Henry Richard, Lord Holland, had been one of Lewis's undergraduate friends.[155] The company of these two men affected his view of life decisively, as appears from the poem he wrote on his return from the burial of Fox, October 10th, 1806. In it he recounts in solemn language and with genuine feeling the most noteworthy deeds of the great statesman, rating highest his struggle against the slave-trade. When his " illustrious shade " approaches the altar of Heaven and the dread Angel of Judgment opens the book of his sins, the whispered word " the slave-trade " moves the Judge to close that catalogue of human failings. It is evident that Lewis had by then formed his opinion of that serious problem in which the principles of universal freedom and humanity clashed with considerations of a material nature. Humane reasons had also been advanced in favour of a continuation of the trade ; they are to be found clearly expressed in Boswell's *Life of Doctor Johnson*. In my view they reflect so well the ideas prevailing in Tory circles during the decades in question and cast so amusing a sidelight on the boundless naïvity of their writer, that I quote them at some length as affecting a problem in which Lewis was directly concerned.[156]

Doctor Johnson, writes Boswell, " had always been very zealous against slavery in every form, in which I with all deference thought that he discovered ' a zeal without know-ledge.' " Johnson was, indeed, so fierce an opponent of slavery and so true a friend of the oppressed, that his well-known animosity against the American colonies and their strivings for independence can be said to have been largely due to their toleration of slave-labour. Lacking the courage to argue out the matter with his adored Master, Boswell wrote the following (at the very latest in 1791, the year in which his *Life* appeared) : " But I beg leave to enter my most solemn protest against his general doctrine with respect to the Slave Trade. For I will resolutely say, that his unfavourable notion of it was owing to prejudice, and imperfect or false information. The wild and dangerous attempt which has for some time been persisted in to obtain an act of our Legislature, to abolish so very important and necessary a branch of commercial interest, must have been crushed at once, had not the insignificance of the Zealots who vainly took the lead in it, made the vast body of Planters, Merchants, and others, whose immense properties are involved in that trade, reasonably enough suppose that there could be no danger. The encouragement which the attempt has received excites my wonder and indignation ; and though some men of superior abilities have supported it ; whether from a love of temporary popularity, when prosperous ; or a love of general mischief, when desperate, my opinion is unshaken. To abolish a *status*, which in all ages *God* has sanctioned, and man has continued, would not only be robbery to an innumerable class of our fellow-subjects ; but it would be extreme cruelty to the African Savages, a portion of whom it saves from massacre, or intolerable bondage in their own country, and introduces into a much happier state of life ; especially now when their passage to the West Indies and their treatment there is humanely regulated. To abolish that trade would be to

' Shut the gates of mercy on mankind.' "

Boswell showed discretion in not putting these arguments, in which a wrong cause finds a beautifully-expressed defence, to the aged prophet in person.

From this battle between conflicting opinions emerged the law against slave-trade, a traffic definitely prohibited in 1807 ; the law did not liberate the slaves.

Lewis Senior owned land in Jamaica on which several hundred negro slaves were employed. Now that Matthew himself became a slave-owner, his liberal and humane views were put to the test. He was publicly opposed to slavery—how was he now to deal with his own slaves? Thus, the problem became acute after his father's death and he did his best to discover a solution from both a humane and a practical standpoint. He sought the society of William Wilberforce a good deal,[157] and ended by deciding that he was unable to liberate his slaves without ruining his estates, the productivity and maintenance of which were based on slave labour, and to preserve his slaves from misery, it was his duty to use other means of securing to them an endurable existence. That he might discover the best way of achieving this object, it would be necessary to study the question on the spot, and on November 10th, 1815, he set out for Jamaica. Byron, with whom he had been much together during these years, wrote to Moore on November

4th : " Lewis is going to Jamaica to suck his sugar canes. . . .
Poor fellow ! He is really a good man—an excellent man—he
left me his walking stick and a pot of preserved ginger. I shall
never eat the last without tears in my eyes, it is so hot." " To
spare each other the unnecessary agony," Lewis said good-bye
to his mother by letter.

He reached Jamaica on January 1st, 1816, and remained
there for exactly three months, embarking on his return
journey on March 31st. During the whole period he kept a
careful diary. As this was written with no thought of publication nor of the demands of his " romantic " public and the
need for satisfying them, his true self is faithfully revealed in
its pages, unselfconscious, unassuming and unaffected. The
book which was the outcome of his visits, *The Journal of a
West-Indian Proprietor*, was published posthumously in 1834,
and gives us an extremely favourable picture of Lewis, both as a
warm-hearted and noble-minded personality and as an author.
It is, as Coleridge affirmed,[158] " delightful " in every respect :
" It is almost the only unaffected book of travels or touring I
have read of late years. You have the man himself, and not an
inconsiderable man,—certainly a much finer mind I supposed
before from perusal of his romances, etc. It is by far his best
work and will live and be popular. Those verses on the Hours
are very pretty, but the Isle of Devils is, like his romances, a
fever dream—horrible, without point or terror." The descriptions in which the book abounds are extremely apt, vivid
and lively. Jamaican nature and conditions are portrayed
impartially and dispassionately with a fine instinct for beauty.
In the descriptions of negro customs one can almost descry
the keen powers of observation of a modern sociologist. The
Journal contains, moreover, an account of the so-called "Nancy-
tales " of the negroes, a series of fairy-tales of which one
was put to paper by Lewis ; it was subsequently published [159]
as *Goose Shoo-shoo's true and marvellous history of a lilly nigger-
man born vidout ed*. The book also includes a poem, " The
Isle of Devils," written on the second journey.

Lewis's measures for the welfare of his negroes, only briefly
referred to here, were concerned chiefly with the prevention of
over-fatigue, and with discipline and accommodation. A
special code of misdemeanours and punishments was to be
strictly followed ; negroes were not to be beaten or otherwise
punished without the consent of certain trusted representatives
and the punishment was in no case to be carried into effect
before a full day had elapsed since the misdemeanour had

been committed. The main feature of all his measures is a conscientious desire to arrange conditions on his estates so that even in his absence any inhuman treatment of slaves would be out of the question. Regarding the existence of the negroes, Lewis came to the conclusion that it was in many respects better than that of English workers.

Lewis drew up his first will on June 5th, 1812, in which he settled on his mother an annuity of one thousand pounds and nominated the trustees who were to administer his property on behalf of his sisters. The will makes no provision for his slaves. Before setting out for Jamaica he added a codicil providing for certain bequests. After his return from that country he went to Italy, where his sister Maria was then living at Naples. The visit to the Villa Diodati to which we have had occasion to refer occurred on this journey. The extensive codicil added to his will on August 20th, 1816, which was witnessed by Byron, Shelley and Polidori, may be regarded as a result of his association and conversation with Byron. In it he enjoins on whoever should become the owner of his estates after his death the duty of personally visiting these estates at stated intervals and of dwelling there for at least three months each time; in the event of his heir failing to comply with these conditions, the estates were to pass to the next-of-kin. The negroes were on no account to be sold, but might be liberated. These injunctions were all dictated by his fear that the slaves might be ill-used in their owner's absence, and are in their somewhat hasty humaneness an honour to their author.

Lewis lingered on his European journey until August 1817, staying as Byron's guest at Venice.[160] Having returned to England he embarked a second time for Jamaica in the beginning of December, a journey from which he was never to return.

He had provided himself with a great number of the latest books, including all that had appeared up to the time of Scott's work, which he specially recommended to his fellow-passengers. His cabin was fitted with a piano, which he would play for hours at a stretch. He was provided, in short, with everything that might serve to enliven a voyage. One of the passengers on board has related that his manners and mode of address were exceedingly polite; sometimes he would be melancholy and abstracted, and walk the decks for hours with a book in his hand, so intent on his own thoughts that he was totally unaware of his surroundings. The crew loved him, for if anyone fell ill, Lewis would be the first to inquire after his condition, to supply him with medicine and to send him titbits from his own table. The joy of the negroes on his arrival was indescribable and they seemed to look upon him more as a law-giving divinity than as a mere human being. On one estate Lewis found his negroes and his affairs in good condition, but on the other everything had gone wrong, whereat Lewis "soothed, threatened, ordered, stormed, swore, and banged the doors," until he had finally established order. On May the 4th, he set out on his return journey, unaware that an attack of fever brought on by the rainy period had been a grave omen. From the moment of his arrival on board he was restless and nervous and after a few days he was laid low by fever ; he had either had the infection in his blood before embarking, or had been infected by one of the many yellow-fever patients on board. Early on May 14th, 1818, he died after severe protracted sufferings.

For fear that the dangerous disease might spread amongst the passengers, he was buried the same morning at 9 a.m. The coffin was shrouded in a canvas sack and lowered with the usual ceremonies into the sea, but as the weights attached to the coffin chanced to fall off, it failed to sink, but began to float in the direction of Jamaica, the wind distending the enveloping sackcloth like a sail. The supernatural quality of this vision greatly alarmed the crew and passengers, for it seemed a last recognition by fate of Lewis's position as the great creator of spectral effects.[161]

In England, where the true circumstances of his death were not published until later, various rumours circulated regarding the manner of his decease, including one that his slaves had poisoned him in the belief that his death would set them free ; it was generally believed that he had died of sea-sickness and the effects of the remedies applied in such cases, and this account is found in Moore's reminiscences.[162] Nor were there lacking pious persons who knew that Lewis, a declared "doubter," had been in great spiritual agony on his deathbed. Byron remembered him as "his dear defunct friend," "as a martyr to his new riches," and altering Scott's lines, wrote :

> I would give many a sugar cane
> Monk Lewis were alive again !

In 1825 Scott wrote the following : "I would pay my share ! How few friends one has, whose faults are only ridiculous. His visit was one of humanity to ameliorate the condition of his slaves. He did much good by stealth, and was a most generous creature. . . ."

Byron inherited Lewis's faithful valet, who was later present at the poet's own deathbed.

16

And now, in the year of Lewis's death, if we cast a backward glance at the harvest of English literature during the years that lie between publication of *The Monk* and its author's demise, we perceive it to be a rich one. Sir Walter Scott has found time to publish all his poetical works and some of his prose stories, and to reach the pinnacle of his production ; a romantic dwelling, the Gothic "haunted castle" of Abbotsford, has risen on the banks of the Tweed and become the focus of his antiquarian interests. Between the two dates mentioned above lies crowded the essential life-work of Coleridge, his poems and his philosophy, and all that remains to him is the ever-dimming speculation of his decline and an embittered and humbling struggle against the fetters of opium. Robert Southey has seated himself at his desk and with a fine flow of rhetoric written his Oriental poems, *Roderick* and a couple of historical works, and having climbed to the heights of the Laureateship, studiously and with an exemplary use of English continues his life-work. During these years Wordsworth completes the most valuable portion of his work and patiently waits for the acknowledgment which, slowly but surely, is to be granted him. Landor has published his *Gebir*, fought in Spain against Napoleon, tried his hand at romantic building at Llantony Abbey, written his *Count Julian* and departed to Italy, where he quarrels with the authorities and meditates over his *Imaginary Dialogues*. De Quincey passes through his wanderings in Wales, his London inferno, the abnormal delights and terrors of an opium-eater's world, his German metaphysical period—all the aspirations and agonies of a sickly and hypersensitive soul and body, preparing himself for his special niche among the great literary self-confessors and self-revealers of the world. Moore's *Irish Melodies* and *National Melodies* are heard already over the whole English-speaking world ; together with his genial sayings and humorous poems and the Oriental glow of *Lalla Rookh*, they have made him famous. Lamb has tried his hand at poetry, fiction and drama, and has suffered with his sister from the effects of poverty and the depressing atmosphere occasioned by the latter's ever threatening madness; he has discovered his true vocation and 1818 sees the publication of his collected works. Maturin has completed his earliest phase and has proceeded so far on his pilgrimage that only three more works are yet to come, of which one, his most famous romance *Melmoth*, is already emerging into sight. Of Godwin's romances three have appeared, amongst them being *St. Leon*, which later became famous. Byron has lived through the first stormy period of his existence, and presents his jewels of poetry to the world with such rapidity that by 1818 he has already concluded the first canto of his immortal *Don Juan*. Shelley, too, has passed through the tempests of his youth, and having written his *Revolt of Islam*, leaves England, in 1818, never to return. Keats has published his *Poems* and *Endymion* and has been severely handled in the reviews; oppressed by the burden of unfeeling criticism and a wasting sickness, he fares onward towards an early grave.

These "years of promise," as we termed them when looking forward from the year 1794, have thus fulfilled the hopes attached to them with such an overwhelming wealth of poetry and new ideas of noble standard that without them the world's literature would be poorer by one of its most fertile chapters. From the historian's point of view it now becomes our duty to study in what measure this glittering stream of poetry hid waters from the modest, often muddied springs whose wellings we followed in the present chapter.

LATER DEVELOPMENTS OF THE PICTURE OF THE HAUNTED CASTLE

I

BEFORE proceeding to a detailed investigation of the terror-romantic stage-setting as it appears in Lewis's works and in those of the period already dealt with, I would like to draw the reader's attention to a matter of style in terror-romanticism. It will be remembered that in the first chapter of this book I remarked on the refinement that stamps the species of romanticism inaugurated by Walpole, apparent alike in style and subject-matter, which reveals an instinctive aversion to the realistic portrayal of the horrors of life. The latter method, rendered familiar by Shakespeare and the picaresque authors, was too coarse for Walpole's school. Lewis's *The Monk* denotes a change in this respect, for in that as in all his productions, he casts amidst the Radcliffesque, languishing, emotional romanticism that relied for its effects on the artificial creation of suspense, a series of themes calculated in themselves, when presented in all their fearful nakedness, to evoke a sensation of terror. So much feeling for reality and pitilessness is revealed in the present-ment of these themes that the new style introduced by Lewis from the German might well be called " terror-romantic realism."

This new stylistic phase denotes in the first place a dis-integration of the conceptions developed by the Walpole-Radcliffe school, which had been exploited to the full and in many respects brought already to their consummation; in the second place it marked the dawn of a period of emancipa-tion due to this disintegration, without which a new line of development could hardly have been begun. In the following pages I shall attempt to trace the development of the haunted castle through disintegration to new paths. For the sake of caution I must point out that this applies only to the general tide of development, from which there are numerous exceptions, and that the material used to support my elucidation is merely a selection from a huge mass of similar examples, too numerous to be included in their entirety.

2

As will have appeared in the preceding chapter, Lewis was not a direct, puristic follower of Walpole's school within the limits of its special characteristics, but the welder into English form of a coarser, German, primitive type of romance. Thus the picture of the haunted castle, clear already in outline and of established tradition, falls to pieces in his hands ; one can still encounter the typical haunted castle of the Walpole school, but we find a kind of general setting of terror, created partly by an expansion of different features of the haunted castle, partly by the additions and alterations necessitated in this stage by new themes of terror. Disintegration is apparent already in *The Monk*.

In the above-ground portion of its stage-setting—a monastery in Madrid—where the action takes place mostly in the daytime, a comparison with the haunted castle already familiar to us reveals nothing new ; we are compelled, indeed, to admit that the clarity and matter-of-factness of Lewis's realistically-inclined descriptions cause it to lose in romantic atmosphere when compared with the work of his predecessors. In contrast, the Castle of Lindenberg which appears in the book is a faithful rendering of the haunted castle. " The night was calm and beautiful ; the moonbeams fell upon the ancient towers of the castle, and shed upon their summits a silver light. All was still around me ; nothing was to be heard except the night-breeze sighing among the leaves, the distant barking of village dogs, or the owl who had established herself in a nook of the deserted eastern turret. I heard her melancholy shriek, and looked upwards ; she sat upon the ridge of a window, which I recognized to be that of the haunted room." Lindenberg Castle has its own bell that proclaims midnight and the hour of ghosts ; it has creaking, heavy doors and shutters, narrow passages and big, moss-grown gates. Seen in the moonlight it is both " awful " and " picturesque " : " Its ponderous walls, tinged by the moon with solemn brightness ; its old and partly ruined towers, lifting themselves into the clouds, and seeming to frown on the plains around them; its lofty battlements, overgrown with ivy, and folding gates, expanding in honour of the visionary inhabitant; made me sensible of a sad and reverential horror." [163] In his description of Lindenberg Castle, Lewis is clearly influenced by impressions gathered from Mrs. Radcliffe.

This traditional type of haunted castle survives unaltered in *The Castle Spectre*, the setting of which, Conway Castle in Wales, reveals all the characteristic features of the type. It has a haunted tower, a great hall with its own ghost, a chapel and gloomy subterranean dungeons. In this play Lewis brought the haunted castle on to the stage, and similar castles form the setting of most of his plays, such as *Adelmorn* and *Alfonso*. They appear also in his ballads, in *Alonzo the Brave* and in several of the *Tales of Wonder*, now powerfully, now vaguely delineated. In his ballad *The Stranger*, for example, we note the " deep-sounding bell," " the slow monks moving through the cloister's thick gloom," the " deep-vaulted tomb," the " moon-silvered battlements frowning over the glade " ; in *The Wanderer of the Wold* " the crackling old staircase of Ethelbert's tower," " the castle dismantled by time," " the bells that chime from the abbey," " the old castle falling to decay," " his father's old castle with dark ivy spread," " the owl's screeching note," " the ivy spreading wide over a huge heap of stones," etc. In *The House upon the Heath*, a ballad to which we shall have occasion to return, the following effective features are given :

> Fast by the moor a lonely mansion stood ;
> Cheerless it stood ! a melancholy shade
> Its mouldering front, and rifted walls arrayed ;
> Barred were the gates, the shattered casements closed,
> And brooding horror on its site reposed ;
> No tree o'erhung the uncultivated ground,
> No trace of labour, nor of life around.

Without adding to these examples I can thus affirm that though it is no longer the sole setting and the primary factor, the haunted castle of the Walpole school persists in Lewis's production, retaining its chief characteristics even where new features have been superimposed.

As for the other settings created by Lewis, I regard them as being so far related to the picture of the haunted castle that their origin must be sought within its precincts. The haunted castle has two actual sources of terror at command— its supernatural element and its dungeons. Finding himself unable to endow the above-ground portion of his monastery with the necessary romantic half-light, in conformance with the cabbalistic nature of certain of his themes Lewis dived into its subterranean storeys, where all the horrors of funeral vaults and secret dungeons were at his beck. In exploiting these he appears as a ruthless and undeterred exponent of terror-romantic realism, rioting in horrors to an extent hardly to be found elsewhere than in some of Shakespeare's most pungent scenes and, later, in Maturin's work. This side of his literary talent brought from Byron the epithet of "Apollo's sexton." The following is a brief exposition of Lewis's charnel-house material.

The subterranean portion of his monastery possesses vast and dark vaults, illumined only by a ceaselessly-flickering grave-lamp, whose faint, wan rays reveal the mighty pillars which bear up the roof, but are unable to combat the deep gloom in which the vaulted arches are hidden. Growing gradually accustomed to the darkness, the eye sees nothing but the most repulsive objects ; skulls, bones, graves, and effigies of saints that seem to stare in horror and amaze. Still deeper lie the hidden dungeons of the monastery, the entrance to the passage leading to these being cunningly concealed. Fettered in one of these secret cells, cut off from light and human society, their only support the consolation provided by religion, the hapless captives of the monastery linger through the final chapter of their existence. No one hears their voices, no friendly word comes in reply to their speech, only a deep, unbroken silence wraps them round. In their vicinity there may be a human head which worms are devouring and which can be recognized as the head of some lately dead monk or nun.

Terrible is the fate of the fallen nun sentenced to such imprisonment. The air is raw and moist, the walls green with mould and the wretched straw pallet lonely and inhospitable. She is bound to the wall by fetters and horrid reptiles of every kind that swarm around terrify her until her brain can no longer stand the strain. A repulsively-swollen and slimy toad clambers across her breast, a cold and agile lizard darts over her head, entangling itself in her hair, and on awakening she will find, coiled round her fingers like rings, the same long worms which feast on the rotting corpse of her child.[164] When Ambrosio accompanies Matilda to these vaults to perform her cabbalistic rites, the cold vapours which stream out to meet him seem to freeze his heart, and for a space he listens sorrowfully to the howling of the wind in the deserted passages.

As he stands there, on the threshold of new crimes, doubting and in spiritual agony, the monk feels his fears increased by the dreadful voices of the night, the owl's cry and the creaking of a loosened shutter.

In such descriptions of places and objects intended to evoke horror and disgust, it would be difficult to find the equal of this pitiless and tastelessly detailed realism. It was something totally different from the innocent attempts at horrors, the bygone murders and skeletons discovered in fetters, of Lewis's predecessors, something new and strange in English romanticism. Indeed, we can regard this phase of it as German, for what else is this awful prison and charnel-house, where victims disappear without leaving a trace, but the famous *Burgverliess* of the German romances of chivalry and terror, the "Tower of Hunger," *Torre di fame*, described by Dante in his Ugolino-episode and in the dawn of romanticism raised by the agitating realism of H. W. von Gerstenberg in his play *Ugolino* (1769) to the position of the central stage of such fearful happenings. The word *Burgverliess* was an invention of writers of this category and denoted a spot from which there was not the remotest possibility of escape, a place without an exit.[165]

This atmosphere of dungeons and graves expands in Lewis's later work, notably in his ballads, into a general romanticism of the graveyard, into a kind of dance of death in spectral moonlight. Typical of this side of his work is the ballad *Grim, King of the Ghosts; or, the Dance of Death*, styled by its writer "a churchyard tale," which has as motto a line from *Othello*—"On horror's head, horrors accumulate." The dignitary referred to in the title takes the grave-digger's daughter to his "charnel-house palace," where a ball and rout of skeletons takes place; in depicting the subsequent horrors, piled up to the verge of caricature, Lewis displays the power of his realism. Chiefly in his ballads, German and original, Lewis gradually withdraws farther and farther from the confines of the actual haunted castle, taking for his settings the snows of Lapland, the madhouse, the rivers and mountains of Scotland, and romantic enchanted forests, renewing in the last the romantic settings of Percy's and Herder's ballads.

The part played by nature in Lewis's settings is neither as extensive nor as finely-calculated as in Mrs. Radcliffe's works, but though nature as seen by Lewis contributes little to the general development of this side of romanticism, it is yet worth reviewing briefly. His scanty descriptions of landscape are derived from Mrs. Radcliffe, a fact evident in the passage wherein he depicts the site of Ambrosio's death : " The disorder of his imagination was increased by the wildness of the surrounding scenery—by the gloomy caverns and steep rocks, rising above each other, and dividing the passing clouds ; solitary clusters of trees, scattered here and there, among whose thick-twined branches the wind of night sighed hoarsely and mournfully ; the shrill cry of mountain eagles, who had built their nests among these lonely deserts ; the stunning roar of torrents, as swelled by late rains they rushed violently down tremendous precipices, and the dark waters of a silent sluggish stream, which faintly reflected the moonbeams, and bathed the rock's base on which Ambrosio stood. The abbot cast round him a look of terror.[166] This is pure Radcliffe, fortified by a deeper gloom. As the quotation concerning Lindenberg Castle revealed, Lewis makes use of moonlight, the night-wind and the owl ; add to these thunder, lightning and storm, and the inventory of his arsenal of natural effects is complete. The last-named factors are particularly important in his ballads : " The moon shone bright on Lapland's snows, when grim the Winter King arose " ; " The moon grows dark, the night grows foul, thick snows descend, and tempests howl " ; " The dashing surges gently break, the moon illumes the watery plain " ; " Full dark the clustered columns stand, the moon gleams bright between " ; " When the wind 'gan to howl, and the welkin to lour, and the moon, through the woodbine, shone dim," etc. ; his winds are " whispering," " murmuring," " dismal," " loud-roaring " ; in the monastery corridors they howl " dismal and drear," causing a troubled conscience " to start at every gust of the blast" ; " the lone owl pours her death-boding note " ; " No longer the moon on the battlements beamed, and the owl, at her window, ill-ominous screamed " ; " Hark ! a loud peal of thunder shakes the roof, round the altar bright lightnings play " ; " When thunders roll round thee, and blue lightnings flame " ;—

> And each damp dismal eve will he stalk through the gloom,
> To wail, 'midst the storm, his sad plaint at the tomb.

Of the furnishings of the haunted castle, the one that seems to have taken Lewis's fancy most is the clock, which, as we have seen, has its own romantic task. " Scarcely had the abbey-bell tolled for five minutes, and already was the church of the Capuchins thronged with auditors," is the opening sentence of his romance, in which the clock regularly ushers in the hour of ghosts. It appears in nearly every one of his ballads, usually to proclaim the advent of the dark hour of midnight. " For whom tolls the deep-sounding bell, why move the slow monks through the cloisters' thick gloom ? " ; " When at eve tolls the slow passing bell, at the soul-chilling sound sad remembrance shall rise " ; " He sighed at each note of the iron-tongued bell, that told the sad fate of the fair Josephine " ; " His limbs, so athletic, were palsied by fear, as midnight's dark hour was proclaimed by the bell " ;

> O'er ocean, when the midnight bell
> Its sad and sullen murmur flings,
> Will Marion strike, with wildest swell,
> Her shadowy lyre's fantastic strings !

We have noticed, moreover, how Lewis bases the whole plot of one of his plays on the chiming of a clock.

3

Passing by Mrs. Radcliffe's *The Italian*, the setting of which does not differ from what has been already analyzed in connection with her work, let us now proceed to the subsequent fortunes of the haunted castle. This brings up the question of the relationship of Sir Walter Scott, who at the beginning of his career was closely affiliated with Lewis, to the chief stage-setting of the terror-romanticists. His poems provide much illumination in this respect.[167]

Branksome " tower " in *The Lay of the Last Minstrel* (1805) is just such a stage-setting of terror. Its mistress has her secret chamber, protected by fearsome spells, while the castle itself, with its knights, its ancient hanging shields and its general air of medievalism, is the familiar haunted castle. The right leavening of fairy-tale and necromancy is provided by the information that the father of the castle's mistress had gained his hidden knowledge by means that bereft him of his shadow. A heavy, moaning voice is heard around the mossy towers, causing the dogs to howl and the owls to fly whooping from their retreats, while the dwellers in the castle surmise that a storm is approaching. No such result ensues, however, the dismal sound being the noise of a conversation between the spirits of the flood and the mountain regarding the fate of the beautiful Margaret, the oppressed daughter, who is forbidden to marry her beloved because he belongs to a hostile clan.

The arrival of William Deloraine at Melrose monastery church provides the opportunity for truly romantic paintings of moonlight and terror. The cold night-wind agitates the old banners hanging over the altar and fans the tiny flames of the grave-lamps, the moonlight lends a mystic aspect to the vaults and casts on the pavement a bloody stain. The old monk tells how he buried the famous necromancer Michael Scott in that very church at one o'clock in the morning, when strange noises were heard and the banners fluttered without a breath of wind to stir them ; a lamp burns now on the grave until the Day of Judgment shall see it finally extinguished. When William Deloraine takes his " Book of Might " from the sorcerer's hand and leaves the church, he hears behind him strange voices, laughter and a sound of sobbing. Half fairy-tale, half an approach to a truly medieval conception of life, the poem proceeds with its record of knightly pride and bravery, magic and marvels, love and female beauty. Here too we find the castle clock ushering in the hour of midnight and proclaiming thereby the advent of night's most mystical moment.

A similar setting reappears in *Marmion* (1808), the first canto of which paints a clear picture of Norham Castle, of its battled towers, its deep moat, the loophole grate where the captives weep, the flanking walls and the warriors silhouetted on the summits of its towers against the sunset sky, their armour flashing back " the western blaze, " the gates barred, and under their gloomy arches the warder, humming some old Border gathering song and with the blast of his bugle-horn announcing the arrival of Lord Marmion. A change of scene brings us to a convent recalling all the horrors of Ambrosio's abode. It has the same vaults for prisoners, darker and more solitary than any real vaults. The horror awakened by this dungeon, which was called the " Vault of Penitence ", froze the senses ; it was used as a place of punishment and torture. Few were aware of its situation, the victims and judges being taken there blindfolded ; its vaulted ceiling hung threateningly low, the floor consisted of grave-stones, and a single torch illumined it. On a seat of stone, attired in long black gowns, the inexorable judges sat to pronounce irrevocable sentence on the woman who has broken her vow. The severity of her sentence is reflected in the screams which echo through the winding passages after the departing judges.

Especially in *Marmion* do we find in each of the castles depicted the familiar features dealt with at length in the foregoing pages. Tantallon Castle, for instance, is broad, stout and high ; its towers soar defiantly from a mountain jutting into the sea ; it is defended on its landward side by deep moats, a narrow drawbridge and staunch outworks. Around it the storms rage, casting the foam on high, and on the top of its old tower, whither a winding passage leads

> Sometimes in dizzy steps descending,
> Sometimes in narrow circuit bending,
> Sometimes in platform broad extending—

the oppressed maiden can fittingly repair :

> And muse upon her sorrows there,
> And list the sea-bird's cry. . . .

Or we see it in the moonlight, which bathes the towers and walls in its silvery sheen. It must be admitted that in this poem, as will be discussed in another connection, on the one hand Scott reveals a typical leaning towards the stage-setting of contemporary ghost-romance, on the other he raises it with his more exact historical knowledge a step nearer to reality.

This old ghostly setting recurs again and again in certain of his romances, showing an advance in the direction of greater historical verity. It is everywhere based on direct historical research, on that " knowledge of ruins " which his indefatigable antiquarian studies had provided him with, but in weaving this material into his romances he could not, for such was the spirit of his age, refrain from embellishing it with traits and colours from the traditional haunted castle.

To take an example, Scott had at his disposal, while writing *Woodstock* (1826), reliable information regarding the real Woodstock during the period of his romance, yet the impression he finally gives us recalls the " haunted labyrinths " of his forerunners. " What sort of a house is Woodstock ? " asks Cromwell, receiving from the madcap Wildrake the pertinent answer : " An old mansion, and, so far as I could judge by a single night's lodgings, having abundance of backstairs, also subterranean passages, and all the communications under ground, which are common in old raven-nests of the sort." When Cromwell searches for Charles Stewart in its mazes, he discovers that the builder had truly done his best to create the most bewildering tangle of rooms and corridors possible. Staircases seem to lead upward only for the purpose of preparing a sudden downward flight ; the corridors lead the stranger by intricate ways back to his starting-point ; and everywhere the way is blocked by stout doors and iron bars, the purpose of which it is impossible to surmise. In addition to its dwelling-rooms the castle contains a royal suite that has long been closed and unaired. There we find stained-glass windows through which mysterious patterns of colour are filtered, and a room with the inevitable ancestral portrait on its wall; yet time has rendered it so pale and indistinct that it seems to depict a being from another world, though its features still reflect pride and triumph. The portrait is further notable for the reason that behind it begins a secret passage. At the summit of the adjacent Rosamunda's Tower—to which attaches a mysterious legend of the fateful love-story of a king and a beautiful maiden—a strange light is seen at night that cannot be accounted for. Its bluish tint shows that it is no ordinary light. That various evil spirits have infested the building is known of old. Sometimes the sound of a pack of hounds in full cry, accompanied by blasts of a hunts-man's horn, is heard from the park, with all the outcry of a real hunt, though nothing can be seen; sometimes also " The White Woman of Woodstock " may appear. The effect on the visitor, when confronted in the twilight by the castle, rising with its pointed towers and mighty walls from its park, is solemn and awesome. The impression is deepened by the dismal chiming of the old castle clock, itself a familiar feature.

When, on such a stage, we are treated to a series of apparently supernatural events, with doors that close of their own accord and other marvels, our conclusion may well be that the fare set before us is haunted-castle romanticism of the Radcliffe type, only raised to a higher level by the inclusion of historical material.

An illuminating example of Scott's success in raising the haunted castle to regions of greater historical trustworthiness and clarity is seen in *Ivanhoe* (1820), which provides, in my opinion, fitting testimony of the extent to which a later age sifted and refined the materials of terror-romanticism. Let us trace its connection with the test-setting.

I have already had occasion to remark on the relationship of the scene and characters of Lewis's play *The Castle Spectre* with Otranto Castle and Manfred and Isabella. Lewis's setting, Conway Castle in Wales, the feudal home of Osmond, is a perfect example of the haunted castle in the meaning with which we have invested the term. Osmond himself is a feudal tyrant of Manfred's type, who intends, despite their relationship, to marry Angela, the daughter of his brother Reginald, recognizing only his own passion as his law : " What though she prefer a basilisk's kiss to me ? Because my short-lived joy may cause her eternal sorrow, shall I reject those pleasures sought so long, desired so earnestly ? That will I not, by Heaven ! Mine she is, and mine she shall be, though Reginald's bleeding ghost flit before me and thunder in my ear. Hold ! Hold !—Peace, stormy heart, she comes." Osmond believes he has killed Reginald, though actually the latter has been buried alive in the deepest vault of the castle. In the fifth act, when Percy, Angela's lover, storms the castle, Reginald is discovered " emaciated, in coarse garments, his hair hanging wildly about his face, and a chain bound round his body." The ghost of his murdered wife Evelina is one of the characters in the play, appearing at the critical moment to save her daughter and administering several shocks to Osmond. She comes on the stage attired in blood-stained white garments. Conway Castle had, moreover, an evil reputation for being haunted ; Earl Hubert rides round the castle each night on a white steed ; Lady Bertha's ghost walks in the western tower ; Lord Hildebrand plays with his own head in the great hall every night ; and the ghost of the dead countess appears as regularly in the castle chapel, where she croons her baby to sleep. To come to my point, the other characters of the play include a fat, merry and talkative epicurean monk whose full-flavoured, quasi-theological speech reminds one of Friar Tuck of Robin Hood fame, and the fool Motley, whose conversation has a familiar ring ; consequently, when we find Scott defending the Saracens in *Ivanhoe* by a reference to the negroes in *The Castle Spectre*, it is borne in upon us that what we are confronted with in the chief setting of *Ivanhoe*, the far-famed robbers' castle of Torquilstone,[168] is neither more nor less than a glorified version of the haunted castle, traceable in the first instance, to the form given in *The Castle Spectre*.

It is " hoary and ancient " and its mossy towers and other defences denote a serious plight for the captive Cedric. We are shown its square towers, walls, outworks, moat and draw-bridge, all as in any medieval castle. Isaac of York is taken to a dungeon situated deeper than the moat and therefore exceedingly damp. The light percolates through two peep-holes placed high up. Rusty fetters with mouldy bones clinging to their links hang on the walls, suggesting that some former captive had been allowed to die and rot in his chains. At one end of the room is a large gridiron for torturing prisoners ; its use is revealed by Front-de-Boeuf's plan to extort money from Isaac by its aid. The castle boasts, likewise, a dreadful hidden crime whose perpetrator, old Urfried, still wanders among the living like a phantom from the past. The clash of romantic strife echoes around the castle, and within its walls two beautiful maidens, Rowena and Rebecca, are threatened by a cruel fate. The stern master of Torquilstone, the knight Front-de-Boeuf, is clearly the counterpart of Osmond of Conway Castle, a direct descendant, in the crudest form, of Manfred; he has murdered his father as Osmond believes himself to have murdered his brother. Old Urfried appears beside his deathbed like a ghost—to Osmond it is the ghost of Evelina who appears. Lewis's monk and fool are found as such in *Ivanhoe*: the negroes become Saracens and are given as master a Good Templar knight of the line of Ambrosio; Ivanhoe's friends besiege Torquilstone with the intention of befreeing Cedric, Rowena and Athelstan just as Percy besieges Conway Castle to set Angela free. The general atmosphere, characters and events connected with Conway Castle thus bear a striking resemblance to those concerned with Torquilstone. Add to this Isaac of York and Rebecca, belated offspring of Shylock and Jessica; the conflict between Saxon and Norman, a glimpse of which is caught, for instance, in Southey's *Madoc*; the chivalry as of Percy's ballads, embodied in this case in Sir Cauline, who returns unrecognized from his banishment, overcomes his opponent in a tournament inaugurated by the King, sets free his beloved and dies on her behalf; and then in the light of the lines

> His acton it was all of blacke,
> His hewberke, and his sheelde,
> Ne noe man wist whence he did come,
> Ne noe man knewe where he did gone—

recall to memory the Disinherited Knight and the Black Knight; added together, all these and the numberless other features that can be traced back to earlier romanticism, be it to folk-poetry or artistic literature, form a graphic illustration of how Sir Walter Scott, aided by an unusual energy and a retentive memory, had absorbed everything that was able to awaken romantic response in his soul, and in the furnace of his powerful imagination exalted and refined this material, imparting to it a new value.

Our pursuit of the picture of the haunted castle from *The Castle of Otranto* and still earlier periods has thus, stage by stage, brought us to the historical novel. Its mysterious " Gothic " twilight has, at least as a leading feature, disappeared in Torquilstone ; its walls, towers, moats and draw-bridges, rooms and the dwellers therein, appear clearer and clothed in greater verity than hitherto ; the attacks of besieging forces, the encounters between knights in armour and other similar events are no longer wholly theatrical in nature, but in great degree actual illustrations of the life of bygone days. Muddled, indeterminate, styleless Strawberry Hill has yielded to the correcter Abbotsford.

In no case, however, may the line we have followed in this pursuit be regarded as the only one to be considered in study-ing the origins of the historical novel ; the species of literature in question has also another source, the elucidation of which lies outside our present purpose. What is of importance for us to know is that it was the haunted castle that brought to the historical novel those features which entitle it to the name " romance," namely, the colouring, the atmosphere conveyed by the phrase " frost of time," an element that has often been termed an essential factor in the success of the historical novel and is regarded by some as its finest and only poetical feature.[169]

4

An attempt has been made in the preceding section to depict the development of the haunted castle as a clearly-defined romantic stage-setting of ever-increasing historical verity. A more difficult task is the elucidation of the simultane-ous disintegration of the picture into the setting for different varieties of romantic works. Seeking to follow the track of the original picture as far as possible, let us begin with S. T. Coleridge's *Christabel* (1816), the setting of which is a medieval castle with the typical " Gothic " appendages.[170]

The opening lines describe the castle clock announcing the hour of midnight, when the owls awaken by their cries the crowing cock. A mastiff bitch howls in echo to the chimes— " some say she sees my lady's shroud." The picture of the haunted castle is in the mind of this author when we least expect it ; for instance, in the final setting of *The Ancient Mariner*, after the dreadful nightmare visions have passed, we find the traditional hermitage with its inhabitant, who is a characteristic property of the " Gothic " school. Coleridge's plays *Remorse* (1813) and *Zapolja* (1817) are typical " Gothic " tragedies, based on echoes of Shakespeare and tragedies in Lewis's style. The theme of both is usurpation. Their settings—the seashore; a wild and mountainous district; a farmhouse interior; the armoury of a castle with an altar in the background; a castle chapel; a dark cave with a crack in the roof emitting a ray of moonlight; the courtyard of a " Saracenic or Gothic " castle and the iron door of a prison; moonlit mountains; prison vaults; the courtyard of the royal castle of Illyria with guards; a mountainous landscape and an outlaw's hut; a gloomy forest and a cave shadowed by ivy; a hall and bedchamber in a castle; a forest glade; an open space before a cave—are all traditional elements of the haunted castle, to which Coleridge has only added his fine perception of nature. His romanticism will not, however, suffer itself to be tied to the unyielding contours of any imaginary castle, but turns, as in Southey's and Wordsworth's case, to the poetry of the surrounding landscape, as we shall later discuss at greater length. A poet more faithful to tradition in this respect is Byron.[171]

In spite of his mocking attitude, Byron was connected with the terror-romanticists both by personal ties and inclination as well as by his choice of literary material. He knew the works of the school and the effect aimed at did not leave him unmoved. Although he affected an ironical, even a contemptuous attitude, terror-romanticism with all its well-known phrases flowed at frequent intervals from his own pen, showing that in spite of his mockings he was himself influenced by the literary images of his day. A brief glance at his production is sufficient to prove the truth of this assertion.

Among the poems of his youth, collected as *Hours of Idleness* (1807), we meet in the opening lines with a " King of Terrors " who has " seized as his prey " some beloved person. Newstead Abbey is shown in a purely haunted-castle illumination: hollow winds whistle through its battlements, and in its once smiling garden, where once the roses bloomed, the thistle now grows; around its ruins glide pensive shades of warriors, monks and dames; its vaulted hall seems to frown proudly majestic, scowling defiance on the blasts of fate. In its gloomy cells and profound shades the monk once abjured the world; there the soul repenting of blood-stained guilt found consolation and oppressed innocence a shelter. Since its decay desolation holds her dreary court and " sable horror guards the massy door." A yawning arch shows signs of increasing decay, which the youthful owner is powerless to prevent.

Line for line and word for word, these poems dedicated to his family estate are like the echo of a mournful ballad of chivalry. *Lara,* in particular, provides a powerful example of terror-romanticism as seen by Byron. The setting is a Gothic castle, on the walls of which the owner's portrait " darkens in its fading frame " while awaiting his return. When at last he returns, he is heard to wander restlessly to and fro in a room where the portraits of his ancestors look down threateningly from the walls and where he too stares at the skull placed beside his book. The moon shines through the dim windows of the old castle hall, lighting up the stone floor, the lofty ceiling and the kneeling saints above the Gothic windows, seeming to transform them into weird beings of another world. In this light, Lara's dark curls, his sombre countenance and the broad shadow cast over it by the nodding plumes of his helmet, appear to belong to a ghost and suggest all the terrors of the grave. At midnight, when all are asleep and the flame of a solitary light trembles as though fearing to pierce the night, a cry is heard from Lara's hall like to a shout—" a sound, a voice, a shriek, a fearful call ! "—followed by deep silence ; Lara has seen a vision which has bereft him for the time of his powers. This fateful hall is shunned henceforward by all and sundry, the place where

> The waving banner, and the clapping door,
> The rustling tapestry, and the echoing floor ;
> The long dim shadows of surrounding trees,
> The flapping bat, the night song of the breeze ;
> Aught they behold or hear their thought appals,
> As evening saddens o'er the dark grey walls.

In these poems and especially in the *Prisoner of Chillon* and *Mazeppa,* Byron puts to use the realistic depictment of suffering learned by him from Lewis, thus attaching himself, in this respect, to the terror-romanticists.[172]

In planning his romantic settings Byron adheres in general to the ground-plan of the haunted castle ; though in his Oriental legends he is compelled to deck it with Oriental properties, for the most part easily recognizable as products of the scene-painter's art. His seraglios of Turkish pashas and half-lit corridors of harems, his prisons, minarets and crescent moons, lonely castles on the rocky coasts of stormy seas, his luxuriant palace of Sardanapalus with its statue of Bacchus, (reminiscent of Otranto) in the forecourt, Werner's castle in Silesia and Prague, Manfred's gloomy Alpine castle with its alchemist's laboratory—these are but facets and enlargements of the essential invention of the terror-romanticists.

In Byron's romanticism the atmospherical and other nature-effects related to the terror-romanticist stage are well represented. While they thus connect Byron with his predecessors they are often expanded into almost the predominant elements of his poem, by the use of which he aspires to create sublime and wildly romantic effects. In the spirit of Ossian, Byron admires high mountains, dark chasms, stormy waves, solitude amidst magnificent scenery, whose wildness fills his soul with an austere delight :

> England ! thy beauties are tame and domestic
> To one who has roved on the mountains afar :
> Oh for the crags that are wild and majestic !
> The steep frowning glories of dark Loch na Garr.

He desires to sit on a rock in the desert, to gaze on a river or a foaming cataract, lost in thought, at his leisure to examine shady forests where human feet have seldom trod and to climb trackless mountains. There one is not alone, for the graces of nature are friends ; loneliness is to wander wearily through the crowded world, with none to bless or to be blessed by. Nature is his loving mother, who has never weaned him from her breast, even if she has not showered her favours upon him ; she is most beautiful when she turns to him her wildest aspect and rages in turmoil. Where mountains are, there are his friends ; where the ocean storms is his home. The desert, forests, caves, foaming breakers are his comrades, speaking a language clearer than his mother-tongue. Ann Radcliffe's nature-romanticism, deriving from Ossian, among other sources, was feminine and sentimental ; Byron's emotional side grasped the manly, defiant qualities of nature ; nevertheless, at bottom, both hail from the same source ; Byron's debt to Mrs. Radcliffe is not to be despised. Finally I would point out that Byron, as the ultimate conclusion of his sublime sense of nature, paints cosmic visions of eternity, rising wholly above terrestrial nature to Milton-like dimensions of space and time.

Amidst this setting of sublime, tempestuous nature, of savage mountains, ocean waves, dim corridors of harems, glittering lagoons of Venice with their enchantments of barcaroles, love and moonlight, at the foot of marble pillars and sorrowing cypresses, appears the character known as the Byronic hero, who absorbs into one individuality all the romantic conceptions of a tragic hero which the preceding decades had slowly, feature by feature, developed.

5

That we should have encountered Byron within the precincts of the haunted castle and amid the sublime scenery around it was in no way astonishing, for we might have expected to find him there; more surprising is it that Shelley, who, in his chief works, dwells in a world of spirit, should at any time have been wholly under the spell of the most typical terror-romantic material, a fact to which attention was drawn in connection with the life of Lewis.[173]   In the poems of his youth phrases such as " twilight grove," " the pale moonbeam that sheds a flood of silver sheen on tower and stream " (*To the Queen of my Heart*, 1810) ; " Cold, cold is the blast when December is howling, cold are the damps on a dying man's brow " ; " the ravens that croak from afar " ; " rocks where the thunder peals rattle " ; " her grave over which waved the desolate form of a storm-blasted yew and around which no demons or ghosts dare to rave " (*Victor and Cazire*, III. Song, 1810) ; " the shrill whistling wind which wanders mournfully over the hill " ; " the thunder's wild voice " ; " the drear tomb of my ancestors' bones where I must dig their remains from beneath the cold stones, for the spirit of Conrad there meets me this night " ; " the echoing sound that fearfully rolled 'midst the tombstones around, the blue lightning gleaming over the dark chapel spire, and the storm clouds tinged with sulphurous fire " ; " a strange silver brilliance—a tall figure as light as a gossamer borne on the storm—celestial terror sat throned in his gaze, like the midnight pestiferous meteor's blaze " (*Revenge*, 1809) ; " the owlet flaps her wing " ; " night ravens loudly sing tidings of despair and death " ; " horror covers all the sky " ; " the tolling village bell tolls the hour of midnight when the powers of hell can blast and fiend-like goblins roam"; a phantom woman, who obeys the commands of a strange being with a fiery cross on its brow, claiming a knight as her own (*Ghasta*, 1810).   These examples, all of them characteristic of his youthful poems, suffice to show that Shelley began his experiments in poetry wholly under the influence of terror-romanticism; his models were no other than Lewis's *The Monk* and ballads of that writer, and, especially as regards the depictment of the haunted castle, Mrs. Radcliffe.

The prose romances of Shelley's youth, *Zastrozzi, a Romance* (1810), and *St. Irvyne or the Rosicrucian, a Romance*

(1811), are typical of the unripeness and naïvity that stamp his first excursions into literature. They reveal no flash of what was to become the chief characteristic of his personality as a poet. Although written in a deeply serious vein and under the influence of solemn feeling, they are such that the present-day reader would find it difficult to write better and more apt parodies of the terror-romantic works of those days. The theory has been broached that they are possibly translations from some German original,[174] but this is not so : Lewis and Mrs. Radcliffe are so clearly reflected in all their chief features that we are compelled to regard them as the imitative products of an unripe youth, the work of a schoolboy whose imagination has been fired by reading romantic scenes of terror ; their appearance in print is probably due to the strangeness of their contents and the accident of their reaching an enterprising publisher. In reading them, one must bear in mind that the author was only seventeen.

Zastrozzi takes Verezzi, the victim of his vengeance, to a " cavern, which yawned in a dell close by," " into a damp cell, chaining him to the wall." There a period of suffering in the style of Lewis's terror-romantic realism, begins for Verezzi : "He scarcely now shuddered when the slimy lizard crossed his naked and motionless limbs. The large earth-worms, which turned themselves in his long and matted hair, almost ceased to excite sensations of horror . . . His bones had almost started through his skin ; his eyes were sunken and hollow ; and his hair, matted with damp, hung in strings upon his faded cheek." The haunted castle and the names of most characters are copied from *The Monk* and from *Udolpho* : " They entered the Venetian territory, where, in a gloomy and remote spot, stood the Castella di Laurentini. . . . It was situated in a dark forest . . . lofty mountains around lifted their aspiring and craggy summits to the skies. The mountains were clothed half up by ancient pines and plane trees, whose immense branches stretched far. . . . Castella Laurentini, whose grey turrets and time-worn battlements over-topped the giants of the forest. . . ." Another description of a Gothic castle runs as follows : " He beheld a large and magnificent building, whose battlements rose above the lofty trees. It was built in the Gothic style of architecture and appeared to be inhabited. The building reared its pointed casements loftily to the sky, their treillaged ornaments were silvered by the clear moonlight, to which the dark shades of the arches beneath formed a striking contrast." The captive in this castle is placed " in the lowest cavern of those dungeons which are under this building." Even the romantic cottage appears : " The cottage stood on an immense heath, lonely, desolate, and remote from other human habitation." And the surroundings of the castle are no less familiar : " The tops of the lofty forest trees waved mournfully in the evening wind ; and the moonbeam, penetrating at intervals, as they moved, through the matted branches, threw dubious shades upon the dark underwood beneath " ; " the grass which grew on the lofty battlements waved mournfully in the rising blast " ; " the terrific grandeur of the Alps, the dashing cataract, as it foamed beneath their feet. The lofty pine-groves " ; " the evening was calm and serene : gently agitated by the evening zephyr, the lofty pines sighed mournfully. Far to the west appeared the evening star, which faintly glittered in the twilight. The scene was solemnly calm, but not in unison with Matilda's soul. Softest, most melancholy music, seemed to float upon the southern gale . . . it was the nuns at a convent chanting the requiem for the soul of a departed sister." The music is fully in accordance with Mrs. Radcliffe's ideals : " Soon sounds of such ravishing melody stole upon the evening breeze, that Verezzi thought some spirit of the solitude had made audible to mortal ears ethereal music " ; the instrument most in favour is the harp. The romanticism of the plot leaves nothing to be desired : Verezzi is in love with Julia di Strobazzo, whom Matilda di Laurentini, aided by Zastrozzi, succeeds in ousting from his affections ; Zastrozzi hates Verezzi because the latter's father had betrayed his mother. These and other names of characters, such as Ugo, Bernard and Bianca, together with the descriptions of the haunted castle quoted above, reveal clearly enough, in com- bination with certain other traits to which we shall return later, that the book was written under the influence of *Udolpho* and *The Monk*.

The same stage recurs in *St. Irvyne*, displaying still clearer tokens of Mrs. Radcliffe's influence. Thus, we note the typical atmosphere of ruins : " In melancholy fallen grandeur its vast ruins reared their pointed casements to the sky. Masses of disjointed stones were scattered around, and, save by the whirrings of the bats, the stillness was un- interrupted." Nature-romanticism is presented in its strongest form : red thunderclouds, midnight whirlwind, crimson- coloured orbit of the moon, rising fierceness of the blast, blackened expanse of heaven, bluish flashes of lightning which disclose the terrific scenery of the Alps, gigantic and misshapen summits, rain, the deafening crash of thunder peals and the sulphuric smell of thunderbolts, the elements battling in wild confusion—these represent the contents of the first few pages, but—" fiercer than nature's wildest uproar were the feelings of Wolfstein's bosom." The romanticism of *The Arabian Nights* is revived : at the touch of a robber chieftain a door of rock opens in the mountain-side, revealing bluish mould, dampness, impenetrable darkness, and ultimately a broad and high cave, the subterranean gloom of which is alleviated by lighted lamps. Hither the romantic maiden Megalena di Metastasio is dragged : " The sole light in her cell was that of a dismal lamp, which by its uncertain flickering only dissipated the almost palpable obscurity, in a sufficient degree more assuredly to point out the circumambient horrors "—quite as in the prison grave in the Madrid monastery where Agnes was immured. Solitude affects Megalena as it did Mrs. Radcliffe's maidens : " The melancholy wind sighing along the crevices of the cavern, and the dismal sound of rain which pattered fast, inspired mournful reflection " ; seizing a pen she writes on the wall of the cave a poem beginning :

> Ghosts of the dead ! have I not heard your yelling
> Rise on the night-rolling breath of the blast—

and continuing with storm, whirlwinds, crashes of thunder, the gloomy heights of the Jura which threaten the valley below, with bitter night-winds and the murmur of death, unaware that her opening lines were memories of Byron, who had written :

> Shades of the dead ! have I not heard your voices
> Rise on the night-rolling breath of the gale.[175]

This habit of lapsing into rhyme in moments of loneliness is found also in Wolfstein, the young hero of the book, who, lost in thought, wanders amid stern and sublime Alpine scenery, with only the " wild hoot of the night-raven and yelling of the vulture " echoing in his ears. At such moments he sinks on some mossy bank, and under the spell of the impressions awakened by his surroundings, writes lines dealing with the deathly silence of night, a glimmering lamp, night-raven's yelling, the howling of storms, thunder and lightning, a chilling murmuring, a heart hard as iron, a low conscience and the ghost of the murdered Victoria.

These dark tones, characteristic of Mrs. Radcliffe's moods

of loneliness, prevail throughout *St. Irvyne* : " Dark, autumnal, and gloomy was the hour ; the winds whistled hollow, and over the expanse of heaven was spread an unvarying sombreness of vapour : nothing was heard save the melancholy shriekings of the night-bird, which, soaring on the evening blast, broke the stillness of the scene. . . ." " The moon had just risen ; its full orb was occasionally shaded by a passing cloud : it rose from behind the turrets of le Château de St. Irvyne. . . ." " Ivy mantled the western tower " :

> Yon dark gray turret glimmers white,
> Upon it sits the mournful owl ;
> Along the silence of the night
> Her melancholy shriekings roll.

The combined effect of all the above shows, beyond any doubt, that in the romantic works of his youth Shelley was under the influence of Mrs. Radcliffe as regards the haunted castle, and under that of Lewis as to the construction of his plot, his characters and other materials. He did nothing to develop the haunted-castle setting, but used it as it had come down to him, heightening its colouring perhaps, in his youthful ardour. In the feeling for nature displayed in his subsequent life-work he casts off the fetters of tradition and becomes the great singer of the sea, the west wind and the crystalline ether, endowing these with colours from the spectrum of a faerie world. It is not impossible, however, that terror-romanticism gave the first impulse to that freedom from all concreteness in the presentment of nature that later characterizes his imagination.

6

Charles Robert Maturin [176] began his production under the spell of Mrs. Radcliffe's stage-setting. In his first work, *The Fatal Revenge, or the Family of Montorio* (1807), a setting appears in the castle of Muralto, which is typically Radcliffesque —the name further revealing that Maturin had read the preface to the first edition of *The Castle of Otranto* (p. 6). This castle and the other settings of terror-scenes are based on Mrs. Radcliffe, helped out by impressions derived from Lewis ; the primary model was probably *The Sicilian Romance*, to which has been added the monk Schedoni from *The Italian*, a type to whom we shall have occasion to return. The setting is a Gothic castle, the uninhabited portion of which, with its mysterious night-prowlers and flashing lights, its hidden doors, secret passages and subterranean vaults, find its counterpart in *The Sicilian Romance ;* the descriptions given in my first chapter of Mrs. Radcliffe's castle can be applied to the Castle of Muralto. Connal O'Morven's ruined tower in *The Milesian Chief* (1812), in which he lives with his old, insane father, is a milder version of the haunted stage, a version that re-appears in an effective and romantic dressing in Scott's *The Bride of Lammermoor* (1819). In the play *Bertram, or the Castle of St. Aldobrand* (1816), the romantic setting greatly resembles that of Lewis's *Adelgitha* as regards its castles, monasteries and caves ; Imogine's plight, and the part as a whole, is also reminiscent of Adelgitha.[177] In *Manuel* (1817) the settings are similarly derived from romantic melodrama, especially the final cave-scene with its daggers and murders [178] ; the Alpine castle in *Fredolfo* (1819) belongs to the same category. In his great romance, *Melmoth the Wanderer* (1820), Maturin depicts settings of terror with stark realism and great suggestive power, achieving here a high standard of effectivity. The lonely, decaying farm in the beginning of the book evokes a haunting atmosphere of desolation, an inexplicable feeling of awaiting strange disaster ; a manuscript telling of fearful matters and a demoniac portrait connect it with the traditional picture of the haunted castle. The monastery in Madrid which forms the scene of *The Spaniard's Tale* is directly descended from the corresponding setting in *The Monk*, the sole difference being that Lewis's horrors, his crypts and smell of rotting corpses, pale beside Maturin's gruesome realism and suggestive power. Not content with being a matchless colourist in the realm of terror, Maturin strove by means of his philosophical problem-themes to awaken feelings of moral horror, a striving that gains the upper hand in his chief romances. From the point of view of the setting, his great significance lies in the fact that he was better able than any of his predecessors to invest it with suggestive power.

Maturin tried to pose as a thinker engaged in investigating the secret forces that uphold human life. In this respect he reminds one of an older contemporary, William Godwin, whose romances *Caleb Williams* and *St. Leon* [179] are usually classed as terror-romanticism. If examined in the light of the haunted castle they will be found, however, to fall for the most part outside the sphere of the present study, though certain terror-romantic traits in *St. Leon* establish a connecting link between it and our theme. *Caleb Williams* is not, as a matter of fact, a terror-romantic work, but both in contents and purpose, a novel of social tendencies, its spirit of revolt against existing institutions, laws and justice giving it a distinctly modern flavour. This spirit of social philosophy,[180] the question of the wrongs to which the poor and weak are subjected under the pretext of justice, is a subordinate feature also of *St. Leon* and plays an effective part in *Frankenstein*, the work of Godwin's daughter, Mary Shelley ; descriptive of the status of social philosophy in English romanticism is the fact that *Caleb Williams* obviously contains the fundamental motive of Victor Hugo's great romantic social novel *Les Misérables*.[181] *Frankenstein* enriched the stage-setting of terror-romanticism by making its mysterious centre, hitherto the haunted room, the laboratory of a cabbalistic seeker after knowledge—Manfred—a laboratory in which the deepest of all secrets, the skill to awaken life in inorganic matter, is ultimately discovered.

7

Robert Southey tells us [182] that in his youth he began to understand poetry after reading Spenser and other poets, the impressions thus derived being strengthened by acquaintance with Percy's *Reliques*, Gray, Mason, Akenside, Cowper, Bowles and Collins, in other words, with the whole early Romantic school of the Miltonic group to which reference was made in the first chapter of this book. These sources and the romanticism that flourished everywhere around him doubtlessly inspired the idyllic feeling for nature which runs through his production, with results resembling the idylls used by Mrs. Radcliffe as contrast to her scenes of sublime grandeur.

It might be averred that the idyllic brook-scene with which we are about to deal is not a feature of the haunted-castle setting but a direct continuation, unaffected by terror-romanticism, of the landscape school of poetry. This is not, however, the case ; as already pointed out when speaking of Mrs. Radcliffe's works, an essential feature of the landscape surrounding the haunted castle is an idyllic scene, intended to form a contrast to the austere and sublime, to act as a soothing element between the storms of passion. Without it the picture would lack the balance upon which the romanticist sets special value. In addition, it is reasonable to assume that if the idyllic landscape had attempted to exist solely on its past, it would inevitably have become worn and ineffectual ;

whereas by its revival as a contrast to the sublimity and beauty in wildness discovered by the romanticists, it was given the vitality needed for it to develop into the " naturalism " usually attributed to the Lake Poets, though the term, in its strictest sense, can be applied only to Wordsworth's production.

A feeling for nature is liberally represented in Southey's early poem *Joan of Arc* (1795), in which names like Theodore and Conrad suggest affinities with Walpole's romanticism. Estranged from mankind, Joan feels a frequent desire for silence and solitude. She breathes the mingled odours of Spring wafted on the evening breeze and listens to the wild wood melody. Night falls and great rain-drops fall heavily, while the gale sweeps over the wood. We are continually coming across phrases such as " purple softness," " winding stream," " twilight dimly shrouds all beside," " dews of night descend," etc. A little brook that meanders through an idyllic landscape is a common sight : " The rivulet whose murmuring was silence to my soul " ; " She watched the tranquil stream flow with a quiet murmuring by the clouds of evening purpled. . . ." " The perpetual flow, the ceaseless murmuring, lulled her to such dreams as memory in her melancholy mood loves best " ; " she saw the forest brook, the weed that waved its long green tresses in the stream, the crag which overbrowed the spring, and that old yew. . . ." " There, by streamlet on the mossy bank reclined, she saw a damsel, her long locks with willow wreathed, upon her lap there lay a dark-haired man, listening the while she sung sad ditties." This view of nature, the brook-idyll, is retained by Southey irrespective of the continent in which his setting may be placed. In *Thalaba the Destroyer* (1801) we note " a vernal brook in the breathings of the stirring gale " ; " Heavy and dark the eve, the moon was hid on high, all living souls had ceased, only the flow of waters near was heard, a low and lulling melody " ; fleeing from the sensual pleasures of Aloadin's garden, Thalaba ran " to the solitude, where the rills rolled their collected waves " ; " A fount of fire that in the centre played, rolled all around its wondrous rivulets and fed the garden with the heat of life." In *Madoc* (1805) we are taken " up mountain paths, beside grey mountain stream, and lonely lake, and through old Snowdon's forest-solitude." In the ballad *St. Gualberto* no sound disturbs the deep silence, " save when a falling leaf came fluttering by, save the near brooklet's stream that murmured quietly." In *The Curse of Kehama* (1810) " every herb and flower was fresh and fragrant with the early dew; sweet sung the birds in that delicious hour, and the cool gale of the morning ruffled the surface of the silvery stream"; we note also "a brook, with easy current, that murmurs near." In *Roderick, the Last of Goths* (1814) "a rocky hill, rising with deep ascent, overhung the glittering beach"; as in Spenser on its top we find "a little lowly hermitage and a rude cross, and at its foot a grave"; "There he stopt beside a little rill," is said of a wanderer, to whom "sweetest of all sweet sounds" was the constant fall of water and its "perpetual gurgling." This idyllic landscape, the essence of which is a forest brook, a mountain stream or a river, is the focus of Southey's conception of nature; it denotes a return to a truer, deeper interpretation of nature than Mrs. Radcliffe was capable of giving, but it is nevertheless a development of the idyllic features of the haunted-castle landscape.[183]

As for the actual haunted castle and its atmosphere, Southey's production reveals to us that notwithstanding his independence, he, too, has set out from this central conception of the terror-romanticists. In the epilogue to *Joan of Arc— The Vision*—we find the following familiar picture : "There a mouldering pile stretched its wide ruins, over the plain below casting a gloomy shade, save where the moon shone through its fretted windows, the dark yew withering with age, and the melancholy cypress"; "through the roof the moonbeams entered, the ivy twined the dismantled columns . . . overhead roared the loud blast, and from the tower the owl screamed." The same poem provides a dismal picture of the abodes of Death, "the skull, the eyeless sockets, and the unfleshed jaws," a burial vault, tainted cold air heavy with unwholesome dews, and the decaying remains of flesh from rotting corpses, which display the holes made by worms. The vision expands subsequently to the mighty image of a kingdom of death, a wide cave, hewn amid the entrails of the earth. In his youth (1791) Southey had written an ode *To Horror :*

> Dark Horror, hear my call !
> Stern genius, hear from thy retreat
> On some old sepulchre's moss-canker'd seat,
> Beneath the Abbey's ivied wall
> That trembles o'er its shade.
> Where wrapt in midnight gloom alone,
> Thou lovest to lie and hear
> The roar of waters near,
> And listen to the deep, dull groan
> Of some perturbed sprite
> Borne fitful on the heavy gales of night.

This by no means exhausts Southey's horrors and settings for scenes of terror : the poem reflects the terror of the lost wanderer in a snowstorm at eve, the sufferings of a shipwrecked mariner on the coast of Greenland, the death-agony of a forsaken wounded soldier, the tortures of negroes. Southey's relation to his forerunners finds apt illustration in the poem *To Contemplation* (1792), the materials of which include a bat flying in short, quick circles, a sober twilight, soft radiance of the moon, low gales of evening, wanderings in pathless forest wilds, the low murmur of trees, the broken streamlet, the drowsy flight of a beetle, a tube-eyed snail, a glow-worm, a ruined abbey, a half-demolished tomb, a vaulted arch wreathed with ivy and the light percolating through it, the blast moaning along the darksome aisle, a lonely romantic glen and the down-dashing torrent. The poet has seen (*The Ruined Cottage*, 1799)

> Many an old convent reverend in decay, the roof
> Part moulder'd in, the rest o'ergrown with weeds,
> House-leek, and long thin grass, and greener moss. . . .

As late as 1821 he returns in his *Stanzas* to the romantic conceptions of nature of his youth, reviewing in memory his visits to ancient ruins,[184] where alone, lost in thought, he was moved almost to tears, admiring even in their ruined state the majestic monuments of the great dead.

The transition to Oriental themes merely alters the colouring of this terror-romantic setting, leaving it in all essentials the same. Shedad's overwhelmingly magnificent castle (*Thalaba*) reminds one of that of Eblis in *Vathek*. Domdaniel's caves, abodes of spirits of darkness, are situated " under the Roots of ocean " ; the council of evil spirits held there is reminiscent of Milton, and the chief witch, Khavla, of Vathek's mother. For the ruins of Babylon the broken portals, the grass-grown fragments of dwellings, twilight and moonlight, fallen pillars, are descriptive features. The scene can be " wild and wondrous, strange and beautiful." The silence in the lonely, voiceless valley is so perfect as to be alarming. Beside the gate hangs a horn, " ivory-tipt and brazen-mouthed," as in the castle of Otranto. The atmosphere of desolation extends even to an Oriental tent : " Our tent is desolate ! The wind has heaped the sands within its door ; the lizard's track is left." The repulsiveness of a prison is depicted with a bat, a toad and a snake as material. The stage of *Thalaba* stretches to comprise the horrors of ice and eternal snow.

Madoc takes us to corresponding haunts of terror in the west, in the land of the Aztecs. With terror-romantic realism Southey paints a crypt in which are hung the dried and withered bodies of Indian chiefs. The *Burgverliess* of German writers is represented in an Aztec cave high up on a mountain-side : " No human foot had trod its depths, nor ever sun-beam reached its long recesses and mysterious gloom " ; the prisoner immured there is left to die in solitude and dark-ness. In *Kehama* the haunted castle is seen as a huge pagoda, which with its " turret and dome and pinnacle " seems to " load the land " ; when the " Ancient Towers " with their golden summits appear at last in the noonday light, shining over the dark green deep that roll between, the sight of their domes and pinnacles and spires peering above the sea was a mournful one :

> In solitude the ancient temples stood
> Hearing no voice save of the ocean flood,
> The lonely sound of winds, that moan around,
> Accordant to the melancholy waves.
> For never traveller comes near
> These awful ruins of the days of yore.

The Diamond City of Hell, with its towers, defences and walls, glows on its mound like a wondrous vision. As an aid to atmosphere the moon is everywhere present :

> Oh what a gorgeous sight it was to see
> The Diamond City blazing on its height,
> Its towers and domes and pinnacles and spires,
> Turrets and battlements. . . .
>
> . . . . .
>
> How calmly gliding through the dark-blue sky
> The midnight moon ascends—shine upon
> The crags, deepening with blacker
> Night their charms—
> The watchman on the battlements partakes
> The stillness of the solemn hour ; he feels
> The silence of the earth, the endless sound
> Of flowing water soothes him. . . .

The reader will note that no attempt has been made to distinguish between Southey's Oriental and his " Gothic " themes ; the difference is only superficial. A study of the settings shows them to be, like Byron's Oriental poems, simply founded on the same Gothic romanticism, and exposes their Oriental dressing as a transparent surface disguise. This is substantiated in part by that special feature of the haunted castle, the clock, which in Southey's poems has its usual important duty assigned to it ; its momentary transformation into a muezzin calling to the faithful from his minaret signifies nothing when we find the muezzin announcing the hour of midnight (*Thalaba*). In *Kehama* this duty has been entrusted to a Brahmin, who announces the beginning of the fateful hour by striking three chimes before a golden palace. The clock can also become a magic object :

> Behold the Silver Mountain !
> Lo, there the Silver Bell, that, self-sustained, hangs buoyant in the air before
> the mystic rose.

Without wearying the reader by a further accumulation of details, I will summarize what they show : firstly, that Southey's poetry emanated from the sphere of "Gothic" romance ; secondly, that he frequently preserved its stage unaltered, but still more frequently, by a kind of outward inventiveness, enriched it with new features and possibilities ; thirdly, that in so doing he showed the terror-romanticists a way out from their original narrow conception of the haunted castle, thus laying the foundation upon which the later New Romantic school was able to build ; fourthly, that while engaged in this pioneer work, he still retained, irrespective of the continent to which his action took him, his affection for that idyllic brook-landscape which is of old a typical feature of English interpretation of nature, and which played so important a part in the surroundings of Mrs. Radcliffe's castles and her landscapes. Thus, the pursuit, step by step, of the romantic landscape leads finally to that "naturalism" whose special representatives, besides Southey, were Coleridge and Wordsworth.

The central feature of Coleridge's conception of nature, especially in his lyrics, is the brook meandering through a forest or an idyllic grove, which we have seen to be such a peculiar feature of English poetry.[185]

> 'Tis sweet to hear a brook, 'tis sweet
> To hear the Sabbath-bell
> 'Tis sweet to hear them both at once,
> Deep in a woody dell—

the poet sings in his poem *The Three Graves*. *The Songs of the Pixies* reflect romantic moods : the murmuring throng of wild bees humming their drowsy song ; " a youthful bard wooing the queen of solemn thought " ; tearful eye ; evening, " the visionary hour " ; eve, saddening into night ; pale moon, etc. In his *Lines on an Autumnal Evening* the poet apostrophizes the brook as follows :

> Dear native brook ! where first young poesy
> Stared wildly-eager in her noontide dream,
> Where blameless pleasures dimple Quiet's cheek,
> As water-lilies ripple thy slow stream. . . .

In his poem *The Picture, or the Lover's Resolution,* he says :

> Here will I seat myself, beside this old,
> Hollow and weedy oak, which ivy-twine
> Clothes as with network : here will I couch my limbs,
> Close by this river, in this silent shade—unheard, unseen,
> And listening only to the pebbly brook,
> That murmurs—
> Or to the bees—

A waterfall with a " weeping " silver birch on the edge of the high rock beside it, a valley seen from afar, a brook and bridge, grey cottages half-hidden by trees and smoke rising straight to the heavens in calm weather ; an old moss-grown bridge, the gleam of a river in the moonlight, a mossy forest-dell beside a brook ; a glow-worm lighting its torch of love in the dusk ;—

> I see a fountain, large and fair,
> A willow and a ruined hut,
> And thee, and me, and Mary there—[186]
>
> .   .   .   .   .
>
> A wild-rose roofs the ruined shed . . .;
> Sister of lovelorn poets, Philomel ;

an Æolian harp—

> How by the desultory breeze caressed,
> Like some coy maid half yelding to her lover
> It pours such sweet upbraiding, as must needs,
>   The long sequacious notes
> Over delicious surges sink and rise,
> Such a soft floating witchery of sound
> As twilight elfins make . . .

these build up the scale which, attuned to many different keys, ranging from the bright calm colouring of summer and the peaceful brook of the meadows to autumn's dark tints, to the coldness of frosty nights, the gloom of cavern waters, the roar of mountain rapids, austere rocks and the cry of an eagle, serves Coleridge for material wherewith to create the settings and moods of his lyrical works. His feeling for nature is to some extent literary, theoretical, inherited, but it is more sensitive and poetically conceived than Southey's, who in all his poetry fashioned and constructed rather than felt. By tracing the picture of the haunted castle we have found, to put the matter briefly, that Coleridge's poetry partly falls within its circle, partly rests on the idyllic margin of the ring.

The application of this stage-setting test to the works of Wordsworth may seem to some like sacrilege, but it proves an extremely interesting task as soon as the obvious relationship is grasped. In his play *The Borderers* (1796) for example, one of the earliest works of his youth, the influence of Shakespeare, chiefly that of *King Lear*, and of Schiller's *The Robbers* [187] is clearly apparent, combined with a typically romantic conception of a sombre, saturnine, philosophizing person with a soul above moral laws and a dark mystery in his past. The settings of this work :—a forest path, a forest, a half-ruined castle and the door of a dungeon, a desolate moor, " a desolate prospect—a ridge of rocks—a chapel on the summit of one— moon behind the rocks—night stormy—irregular sound of a bell "—reveal, taken together with the whole construction of the play and its characters, the relation between it and the romantic influences by which the author was surrounded. Born wholly under Lewis's star and displaying marked affinities with terror-romanticism is the story of the betrayed maiden who lives in a " ragged dwelling, close beneath a rock by the brook-side " and who " every night at the first stroke of twelve quits her house, and, in the neighbouring churchyard upon the self-same spot, in rain or storm, paces out the hour 'twixt twelve and one round an infant's grave." She has been seen there " at midnight . . . when the moon shone clear, the air was still, so still, the trees were silent as the graves beneath them." The castle of her seducer, where he holds his hellish orgies, " hangs from a beetling rock " beside a barren moor, a site whose superstition-awakening gloom makes the horror of his dark crimes worse. The atmosphere of storm is heightened by the thunder that crashes " with hell-rousing force." To blind Herbert, as he gropes his way in the storm towards the erratic sound of the bell, it is as though no human hand, no peasant who might aid him, were ringing it, but an evil spirit. He also wanders, guided by the rippling of a brook, to an old oak, in whose shade he seats himself ; in his wanderings in Syria the cruel Oswald fares " through woods of gloomy cedar, into deep chasms troubled by roaring streams " and gazes from the summit of Libanon at the " moonlight desert, and the moonlight sea."

In writing the above, Wordsworth was not, however, the poet he was soon to become—one who " with modest looks, and clad in homely russet brown, murmurs near the running brooks a music sweeter than their own," who :

> The outward shows of sky and earth,
> Of hill and valley, he has viewed ;
> And impulses of deeper birth
> Have come to him in solitude.
> In common things that round us lie
> Some random truths he can impart—
> The harvest of a quiet eye
> That broods and sleeps on his own heart.[188]

He was soon to become

> A poet, one who loves the brooks
> Far better than the sages' books [189]

who like a rambling naturalist, with observant eyes possessing their own individual conception of beauty, notes down all he sees of nature or man that in any way stirs his humanity. Between nature, human life and the poet's soul a secret link was forged, his soul was pantheistic, dissolved into oneness with nature; his muse had to forsake all outward "glitterings of poetry " [190] and to rise through a compliant, calm yet loving sympathy and meditation to a simple patriarchal humanity encompassing all the joys and sufferings of the world.

In my opinion Wordsworth is the only one of the Lake Poets who merits the attribute of " naturalist," for only in his poetry is nature the actual sounding-board above which the strings of his moods and meditations vibrate. Thus, despite his ever-recurrent forest brooks, mountains, roaring waterfalls, old oaks and yews, moss-grown stone seats and other familiar materials, Wordsworth sounds the depths behind these images of the idyllic outer verge of the haunted castle, and reaches ultimately beyond the charmed circle into a true, free and " natural " nature.

In conclusion, I cannot resist a glance at Thomas Moore,[191] from whose flute surges a veritable lyricism, delightful in its light, crystalline, carefree melodiousness. Although the foundation of his poetry is rather Irish national melody than any conventional romanticism, he is not wholly independent of the general materials and poetical images of his day. The poems of his youth include the ballad, the elegiac march-music of ghosts so typical of his period. " The darkness that hung upon Willumberg's walls had long been remembered with awe and dismay," he sings in his ballad *Reuben and Rose*, picturing in his mind " a spirit that shall toll the great bell of the mouldering abbey." The ballad called *The Shield* tells of a shield hung up long ago on the branch of a yew, which " is blushing with murderous stains " that neither storm nor rain can wash away.

> Oft by that yew, on the blasted field,
> Demons dance to the red moon's light,
> While the damp boughs creak, and the swinging shield
> Sings to the raving spirit of night.

In his Indian ballad *The Lake of the Dismal Swamp* he sings of the ghosts of an Indian maiden and her faithful swain which float at midnight on the surface of the dread lake in their white canoe, and the light of the fireflies. He sings to " the Evil Spirit of the wood," and is deeply sensitive to the solitude of forests (*Ballad Stanzas*) :

> It was noon, and on flowers that languish'd around
> In silence repos'd the voluptuous bee ;
> Every leaf was at rest, and I heard not a sound
> But the woodpecker tapping the hollow beech tree.

The romantic instrument favoured by him is the harp, among whose cords " mournfully the midnight air doth sigh." When he devotes himself to the Oriental colours of *Lalla Rookh* (1817), he takes with him, like Byron and Southey, his romantic images. The place where Mokanna and Zelica are wedded (*The Veiled Prophet of Khorassan*) is depicted with a terror-romantic realism learned from Lewis : " He hurried her away—to the dim charnel-house, through all its steams of damp and death, and, passing through upright ranks of Dead, which to the maiden, doubly crazed by dread, seem'd, through the bluish death-light . . . to move their lips in mutt'ring as they passed. There, in that awful place, when each had quaffed and pledged in silence such a fearful draught—red bowl—he bound her soul by a dark oath." While wandering in Mokanna's brilliant fairy-palace, young Azim experiences a gentle, soothing enchantment and hears the pleasant murmur of the waters as the song of Indian bees at sunset and distant delightful dream-music. In *The Fire-Worshippers* a Radcliffesque castle on a steep mountain beside the sea is depicted, in the conception of which, as in that of its young ruler, the spirit of Byron is nigh :

> There stood—but one short league away—
> A rocky mountain over the sea ;
> On its peak that braved the sky,
> A ruined temple towered, so high ;

Beneath, terrific caverns gave
Dark welcome to each stormy wave.
And such the strange, mysterious din
At times throughout those caverns rolled,
And such the fearful wonders told
Of restless spirits imprisoned there,
That bold were Moslem, who would dare,
At twilight hour, to steer his skiff
Beneath the Gheber's lonely cliff.
On the land side, those towers sublime
Were severed from the haunts of men
By a wide, deep and wizard glen,
So fathomless, so full of gloom,
No eye could pierce the void between ;
Like distant thunder, from below
The sound of many torrents came.

At midnight a maiden goes to the highest tower to weep in solitude, to watch and to seek on the depths below the one whose smile had first melted her heart. But her tears and watches are in vain, for she is nevermore to see his sail.

The owlet's solitary cry,
The night-hawk, flitting darkly by,
And of the hateful carrion bird,
Was all she saw, was all she heard—

Even the horn from the Castle of Otranto is present in this nest of pirates :

To the tow'r-wall, where, high in view,
A pond'rous sea-horn hung, and blew
A signal, deep and dread—
And there, upon the mould'ring tow'r,
Hath hung this sea-horn many an hour,
Ready to sound o'er land and sea
That dirge-note of the brave and free.

These materials entitle Moore to a place in the ranks of the terror-romanticists.

8

While on the one hand the haunted castle had thus gained in historical verity and become an important setting in historical novels, instilling into these a breath of romantic poetry, on the other it either clung tenaciously to its traditional outward aspect or broke up into a general setting of terror which was no longer tied to the picture of the haunted castle. When the limits of this disintegration had been reached, the picture disappeared altogether, leaving behind it chiefly the feeling for nature which had throughout formed part of it and whose idyllic propensities now became the special field of the Lake Poets. An additional glimpse or two at the further development of the haunted castle may make the purport of the present chapter clearer to the reader.

Examples of the tendency of the haunted castle to keep, even in later years, to the types created by Mrs. Radcliffe include Edward Bulwer-Lytton's *Zanoni* (1842) and Nathaniel Hawthorne's *The Marble Faun* (1860).[192]

When Glyndon in *Zanoni* approaches " the Castle of the Mountain " where he was to meet the one who was to guide him in the deepest secrets of occult knowledge, he is at first charmed by the delightful view opening out at the foot of the mountain. But when he turns, he sees before him the grey decaying walls of the castle within which he purposed to find the wisdom of the future. Even in its decay the castle is majestic, stern and threatening. Within are rooms displaying traces of former splendour—faded tapestries and heavy tables of marble. From the balcony he admires the " fearful beauty " of the surrounding mountainous nature. Such is the spot in which he makes the acquaintance of the most mysterious of all the terror-inspiring beings of romance.

When Kenyon draws near to Donatello's home, the castle of Monte Beni, in *The Marble Faun*, he sees a mighty tower, decked out by Time in a covering of yellow moss. Here and there are openings for windows and little loopholes, everything seeming to denote that the place had once been a fortress. Many an archer had shot his bolt through those loopholes, and on festival nights the light of hundreds of lamps had shone far into the valley. The remainder of the castle consists of suites of forsaken rooms, all witnessing to past splendour and might. The apartments had been built as strongly as possible ; sturdy pillars supporting high arched vaults rise from the marble floors. The walls had been covered by frescoes which time had now partly obliterated ; cheerful as their effect had once been, so much more sombre is it now in decay. Old parchments relate marvellous matters concerning the family history.

The tower is called " The Owl Tower " and houses two such birds. The way thither leads through many bewildering chambers and corridors before a little low gate is reached. Here begins the narrow staircase that winds upward, storey by storey. Concerning the prison room a legend is told of the ghost of a monk who was once burned for his faith and who still creeps about the tower. In the topmost storey is a skull of alabaster which the lords of the castle have been compelled to procure and to keep in constant view as a punishment for some crime (*Udolpho*). The castle is surrounded by an Arcadian Italian landscape with villages, castles and monasteries, the bells of the latter adding an idyllic touch to the peace of evening. The reader of Mrs. Radcliffe will find all this familiar.[193]

Proof of the capacity of the terror-romanticist stage for remaining rooted in the old haunted castle even while increasing in extent until it encompasses the entire gamut of themes of terror is provided by the production of Edgar Allan Poe.[194]

Poe's stage comprises numerous features from the haunted castle. William Wilson [195] goes to school in an old convent-like building in which he thrills " at the deep hollow note of the church-bell, breaking each hour, with sullen and sudden roar, upon the stillness of the dusky atmosphere in which the fretted Gothic steeple lay imbedded and asleep." It is surrounded by a high wall pierced by a threateningly dark gate that inspires him with a respectful terror. " But the house !— how quaint an old building was this !—to me how veritably a palace of enchantment ! There was really no end to its windings—to its incomprehensible sub-divisions." Its plan is so bewildering that although he lived there for five years, the narrator could not have explained it. | In *Ligeia* [196] the narrator purchases an old abbey, whose " gloomy and dreary grandeur " affects him strongly. In this building is a mysterious tower-room which he furnishes as a bridal chamber, a room especially descriptive of the quality of the author's imagination. It has only one large window, the Venetian leaded glass of which gives to the light a " ghastly lustre " ; the panelling is a sombre oak, adorned with wild and grotesque half-Gothic, half-Druidical carvings ; the room itself is high and vaulted and wears a melancholy aspect. Its most impressive feature, however, is its tapestries, which are of heavy, carpet-like cloth-of-gold. They teem with strange arabesque-like designs which alter as the spectator moves from place to place. Thus, to one walking in the room it seems as though he were surrounded by an endless series of those " ghastly forms which belong to the superstition of the Norman, or arise in the guilty slumbers of the monk." The eerie effect is increased when the draught sets the tapestries slowly moving, awakening those terrible beings to life. Here, too, it is clearly a question of the wind that infested the passages of the old haunted castle, but brought into much more suggestive activity, transformed almost, one might say, into a living personality. The story of *The Assignation* [197] deals with a peculiar room of this type, which is simply the former secret chamber of the haunted castle, the room in which devils were conjured up or the art of alchemy practised. There " the eye wandered from object to object, and rested upon none— neither the *grotesques* of the Greek painters, nor the sculptures of the best Italian days, nor the huge carvings of untutored Egypt. Rich draperies in every part of the room trembled to the vibration of low, melancholy music, whose origin was not to be discovered. The senses were oppressed by mingled and conflicting perfumes, reeking up from strange convolute censers, together with multitudinous flaring and flickering tongues of emerald and violet fire."

The Oval Portrait [198] is begun by Poe as follows : " The château into which my valet had ventured to make forcible entrance, rather than permit me, in my desperately wounded condition, to pass a night in the open air, was one of those piles of commingled gloom and grandeur which have so long frowned along the Apennines, not less in fact than in the fancy of Mrs. Radcliffe " ; [199] an old portrait found in this castle gives him an opportunity to deal with the portrait-theme in the light of his own weird and individual imagination, which imparts to it new and agitating contents. *The Masque of the Red Death* [200] shows us Prince Prospero's castle, whither he flees to escape the plague ; we find here the old spectral stage renewed in characteristic, fantastic fashion. The " castellated abbey " is entirely surrounded by a high wall in which are iron gates ; it comprises altogether seven truly imperial rooms, which can be combined by opening the great intervening doors, placed so that only two rooms at a time are visible to any guest. Of these rooms, one was wholly blue, even to its windows, the second was purple, the third green, the fourth orange, the fifth white, the sixth violet, the seventh black.

In each room the windows were of the same colour as the rest of the room, except in the black room, which had blood-red windows. The illumination was spectrally flickering and uncertain. Against the western wall of the black room stood a gigantic clock of ebony, its pendulum swaying " with a dull, heavy, monotonous clang " ; its brazen lungs emitted a deep, full and musical note, which was so peculiarly solemn and majestic that on hearing it the musicians were impelled by some inexplicable influence to interrupt their playing to listen ;

the dance, too, broke off, and a mood of melancholy descended for a moment over the merry company. While its chimes were sounding, the most light-hearted were seen to turn pale, while the oldest and wisest of the company passed their hands across their brows as though to banish bewildering dreams or unpleasant thoughts. Hardly, however, have the chimes ceased before the company breaks again into merry laughter. To such heights of effectivity as this had the old castle clock been raised.[201]

Poe based his work on the old haunted castle of the terror-romanticists, revivifying it with the aid of his rare imagination to serve his own purposes. Even where the castle is not directly brought into the picture, as in *The Fall of the House of Usher*, which in mood and partly even in its contents greatly resembles Lewis's poem *The House on the Heath*,[202] by the skilful use of meteorological and other outward aids to atmosphere he achieves an enigmatical sense of terror akin to that evoked by the haunted castle. This exploitation of the power of suggestion—with the aid of which, gradually and of set purpose, making full use of the power of words and tricks of style, he hypnotizes the reader into entire compliance with his fantastical themes—liberated terror-romanticism from its dependence on the haunted castle and gave to it the power of choosing its settings at will.

9

It is needless to proceed further in the search for examples, for we have given enough to show the great importance for later literature of the haunted castle of the terror-romanticists. In the historical novel it still survives and in romantic stories depending for their material on the past it is easily recognizable ; in the pictures drawn by later romanticists of scenes intended to evoke a sensation of horror, its influence can be sensed in the background. Its haunted room becomes the laboratory of workers of magic, of alchemists, the secret research room of a modern scientist—becomes, in general, the mysterious hidden chamber where the terrifying element is housed. Each age fashions this centre of suspense to conform with its own new experiences and inventions, but for the reader aware of its history it is an easy task to strip off the modern equipment, when it stands confessed as merely a new rendering of the old picture of the haunted castle.

THE HAUNTED CASTLE

I shall now return to the characters connected with the haunted castle and to the various conceptions attached to these. Thus we shall deal with Lewis's monk and his descendants, Lewis's Wandering Jew and related conceptions, the group of tyrant-types known as Byronic heroes, with ghosts and demoniac beings, terror-romantic eroticism, the young hero and heroine and other characters—with all the chief themes, in short, which in the foregoing pages have been found to possess a natural right to appear on the stage of the haunted castle.

IV

THE CRIMINAL MONK

I

IT has become clear from the life-story of Lewis that the leading position assigned to the monk in his novel was due to the influence of Monvel's play, *Les Victimes Cloitrées*, in which an erotic monk plays an important part; in English romanticism the idea was new, for the ecclesiastic who makes his appearance in the novels of Walpole and Ann Radcliffe is usually worthy of respect and in full accord with fine traditions. In Walpole's play *The Mysterious Mother*, there are, certainly, two criminal monks, but these remain exceptions, the more so as the play itself was very little known and its chief interest centred elsewhere. For the entry into English literature of the romantic monk of criminal tendencies and the interest and horror awakened thereby, credit is due to Lewis. His influence stretches to France and Germany, for it was the numerous translations of his novel that, together with Mrs. Radcliffe's *The Italian*, made the criminal monk widely known in France, giving rise there, as in Germany, to a rich series of imitations and variants.

The depravity and vices of monks and priests is an old theme in literature, providing, particularly in the days of the Reformation, a fount of material for blame and satire. The fleshy and lazy monk with a bent for amorous adventure had become a veritable scapegoat in folk-tales, which invariably imposed on him greatest discomfiture in the end. In such tales he usually plays a humorous part, but as soon as the narrator transfers his attention to graver matters, to the depictment of crime and horrors and every description of dangerous intrigue, the monk is ready to appear as an instigator of evil and a master of duplicity. Thus in Germany, when at the latter end of the eighteenth century a vogue arose for the so-called " historical " and other " romantic " novels of which mention has already been made, with their descriptions of former Teutonic greatness, of the romantic splendour of the days of chivalry, of struggles against papal treachery, the whole being illustrated with more or less accurately depicted historical events, the monk takes on the guise of a Prince of the Church, engaged in the basest crimes. Even where the historical padding is restricted to an arbitrarily-concocted knight and monk with fictitious adventures, the monk retains his evil character, being depicted as the lover, helper and ally of some false woman who plots against the brave and guileless German knight. All evil proceeds from the cowl, and the virtuous knight can conceive of no crime too base for the monk to commit. Woman is his greatest weakness ; he is guilty of adultery, rape and even incest. According to one of the most prolific of this class of writers, Cramer, the monk represents nothing less than the principle of evil. To him, monks are " holy monsters " (*die heiligen Ungeheuer*), " God's devils," whose slinking footsteps are like—*die Schritte der Blindschleiche über dürres Heidemoos ;* their glance is " mortally poisonous " like that of the basilisk, and their hearts *ein verfluchter Rustsaal aller Laster.* The knight, too, can be wicked and commit crimes, but that is a totally different matter ; his sins are the outcome of mighty temptations and the strayings of a kindly, though weak being, while the monk is by nature a born criminal.[203] In all this one can discern an influence, antagonistic to the papacy, natural enough in view of the history of Protestant countries, and expressly calculated to please Lewis, whose views, while in Paris, had become tinged with revolutionary anticlericalism.

In constructing Ambrosio, Lewis took for his model Laurent from *les Victimes Cloitrées*, heightening his colours from the palette of German monk-romanticism, for it must be remembered that he possessed expert knowledge of this branch of literature. Nor did his memory fail him with regard to the rest of his reading : fresh in his memory were such tyrants of the English school of romantic terror as Montoni, a type with possibilities, in its sombreness and beauty, of appealing to the memory with lasting force. In depicting Ambrosio's outward appearance—the aquiline nose, large, black, sparkling eyes, and dark brows joined almost together, the burning, piercing glance that few could withstand—he gives to him that general darkly romantic mask which, beginning with Hamlet and drawing unto itself Manfred and the youthful hero, runs through the whole of Mrs. Radcliffe's production. That piercing gaze reawakened memories of the Caliph Vathek and Eblis, even perhaps of Milton's Satan, and henceforward the attention of the school of romantic horrors was especially directed to the power inherent in the human eye. To his Ambrosio, Lewis further attached the youthful hero-motive of a mysterious birth, for Ambrosio is a foundling and as such become the ward of a monastery.[204] For greater clearness it is necessary to return once more to his story.

When first introduced to the reader he is the Abbot of a Capuchin monastery in Madrid. He is in the full flower of his early manhood, a proud and refined figure, skilful as a preacher and known throughout the town as the " Holy Man." Whenever he preaches the monastery church is thronged with devout listeners, especially women, whose favour he enjoys in the highest degree. He is the radiant focus of Catholic devotion in his town and towards him the eyes of all believers are turned. His fall was therefore destined to be from on high and visible from afar, a crushing blow to thousands of souls, for which reason he is chosen as victim by Lucifer. Examining Ambrosio's most secret thoughts, he perceives his devotion to be spiritual conceit and pride, his virtue to be based solely on lack of opportunity. Thereupon Lucifer directs his blow, causing, as already related, a beautiful woman, Matilda de Villanegas, first to fall in love with the Abbot, then dressed as a novice to penetrate into the monastery on purpose to tempt him. On the whole, the plan succeeds easily, and when, shortly afterwards, the monk tires of her, she barters her chance of salvation for infernal pleasures and as the agent of Lucifer begins to beguile her victim ever deeper into crime. Thus Ambrosio is led to become first the murderer of his mother, then the seducer and murderer of his sister, until, fallen into the hands of the Inquisition and dreading punishment, he sells his soul to Lucifer, who releases him from confinement only to kill him.

Such, in all brevity, is the main plot of the novel. Its weakness lies in the insignificance of the spiritual struggle which precedes the monk's fall, and also because it makes him too great a sinner, whose bestiality is almost enough to kill the pity aroused by his fate. Compassion is kept awake only because Ambrosio is helpless and altogether abandoned to the temptations threatening him, so that any balance of conflicting powers or even the possibility of a better fate seem out of the question. The only positive emotion to be gained by reading the book is the somewhat Biblically-tinged state of mind which can be evoked by stories of terrible crimes with their ensuing retribution of everlasting misery, though this has been rendered impossible in places by the extremely powerful and daring treatment of erotic scenes which is such a feature of the novel.

The pictures of horror demanded by a plot of this description occur in the surroundings already depicted. The general impression is a feeling that instead of Walpole's legend-like, naïve narration of events and the innocent artifices of Mrs. Radcliffe, the question hinges now on the interference in human affairs, according to Biblical traditions of a personified Tempter, of supernatural powers, and the evocation of such powers by magic. The conception of an absolute Evil Being and his relation to mankind has been accepted as a fact ; Lucifer with all his might and auxiliaries, his methods and aims has been compressed into a character of the novel, and a tale is thus created of events contingent to such a phenomenon and the fate of their victim, with the intention, as shown by the concluding lines of the story, of exposing the danger of narrow-minded and self-righteous judgments and the hollowness and impotence of all pharisaical virtue. The drawback in the method is, that temptation proceeds too far from without the victim's own soul and in such intensity that he is left helpless ; it arises not from the heart, although for its success it depends on weaknesses dwelling therein.

2

We have dealt already with the storm awakened by the appearance of *The Monk*. The cause of the outburst was Ambrosio, his unquenchable licentiousness and the events occasioned thereby ; and in general, the undismayed realism of the narration and the pitilessness of the author in eliminating every hope and possibility of salvation for his monk ; these served to arouse in the reader's mind moral indignation and a sense of opposition, though fundamentally the extremely agitating effect of the book was the cause of this. However hard the reader might try to regard the work as the unripe creation of a mere youth, scarcely deserving of attention, he was compelled to admit that it revealed in a perturbingly merciless manner the hidden lust of pleasure biding its opportunity, which bereft of control, exposed to strong temptations, can sweep human beings to destruction. The argument

PLATE VI

THE TEMPTATION OF AMBROSIO

(From M. G. Lewis's *The Monk*)

[face p. 176

of the book, that the most pious person can, in suitable circumstances, become the slave of his passions is one of the silent truths we are prone to ignore and which, over-boldly expressed, gives rise to hypocritical wrath.

The best proof that the basic argument of Lewis's novel did accord with one of the truths thus silently acquiesced in, is the fact that, as though sprung from the earth, a series of sombre, tragic phantoms of monks appeared to keep Ambrosio company, introducing into the romantic literature of England and the rest of Europe a ghastly, graveyard atmosphere. The passion of the romanticists for the past found in the monk a suitable character, in whose heart deep human conflicts could be laid, making of it a stage for the struggle between good and evil for the ultimate mastery over the human soul. For the romantic movement this denoted a setting aside of mere outward effects and the transference of psychological phenomena into the foreground. Also from this point of view does the appearance of the monk inaugurate a new phase in romanticism, a concentration of interest on the romanticism inherent in tragedies of the soul, which, as a source of " terror-awakening beauty," provided more effective means than those hitherto used. The line of development thus begun by Ambrosio is one of extreme interest in the history of romanticism, and carried to its utmost limits is responsible for many weird literary monsters.

The first author to feel the fruitful impulse of the book was Ann Radcliffe. Having written her *Udolpho* she was doubtlessly aware that a romantic hero of the type of Montoni had exhausted its possibilities for her. Now that Lewis had spread before her the scenery of those Latin countries which to Mrs. Radcliffe were already so familiar and well-loved, but with a new shimmer of terror derived from monastic worlds over them, she was quick to take the cue for a new romantic central character. To me it is obvious that *The Italian* was created under the revivified romantic impulse supplied by the tragic monastic story written by Lewis, even if Mrs. Radcliffe did choose the setting for her book from Monvel's play.

The central character of *The Italian*, the confessor of the Vivaldi family, Father Schedoni, is conceived differently from Ambrosio. He is no longer a young and inexperienced saint preserved from temptations, but a person long hardened in the ways of crime and vice, alarmingly gifted and strenuous, hypocritical, unfeeling and merciless, more like Monvel's Laurent. It was impossible for Mrs. Radcliffe to write a novel dealing with erotic strayings, and so such sins were relegated to the monk's past, and a dark mystery in that line only hinted at with faint suggestions. Thereby the romantic effect of the character was increased. If Schedoni had only possessed a high guiding principle he might have become a truly magnificent tragic creation ; but as Mrs. Radcliffe's talent was unequal to making of him anything more than a tool in the hands of the Vivaldi family for the persecution of young Vivaldi's beloved (note the influence of Laurent), he is left outside the circle of great tragic figures, in the gallery of sombre criminals. But even as such, there is more of the atmosphere of romantic terror around him than in any single preceding type, and the picture of the criminal monk is raised by him to more dreadful heights. This is even clear from his appearance.

In describing his person Mrs. Radcliffe betrays labours of intellect and imagination, the starting-point for which has been the character of the romantic tyrant already dealt with ; but she deprives it of its essential beauty and makes the criminal past become mirrored in facial expressions, at the same time preserving the most effectual feature of that romantic countenance, the gloomy, keen and burning glance which is in alarming contrast to the unnatural pallor of the face and is an impressive trait already seen in Eblis (*Vathek*). Her imagination has evidently been occupied to a greater extent than in her earlier work with the outward apparition of the tragic, romantic figure, and in accordance with her personality she develops it in the direction of greater detail and exactitude. Schedoni's " figure was striking, but not so from grace, it was tall, and, though extremely thin, his limbs were large and uncouth, and as he stalked along, wrapt in the black garments of his order, there was something terrible in his air ; something almost superhuman. His cowl, too, as it threw a shade over the livid paleness of his face, increased its severe character, and gave an effect to his large melancholy eye, which approached to horror. His was not the melancholy of a sensible and wounded heart, but apparently that of a gloomy and ferocious disposition. There was something in his physiognomy extremely singular, and that cannot easily be defined. It bore the traces of many passions, which seemed to have fixed the features they no longer animated. An habitual gloom and severity prevailed over the deep lines of his countenance ; and his eyes were so piercing, that they seemed to penetrate, at a single glance, into the hearts of men and to read their most secret thoughts ; few persons could support their scrutiny, or even endure to meet them twice. Yet, notwithstanding all this gloom and austerity, some rare occasions of interest had called forth a character upon his countenance entirely different, and he could adapt himself to the tempers and passions of persons whom he wished to conciliate with astonishing facility, and generally with complete triumph. This monk, this Schedoni, was the confessor and secret adviser of the Marchesa di Vivaldi."

To my mind the description given of Schedoni's character suggests as its model a person whose shadow has up to the present day hovered over the romantic tyrant, ready at the first suitable moment to slip into his garments—Richard III, in whom practically every one of the characteristics enumerated are represented. Richard III was no monk, yet when needed he could with masterful hypocrisy appear a devout man ; he was energetic, gifted, ambitious, unscrupulous, cruel for cruelty's sake and wicked for the sake of wickedness, an obvious Schedoni, the only difference his hunched back, and instead of the monk's cowl his crown and mantle. The credit of divining the possibilities of romantic terror in the type is thus Mrs. Radcliffe's ; none the less as she proved able to cultivate it anew in the soil of romanticism, with new artifices, a new form and surroundings and new purposes, which give to it an original appearance. When, under the influence of Ambrosio and Laurent, Mrs. Radcliffe became inspired to create her own impressive, tragical monk, the basis that unrecognized suggested itself to her was Shakespeare's ever-effective, genial usurper and regicide, now become a universal type of heroic evil.

The close influence of Ambrosio is otherwise clearly apparent in the fact that when Schedoni fails to encompass the persecuted maiden's death through his assistants, he decides to carry out the murder in person ; looking on the sleeping girl, his passions are awakened, but before he has time to carry out, like Ambrosio, his criminal intention, he perceives her to be his own child (a discovery that unhappily proves to be unfounded when the end of the novel is reached). The ghastly themes from Ambrosio, incest and the murder of the victim, hover thus in the vicinity. The unravelling of the plot and Schedoni's seizure by the Inquisition, follows the line of Ambrosio's fate.

3

Mrs. Radcliffe raised the type of criminal monk into perhaps greater prominence than it had been brought by Ambrosio ; both retained their suggestive power and it was within the charmed circle of this power that Maturin began his literary activity. His first novel, *The Fatal Revenge*, rises from the romanticism of Mrs. Radcliffe, and its chief character, the object of greatest interest to the author, is the pseudo-monk Schemoli, connected already by name with the line of Ambrosio and Schedoni. In other respects the book is a complete arsenal of romantic terror, in which the whole Walpole-Radcliffe battery of themes has been conscientiously assembled, increased and developed both in extent and suggestive atmosphere. In revenge for his refusal by Erminia, distantly resembling Desdemona, the beautiful wife of his brother Orazio, the wicked brother, like a second Iago, succeeds in inflaming Orazio-Othello to a catastrophic jealousy, using as his assistant his own base-minded wife and acting with her the part of the persecutor-couple played earlier by Ambrosio and Matilda against Antonia. After the death of Desdemona-Erminia comes a continuation of the Othello-story, in which the deceived Orazio, having learned the truth, sets out disguised as the monk Schemoli to seek a fateful revenge on his brother. In his person the author has created an impressive and worthy successor to Ambrosio, even though he lacks the stamp of true originality.

The basis of Ambrosio's actions was erotic passion, that of Schedoni congenital wickedness ; the origin of Schemoli's activity is the lust for revenge stirred up by a wrong done to an innocent woman ; but as vengeance is the Lord's (Maturin was in Holy Orders) the deed brings about his own destruction, for all unknowingly he has incited his sons to commit murder. But as in so doing they only mete out to the villain his deserts, the tragedy of the plot is left weakly established, despite the fact that Schemoli takes the guilt upon himself and dies. As a matter of fact his impressiveness depends less on the story of his fate than on the romantic gloom and mystery with which the author, by developing the sombre exterior of Schedoni, succeeds in endowing him. By adding to the powers possessed by Schedoni, he makes of Schemoli, with the Wandering Jew from *The Monk* and Godwin's *Leon* as model, a student of magic and an " adept," thus providing him with supernatural physical and psychic powers which naturally, used with Maturin's suggestivity and contempt for verisimilitude, increase the mystery surrounding the character. An effective addition to Schedoni's nature is the self-control and cold, unflinching calm displayed by Schemoli on every occasion, whereby his value as a character is enhanced. In outward appearance and build the two monks are in general alike.

In Maturin's third novel, *The Milesian Chief*, the now traditional monk bears the name Morosini and, as the influential and callous confessor of an aristocratic family, continues the work of Schedoni, darkening with his intrigues and sombre apparition the already terror-filled romantic colouring of the novel.

Even at the heels of Walter Scott's muse can the shadow of the criminal monk be discerned, although his healthier romanticism declined to accept the type in the fantastic form depicted above. The nearest approach is in *Ivanhoe*, in the shape of the Good Templar Brian de Bois-Guilbert, soldier and priest, who in the manner of Ambrosio joins the band of monks as the victim of a broken promise and a conflict between a forbidden, unhappy love, passion and duty. Of all the types here dealt with, his is the fate most consequently and logically developed and described, rising to true tragedy. In creating his character, Scott used with fine discretion traits from the composite tragical monk, at the same time joining to them such features from the tyrant-type as manlihood, cruelty and wildness ; the keen, searching gaze has not been forgotten, any more than the surrounding mysterious gloom.

Walter Savage Landor, whom Southey "discovered" owing to the circumstances that the poem *Gebir* (1798) was in theme, in the romanticism of its imagery and general atmosphere a realization of his own dreams, an obvious precursor of his Thalaba and Kehama, differing from these only in its poetical vigour, is another English poet whose imagination was touched by the sombre figure of the criminal monk. In his old age he wrote a great poetical drama, his trilogy *Andrea of Hungary, Giovanna of Naples*, and *Fra Rupert* (the two first in 1838, the last in 1840), in all of which the ruling character is the monk Rupert. He is descended from Schedoni, but behind his adventures and actions one discerns sometimes Ambrosio and the traditional figure of Richard III. Previous to the period dealt with in the plays, Rupert has passed through an erotic experience : he has been the pious adviser and mentor of the beautiful Agatha, whose mother he frequently visits to pray and to hear long confessions, precisely like Ambrosio with the mother of Antonia. When he becomes the teacher of Agatha he soon thrusts religious works aside, to hum in the ear of his pupil " Florentian tales and songs of Sicily " and to accustom her to speak " the only soft language of love " which brings a blush to the maiden's cheek—again like Ambrosio in his attempts to seduce Antonia. Rupert is able however to conceal his sin, and when the trilogy begins he appears as " the holiest monk on God's earth," and especially as a strict woman-hater. He has, indeed, by this time a new love, the love of power, which he is desirous of retaining altogether and undivided in his own hands. For this reason he tries to estrange Andrea from the consort intended for him, Queen Giovanna, to prevent her from influencing the course of government, which would then be left entirely to Andrea : in reality to Rupert. Andrea, however, is in love with Giovanna and begins to fear Rupert, afraid of the uncanny, staring glance and great influence of the monk. Noticing this, Rupert murders him during the wedding festival and begins to intrigue against Giovanna, with the result that she and her whole family are brought to ruin, the monk ever keeping one aim before his eyes : power and worldly honours. When finally the burden of dreadful crime becomes too heavy for his soul, like Richard III he sinks into gloomy introspection : " I am more a man than others, therefore I dare more and suffer more. Superficial men have no absorbing passions."

He remembers Giovanna at the moment when the bridal wreath was twined around her crown and wishes he had never laid eyes on her. Then would Andrea, " his comfort and help," still be alive ; " divided power I could never brook." He was bound to his ward by a deep love and yet in the grip of ambition murders him, laying bare his own soul to gnawing remorse, which his subsequent crimes continue to swell ; the reader is led to suspect that he nourished warmer feelings towards Giovanna, so that the death of the Queen denotes for him the death of his latest love. In Rupert two strong passions struggle for mastery, and he falls into the pit between the two. He is a revised version of Shakespeare's strong natures, whose dimensions are mighty and awe-inspiring in all their fear-fulness. As to exteriors : " stout is he, nor ill-built, tho the left shoulder is half a finger's breadth above the right "—a description reminiscent of Richard III ; another hint in the same direction is Rupert's extraordinary power of dissimulation and his talent for attracting people by masterly speeches and turns of speech when it is in his interest to do so. In its dimensions, colouring, tragedy, and in its wealth of thought shot through with flashes of insight, Landor's trilogy is an unforgettable creation of a powerful and masculine mind.[205]

4

In the various phases of Ambrosio's fall there are certain subsidiary features which gradually attract the attention of the reader. As soon as the passion inspired by Matilda takes possession of the monk, a strange double-life begins. In the daytime the abbot is the most devout priest of his town, a model of impeccability, but his nights are spent in unbridled licence with his beloved. None would suspect him of traffic with the powers of evil, yet in the darkness he weaves dreadful spells and practises magic. He who is most virtuous and pious in the eyes of his fellows slinks through the night like the worst criminal, seeking an opportunity to attack the innocent maiden chosen as his victim. At times this double-life awakens his own horror ; he feels as though another person, some evil being, has taken possession of him, subduing him to its will. While reading the novel a conception is gradually formed of the evil that has hitherto slept in the depths of the monk's soul, to expand at the first opportunity into a second personality, thereby cleaving his spiritual being into two. This feature of a double inward and outward existence was to prove fruitful for the romanticism of terror in the period which followed, leading at length to that strangest invention, the conception of a division of the ego into a good and an evil being. Alongside Ambrosio rise thus such figures as Medardus, the chief character in E. T. A. Hoffmann's novel *Die Elixire des Teufels*,[206] a character of whom, to permit myself a brief digression from the domain of English literature, I shall say a few words in the following paragraph.

Comparing the theme and construction of the two novels, one soon notices that Hoffmann borrowed a good many outward traits from Lewis, and that but for the earlier work the later could hardly have been given its present contents. Medardus is a Capuchin monk who, as the ward of his monastery, soon becomes famous for his learning, his devoutness and gift for preaching. But having drunk the mysterious elixir of the Devil, temptation begins its work in his heart, his sermons are transformed to words of self-righteous hypocrisy, and within him is born a longing for carnal pleasures. He meets with an erotic experience (similar to that of Ambrosio) on seeing his music-teacher's daughter *mit beinahe ganz entblösster Brust.*[207] Like that of Ambrosio his reputation spreads rapidly and the eagerness of the public to hear his sermons is depicted in like manner : " An hour before the bells for assembling, the most aristocratic and cultured portion of the town's inhabitants crowded into the not very large monastery church to hear the sermon of Brother Medardus." Honour is shown him as to a saint and he too, like Ambrosio, possesses the picture of a beautiful woman, Saint Rosalie, with which he is in love and which proves in the end to have been sent by the Devil. Again, to him does a young woman declare her love in the monastery. The result of all these spiritual experiences is that Medardus leaves the monastery and is led to commit a series of appalling crimes. At the moment when lust for pleasure and delight in this world are at their height in his soul, and a discharge of the tension seems necessary, he meets his double, in reality his own brother who is like him in appearance, and having hurled him down a crevice, he dresses himself in his brother's garments and begins in cold blood to impersonate his victim.

Sensual pleasures open out to him, while in his heart a longing for pure love awakens, when suddenly in what is to him an inexplicable manner, his whole being is divided into two. Beside him appears a new Medardus (his brother whom he believes he has murdered), and his conception of his ego is shaken ; he no longer knows whether he dreams he has committed those dreadful crimes, or whether they were the work of the new Medardus, that mysterious, incomprehensible being who never leaves his side. A kind of cloud of horrible delirium seems to descend over the novel, and the reader dimly discerns a series of insane thoughts and actions, feverish visions and presentiments, which convey an oppressive, mystical, enigmatical feeling. Throughout it looms the idea that at the side of good there is everywhere evil to frustrate its endeavours, and that the second Medardus is the embodiment of all the inherited and acquired evil in the real Medardus, wrenched apart at some moment of moral apathy to an individual existence. With this diseased fancy of his weird imagination, with which is bound up a suggestion of the fateful influence (as though from beyond the confines of his own ego) of inherited impulses on the actions of an individual, Hoffmann has achieved effects which oppress the reader with the dreadful weight of probability. The merciless exposure of the most secret impulses of the human soul, which forms the undercurrent of this terrible novel, lends to it a strange and agitating power, the influence of which is penetrative and provocative of thought. In Hoffmann's hands Lewis's theme became endowed with a depth of thought and, in all its weirdness, with a deep humanity.

Hoffmann's novel reminds one of Lewis in other respects also. Matilda has her counterpart in the criminal and lewd Eufemia, who helps Medardus to realize his plans. Aurelie, who like Antonia, represents pure womanhood, worthy of and supported by heavenly love, and with whom Medardus is in love, meets her death at the hands of her lover's mysterious double. The counterpart of the Wandering Jew in *Ambrosio* is a certain enigmatical painter whose conduct bears the same stamp, but who, in reality, is intended to represent Medardus's father. But everything has been transferred to a world apart from the normal sphere of healthy senses, a world where the usual self-revealing characteristics of men are dissolved in air. By these means a complete and harmonious work has been created, fulfilling what was probably always Hoffmann's intention—to hurl the reader into a world where he can no longer make his way with the weapons of common sense and where he becomes the plaything of strange instincts hidden in the remote depths of his soul.

To give a complete exposition of Hoffmann's novel is outside of the boundaries of my present task, nor is it indeed possible to give any clear account of it by description ; the book must be read. One cannot affirm it to be based on Lewis in other than the superficial features referred to, or that *Ambrosio* supplied more than perhaps the first impulse in Hoffmann's mind to create a work of this description. Yet the two books are related, and Medardus marks an epoch in the story of the criminal monk, besides being one of the most effective products of the romanticism of terror, a product which with its spiritual content has developed and interpreted an actual, inexplicable and irresistible atmosphere of romantic terror, welling forth from the depths of its own being in a manner that, at least up to the present, has neither aged nor become ineffective.

Another work to be mentioned in connection with *Ambrosio* is Victor Hugo's *Notre Dame de Paris* (1831). The plan of this work seems difficult of explanation without recourse to Lewis's work. From his earliest youth the Arch-Deacon of Notre Dame, Claude Frollo, has dedicated his life to the Church and

to science, and his devoutness and learning awaken general
respect and procure for him a great reputation. He has
governed his imagination by a severe control of his will, so that
until he meets Esmeralda he has evaded the temptations of
love. At the meeting he is overwhelmed by a superstitious
premonition that the maiden has been sent by Satan to tempt
him, and in his struggle against his passion he is finally led to
destroy the object of his love. Outwardly there is thus a
considerable resemblance, but that is all. Yet it is difficult to
deny to Ambrosio the status of elder brother to Medardus and
Claude Frollo, and thus they form a trio around which the
thrilling material of the romantic movement was spun and
perhaps the highest literary achievements of the school of
terror. A work in itself insignificant can, as described above,
contain the fundamental elements of the highest literary
successes of a later epoch.

The idea of a double life, a parting of good and evil as
though into two separate entities in the same individual, and of
veritable doubles, became an extremely vital theme of terror in
romantic literature. Although there is no longer any question
of monk or priest, one must consider Hoffmann's second powerful novel *Das Fräulein von Scudery* in connection with this same
primary motive. Its chief character, the greatly-respected
and trusted goldsmith Cardillac, lives his days blamelessly, only
to become transformed at the outbreak of night to a monster
who prowls through the streets seeking his victims. True, he is
not driven thereto by the passion of love, but by the desire to
regain the jewels he has sold. This is not due to avarice, but to
some unaccountable attachment to the beauty of the gems, to
a kind of abnormal falling-in-love with the fascination radiat-
ing from jewels. The story of the criminal goldsmith awakens
particular interest because it forms a bridge back to English
literature.

If we consider the possibilities which open out to this
particular school of romanticism for the further development of
the double-life theme, the conflict between good and evil and
the cleavage of the ego into two separate entities, the first
artifice to offer itself is that represented by Medardus. In
his case the division has actually occurred in his imagination,
although by straining his perceptions the reader can conclude
the double, unknown to Medardus, to be his real twin-brother.
A more practical Scot, working in colder blood with the
elements of terror, proved able to deal more clearly with
similar material and yet to achieve as agitating results, though

in a literary sense his success was more modest. An example of the case in point is Stevenson's novel *The Strange Case of Dr. Jekyll and Mr. Hyde* (1886).

Here the element of evil is actually wrenched apart from a human being and transmuted into a new being, not only in a spiritual sense but bodily. The division, or more rightly, transformation is effected by the invention, in itself a little mysterious, of an unknown drug. So Stevenson rejects the Devil's elixir and turns for help to science, whereby he eliminates the mystical element from his story and substitutes for it that instinctive impression aroused in the mind by the mention of strange and terrible unknown drugs discovered by the " adepts " of science. The effect of the drug on Dr. Jekyll is to cause everything good in him to disappear. His noble appearance becomes the prototype of wickedness, his soul a nest of baseness and iniquity ; for this new being sinning is fraught with devilish joy. His pleasure is increased by the knowledge that he need never fear being brought to book for his excesses, as he can at any time regain his former respect-awakening exterior simply by a new dose of the same drug. The position could not have been better for a personation of human wickedness.

A double life now begins. Like Ambrosio or the gold-smith, Dr. Jekyll maintains his former reputation and personality in the daytime, to prowl at night, in the shape of Mr. Hyde, the roads of crime and vice. Horror-stricken, Dr. Jekyll views in the day the deeds of Mr. Hyde, but the temptation to continue is too strong to be overcome ; again and again he resumes the likeness of evil, falling each time deeper into its power. Owing to this, or a too frequent use of the drug, the return to a normal state becomes increasingly difficult. The final catastrophe comes when the supply of the drug is exhausted and to procure more seems impossible. The good in Dr. Jekyll cannot however go on living as Mr. Hyde and elects to leave this life altogether.

The merit of this tale of horror, put together with cool-headed Scotch calculation, lies in its power of affecting the reader, even though it lacks the suggestive power of the story of Medardus, with its realistic, human and yet demoniac representative of the principle of evil and with the allegorical force with which the growing power of evil over its proselytes is depicted. The detachment and quasi-scientific stamp of the novel tempt one to deny to it the atmosphere of romanticism, but its masterly manner of depicting evil in the guise of a human being, capable of being evolved from the noblest soul, awakens a series of compelling moods.

Another of Stevenson's novels, *Markheim* (1885), deals with the dual personality theme. On commencing to rob his victim, a murderer incorporates his own fear and horror and the criminal element within him in the person of a new being who calmly proceeds to advise him, to warn him of the approach of a servant and to bid him hasten. Here also, the materialization of evil awakens the opposition of the good in the man, to such a degree that he decides to give himself up to the police. As soon as the promise of atonement is made the evil being vanishes.

It is not difficult to perceive in Oscar Wilde's *The Picture of Dorian Gray* a modern version of the theme of dual personality in *Ambrosio*, treated with successful romantic colour and suggestivity.

5

With the fallen monk Ambrosio there is thus connected a series of sombre, romantic figures, which seize now upon one now upon the other tributary feature of the general idea for their own particular territory. His direct descendants are those which deal with the conflict between vows and passion waged in clerical bosoms, with passion gaining the victory, a theme recurring frequently in literature.[208] With Faust and Medardus the conception rises of the duality of the human spirit, a conflict which finds allegorical expression in the mysterious doubles of the romanticists. The idea of dual beings is dealt with by Poe in the story of his already referred to *William Wilson*, much in the style of Medardus ; the conception of the materialization of evil as a separate entity is lifted into a wider sphere in his *The Man of the Crowd*.[209] Watching the London crowds, the narrator is drawn to a certain face which attracts his attention in special degree. It is the face of an old man, and in it are depicted a powerful intelligence, caution, parsimony and greed, cold-bloodedness and malice, bloodthirstiness, triumph, merriment, utmost terror and despair. Beginning to follow the old man, the narrator always finds him where crowds are assembled, where either in thought or deed crimes are being committed, and he grasps that the old man is crime personified, the type and spirit of crime, an incarnation of the evil impulses of the crowd, unable to exist in solitude, apart from men. We see here the flashing of a vision of the whole of mankind as a dual personality of good and evil, the effect of which, owing to the dimensions of the vision, are more crushing than a like idea in a single individual.

In the end we find the idea of duality linked up with the study of heredity; a group of motives appears in which a later generation often represents in material form the vices and evil inclinations of its predecessors. Thus in the course of time, from a seed modest in itself but rich in impulses fertilizing to the imagination, a stately tree of motives has grown. The present-day reader, sunk in enjoyment of the exalted mood awakened by the interpretation in music of Tannhäuser's struggle between purity and passion, will do well to recollect that at Tannhäuser's side stands the invisible, gloomy and mournful figure of Medardus,[210] a tragic victim of the same struggle, symbolical in his way of that chain of conflicts between good and evil which never ends in the human heart.

V

THE WANDERING JEW AND THE PROBLEM OF NEVER-ENDING LIFE

I

THE records of the legend of the Wandering Jew begin early. The first written account of it is in Roger of Wendover's *Flores Historiarum*, a chronicle that begins with the Creation and continues to A.D. 1235. The writer, a monk of the monastery of St. Albans, remarks that in the year 1228 a certain " Armenian archbishop " arrived in England, who had with his own eyes seen a famous personage, none other than the man who had witnessed the death of Jesus and was still among the living. The bishop had, indeed, partaken of a meal in his company shortly before his journey. The man had been a guardian at Pilate's gate and was named Cartaphilus ; while Jesus was being taken past him from the place of judgment, he struck the Redeemer on the back with his fist, saying, " Go faster, Jesus, go faster : why dost thou linger ? " Whereat Jesus looked upon him reprovingly (*severo oculo*) and said, " I, indeed, am going, but thou shalt tarry till I come." Soon afterwards Cartaphilus was baptized and was given the name Joseph. He never dies, but at the end of each hundred years he is seized by a sickness culminating in a trance, from which he emerges once again as a man of thirty,— the age he was when Jesus suffered. He remembers every detail connected with the sufferings of Christ and His Resurrection, and is a very grave and pious person. Another friar of the same monastery, Matthew of Paris (d. 1259), copied Wendover's account verbatim into his own *Chronica majora*.

The Biblical foundation of the legend—to start from that point [211]—is to be found in Matthew xvi. 28 : " Verily I say unto you, there be some of them that stand here, which shall in no wise taste of death, till they see the Son of man coming in his kingdom." This mystic prophecy is connected elsewhere in the Bible with the best beloved among the disciples, St. John, as will be seen from John xxi. 21-23: " Peter therefore seeing him (John) saith to Jesus, Lord, and what shall this man do ? Jesus saith unto him, if I will that he tarry till I come, what is that to thee ? " Posterity refused to pay attention, however, to the conditional in this saying and believed that St. John was to live until the second coming of the Saviour. Even when time showed this to be a mistaken interpretation, the belief persisted ; St. John was either alive in his grave or had risen and unknown to the world was living and bearing witness to the words and teachings of Christ. This belief was so tenaciously adhered to that even as late as the seventeenth century a sect existed in England which believed in a coming restoration of the Church to be brought about by the arrival of St. John.[212]

But long before this saying of Jesus had become known through the Gospels, an Oriental tale of similar import was in existence, concerned with Buddha. According to this, a disciple of Buddha, Pindola by name, had transgressed the Master's will and was told that so long as the law held he would not fully attain to Nirvana ; so Pindola went on living in witness of his Master and was still alive in the days of King Asoka. This legend is to be found in Chinese and in Buddhist literature. Carried by Buddhist monks it spread westward until it reached Palestine, where it became interwoven with the legendary material accumulated around the sufferings of Jesus, to be ultimately reflected in the Gospels. Its Oriental origin is further shown by its inclusion in the Koran ; Sameri, the friend of Moses, takes part in the construction of the Golden Calf and is sentenced by Moses to wander eternally over the face of the earth, with fever and plague as companions—a variation in which the element of wandering appears more clearly than in the Buddhist legend. This, however, may be taken from the history of Cain.

In this way a group of Christian legends concerning eternal life on earth came into being, grouped around St. John. A certain record in the Bible served, however, to give a new direction to these imaginings. In John xviii. 22-23 we read : " But when he had said this, one of the officers standing by struck Jesus with his hand, saying, Answerest thou the high priest so ? Jesus answered him, If I have spoken evil, bear witness of the evil: but if well, why smitest thou me? " Christian indignation at such cruelty gave rise to a chain of ideas regarding the punishment suited to such a deed, and resulted in a group of legends concerning the striker of Jesus, who is compelled in these to revolve for ever under the earth around the pillar to which Jesus was bound when He was scourged. Curiosity next arose as to the identity of this monster, and before long the name of a suitable " officer " had been discovered in John xviii. 10 : " Simon Peter therefore having a sword drew it, and struck the high priest's servant, and cut off his right ear. Now the servant's name was Malchus." This man now becomes the striker of Jesus, a darker light being cast on his deed by the fact that a little earlier Jesus had healed the striker's ear at Gethsemane. The legend thus depicts eternal life on earth as a punishment and not as a reward, as in the legend applied to St. John.

From the merging of these two conceptions, and with the basis of the ancient legend of the eternal Wanderer, which had possibly spread to Europe during the Crusades, sprang the legend of the Wandering Jew. The detail found in Spanish variants of a mark of God, a flaming cross, on the Wanderer's brow, reveals the added influence of the story of Cain. " A fugitive and a wanderer shalt thou be in the earth," ran the curse of the Lord, " And the Lord appointed a sign for Cain, lest any finding him should smite him." [213]

The name Cartaphilus which appears in the chronicle of Matthew of Paris hints directly at St. John, who rested in His bosom, for the name Cartaphilus denotes " greatly beloved." In other legends dating back as early as the thirteenth century, the mysterious Wanderer is definitely called John, with the added attribute, however, of " Buttadeus," the first part of this somewhat obscure word being possibly derived from the Italian word *buttare* (to throw, to strike). " Buttadeus " would thus denote " striker of Jesus," and consequently the name John Buttadeus would reflect exceedingly well the merging of the two groups of legends ; both being represented in the name and in the element of eternal wandering, which the legend of Malchus presented in the light of a punishment.

So the legend persists in the three forms represented by Malchus, Cartaphilus and John Buttadeus, now separately, now merged into one another, with different names for the chief character in different countries. On the whole, it seems to have thriven best in the folk-lore of Italy and Spain. In Germany it was practically unknown until the beginning of the seventeenth century, when among those books dealing with miracles which sprang into being as a result of the sudden submersion of Europe in fear of the Antichrist and the end of the world, a work appeared called *Kurtze Beschreibung und Erzehlung von einem Juden mit Namen Ahasverus* (A Short Description and Story of a Jew called Ahasuerus), 1602. This book, of which several editions appeared, tells of a certain bishop whose attention was attracted by the appearance of a strange-looking man of about fifty whom he saw in a church at Hamburg, in 1542. He was tall in stature, with hair hanging to his shoulders, barefooted, dressed in torn nether garments and a cloak reaching to the ground. On being questioned he confessed to being Ahasuerus, the shoemaker of Jerusalem, who had forbidden Jesus to rest before his house on the way to Golgotha and had therefore been doomed to wander eternally. This book helped to make this version of the Ahasuerus legend extremely popular, and was responsible for the accumulation of a considerable mass of literature for and against the story. The name Ahasuerus is taken from the Bible, where in the Book of Esther it is used to denote Xerxes [214] and other rulers of Persia. In France the Wandering Jew became known in the form spread by the popular German version of the legend since the year 1604. A book of special interest is the *Histoire admirable du Juif Errant*, in which certain noteworthy features are added to the wanderer's biography: " I have been struck over a thousand times with swords in battles, for my body is hard as rock. I was at sea and was often shipwrecked; I floated on the water like a feather, although I cannot swim." These qualities bring him nearer to the picture of Ahasuerus provided by later fiction. Such, approximately, is the development of the legend of the Wandering Jew. What the popular belief is on which the idea originally rests has not yet been ascertained.

2

The atmosphere of the seventeenth and eighteenth centuries was unpropitious for the flourishing of so romantic a theme as Ahasuerus; even where this fabulous personage was admitted into literature, it was as a comic character. Thus, Ahasuerus appears in French comedies as a buffoon and a singer of couplets. In *Le Diable Boiteux* Le Sage tells of a wily author who had sold his comedy *The Wandering Jew* to three different publishers. In England the theme fared no better. A book of a satirical tendency appeared in 1640 entitled *The Wandering Jew telling Fortunes to Englishmen*,

PLATE VII

THE WANDERING JEW

(After Gustave Doré)

[*face p. 194*

and as late as 1797, after *The Monk* had seen the light, the publication of Andrew Franklin's comedy *The Wandering Jew or Love's Masquerade*, in which the wooer attires himself as that famed Wanderer, shows that the romanticism of the Ahasuerus legend had never struck a sympathetic chord.

Not until the '70s of the eighteenth century did the legend begin to exert influence on poetry. It touched Goethe's imagination; his notes reveal his intention of writing a poem in which Ahasuerus was to be the chief character, and in his *Wahrheit und Dichtung* he informs us that in his childhood he had obtained a living conception of the Wanderer, from popular books on the subject. He intended his poem to deal with the most noteworthy events in the history of religion and the Church, and imagined a meeting between Ahasuerus and Spinoza, to be depicted in a canto that was to extol the philosophy of the latter. These ideas resulted, however, only in a few fragments written in 1774 and published after the author's death. Its lightly satirical form makes it impossible to divine what Goethe's conception of Ahasuerus had been in that late hour of night during which he hastily wrote his fragment; the Wanderer does not emerge enough to permit us to draw conclusions as to his ultimate rôle. Goethe subsequently used up all his ideas on the subject in working out the parallel legend of Faust.

At that time, however, there was another poet in Germany whose imagination had been touched by the legend of the Jew, namely, Chr. D. Fr. Schubart, who would occasionally forecast to his friends with some enthusiasm the great poem he intended to write around Ahasuerus. He did actually write, in 1783, a " lyrical rhapsody " entitled *The Wandering Jew—* a short work bearing the stamp of sudden inspiration and lacking polish and careful consideration, but for that very reason unaffected and effectual. The agony of Ahasuerus as death evades him becomes impressive as details are accumulated regarding this strange faculty of his ; thus, creeping forth from his dwelling-place in a cave under Mount Carmel, he laments : " I cast myself into the sea from a rock besieged by the clouds, but was dashed by the foaming waves to the shore—I hurled myself into the flaming maw of Etna and was spurned thence on an angry stream of lava," and so on through a long catalogue of seekings after death. With this poem, published in 1787, Schubart lifts with unerring hand the Ahasuerus-theme from the region of folklore into that of artistic literature.

The theme was then taken up by Schiller. In *Der Geister-*

seher (1789) appears a strange Armenian who is responsible for most of the mystery in the work. The chief character, a prince, is pursued in Venice by a mask who bewilders him with his strange prophecies. Later, the same person appears as a Russian officer. " Never in my life had I seen a face of such varying expression and of so elusive a character, so much attractive good-nature paired with repellent coldness. In it every passion seemed to have raged and again to have forsaken it. All that remained was the calm, penetrating glance of the perfect psychologist, which no one might withstand. This man could be anything the moment demanded. No mortal had ever discovered his real identity. No class, no type or nationality existed whose dress he had not worn. I can neither deny nor affirm what is said of him, namely, that he has dwelt for long in Egypt and learned his secret wisdom in a pyramid there. Here he is known only as The Unknown. Trustworthy people relate of his having been seen simultaneously in different parts of the world. The point of a sword cannot pierce him, poison has no effect on him, fire burns him not, the ship on which he travels cannot sink. Time has lost its hold on him, the years cannot dry up the juices of his body nor make gray his hair. No one has seen him eat, he touches no woman and sleep never closes his eyes. So soon as the clock strikes twelve he is no more among the living. This dread hour tears him away from the bonds of friendship, from the very altar, ay, it would recall him from his death-agony. Whither he goes then and what his experience is no one knows. None dare to inquire of him, much less to follow him, for at the advent of that fateful hour his face suddenly takes on so sombre and awesomely solemn an aspect that none are bold enough to look upon him or to address him. The merry conversation of his companions is hushed in a deathly silence and all await his return in respectful terror, without daring even to rise from their seats and to open the door through which he departed. Once only has he neglected to obey his mysterious summons. When the fateful hour struck he was suddenly silent and turned stiff ; his limbs lost their elasticity and his veins ceased to pulse. All the methods used to resuscitate him were in vain. In this state he remained the whole of that hour. When it ended he suddenly regained consciousness, opened his eyes and continued his speech from the syllable at which he had been interrupted."

It is difficult to guess at the part ultimately designed for this character by Schiller, as the story was never completed.

No mention is made of the name Ahasuerus, and, as the reader can see, the picture contains features developed beyond those of the traditional Ahasuerus. Nevertheless, the Armenian is obviously founded upon the legend.

The Wandering Jew emerges into view about this time also in Percy's ballads. The *Reliques* contain a ballad of the Wandering Jew, the preface to which gives an account of the Cartaphilus-legend as depicted by Matthew of Paris, together with the information that the ballad itself is based on the popular German book referred to earlier. His crime and wanderings are described, and it is stated that he has never been seen to smile or laugh ; if he hears anyone swear or take the Lord's name in vain, he invariably chides the culprit, as by such words the Redeemer is crucified anew ; no one, he says, would wish to do so who had seen, as he has, the death of Jesus. In 1785 came the publication at Riga of Reichard's *Der Ewige Jude*, "a historical or a popular romance as the reader wishes," and in 1791, came M. Heller's *Briefe des Ewigen Juden*, in two volumes.

3

All this literary material was available to Lewis when he began *The Monk*. The picture given of the Jew in the episode of Raymond can be traced, in the first instance, to the outlines supplied by Schubart and Schiller. He is looked upon as an alien, but no one knows whence he hails ; he has not a single friend in the town ; he speaks but rarely and never smiles ; he has neither servants nor goods, but his purse is well furnished and he does much good among the townspeople. Some regard him as an Arabian astrologer, others declare him to be Doctor Faust himself. He is of majestic appearance, with powerful features and large, black, flashing eyes ; something in his glance awakens a secret awe akin to horror. His costume is ordinary, his hair hangs in disarray over his forehead, over which a band of black velvet is drawn, adding to the sombre effect of his countenance. His expression reflects a deep melancholy, his steps are slow, his demeanour grave, noble and solemn. He speaks of nations long extinct as though personally acquainted with them. It is impossible to mention a country, however distant, where he has not been, and one cannot sufficiently admire the extent and variety of his knowledge. "No one is adequate to comprehend the misery of my lot ;

Fate obliges me to be constantly in movement; I am not permitted to pass more than a fortnight in the same place. I have no friend in the world, and from the restlessness of my destiny, I never can acquire one. Fain would I lay down my miserable life, for I envy those who enjoy the quiet of the grave; but death eludes me, and flies from my embrace. In vain do I throw myself in the way of danger. I plunge into the ocean; the waves throw me back with abhorrence upon the shore: I rush into fire; the flames recoil at my approach: I oppose myself to the fury of the banditti; their swords become blunted and break against my breast. The hungry tiger shudders at my approach, and the alligator flies from a monster more horrible than itself. God has set his seal upon me, and all his creatures respect this fatal mark." [215] This mark is the flaming, gleaming cross on his brow, which awakens the utmost terror in the beholder. Hence the velvet ribbon across his forehead.

Such is Lewis's painting of the mysterious hero of a romantic tradition; one discerns in it features gathered promiscuously from legends and the literature that had previously appeared on the subject. As Lewis's own contribution I am inclined to regard the Jew's large, black, flashing eyes, whose glance awakened horror, his melancholy and his noble majesty. Lewis obviously modelled his Ahasuerus to conform with a conception inspired by the figure of Montoni, adding with romantic inventiveness a number of extremely effective traits. Thus the deep and penetrating glance found already in Ambrosio is heightened in Ahasuerus to a source of demoniac terror; the monk's countenance, which reveals the general traits of romantic beauty, becomes a mask of tragic melancholy; and finally, the flaming cross sets him apart from common humanity as an individual endowed with superhuman attributes.

The glance of the Wandering Jew, whose sinister power Lewis has so well expressed, is a special characteristic of romantic, saturnine persons, from Eblis (the Oriental Lucifer of *Vathek*) onward, increasing in significance as a source of mysterious influences as attention is drawn to the general possibilities of power in the human eye. The latter half of the eighteenth century was the heyday of Mesmerism, [216] a time when "animal magnetism" and quackery based on that idea were extremely fashionable; the species of "magnetism" which flowed, according to Mesmer, from the human eye, in other words, the hypnotic power of the eye, was adopted by the romanticists to serve their own purposes, its source, the eye, being endowed by these writers with a dark mystical colouring harmonizing with their own special conception of beauty. Whether or no they were influenced by earlier written accounts of a famous glance need not be dwelt upon here ; I will only mention that the Bible provides an account of a glance that has deeply impressed the mind of man : " And the Lord turned, and looked upon Peter. And Peter remembered the word of the Lord, how that he had said unto him, before the cock crow this day, thou shalt deny me thrice. And he went out, and wept bitterly."

Young has depicted this glance in his *Night Thoughts* in the following passage :

> When the cock crew, he wept—smote by that eye,
> Which looks on me, on all : that power, who bids
> This midnight sentinel, with clarion shrill,
> Emblem of that which shall awake the dead,
> Rouse souls from slumber, into thoughts of Heaven.

4

When the legend of the Wandering Jew had reached this stage of development in artistic literature, it was joined by the legend of Doctor Faust. In a way, Lewis had already pointed the road to this legend by allowing his Ambrosio, after the monk had fallen into the power of the Inquisition and suffered torture, to agree to sell his soul to Satan. Matilda, who had already taken this step, appears to the monk in his prison and begins tempting him : " I have sold distant and uncertain happiness for present and secure. I have preserved a life, which otherwise I had lost in torture ; and I have obtained the power of procuring every bliss which can make that life delicious ! The infernal spirits obey me as their sovereign ; by their aid shall my days be passed in every refinement of luxury and voluptuousness. I will enjoy unrestrained the gratification of my senses ; every passion shall be indulged even to satiety ; then will I bid my servants invent new pleasures, to revive and stimulate my glutted appetites. . . . Shake off the prejudice of vulgar souls ; abandon a God who has abandoned you, and raise yourself to the level of superior beings ! " But the monk only succumbs after renewed tortures and after sentence to be burned has been passed on him. Opening at its seventh page the book of incantations given to him by Matilda he reads the first four lines, upon which Lucifer immediately appears, " in one hand a roll of parchment, and in the other an iron pen," offering to take him to pleasures that would last his life through, if he would sign the parchment, in other words, assign his soul to Lucifer. The monk still draws back with horror and Lucifer vanishes, but when the guardians are already, as he believes, on their way to fetch him to the place of execution, he conjures up Lucifer anew and signs the deed with blood from his left hand ; nor is this enough, he has yet to make a verbal promise to belong to Lucifer " for ever and irrevocably." Only then does Lucifer liberate him, though as the reader is aware, it is but to betray and kill him.

The bargain thus made by Ambrosio with his soul as price is an old feature of Christian legends. The first ecclesiastic to escape from a sore predicament by means of a written bargain with Satan was Theophilus, Bishop of Adana ; he was freed, however, by the Virgin. The legend of Theophilus,[217] known already in the tenth century, formed a subject for literature in the Middle Ages, and was one of the forerunners of the legend of Doctor Faust. Marlowe's Doctor Faustus signs with his own blood a deed relating to the sale of his soul. In Number 148 of *The Guardian* (1713) we find " The Story of Santon Barsisa," which Lewis himself states was his source. Alarmed at the great holiness of Barsisa, Satan sends him a king's daughter to heal, thereafter tempting him to sin and ultimately kill his victim. Barsisa is caught and in his danger acknowledges Satan as his god ; in return, Satan promises to save him, but ends up by betraying him.

In 1751 the Benedictine friar Augustin Calmet's work *Dissertation sur les apparitions des anges, des demons et des esprits* was published in Paris, an English translation appearing in 1759. It contains an extensive account of the contract made with the Devil by a German nobleman, Michel Lovis. As regards the deed of sale drawn up between the Frenchman Urban Grandier and the Devil, even the wording has been preserved. Among the legends dealing with human relations with the powers of darkness and mankind's unquenchable lust for pleasure, the form relating to the bargain for a human soul is probably the widest known ; the belief in the possibility of such a bargain gave a gruesome touch of reality to such stories during the persecutions of witches.

The legend of the Wandering Jew is a story of never-ending life on earth bestowed as a punishment ; that of the selling of a soul to the Devil is based on the idea of an exchange of eternal bliss for temporal sensual pleasures ; combined, the two give rise to the legend of the exchange of eternal bliss for everlasting life and happiness on earth, or to the Faust-group, whose two chief elements Lewis thus came to utilize in his romance. Faust's earthly wisdom and the evil results and vanity of his over-great study are comparatively late additions, derived from the circle of legends that sprang up around the alchemists, particularly, perhaps, from those attaching to Friar Bacon, and display an orthodox horror of occultism. With their philosophers' stones and elixirs of life, Friar Bacon's books and legends are well adapted to lead beyond Ahasuerus and Faust to the idea of man himself defying death by supernatural means. It is on this foundation that the legend of the Wandering Jew and Faust proceeds to develop.

The interest taken in these themes by the romanticists, especially in the idea of eternal youth and the prolongation of life by means of an elixir or a Philosophers' Stone, received new nourishment from the mysteries of contemporary wonder-workers and occultists. Mesmer has already been referred to in connection with the magnetic glance ; the mention of eternal youth and health brings up Cagliostro, who, in his *Egyptian Freemasonry* promised to endow the faithful with lasting beauty and to restore them to the state of images of divinity from which sin had caused them to fall. Romantic themes and legends capable of giving rise to mystical chains of ideas seem to have been much in the air during this famous period of " enlightenment."

5

William Godwin's romance *St. Leon* (1799) is the first noteworthy work after *The Monk* to join, in the person of its chief character, the ranks of those described above. It is the life-story of the French knight St. Leon, its first part a precursor of the historical novel, its central and concluding portions a study of the Wandering Jew, of the elixir of life and eternal youth, of the Philosophers' Stone and inexhaustible gold, of social philosophy and psychology. The author is said to have derived his first impulse towards writing it from John Campbell's *Hermippus Redivivus*, which tells of a certain Gualdi,[218] who attracted much attention at Venice in the year 1687. A special feature connected with this character was that he owned a small, but choice collection of pictures, which he willingly displayed to all desirous of seeing it ; also that he was perfectly acquainted with all the manifestations of the arts and science and could discourse on any subject so freely and discerningly as to astonish his audience ; that he never wrote or received letters, never borrowed or exchanged money, though he paid for everything in cash, and that he lived in comfort, if not in affluence. Curiosity was aroused by the fact that a portrait by Titian obviously depicted Signor Gualdi himself, although Titian had lived some hundred and thirty years previously. Then, without a word of explanation, the mysterious stranger disappeared from Venice. Godwin continues : " It is well known that the philosopher's stone, the art of transmuting metals into gold ; and the *elixir vitæ*, which was to restore youth, and make him that possessed it immortal ; formed a principal object of the studies of the curious for centuries. Many stories, beside this of Signor Gualdi, have been told of persons who were supposed to be in possession of those wonderful secrets, in the search of which hundreds of unfortunate adventurers wasted their fortunes and their lives." In this weird story Godwin believes himself to have created a work unlike anything else in existence. As we are aware, this assumption was only partly true ; the legend of the search for eternal youth and pleasure and their successful achievement had been used, though without the elixir of life and the Philosophers' Stone.

Before the meeting between the possessor of the secret of life, a mysterious wanderer, and St. Leon takes place, the latter has lived through the stormy years of his youth and manhood, and sunk with his family into misery from which escape seems impossible. In outward appearance the wanderer is reminiscent of the Wandering Jew : " He was feeble, emaciated and pale, his forehead full of wrinkles, and his hair and beard as white as snow." His glance is wide-awake and lively, suspicious and timid ; his dress is a brown, corded cloak, his support a staff. He says that his name is not Francesco Zampieri, as he had first stated it to be ; yet he is not the Wandering Jew, for he dies without revealing to a soul his birth and real name. He has wandered through many countries, everywhere experiencing disappointments ; he has sojourned at the courts of kings, followed armies, pined in the filth of prisons, tasted every variety of splendour and misery, and with difficulty escaped the executioner's block. He has become a being hated of mankind, bereft of nationality, home and friends. For this reason he has decided to cease from living and to pass on his secrets to another. These secrets are the art of making gold and of prolonging life to eternity, if desired. How this was to be effected the author declines to say, having of course been forbidden to disclose the secret. In depicting the subsequent career of St. Leon, the author shows how the mystic gifts brought upon him the same consequences that had been experienced by Zampieri; they turn him into a being unnatural in every respect, one who, despite all his efforts to the contrary, awakens terror in all who encounter him. True happiness is thus to be found only within the sphere marked out by nature for mankind, in which death forms the logical and liberating end.

Godwin is a poor romanticist. He lacks descriptive power and a suitable scale of colour, and his monotonous, matter-of-fact, expository style is bloodless. With him romantic materials are merely a decoy to entice the reader into following him through the philosophical dissertations and psychological analyses which form the main interest of his books.

When he wrote *St. Leon* Godwin was already a practised author, capable of avoiding direct imitation of the legend of the Wandering Jew. On the other hand Shelley was an inexperienced youth on whom the story of Ahasuerus made a deep effect, being reflected in his thoughts even after he had left behind him the childish romanticism of his youth. In one of the notes to *Queen Mab*,[219] he informs us that a few years earlier he had chanced upon a German work dealing with Ahasuerus, which his translation shows to have been Schubart's *Wandering Jew*. This had appeared in English in 1802 in a publication called *German Museum*. Together with *The Monk* it forms the source for the conception of Ahasuerus found in Thomas Medwin's narrative poem on the subject, in the writing of which Shelley had participated, and whose lines he used later for mottoes to the chapter headings in *St. Irvyne*. January, 1810, is given as the date of *Ghasta or the Avenging Demon*, a work obviously modelled on Raymond's story. In it an apparition whose " form is Majestic, slow his stride," comes to the rescue of a knight assailed by a ghost. A bright flame burns on its brow as it conjures up the spirits of night; in response, the ghost of Theresa appears and declares that the object of her attack on the knight was to take possession of her faithless lover. At once the flame on the eerie stranger's brow is transformed into a cross of fire, at the sight of which the knight falls lifeless to the ground. *The Wandering Jew's*

Soliloquy, written in 1810, depicts the Jew's agony when death refuses to come, and is based on Schubart. Finally, the romance *St. Irvyne or the Rosicrucian* (1811) contains a graphic conception, based on the group of Wandering Jew legends down to the form dealing with the elixir of life, of a mystic individual of this type, with an added touch of the mystery evoked by the word " Rosicrucian."

The person in question is Ginotti, whose unquenchable curiosity has led him to the gate of wisdom and who, by studying the natural sciences, has come to the conclusion that no " First Cause " exists and that it is possible to prolong one's life. His investigations lead him finally to a method by which a human being can prolong his life to eternity. Existence becomes an insupportable burden to him, however, and he seeks a suitable person to whom to impart his secret, for by that act he would be set free to die. Ginotti believes young Wolfstein to be the right man for his purpose and follows him like a shadow, finally handing him the ingredients of his mysterious elixir : " Take and mix them according to the directions which this book will communicate to you. Seek, at midnight, the ruined abbey near the castle of St. Irvyne." The concluding chapter furnishes only a short scene of terror in which the Devil carries off Ginotti ; as Wolfstein is depicted as dying, he has apparently not had time to drink the marvellous potion. Descriptive of the trend of Shelley's youthful philosophy is the unconditional atheism demanded for the achievement of eternal life, a condition exacted also of Wolfstein by Ginotti.

Of greater interest than the actual story of Ginotti, a story outlined with youthful capriciousness and inconsistency, is his outward appearance, which shows the conception of dark, magnetic eyes and the general aspect of the mystical character to be crystallizing into greater perfection. Ginotti's " superior and towering figure " awakens respect even in robbers. Wolfstein starts at his glance as though it were imbued with the power of some commanding supernatural being. He tries in vain to avoid the burning, fascinating glance, which fills him with a quivering fear. When he gambles, a strange person stands at the other side of the table and gazes at him fixedly. Ginotti is of noble presence ; his voice is resonant ; sternness gleams in his eye ; he is of gigantic stature, yet perfectly developed ; his countenance is exceedingly beautiful, dark, beaming with superhuman amiability. When the moon chances to illumine his face, and his burning glance, unbearably bright, falls on his victim, a freezing terror enters the soul of the unfortunate man.

The picture of such a being had bitten so deeply into the youthful Shelley's soul that he endows even Wolfstein (a type of young hero who succumbs to great temptations) with a similar outward apparition. This depictment of outward characteristics—glance, etc.—intended to produce an effect of solemn mystery, together with the mention of the word "Rosicrucian," was bound to attract a follower who would develop the hints thus provided to a higher pitch of perfection from the romantic point of view and a greater capacity for evoking the sensation of terror. That this was just what did happen we shall soon be shown.

Meditating over the existence of a Supreme Being, Shelley returns to Ahasuerus in *Queen Mab*. In the seventh canto the Fairy conjures up Ahasuerus. He is "a strange and woe-worn wight," and "his inessential figure cast no shade upon the golden floor":

> His port and mien bore mark of many years,
> And chronicles of untold ancientness
> Were legible within his beamless eye:
> Yet his cheek bore the mark of youth;
> Freshness and vigour knit his manly frame;
> The wisdom of old age was mingled there
> With youth's primeval dauntlessness;
>   And inexpressible woe,
> Chastened by fearless resignation, gave
> An awful grace to his all-speaking brow.

To him the Spirit then propounds the question: "Is there a God?" to which Ahasuerus answers: "Is there a God!—ay, an almighty God, and vengeful as almighty!" As the enemy of the Almighty, Ahasuerus depicts Him as "the omnipotent Fiend," who created Man only to inflict evil on him; Jesus is a wolf in sheep's clothing, who pretended to teach justice, truth and peace, yet at the same time implanted in the breast of man

> The quenchless flames of zeal, and blessed the sword
> He brought on earth to satiate with the blood
> Of truth and freedom His malignant soul.
> At length His mortal frame was led to death.
> I stood beside Him: on the torturing cross
> No pain assailed His unterrestrial sense;
> And yet He groaned. Indignantly I summed
> The massacres and miseries which His name

> Had sanctioned in my country, and I cried,
> "Go! Go!" in mockery.
> A smile of godlike malice reillumined
> His fading lineaments—"I go," He cried,
> "But thou shalt wander o'er the unquiet earth
> Eternally."

Fearless and unswerving, Ahasuerus has thereafter trodden his eternal path as the enemy of God, mocking at His impotence. Shelley designates him in the end

> The matter of which dreams are made
> Not more endowed with actual life
> Than this phantasmal portraiture
> Of wandering human thought.

In the autumn of 1821, carried away by enthusiasm over the Greek war of independence, Shelley wrote a lyrical drama entitled *Hellas*, in which the Wandering Jew again appears. He is so old that the mountains and the ocean look younger than he; his glance reflects the power of untiring thought, which pierces the past, the present and the future. Whoso wishes to meet him must sail alone at sunset to the island of Demonesi, where the Jew dwells in a cave. Should Ahasuerus be inclined to answer the suppliant's hail,

> . . . a faint meteor will arise
> Lighting him over Marmora, and a wind
> Will rush out of the sighing pine-forest
> And with the wind a storm of harmony
> Unutterably sweet . . .

after which Ahasuerus will appear at the time and place most suitable. Having appeared in answer to the petition of the Sultan Mahmud, he answers that ruler's questions as to the future by declaring the whole of eternity to be only a vision, the dream-picture of a sickened eye:

> Thought is its cradle and its grave, nor less
> The Future and the Past are idle shadows
> Of thought's eternal flight—they have no being:
> Nought is but that which feels itself to be.

> .   .   .   .   .

Thought alone cannot die. The future is reflected on the surface of the past, and just as Mahmud's ancestors once stormed a great city, so in its turn will his power be overthrown.

The theme of the Wandering Jew was ever alive in Shelley's imagination, yet he never used it except as a subordinate motive; the full poetical value of the idea never really dawned on him. Ahasuerus appeared to Shelley, now in his traditional guise; now as the Prometheus-like victim of the eternal curse of God and as His enemy; now as Thought itself, which pierced through every layer to the core of Truth and found nothing immutable save itself.

6

Southey's *Curse of Kehama* belongs in great part to the sphere of the Wandering Jew theme, although its Oriental setting is at first apt to disguise the fact. Kehama is a mighty sorcerer, an instrument of evil, who desires to overthrow God and to usurp His throne; he is thus a sort of Eastern Prometheus though he lacks the justification of a noble motive. Like Vathek he ultimately achieves immortality, but this proves to be an everlasting burning agony in his veins, which causes his body to glow like molten iron. To avenge himself on Ladurlad, who has killed his son, he endows him with eternal life, the sufferings of which were to be enhanced by the knowledge that death could never bring alleviation; but, like Jehovah in *Queen Mab*, he only succeeds in creating for himself an enemy eternally beyond his reach. The moral of the poem is that a virtuous heart and firm mind ever denote freedom and that the power of good is invincible, since, despite all temporary sufferings, it will emerge the victor. The idea of unending life as the worst punishment conceivable clearly hails from the legend of the Wandering Jew.

Lewis makes his elementary personification of the principle of evil watch over the strayings of its victim, guide him to new pleasures and promise him an eternal continuation of these if he will in return surrender his soul—his right to eternal bliss. With Lewis the introduction of the Devil and the realistic depictment of his outward aspect and bargain for a human soul was more important than any close analysis of the spiritual side of the theme; yet all unwittingly he had taken a step towards that threshold behind which terror-romanticism opens out in its deepest, highest-developed and most spiritual form. The scene in which the Devil appears to the doomed Ambrosio and makes use of the monk's desperate plight to entice him into selling his soul was later expanded in Maturin's *Melmoth the Wanderer* into a study of the stubbornness with which mankind clings, even in moments of the greatest misery, to its right to the highest conceivable happiness, eternal bliss.

A reader with the stamina and determination to wade through the endless pages of the last-mentioned work will find it almost impossible to ward off a certain oppressive and suffocating, nightmarish sensation, which increases the farther he reads. The world depicted is not the familiar one, but one envisaged in the light of a feverishly agonized mood, a world duskily-lit and stormy, behind it always an unknown, enigmatical, undefined terror, a force not to be measured or fought against with human weapons. The ruling atmosphere is a half-light reminiscent of Dante's *Inferno* and a paralyzing dread of some unknown, yet nearby terror. Parallel with this general impression, which etches itself mercilessly on the mind in torturing pictures and descriptions shocking in their realistic exactitude, an ineffaceable portrait is given of Melmoth himself, that sombre and mysterious wanderer. Faust and Mephistopheles seem to be combined, in his person, for he has studied both the lawful and unlawful sciences, achieved contact with the Devil and at the price of his soul purchased a term of youth, and now, in the part of Mephistopheles, seeks new victims ; his wanderings and endless persecution of mankind remind one of a being related to the Wandering Jew, namely, the *Bonhomme Misèr* of French folklore ; [220] on the other hand, his tragic, endless migration from one continent to another, undeterred by considerations of time and space, and his sudden appearance at fateful moments recall to mind the Wandering Jew. His awful aspect and great, dark, gloomy and despairing eyes, which resemble those of the Jew, seem to shine in the dark with an enthralling and bewitching light. Proof of the deep and lasting impression their description is capable of making is the fact that Thackeray thought of them on seeing Goethe's eyes. [221] His tragic fate in being compelled, against his better knowledge, to seek new victims, the resulting moods and even his general appearance, all show affinities with Milton's Satan.

An unquenchable desire for knowledge has brought Melmoth to such a pitch that he has exchanged his soul for youth. The bargain has, however, one individual feature attached to it : if he can induce anyone to take his place of their own free will, he is free from his bargain (Ginotti). Hence his mysterious wandering, the purpose of which is to seek out people who have fallen into such utter distress that, to escape further suffering, they are willing to exchange fates with him. To this fundamental idea can be attributed the pictures of dreadful sufferings, for before Melmoth appears with his offer, the fate of his prospective victims must be dire in the extreme. To keep the interest from flagging, the words

Melmoth whispers at such moments are not revealed until in the closing pages.[222] Yet not one of the unfortunates consents. Before casting himself into the sea from a rock, Melmoth says : " I have been on earth a terror, but not an evil to its inhabitants. None can participate in my destiny but with his own consent—none have consented—none can be involved in its tremendous penalties but by participation. I alone must sustain the penalty. . . . No one has ever exchanged destinies with Melmoth the Wanderer. I have traversed the world in the search, and no one, to gain that world, would lose his own soul."

An identical search for a substitute, with the accompanying possibility of escape from a fateful bargain, forms the theme of such stories as Balzac's *La Peau de Chagrin* and Stevenson's *The Bottled Imp*. Balzac was deeply impressed by Melmoth, and even wrote a sequel entitled *Melmoth Réconcilié*.

7

Melmoth attained to lasting youth by the traditional method of making a bargain with the Devil. This method would seem both inadequate and unsuited to those days when the " Gothic " romance had become a subject for mockery. New possibilities of breaking down the barriers to lasting life and youth, of which the final barrier is death, had thus to be sought. It was at this juncture that terror-romanticism received reinforcements in the form of the occultism woven around the legend of a " Rosicrucian Brotherhood," the first work to profit from the impulse being *Zanoni* (1842).

One might call Lord Lytton a reviver of the " Gothic " romance and find proof for the assertion in the literary form of *Zanoni*. According to its preface, the book is merely the translation of a manuscript given by a mysterious and peculiar old man to the person publishing the work. The translator had made his acquaintance while engaged in studying the origin of the " Rosicrucian Brotherhood," and had found the old man possessed of expert knowledge regarding the doctrines of that secret brotherhood. Concerning his birth and earlier fortunes the old man had been dumb ; he had written his work in cipher, happily furnishing it, however, with a key. Not content with a cipher, closer study of the 940 dreadful foolscap sheets of manuscript reveals that their author had really written two versions of his work, one more comprehensive than the other, thus saddling the translator with the hard task, extending over years, of deciphering and completing their contents.

The nearest source for the study of the origin, fortunes and doctrine of the Rosicrucians, a source open also to Lord Lytton, is Thomas de Quincey's series of articles in *The London Magazine* of 1824, under the heading " Historico-Critical Inquiry into the Origin of the Rosicrucians and Freemasons." [223] I am also inclined to regard it as certain that for many of its details *Zanoni* has to thank Shelley's *St. Irvyne*, whose Wolfstein and Ginotti reappear as Glyndon and Zanoni.

In construction *Zanoni* is a " romantic book," " truth for those who can comprehend it, and an extravagance for those who cannot," as the introduction states. The first part, " The Musician," introduces the reader to the youth of the second chief character of the book, the singer Viola, a character whose whole soul is filled with music ; " associations, memories, sensations of pleasure or pain, all were mixed up inexplicably with those sounds that now delighted, and now terrified— that greeted her when her eyes opened to the sun, and woke her trembling on her lonely couch in the darkness of the night." It is as though the " phantoms of sound " perpetually surrounded Viola, as though she were a daughter of music, a denizen of the invisible world of faerie rather than a being of the material world. Thus the First Part is endowed with a bright yet mystical atmosphere of music. The Second Part is called " Art, Love and Wonder." What God is to nature, so must Art be to Man—majestic, inspiring, delightful and warming. Seeking Truth it ever avoids Reality ; it rises to lordship over nature becoming not its slave. Science discovers, Art creates. Love is wisdom, the greatest gift of life, its full value being manifest only to those who have experienced the futility of all else. It is unselfish and bound up with sacrifice. The Wonder is that world hidden from Man, beyond life and the material, which the door of secrets opens only to the chosen few. The Third Part is called " Theurgia," and introduces the reader to the "Rosicrucian Brotherhood," and to the teachings and fortunes of Zanoni and Mejnour.[224] The title of the Fourth Part, " The Dweller of the Threshold " is derived from the dread being who guards the door to perfect knowledge. The Fifth Part, " The Effects of the Elixir," describes what happens to the novice in secret wisdom who has not been strong enough to overcome the " Dweller of the Threshold." The Sixth Part, " Superstition deserting Faith," is an account of the consequences to mankind of discarding the truths of religion and of giving themselves up to superstition. The Seventh and concluding part, " The Reign of Terror," is a description, written in the spirit of the preceding part, of the terrors of the French Revolution. This division and the frequent use of mottoes quoted from mystical literature is in itself sufficient to impart a deeply mystical quality to the book, an impression heightened on closer acquaintance with its contents.

According to Zanoni, an invisible world peopled by spirits exists parallel with the visible world. The material nature of man prevents him from seeing these beings, which are notwithstanding linked up with his fate. There are spirits both of light and of darkness, the former led by the exquisite Adonai, the latter by the mystical Evil, an indefinable Terror and a mysterious " Dweller of the Threshold." If Man is strong enough to overcome the fetters of the material and to brave the terrors placed in his path by the " Dweller of the Threshold," the laws of mortality will no longer apply and there is no obstacle to his living in the world as long as he desires, ever young and human, yet freed from the fetters enjoined on humanity. But he must take care to prevent any mortal interest such as love from defiling the noble and passionless clarity of his soul, for in that case he will lose in corresponding degree the divine qualities he has achieved and will sink gradually to the level of common humanity. In the dim past, by purifying their souls certain Eastern philosophers had succeeded in becoming increasingly free from the fetters of the material, and by the strength of their intellect and will, aided by secrets wrested from nature, had penetrated so far that they had discovered the means by which the threshold could be crossed. The noble strength of their souls and the purity of their motives had enabled them to endure the terrible final struggle with Evil, and thus they had risen to be lords of Death and mortality.

Such was the origin of the sacred Rosicrucian Brotherhood, whose high purpose was to create a new race in the world, lacking the weaknesses and vices of Man, and by the power of their knowledge, even to conquer new planets. Whether ordinary human life, love in particular, had proved strong enough to exert its fascination on the Brotherhood, is left untold ; in any case, only two adepts are left when the story opens, Zanoni and Mejnour. The former represents youth, the principle of Art in the universe, the latter calculating age and science, being consequently calmer and less disposed to passion than his comrade, keeping his glance fixed on the attainment of increasingly perfect knowledge. He it is who labours for the great aim of the Rosicrucians, and scours the whole world for suitable adepts, though without success, for human beings capable of facing the terrors of the " Dweller of the Threshold " are born but once in a thousand years. This is sufficient to cast a tragic light over the two " Theurgists," who have the interests of humanity at heart, a tragedy subsequently increased by Zanoni's sacrifice of his life in the cause of mortal love.

The first mark of identification that enables us to place Zanoni is his glance. He is able to impart to it such power that he can govern the minds of others, either to purity and uplift or to cast down. The " lustrous darkness " of his eyes is irresistible, and the superstitious aver that he has the true evil eye, *mal-occhio*. Outwardly, Zanoni is indescribably beautiful, majestic in stature, bearing and demeanour, and at the same time he is mysterious and spectral, like an apparition from another world. He has a boundless capacity for enjoying life, which he does in a pure idealistic way, exerting a purifying and uplifting effect on his company. No one knows whence he has come ; the most marvellous tales are related of him ; every race and every country, with all their conditions, customs and languages seem familiar to him. His boundless wealth, his knowledge of Oriental languages, the stately calm that never leaves him even in his merriest moments, the dusky sheen of his eyes and hair, his small, carefully-tended hands, the Arabian contours of his skull, all seem to hint at kinship with some Eastern race. Many old persons profess to have seen him in different parts of the world in the days of their youth, yet his appearance has not changed. It is as though Zanoni were a new Adonis, a youthful symbol of divine beauty and the birth of light. Such is Zanoni's personification of the mysterious wanderer of literature whose track we have followed from Schiller's *Der Geisterseher*. He combines several features of the legends dealt with earlier, but rises to the position of an eternal symbol of Art, a poetical vision of its divine beauty, of its purifying influence, and, not least, of its immortality.

Beside him we find a second mysterious being, Mejnour, the symbol of reflective age, of science, of eternal seeking and investigation. " Mejnour seemed wholly indifferent to all the actual world. If he committed no evil, he seemed equally apathetic to good. His deeds relieved no want, his words pitied no distress. What we call the heart appeared to have merged into the intellect. He moved, thought, and lived, like some regular and calm abstraction, rather than one who yet retained, with the form, the feelings and sympathies of his kind." Thus he is made to symbolize science in its absolute form, elevated above human frailty. His life is devoted to philosophical meditation, as Zanoni's is devoted to pleasure.

With rather more boldness than we have hitherto been accustomed to find in terror-romantic literature, the author endows his wanderers with supernatural qualities. By hypnotic means they can cause a person to prophesy future events, as Zanoni does the author Cazotte, using the opportunity to conjure up a picture of the tyranny and horrors of revolution as the result of and the reaction to the optimism of the age of enlightenment. The laws of time and space no longer apply to them, nor can the elements affect them; they can become invisible at will. In their science they have progressed so far that their apparatus and laboratory resemble those of the alchemists and recall to mind the mysterious rites of the occultists, without being of the nature of either. Mejnour's laboratory is situated in a medieval castle perched in an inaccessible corner of the Apennines. When Glyndon, his pupil, chances to enter without his teacher's consent, he becomes aware of a strange, unrecognizable odour and sees the room filled with a kind of billowing mist. A mortal coldness overwhelms him and he believes himself to see dim, mighty beings in the mist. He is saved by Mejnour and thus learns how dangerous contact with the unknown can be for the uninitiated. Stored away in this laboratory Mejnour preserves mysterious " Rosicrucian lamps," nine in number, an elixir of life with a rejuvenating effect on the organism and a mystical book of knowledge which explains how the frontier to knowledge can be crossed. But in all this there is no magic, only the purest science. Mejnour knows no method of placing death beyond the reach of his own will—he can die if he so desires—but by ceaselessly studying nature he has learned all the secrets of the human body, including the causes of the hardening of the arteries and the slowing-down of the circulation, and finally discovered an elixir by means of which the body can be repeatedly renewed. The matter is merely, says Mejnour, one of the ultimate achievements of medical science.

The vague philosophy of *Zanoni* could be made the theme of endless discussion, but for our present purpose the above account of it will suffice. It shows the dimensions to which a romantic author could expand the old theme of a type of human being entitled to ask in a material sense—" O Death, where is thy sting ? " The conception of the gift of eternal youth had sunk deep into Lytton's soul and was used by him a second time in his famous story *The Haunted and the Haunters, or the House and the Brain* (1859).[225] This story deals with a mysterious person who lives in perpetuity and who has at one time " loaded " a certain house with a fearful spirit of evil that acts inimically on all who enter. This person has ensured the uninterrupted working of his will by a kind of half-magnetic, half-cabbalistic accumulator, which he has concealed in a secret cupboard. Not until the narrator has steeled his will to an extent that makes him able to endure the terrors of a nightly ghost-scene, is the dread influence broken, so that the house can be searched and the terrible apparatus destroyed. Be it noted that this mystery-person, too, has a piercing glance, riveting as a snake's. In him the theme of a human being who need never die brought, in its development to terror-romanticism, the modern features of hypnotism or mesmerism, electricity and the transference of thought or feeling by will-power.

In *Zanoni* Lytton created a work which is in many respects still effective and impressive. Theosophists see in it a manifestation of hidden wisdom, as though one of the invisible spirits mentioned in it had moved the author's pen. Its basic theme, the idea of a human being who has achieved mastery over matter, is still alive in literature, giving rise to a constant output of eerie stories in which the prolongation of life and rejuvenation of soul and body are dealt with in different ways. Its suggestive element is so well thought out, its diction in the most mystical passages so purposely indefinite and bewildering to the critical faculties, and its whole contents, owing to the frequent flashes of paradoxical argument and poetry, so fascinating, that even the present-day reader feels a strange enchantment breathe from some of its pages.

Continuing on the track of the idea so tempting to terror-romantic writers, of eternal life on earth, we come in our own times to H. Rider Haggard's *She, She and Allan* and *Ayesha*. The chief character in these books, Queen Ayesha, has succeeded in acquiring eternal youth and beauty by bathing in a marvellous spring of fire that wells forth in one of the most hidden caves in the heart of darkest Africa. From the historical point of view these works are interesting as reviving the old romanticism of terror, particularly as one cannot help connecting the picture of Ayesha and the Fire of Life with Southey's *Thalaba*. The poem contains mention of a magic garden and " a fount of fire," that fed the garden " with the heat of life." This spring washes away all worldly stains ; the scene of Maimuna's liberation from the fetters of magic and eternal youth, when the added weight of all her years falls suddenly upon her, finds its counterpart in the final scene in *She*. In Laila the basic features of Ayesha are already encountered, while Okba, the " old man " of the poem, assumes an extremely familiar air if we compare him with Rider Haggard's wise old men. The enormous cave in *She*, the ancient repository of the mummies of former generations, recalls to mind the grave-city of *The Curse of Kehama : " So well had the embalmers done their part that each corpse had still the hue of living man—statues of actual flesh—a fearful sight ! Their large and rayless eyes— glazed, fixed and meaningless. . . ."* Comparing Southey's poems with Rider Haggard's novels one cannot help drawing certain conclusions, the correctness of which seems irrefutable, namely, that the novelist has been influenced in his choice of material by the poems, and that in their general character— in the invention of adventures, in settings, battle-scenes and a predilection for exotic romanticism of a fabulous nature— the poems are like *Ayesha*-books in verse form. Finally, Southey's idea of the achievement of eternal beauty by sorcery and of mummies resembling living beings leads via *Ayesha* direct to Pierre Benoit's *L'Atlantide*, of whose imitative relationship with the conceptions dealt with above there can be no doubt.

8

The above depicts in some degree the part played by terror-romanticism in the flights of imagination evoked by the legends of the Wandering Jew and Doctor Faust. As we have seen, the school quickly freed itself from the traditional materials of the legends and invented its own characters to interpret the mystery which attaches to the idea of eternally living human beings. Meanwhile, the story of Ahasuerus persisted in its traditional form, becoming the starting-point for a great mass of literature and by its mysticism ever in- spiring new poets to try the strength of their imaginations and to sound the depths of their philosophies. An elucidation of this extensive literature is beyond the province of the present work, yet a brief review of the ideas which the theme has been used to express is necessary to round off my own exposition.[226]

To deny death to Ahasuerus was to acknowledge the liberating significance of death. Nothing could have been better suited to the ascetic conception of the Christian Faith, for according to this view, human life is at its best but sorrow and suffering. Thus the longing for death experienced by Ahasuerus could be made to interpret the Christian's desire to cast off the fetters of mortal life. The chief idea of Schubart's poem centred around the agony of endless life and the significance of death as a doorway to freedom.[227]

The endless wanderings of the Jew made him a living witness to history and therefore a suitable vehicle for ideas concerning the vicissitudes and future of humanity. This side of the theme was exploited in several narratives at the end of the eighteenth and beginning of the nineteenth century.[228]

His endless life and wanderings could also be conceived simply in the light of a punishment and as a penance for the lack of pity displayed by him towards Jesus. Consequently, he is reflected in Christian thought as an eternal warning against unbelief and sin against God. This is the part assigned to him, despite all the attributes of fabulous romance showered upon him and his high duty, in the lowest type of cheap pedlar-romances. The same conception of his personality can likewise be made to serve as an excuse for making his history depict the conversion of an atheist and a doubter, and for placing in his adventures visionary scenes of the fortunes of mankind.[229]

His nationality gave rise to the conception of him as a symbol of the homeless, wandering, yet indestructible Jewish race. From the Christian point of view he symbolizes the Jews as an accursed race bowed under their punishment ; on their part, the Jews conceive him as the martyr of all the oppression and the wrongs endured by them, and as the symbol of their hopes and strivings. This agony and upward striving of the Jew forms the fundamental theme of many works dealing with Ahasuerus ; [230] and the conception tends logically towards a gradual view of Ahasuerus as the mouthpiece and pioneer of national and social liberty, and as the tragic, vanquished hero of aspirations of this nature. The unresting, scorned vagrant of the world becomes the spirit of Liberty, to whom a resting-place is ever denied.[231]

The Wandering Jew's perpetual sorrow, his loneliness and alienation from mankind, his estrangement from human passions and his eternal longing for peace, all of which burn fiercer as he perceives the hopelessness of his desires, make him the symbol of *Weltschmerz*. This world-weariness and its resulting melancholy are joined by a titanic defiance, by anger provoked by the hardness of fate. Thus Ahasuerus becomes enriched with qualities taken from the picture of Prometheus, and rebels, as the friend of mankind, against the Godhead. Byron and Shelley, the poets of world-sorrow, were themselves homeless wanderers, titanlike in defiance, kin with Ahasuerus, each like Childe Harold,

> The wandering outlaw of his own dark mind.

This conception is a logical outcome of the two preceding ones ; Jewish liberty—national and social liberty—the liberty of all mankind from the fetters that bind it.[232]

Even social reformers have not despised the legend. The poor shoemaker of Jerusalem has been conceived in the light of a symbol of all poverty-stricken and landless wage-earners, for whom peace in death is possible only when the conditions of the poor have been improved and their bonds shattered. Of such nature is Eugène Sue's picture of Ahasuerus, whom he provides, moreover, with a wife, Herodias, the eternal Jewess ; rest in the grave is to be attained by her when the shameful slavery imposed on women is ended.

The foregoing account of the different conceptions to which the legend of Ahasuerus gave rise shows its peculiar adaptability to the most different purposes. This might be esteemed its strongest point were it not at the same time its weakest. It provides material for too many interpretations and lacks one dominant, central idea capable of exhausting its possibilities. Contrary to what happens in the Faust-theme, in which love of life is regarded as the decisive factor in human life, the Ahasuerus-theme reflects too many different facets, each full of inspiration in itself, but leading unfortunately to a mysticism so far beyond the experiences of common flesh and blood that it is difficult to find adequate expression for it in poetry. Owing to this, Ahasuerus must still await the great poet who alone can conclude his wanderings and grant peace both to him and to writers, as Goethe granted peace to Faust.

The history of the theme shows that among Europeans the Germans have worked hardest at it ; in England it never became as popular as the alchemistic and Rosicrucian offshoots which resulted from the combination of the Ahasuerus and Faust legends.[233]

VI

THE BYRONIC HERO

I

THE reader will remember that in *The Castle of Otranto* there appeared a dark, gloomy and passionate tyrant, a type later cultivated with great zest by Mrs. Radcliffe. The outward characteristics include a high, white forehead shadowed by ebon curls, a dark, piercing glance, general beauty of countenance, a manly character and a mysterious past. Behind his melancholy we can discern Hamlet, Eblis in *Vathek* and Milton's Satan,[234] who share with him the dark glance and the defiance that dwells in his soul; Lovelace and Zeluco, too, are not far removed and contribute to the hints of the tragedy that enslaving passions bring their victims. Falkland in *Caleb Williams* and Bethlem Gabor in *St. Leon* loom in the background, representing hatred and a fear of mankind not without a touch of the abnormal. We have further seen the tendency of the criminal monk, the Wandering Jew and the Rosicrucian philosophers to attire themselves in the outward features of this type. Obviously there was formed a kind of approved composite portrait, recognizable as such whenever an author of the period occupied himself with the type.

An indication that this figure is modelled on a purely English literary tradition is the appearance, though admittedly in a tamer and less noticeable form, of Mrs. Radcliffe's dark hero in the works of the Lake Poets. In Wordsworth's play *The Borderers*, written as early as 1795-96, Oswald is a manifestation of Montoni, further equipped with the wickedness of Iago. Tempting his chief to commit murder, he observes, on perceiving the latter to hesitate:

> It may be,
> That some there are, squeamish half-thinking cowards,
> Who will turn pale upon you, call you murderer,

And you will walk in solitude among them.
A mighty evil for a strong-built mind !
                              Solitude !

.   .   .   .   .

The Eagle lives in solitude.

In his youth Oswald has been a general favourite, the
"darling of every tongue " ; he travels to Syria and believing
himself to be the victim of a plot between the captain and
crew of the ship, revenges himself by marooning the captain
on an uninhabited island, subsequently hiding in a convent
until he can join the Crusaders, in whose ranks he does deeds
of valour. Yet he is a lonely being, his path is solitary, his
thoughts are morbid self-analysis and a desire to expand the
intellectual kingdom of mankind. His motive in inciting
Marmaduke to murder is to obtain a comrade in misfortune,
one who will share his loneliness. Wordsworth's play was
published so late that it cannot have influenced any writer of
his day, yet it shows clearly that the existence of this gloomy
dreamer was recognized in England at the end of the eighteenth
century and that attempts were made to depict him in poetry.

This emerges also from Coleridge's work. In his play
Remorse (the first version of which was written in 1797, but
which was not performed until 1819), Ordonio, the usurper
of his brother's inheritance and claimant for the hand of his
bride, is one of these sombre, conscience-ridden criminals ;
the influence of the *Geisterseher* discernible in the plot does not
entitle us to conclude that the picture of Ordonio was derived
from Schiller, for in all its details it can be traced back to
the line Manfred-Montoni. Southey, too, permits this dark
visage to appear in his poetry : Kehama's most characteristic
feature is

His dreadful frown—
His dark lineaments—
Protruded brow, gathered front,
The steady eye of wrath.

A corresponding type appears in Germany about this time
in Schiller's Karl Moor, notable for his Prometheus-like
defiance, his love of liberty and hatred of mankind. He is
more titanic and has higher aspirations than his English
brother, but is devoid of mystery and open-browed, being conceived in all probability under the combined influence of
Milton, Shakespeare and Götz von Berlichingen. *The Robbers*
appeared in an English version in 1792.

The element of hatred finds powerful expression in

Godwin's *St. Leon*, where it is represented according to the Schiller tradition, in the Hungarian robber-baron Bethlem Gabor. In Leon's eyes, Gabor resembles a sullen, mysterious tyrant ; his castle, with its subterranean passages and dungeons being also a perfect replica of the haunted castle of the romantic tyrant. He has not always been the man we find him ; not until a great injustice was done him did he become a misanthropist. As the reasons and motives for deeds are much the same for all men, Gabor sees no reason for discrimination, but hates all mankind impartially. Finding Leon's experiences to coincide with his own, he feels friendship for him, but when Leon, despite his misfortunes, attempts to do good, Gabor's friendship is transformed into a bitter hatred, for he can permit no one to love mankind. In this misanthropy Gabor remains firm until the end, when he is buried under the ruins of his robber's castle.

In France, the line commenced by Rousseau had resulted in a national gallery of heroes representing world-sorrow : Saint-Preux (Werther), René, Obermann and Adolphe. There is more sentimental world-sorrow in the French hero than in the Byronic type, whose predominant features are mystery and defiance. In his *Mémoires* Chateaubriand certainly seems to regard Childe Harold almost as his own invention, but René is in nowise necessary for the birth of Childe Harold. Each of these lines of development reflect different aspects of the same great yearning that possessed the Europe of those days.

The progenitor of the Byronic hero is thus, on the basis of discoveries made in following the line Hamlet-Manfred-Montoni-Bethlem Gabor with their related subordinate characters, a purely English literary type, and even during its development its enrichment from alien sources is doubtful. Especially must care be taken not to place Karl Moor at the head of this family tree, for he is not the father of the Byronic hero but a parallel German phenomenon, a brother sharing a distant common ancestor in Shakespeare-Milton. The English branch leads straight to Sir Walter Scott and his poetical works.

2

To encounter Scott on this voyage of investigation is as natural as it was on our pursuit of the picture of the haunted castle. He had adopted the whole world of Walpole, Mrs. Radcliffe and Lewis, and with bounteous hand proceeded to enrich it from his own treasures of folklore and history. Knowing his admiration for Mrs. Radcliffe, one can hardly be mistaken in expecting his own work to show some Montoni-like character, slightly transformed perhaps by Scott's more virile temperament. A glance at his poetical works shows this assumption to be correct.[235]

The Lay of the Last Minstrel provides only a stray feature or two from William Deloraine and Lord Dacre. The first of these is a border knight, " steady of heart, and stout of hand," who has been outlawed no less than five times. He does no penance and scarce knows a prayer, unless perhaps his " Ave Maria." He is a black-browed man with a proudly-waving plume in his helmet. Meeting an enemy

> Stout Deloraine nor sighed nor prayed,
> Nor saint, nor ladye called to aid.

Lord Dacre is " a wrathful man," " fierce " and " haughty," the latter trait furnishing the permanent attribute attached to his name. We are given, moreover, the sketch of a soldier with a " coal-black hair, shorn round and close," which sets off " his sun-burned face." When Conrad of Wolfstein insults the " hot and hardy " Rutherford and is believed to have been secretly murdered by the latter in consequence, one is instantly reminded of the first impulse for the similar crime in *Lara*.

Marmion brings us nearer to the terror-romanticism of the preceding decades, for it is practically a condensed, poetical exposition of the school in question. Attention has already been drawn to those features which connect it with its pre-decessors and which indicate at the same time the soil whence it has sprung ; next to these, the greatest interest attaches to its chief character, the knight Marmion.

His face reveals him as a stern warrior, who has fought in many battles. His eyebrows are dark, his eyes of fire, their flashing denoting a proud and hasty temper ; on the other hand the lines of thought which seam his face testify to a capacity for hatching " deep design and counsel." His forehead is high, his moustache thick, his hair curly and coal-black, grizzled here and there, due more to toil than to age. His " square-turned joints " show him to be no " carpet-knight," but a " champion grim " in battle and a sage leader in camps. His arrival at the head of his men at Norham Castle reminds one of the sword-bearing procession in *The Castle of Otranto*, especially as attention is drawn to his magnificent plumed helmet and the great lance borne by two men. His expression grows dark when questioned regarding the absence of his beautiful squire, in reality a truant nun, his mistress, who had followed him dressed in male attire. One is again reminded of *Lara* by this female companion who dresses like a man. Later, too, when Marmion goes out at night to break a lance with the ghost of the man he thinks he has killed, only to discover later that his opponent is living flesh and blood, the scene seems somehow to be related to the enigmatical vision of terror seen by Lara in his castle.

A trait shared by Marmion with the barons of earlier terror-romance is the criminality and violence of his nature, but he differs from them in feeling pangs of conscience and remorse, and as he is unable, despite the possession of a conscience, to obey his better instincts, the result is an endless conflict in his soul. It is said that he scarce received for gospel what the Church believed. An atmosphere of mystery and impenetrability is gradually woven around his person. The sombre colouring of the poem is darkened by de Wilton's picture of his lust for revenge, how he broods " on dark revenge, and deeds of blood." But Marmion is clearly an object of admiration to the romantic muse ; his brave nature, the gloom and strangeness of which is perhaps due to his criminality and recklessness of consequences, raises him " in fearful beauty " above the other characters, to dominate at last the whole of Flodden Field—like Lara in his last battle, where he too has a beloved woman to comfort him. When Marmion is laid in a nameless grave, he leaves behind him the memory of a brave and admirable knight.

To my mind, the romantic admiration displayed for Marmion, which is expressed with the utmost clarity and even infects the reader, is in the first place something novel when compared with his predecessors, while in the second place it is exactly what Byron aimed at in his own sombre hero. Marmion thus becomes, in a quite special sense, a bridge between two stages of development ; he emerges from the ranks of conventional tyrants, cast more or less in the same mould of terror-romanticism, to represent that romantic individual of stormy passions and conflicts, crime, heroism and ambition who was later to reap such unbounded admiration.

The Lady of the Lake is brighter and gaudier in general tone and merrier in melody than the dark-hued *Marmion*. Gazing upon a beautiful mountain lake, the poet declaims in fine Radcliffe style :

> How blithely might the bugle-horn
> Chide, on the lake, the lingering morn !
> How sweet, at eve, the lover's lute
> Chime, when the groves were still and mute !
> And, when the midnight moon should lave
> Her forehead in the silver wave,
> How solemn on the ear would come
> The holy matins' distant hum,
> While the deep peal's commanding tone
> Should wake, in yonder islet lone,
> A sainted hermit from his cell.

To the poet the shores of the lake are exactly what he means by the word " romantic." The poem thus reflects the bright lyrical beauty of Loch Katrine, interpreted in the manly spirit and with the love for his native landscape that characterizes Scott. The lyrical effect of the poem is heightened by the picture given of the Lady of the Lake.[236]

Romantic gloom and passion is represented in the person of Roderick Dhu. He is

> . . . brave,
> But wild as Bracklinn's thundering wave ;
> And generous—save vindictive mood,
> Or jealous transport, chafe his blood :
> I grant him true to friendly band,
> As his claymore is to his hand.

But although his noble qualities shine clear,

> They make his passions darker seem,
> And flash along his spirit high,
> Like lightning o'er the midnight sky.

Ellen Douglas relates how, as a child—

> I shudder'd at his brow of gloom,
> His shadowy plaid, and sable plume ;
>   .   .   .   .   .
> His haughty mien and lordly air.

In describing the mountain chieftain the poet makes use of

terms such as " moody aspect," " haughty brow," " darkened brow,"

> . . . where wounded pride
> With ire and disappointment vied,
> Seem'd, by the torch's gloomy light,
> Like the ill Demon of the night,
> Stooping his pinions' shadowy sway
> Upon the nighted pilgrim's way—

" deep anguish of despair " which bursts in fierce jealousy to air ; " goading thought " ; " sullen " ; " he yields not, he, to man nor Fate," and when he dies, he draws his last breath " motionless and moanless," or as the poem says :

> His face grows sharp, his hands are clench'd,
> As if some pang his heart-strings wrench'd ;
> Set are his teeth, his fading eye
> Is sternly fix'd on vacancy.

Depicting her own fate, Blanche describes him in the following words :

> When thou shalt see a darksome man,
>
> .   .   .   .   .   .
>
> With tartans broad, and shadowy plume,
> And hand of blood, and brow of gloom,
> Be thy heart bold, thy weapon strong.

To me these lines reveal that here also the picture of the dark hero of romance confronts us, arrayed as a mountain chieftain. We find him again as the central character of the poem, an object of fearful admiration, exalted with his magnificent gestures, his romantic passion, conflicting emotions and defiance into a " sublime " hero.

In many other features *The Lady of the Lake* reveals its relationship with the themes of the period and with its predecessors. When the unknown knight enters the refuge on the island, the old family sword leaps from its scabbard and falls to the ground, an infallible omen (already familiar from *The Castle of Otranto*) of something important about to happen ; the same knight sees in a dream a phantom whose helmet " slowly enlarged to giant size "—in fact, to the size of the famous helmet of Otranto. When the old bard calls Ellen " The Lady of the Bleeding Heart," one has a momentary vision of a famous nun. Ideal lyrical landscapes are varied occasionally in the poem by wild mountainous romance :

> It was a wild and strange retreat,
> As e'er was trod by outlaw's feet.
> The dell, upon the mountain's crest,
> Yawn'd like a gash on warrior's breast.

Nor does the poem lack our faithful friend the old haunted castle, with the heavy keys of its dungeons hanging on a rusty hook, with torches, fear-awakening corridors echoing with the clanking of fetters and the laments of prisoners, a wheel for breaking stubborn captives, executioners' swords and dreadful instruments of torture. In such a castle the persecuted Ellen suddenly hears a beautiful romantic song, which issues from the lips of a lovesick youth. The youth's confession of love is intended for Ellen's ears. Throughout its whole length we find thus woven into the poem little romantic features already familiar to us.

In *Rokeby* (1813) the dark colouring is varied by the introduction of a number of new themes gladly received by later romanticists. In the first place attention is drawn to Oswald, who is inclined to greed and the most cruel crimes, and whose " conscience, anticipating time, already rues the enacted crime," disturbing his sleep ; a weak and ignoble character. Like the romantic criminal, he tossed on his bed, harassed by tormenting dreams, and

> Woke—to watch the lamp, and tell
> From hour to hour the castle-bell,
> Or listen to the owlet's cry,
> Or the sad breeze that whistles by.

Something in his mistrust and the baseness of his character reminds one of Byron's Werner. There is in Oswald, as in Werner, nothing particularly descriptive of the romantic hero ; both are pitiable creatures, lacking the glamour of poetry. The real hero of *Rokeby* is the adventurous robber Bertram, who is partly responsible for the birth of a character like Werner's son Ulric,[237] and side by side with him his former friend and comrade in battle Mortham, who represents the higher and nobler qualities of the type.

When Bertram visits Oswald in the night, he comes with " heavy stride " ; his face is overshadowed by the plumes of his helmet and around his giant's body a spacious cloak is wrapped. There is much that is fear-awakening in his aspect : life and the torrid sun have set their mark on his dark countenance, furrowing his brow and sowing grey in his hair, but leaving untouched the " lip of pride " which " upward curled " and was never " by terror blenched," and the " eye of flame " which " seemed to scorn the world," knew naught of tears and flashed with swarthy glow, which " mock'd at pain, and knew not woe." He could look coldly and indifferently on blood and danger; long-nourished evil passions have ploughed their furrows on his " swart brow and callous face." Fled are the light-hearted sins of youthful thoughtlessness, giving place to naked vice, which has taken deep root, though not so deep as greed and love of pleasure. Bertram's " swarthy eye," " sullen mood," " stormy mind," " felon deed," " fruitless guilt," " gloomy train," " giant form," recur again and again in the descriptions given of him, of which the following is an example :

> One ample hand his forehead press'd,
> And one was dropp'd across his breast.
> The shaggy eyebrows deeper came
> Above his eyes of swarthy flame ;
> His lip of pride awhile forbore
> The haughty curve till then it wore ;
> The unalter'd fierceness of his look
> A shade of darken'd sadness took,—
> For dark and sad a presage press'd
> Resistlessly on Bertram's breast.

With true romantic defiance he refuses to allow the burden on his soul to compel him to repentance ; firm as a rock he awaits his fate—" My heart may burst, but cannot bend." He maintains this sombre attitude to the end. When he rides to church to avenge himself on Oswald, the poem relates admiringly how " sable his cloak, his plume, his steed," and how his look was " grimly determined " ; when he died, his parting groan " had more of laughter than of moan." For all this he is accorded full romantic admiration after his death :

> Fell as he was in act and mind,
> He left no bolder heart behind :
> Then give him, for a soldier meet,
> A soldier's cloak for winding-sheet.

The other dark hero of the poem is Mortham. His life contains a secret which is revealed at the end of the poem ; in a fit of jealousy he has killed his wife. In his youth wild and wanton he has been, but now his mind is oppressed by this " dark and fatal tale." When his son disappeared he set out to wander through the world, becoming ultimately the leader of a fierce band of pirates, with his friend Bertram as comrade. He behaves in a way that causes even his companions to gaze upon him with horror and dread, and though he sees much human agony and crime, there is none whose sorrow could be matched with his. Bertram describes how Mortham, in his pirate years, had been a gloomy man, despairing and terrible, when he threw in his lot with the others despising life and all human bands ; he loved reckless adventure and danger for their own sakes ; merriment and wine could never smooth a single fold on his brow ; his smile was a dangerous omen, for it occurred only in stern and desperate moments, and when he laughed,[238] he who heard it might regard his fate as sealed. He was the foremost in every battle, only turning his back despisingly when booty was to be shared ; often he would try to influence his old comrades for the better, exhorting them to show pity and humanity. When he returns at last to his own country, he tries to ease his conscience by repentance.

These two dark heroes bring the pirate into romantic literature. The whole field of buccaneer-themes, treasures of exotic lands, the merciless struggles enacted there, famous pirates and all that wild life beyond the pale of law and society, is here depicted in sombre flashes of a truly romantic illumination. The world of Captain Singleton lives anew, but wholly romanticized. From now onward it was no longer necessary for the dark hero to appear in the guise of a knight amid " historical " scene-paintings,—if so desired he might be a contemporary ; the black plumes of the helmet of Otranto, which hitherto had nodded on every hero's head, lost their importance with the iron harness and gigantic sword ; all that was needed now was a dark countenance, flashing eyes, a restless temper that mocked at everything, a mysterious past, a wild and vicious youth, a constantly-gnawing remorse and self-scorn in the inmost recesses of the heart.

In this poem attention is also drawn to a sentimentality alien to Scott's nature, which appears comparatively often and in typically Radcliffesque form. Its chief representative is young Wilfred, the delicate, dreamy, lovelorn son of the tyrant Oswald. Frail from childhood, he dreads warlike pastimes, " mused with Hamlet " and " wept himself to soft repose o'er gentle Desdemona's woes." He loves the quiet joys which " wake by lonely stream and silent lake." While climbing in the mountains he dreams of constant love or endless spring, until he can no longer bear the weight of these fancies, but is compelled to return mournfully to earth. He is passionately and hopelessly in love with Matilda, but keeps silence, his feeling only betraying itself in his eyes. He is most at home " in some wild and lone retreat," where his day-dreams can be transformed into reality and reality into a dream. Lying awake at night, the pale light of his lamp mingling with that of the moon, a hectic flush on his cheeks, he seizes his lute in true Radcliffe fashion, and with mournful air composes over-emotional lines " to the Moonlight," which begin in familiar strain : " Hail to thy cold and clouded beam, etc." He is one of those romantic characters whose emotions are deeply affected by aspects of Nature, especially that which awakens " awful pleasure check'd by fear." When he dies it is suddenly, kneeling before his beloved and in the act of kissing her hand, at the very moment when the purity of his love and the nobility of his intentions have been most strikingly revealed.

A contrast to Wilfred is formed by Redmond, a model of youthful high spirits, virility and bravery. Only love can induce him to dream, at which time he too " sought the lonely wood or stream to cherish there a happier dream." Redmond is the lost heir to the throne, kidnapped in his youth by a treacherous enemy, and now recognized by the gold chain he had worn on his abduction. His kidnapper receives his rightful punishment, which gives occasion for the castle bell to take up its old stern duty :

> One stroke, upon the castle bell,
> To Oswald rung his dying knell.

The old castle appears in its proper part. When Bertram and his pirates creep along a secret passage to the castle hall, where the obligatory minstrel scene of all Scott's poems is in progress, the account distantly resembles that in which Lewis's skeleton knight arrives at a feast, for here too we note " the lamp's uncertain lustre." Mortham, believed to be murdered, appears to his would-be murderer as a spirit, which occasions an eloquent description of the effects of ghost-stories. The whole of the materials of which *Rokeby* is composed show the poem to have been written under the influence of *The Castle of Otranto*, so that it has the effect of being a poetical version of its distant model. Nevertheless, the new material superimposed points to the future, specifically to the dark robber-types of Byron.

In terms of the Byronic hero, *The Lord of the Isles* (1815) is not as yielding as *Rokeby*, although from the first it transports the reader to the romantic atmosphere of a storm-tossed sea and the feudal castles

> Each on its own dark cape reclined,
> And listening to its own wild wind. . . .

Here, too, the first lines to depict the hero of the poem, Robert Bruce—

> Proud was his tone, but calm ; his eye
> Had that compelling dignity,
> His mien that bearing haught and high,
> Which common spirits fear—

show the now familiar picture to have exacted its rights. His younger brother displays the same marks of identification, his glance being " quick, keen, high and fierce." The robbers are

> . . . men of evil mien,
> Down-look'd, unwilling to be seen ;
> They moved with half-resolved pace,
> And bent on earth each gloomy face.

Words such as " dark brow," " dark look," " dark, deadly, long hate," reveal the demands of romanticism as regards character, just as the attributes in the following—

> It is the form, the eye, the word,
> The bearing of that stranger Lord ;
> His locks upon his forehead twine,
> Jet black . . .

originate in the descriptions of the hero in earlier romanticism. A romantic feature is the unrecognized union of a loving maiden in male attire with her hero.

The third canto and the beginning of the fourth show the poet's wildly romantic conception of nature, and reveal, at the same time, certain special features worked out by Mrs. Radcliffe :

> Sublime but sad delight thy soul hath known,
> Gazing on pathless glen and mountain high,
> Listing where from the cliffs the torrents thrown
> Mingle their echoes with the eagle's cry,
> And with the sounding lake, and with the moaning sky.
> Yes ! 'twas sublime, but sad. The loneliness
> Loaded thy heart, the desert tired thine eye ;
> And strange and awful fears began to press
> Thy bosom with a stern solemnity.
>
> .   .   .   .   .
>
> Such are the scenes, where savage grandeur wakes
> An awful thrill that softens into sighs.
>
> .   .   .   .   .

Mrs. Radcliffe's terror-romanticist conception of nature, the essence of which was built up of rocks, mountain cataracts and the eagle's cry, is thus revived in a familiar form.

Harold the Dauntless (1817) resembles a fable of chivalry, in which a fierce and dauntless heathen knight wanders disinherited in alien lands, until he returns to enter into his inheritance by force of arms, to repent and become baptized in the Christian Faith. He, too, is accompanied by a woman disguised as a man, who is secretly in love with him. Covetous priests, a sorcerer and sorcery, a Castle of the Seven Shields reminding one of Poe's plague-stricken palace with rooms of different colour, in which death dwells, copious descriptions of the haunted castle and other familiar materials, make up the contents of the poem. In Harold, despite his character of a pagan of dim antiquity, many of the features of the romantic hero are found :

> His shaggy black locks on his brow hung low
> And his eyes glanced through them a swarthy glow.

He is " Harold of harden'd heart, stubborn and wilful," accustomed since childhood to care little for logic or truth. The usual attributes, too, are all there : " dark brow," " sullen mood," " gloomy brow," " his helmet's gloomy pride," " his dark habitual frown," " his gloomy soul," " dark and sullen hour," " his broad sable eye," etc. Harold greatly resembles Bertram ; the only addition is the bold " Berserker's wrath," characteristic of Vikings and apparently regarded with affection by the romanticists.

Passing over the rest of his poetical production as less interesting from the point of view of the Byronic hero, I may add that by these poems Scott made the romantic " lay " or " legend " extremely popular, in both meanings of the word, and thus inaugurated a fruitful era of poetry. It must expressly be admitted that Scott's broad manner of depicting his heroes was well calculated to touch the imagination and evoke admiration for a type that impressed readers by its novelty and fascination. With Scott's hero still in memory let us now proceed to the study of Byron's own hero, from whom the type derives its name.

3

The presence of Byron is as natural here as was that of Scott. He, too, had been a zealous reader of terror-romanticism and had steeped himself in the atmosphere of ancient crimes and decay and a sense of the sublime in nature. The field was as familiar to him as it was to Scott. He had no need to go to Schiller for his type of romantic hero, for it already existed in embryo in the works of Mrs. Radcliffe and Moore (Zeluco), both of whom he had read. Besides, Karl Moor lacks the mystery that is so essential a feature of the Byronic hero, whereas the first mists of this quality were already clouding around the English type. Now that Scott had begun to strike water from a rock, inaugurating a new, lyrical, narrative style of poetry and achieving with it a great success, the path was opened to Byron whereby he could interpret the pent-up visions and images sown in his own soul by the romantic period. Thus were born in swift sequence the shorter of his narrative poems, in which the hero-ideal of the earlier period is clearest discernible. Investigation of these casts light upon his relation to Scott and Mrs. Radcliffe, which must be kept in view while tracing the genealogy of his hero-type.

The young *Giaour* (1813) [239] rides forth " on blackest steed," somewhat in the style of *Lenore*, " lash for lash and bound for bound," diffusing around him an atmosphere of horror akin to that awakened by a phantom. The narrator says of him :

> I know thee not, I loathe thy race,
> But in thy lineaments I trace
> What time shall strengthen, not efface :
> Though young and pale, that sallow front
> Is scathed by fiery passion's brunt ;
> Though bent on earth thine evil eye,
> As meteor-like thou glidest by,
> Right well I view and deem thee one
> Whom Othman's sons should slay or shun.

He is " like a demon of the night," " of foreign garb and fearful brow," a flash of dread visits his face, only to become transformed into hatred—not the reddening flush of transient anger, but a paleness of marble over a tomb, whose ghastly whiteness aids its gloom. When he reins in his raven charger on the summit of a rock and looks with frowning brows and " glazed eyes " at the scene from which he has fled, it is as though at that moment the "winters of memory" were crowding into his soul, gathering in that drop of time a life of pain, an age of crime. His mind, that broods o'er guilty woes, is like the scorpion girt by fire [240]—unfit for earth, undoom'd for Heaven, darkness above, despair beneath, around it flame and within it death. When he meets his enemy Hassan, the latter exclaims :

> 'T is he ! 't is he ! I know him now ;
> I know him by his pallid brow ;
> I know him by the evil eye
> That aids his envious treachery ;
> I know him by his jet-black barb.

After the battle, when the Giaour stoops to gaze upon his fallen enemy, full scope is given to the dark tones :

> And o'er him bends that foe with brow
> As dark as his that bled below.

To this picture, gloomy enough in itself, is added the hope that the mysterious, faithless Giaour might become after death a vampire, to haunt his native place and suck the blood of his kin. The gloom of the narrative increases as the poem proceeds to depict the Giaour's life in an alien land, in the monastery which has granted him a refuge, apostate as he is. He is shown standing alone on the summit of a rock and raging inwardly ; the glowing glance and air of mockery visible under the dark cowl make a gloomy and supernatural impression (Schedoni) ; they terrify the beholder because of the nameless fascination that dwells in them, bespeaking a still undaunted, arrogant spirit. Were the Angel of Evil to take on human form, so would he look, for his appearance is neither of earth nor of Heaven. Later, when the Giaour gains absolution on his deathbed, his confession becomes the reminiscence, borne up by a dark, southern passion, of an Oriental love-story abounding in romantic, furious episodes of vengeance.

> The cold in clime are cold in blood,
> Their love can scarce deserve the name ;
> But mine was like the lava flood
> That boils in Ætna's breast of flame.

So dies the mysterious Giaour, whose whole life had been devoted to one great passion, that of love, leaving no trace of his identity or origin.

Compared with his predecessors, the Giaour can show a

number of new features. The main effect of the whole poem is from the first one of sombre, concentrated passion, which can " but to obtain or die," and which causes its lines to vibrate with a suppressed, only half-hidden torturing agony. The mysterious nocturnal gloom which had already begun to gather around the hero of romance is here developed to its ultimate conclusions : to the vicissitudes of the Giaour attaches an impenetrable mystery, which he takes with him to the grave, and the whole narrative of his life and love is told in a style purposely avoiding clear-cut descriptions, a style fragmentary and indirect.[241] Thus the passion of the poem is accompanied by a hidden suspense which adds to the fascination evoked by the deep metaphors and flashing paradoxes and its undertone of suppressed sobbing. The historical trappings, the display of helmets, lances and armour, have all fallen away ; the period might be the poet's own. Romantic colour is furnished by the glow of the Orient, by minarets, turbans and curved scimitars ; the sentimental atmosphere of decay has been preserved in the masterful lines depicting Hassan's castle :

> The steed is vanish'd from the stall ;
> No serf is seen in Hassan's hall ;
> The lonely spider's thin gray pall
> Waves slowly widening o'er the wall ;
> The bat builds in his haram bower,
> And in the fortress of his power
> The owl usurps the beacon-tower ;
> The wild-dog howls o'er the fountain's brim,
> With baffled thirst, and famine, grim.

Thus, although its derivation from the past can be clearly demonstrated, *The Giaour* so far denotes a new phase in the development of the Byronic hero that, without neglecting the " pale gloom " brought down from earlier pictures, his passion and mystery have become expanded into the chief characteristic. We shall now see what variations Byron was capable of sounding on this new keynote.

The Goethe-inspired opening lines of *The Bride of Abydos* (1813), which brim over with romantic admiration for the Orient, lead us into a bright atmosphere, flooded with the sun-haze of the Bosphorus and the Sea of Marmora. The Byronic hero of the poem, Selim, is correspondingly of more delicate texture and more lyrical than the Giaour, even though the defiance of his glance does cow his father. His true character emerges, however, at the threat to deprive him of his beloved, his " sister " Zuleika. As the setting is transformed in the second canto into a night of storm, in which the only illumination comes from the light in Zuleika's chamber, so does the apparently delicate Selim become transformed into a romantic pirate. He is not really Zuleika's brother, but her cousin, and his history is a dark story of fraternal hate and fratricide. His whole life centres around his love for Zuleika and his desire to be revenged upon her father. A repressive upbringing and an unquenchable thirst for liberty make him turn pirate. As the poem proceeds this gloomy nocturno is then expanded into the lurid death-tragedy of Selim, by which he is deprived of both love and revenge, whereafter the dark colours subside into a note of yearning expressed in a cypress, which " withers not, though branch and leaf are stamped with an eternal grief," marble and "a single rose" which looks " as planted by Despair." The outward marks of the Byronic hero are thus lacking in the poem, but it shows, in a manner, those of *The Giaour*, keyed however to a tenderer and much more sentimental pitch ; without the gloom evoked by descriptions of character or outward apparition, yet filled with the passion of love, revenge and mystery, with the further addition of the romance of storm. The poem plays therefore little part in the development of the Byronic hero.

The story of Selim encroaches in great measure on the theme whence sprang *The Corsair* (1814), the poem of " the glad waters of the dark blue sea." [242] After depicting with a romanticist's liberty the life of the corsairs and the gaudy camp on their island, the poem goes straight to the mystery which enwraps Conrad, their chief. " But who that chief ? His name on every shore is famed and fear'd." No answer is vouchsafed. His words are few, yet all obey him and rarely question his commands. He often stands in meditation on the crest of a rock, and at such moments must be approached with caution, as in this mood he cannot bear intruders. He is " the man of loneliness and mystery," who is scarce seen to smile and seldom heard to sigh ; in his being there does not seem to be much worthy of admiration, although " his dark eyebrow shades a glance of fire."

> Sun-burnt his cheek, his forehead high and pale
> The sable curls in wild profusion veil.
>
>   .   .   .   .   .
>
> His features' deepening lines and varying hue
> At times attracted, yet perplex'd the view,
> As if within that murkiness of mind
> Work'd feelings fearful, and yet undefined.

Too impertinent a curiosity is stifled by his stern glance, whose searching expression few can withstand :

> There was a laughing Devil in his sneer,
> That raised emotions both of rage and fear ;
> And where his frown of hatred darkly fell,
> Hope withering fled, and Mercy sigh'd farewell !

" Feared, shunned, belied," he has learned to hate mankind even before his youth is over ; he regards his hate as a sacred call to avenge the sufferings of the individual on the whole race of man. He knows himself for a villain, but believes all others to be no better, and thus he lives his life :

> Lone, wild and strange, he stood alike exempt
> From all affection and from all contempt ;
> His name could sadden, and his acts surprise ;
> But they that fear'd him dared not to despise :
> Man spurns the worm, but pauses ere he wake
> The slumbering venom of the folded snake. . . .

It would be difficult to find a more powerful portrait of this dark type of hero than that provided by Byron in the lines quoted above. In gloom and mystery Conrad ranks with the Giaour, whom he excels in hate for mankind, which trait, accentuated to this degree, is a new addition to the character of the Byronic hero. When he bares his " mail'd breast " and flashes " his sabre's ray " the Moslems regard him, with his " glittering casque and sable plume, more glittering eye, and black brow's sabler gloom " as an evil spirit ; but to us he is Scott's romantic knight at the climax of his career. When he falls captive his stern and controlled expression has more of the victor in it than of the vanquished, a fact reflected in the secret fear of his guardians. The sombre passion that upholds the whole poem crystallizes finally around its hero in the scenes of terror which result in Conrad's outward deliverance, though they deprive him of the last motives for continuing to live. So, as we are given to understand in enigmatical hints, he vanishes without a trace :

> He left a Corsair's name to other times,
> Link'd with one virtue, and a thousand crimes.

The gloomy side of the romantic hero's outward aspect, character and fate is revealed, if possible, in a still darker and more mysterious form in *Lara* (1814). This poem can be looked upon as a sequel to and conclusion of *The Corsair.*

Lost from sight since youth, Lara appears (after his piratical career is over) in the decaying haunted castle of his father in " sudden loneliness " ; the whole long period of his absence remains wrapped in deepest mystery, a mystery enhanced by the appearance of a woman (Kaled-Gulnare) dressed as a man, and by the accusation of some dreadful crime, which remains unformulated because of the accuser's enigmatical death at Lara's hand. Thus, the whole poem is pervaded by an atmosphere of crime and unfathomed guilty secrets, by the oppressive air of terror-romanticism, which even the element of love does little to lighten. In Lara Conrad lives again. The lines on his brow have become fixed, telling of past passions ; they reflect the pride of youth—but not its ardour—coldness, indifference and mockery. Around him is a cloud of mystery that wards off the curious ; often he will shut himself up for days at a time. He is a stranger to this world, as though suddenly cast there from elsewhere ; " there was in him a vital scorn of all." In moments of anger his romantic gloom becomes impressive :

> For Lara's brow upon the moment grew
> Almost to blackness in its demon hue,

and at the moment of death he is—

> So unrepentant, dark, and passionless.

With forbidding mien he thrusts away the hand that proffers him the last Sacrament, as though it disturbed his dying. The mystery that surrounds him includes Kaled-Gulnare, who dies to keep him company. Lara is mostly Giaour, seen in the light of Conrad, and owing to his lack of Oriental qualities akin to Scott's Marmion, as we have previously remarked. The Byronic hero is not much developed by him beyond the stage already reached in Conrad.

In these poems Byron had squandered so prodigally the attributes of gloom and mystery on his dark hero that he now saw himself compelled to economize, if he was to avoid repetition. Thus they are almost entirely lacking in *The Siege of Corinth* and *Parisina* (both 1816). The passionate apostate Alp of the former poem is nevertheless closely related to Conrad, while its stern Venetian elder Minotti recalls, like Prince Azo in the latter poem, the grand Giaffar of *The Bride of Abydos* ; Prince Hugo is Selim, altered to conform with the court of a condottiere. The terror-romantic element of *The*

Siege of Corinth is, despite the ghost and the realistic scenes of carnage, not as consistent as usually ; the whole poem, as a matter of fact, makes a somewhat incoherent and crowded effect, in contrast to *Parisina*, which is given an individual character by the gloom of the predominant romantically dusky atmosphere of death, where mighty passions, cruelty, crime and the ultimate dreadful end of the whole of its characters blaze like a holocaust in the night. The materials used in *The Prisoner of Chillon* (1816) deserve particular attention owing to the inclusion amongst them of spiritual sufferings bordering on insanity and the bodily torments that the victim of this terror-romantic *Burgverliess* has to endure. Likewise *Mazeppa* (1818) is noteworthy for its almost unbroken portrayal of suffering, a theme tempting only to a terror-romanticist in search of " the beauty of cruelty." In *The Island* (1823), a poem full of the horrors of mutiny and the idyllic lovemaking of tropical Otaheiti,[243] Christian, leader of the mutineers, appears in the dark hero's trappings, side by side with a gentler, conciliatory character in the person of young Torquil.

> Stern, and aloof a little from the rest,
> Stood Christian, with his arms across his chest.
>
> .   .   .   .   .
>
> Still as a statue, with his lips comprest
> To stifle even the breast within his breast,
> Fast by the rock, all menacing but mute,
> He stood . . .
>
> .   .   .   .   .
>
> Like an extinct volcano in his mood ;
> Silent, and sad, and savage—with the trace
> Of Passion reeking from his clouded face. . . .
>
> .   .   .   .   .
>
> For me, my lot is what I sought ; to be,
> In life or death, the fearless and the free.

As he waits, gun in hand, he is

> Dark as a sullen cloud before the sun.

4

These examples are sufficient to reveal the affinity between the Byronic type and the romantic past, even its direct derivation by way of Scott.[244] But the picture of the Byronic hero would be incomplete if only this aspect were dealt with, and confined in great measure only to those traditional outward features which had become fashionable ; in a word, it would seem " hollow," lacking in the spiritual contents on which its later fame rested. To complete the picture it is necessary to ascertain how Byron breathed into it the breath of life.

In the study of his hero-type, Byron's youthful poems *Hours of Idleness* are of great interest, for in them we catch the occasional echo of a melody which was later to become the *leitmotiv* of his symphonies. In the poem *Remembrance* he takes leave of love, hope and joy, desiring to add to them even the memory of their existence. As typical products of a precocious youth they reveal the kind of insincere, sentimental yearning over the lost joys of youth and a present sense of emptiness which hardly convinces. But between these poems and the first two cantos of *Childe Harold* much had happened that gave to the words of the latter a lasting and effectual influence. The poet's youth with all its vices is luridly revealed in the opening lines, the youth of one

> Who ne in virtue's ways did take delight ;
> But spent his days in riot most uncouth. . . .[245]

As a result of this dissipation he soon felt the " fullness of satiety " and began to long for other scenes than his fatherland could provide, which now seemed to him more lonely than a hermit's sorry hut. " The sullen tear " rises at times to his eye, but pride bids him conceal it, and thus he draws apart to " joyless reverie " and makes up his mind to flee ; he has experienced so much pleasure that he almost yearns for suffering, and if no other change of scene were possible to him, he might even have sought the abode of the dead. The shadows that flit across his brow at the moment of his departure remain unperceived ; he is no open-minded, guileless soul for whom alleviation is possible by relating his sorrows, nor does he seek the advice and consolation of friends. Unloved, he leaves his native shore without a sigh. He has already learned the lesson that

> When all is won that all desire to woo,
> The paltry prize is hardly worth the cost :
> Youth wasted, minds degraded, honour lost. . . .

In the third canto he returns to this " wandering outlaw of his own dark mind," in whose story he discerns " the furrows of long thought, and dried up tears." He has aged more on account of his deeds than of his years ; studying the sources of life, he no longer expects to meet with marvels ; love, sorrow, fame and ambition cut no longer at his heart. Looking into his past he finds that he had become too deeply involved in his own gloomy thoughts and has attempted to re-enter the whirlpool of human life only to discover anew that he is unsuited for the attempt and that he must withdraw again into his voluntary banishment.

From the point of view of the Byronic hero it is clear that in the person of Childe Harold the poet imparts a new inner man, conforming with his own spirit of opposition and fashionable spleen, to a romantic hero-type which was, in all essentials, already in existence. An added feature of special interest is the use of Childe Harold as an extremely thin disguise for Byron's own posing ego. His use of his hero to display, proudly and defiantly, his own sinfulness ; his exploitation of the themes furnished by his travels to illustrate his pessimism and to cry out his protest against the misery of the world and all mankind, to voice the radicalism and love of liberty whose prophet he had made himself, raised that romantic dark hero of the pale countenance, with all his mystery and recklessness, to the dignity of a combative force in the poet's own period. In the public mind the spiritual development of Childe Harold became easily superimposed on the demoniac being of Byron's Oriental poems, and resulted in the conception known afterwards as the " Byronic hero," a type which the poet's own age, particularly the world of women, had good reason for supposing the poet himself to represent. The amalgamation was rendered easier by the lack of that cynical, all-pervading mockery which later gives to *Don Juan* its special character. In *Childe Harold* we hear an echo, rather, of something grave and solemn, even mournful, hinting, notwithstanding the general pose of its hero, at a hidden belief in the noble ideals of mankind.

The type thus created, the gradually-developed offspring of romantic literature, is the central personage of all Byron's poetry, a type with whom he deals from varying points of view, in varying lights, endowing it with ever new tasks, infusing into it, as in Cain and Manfred,[246] a shade of Prometheus, defiance of the gods and a demand to know the secrets of the cosmos ; but always keeping it fundamentally the same, for his poetry is in its essence self-revelation, which in some mysterious fashion invariably conforms with what one might expect of the " hero " in question. When, in the beginning of *Don Juan* he speaks of his need for a hero and mockingly waves aside the types which the world has sanctioned as such, choosing instead Don Juan, the choice is in reality inevitable; he could have found no other bearer for his message than the central heroic personage of his imagination, conceived in the light of his own advanced development. Compared with the past, the hero of *Don Juan* is changed; he has been stripped of his dark-hued romanticism, and at the same time of his pose, that rostrum from which so much of Byron's earlier work had been declaimed.

Don Juan is, in a way, one of Fortune's favourites, seen and depicted with a rare feeling for reality, one to whom romance attaches only by reason of his strange experiences in the field of passion and the extraordinary adventures which the poet paints with such highly-coloured, terror-romantic realism. The stamp of the whole poem is, nevertheless, given to it by the pitiless, cynical analysis which finds nothing sacred or enduring, and in which judgment is passed on the whole of the poet's age.

Such, broadly viewed, is the development of the Byronic hero as reflected in English literature.[247] We have seen that the type had a distant ancestor and that it passed through a period of crystallization before Scott finally made it widely known and Byron endowed it with its ultimate form and contents. Not until then did its pilgrimage begin through the literature of the rest of Europe, where it raged for long, passing from country to country and sowing everywhere a crop of " pale and interesting " heroes whose foreheads are shadowed by dark curls and in whose eyes gleams a deep world-sorrow.[248]

VII

GHOSTS AND DEMONIAC BEINGS

I

IN dealing with the central setting of the terror-romantic
school I have given to it the generic name of the haunted
castle.

The ghost, as such, is no new invention of the romanticists, for it has recurred in literature ever since the Witch of
Endor inaugurated the series. Euripides and Seneca made use
of ghosts ; they were not unknown in French classical drama,
and as the previous quotations from Addison and Steele have
shown they played a part in English drama. The belief in
ghosts is a general feature of all folklore ; even where the
development of civilization has extinguished legends, ghost-
lore survives tenaciously both among the uneducated and the
cultured classes. This survival is helped by a tendency to
attach itself to particular localities and families, by the
nourishment it draws from the superstitious dread with which
death is regarded and from beliefs connected with a life beyond
the grave. Ghost-lore had thus, like all other ancient things,
a natural right to the admiration of the romanticist for
everything old. As it has, in addition, a well-proved power to
agitate the senses, it is clear that a literature which aimed at
beauty through terror, would find in it a welcome means to
this end.

So began the use of ghost-material in its first and most
primitive stage ; popular ghost-stories connected with some
definite locality or family were introduced in their traditional
form into literature, on their own intrinsic merits. An
example of the method is Lewis's " Legend of the Bleeding
Nun." Soon, however, attention had been attracted to
another feature of popular ghost-lore ; it was observed that
some moral reason lay behind the appearance of a ghost.
Where a crime had remained unpunished during life, the only

chance for outraged justice lay in an appeal from beyond the grave. As soon as this had dawned on the romantic author, the ghost became to him, metaphorically speaking, the avenging conscience of the delinquent, which at the critical moment dashed the whole of his plans and made good the injury to moral order. These are the main purposes for which a romanticist uses ghosts ; in the first place, to create a general atmosphere, and in the second, to achieve a moral purpose unattainable without some such *deus ex machina*. This appearance of the ghost as an important active element in romantic circumstances opens a new chapter in its history.

In the first chapter of this book I have already dealt briefly with the ghost in English literature—in Shakespeare's dramas and elsewhere—and with the general interest accorded to the subject.[249] The remarks relating to Percy's ballads call for further elaboration, as at a time when romanticism was still in its infancy this collection brought to light a selection of popular songs on ghost-themes, with a special flavour of romanticism about them. Percy's ballads stress the tragic side of love, the unhappy fate of lovers, with all the unaffectedness and simple elegiac quality of the folk-song, revealing thereby the key and method of interpretation essential to success in this line.

> When day was gone, and night was come,
>   And all men fast asleep,
> Then came the spirit of fair Marg'ret,
>   And stood at William's feet

runs the mournful poem called *Fair Margaret and Sweet William*. In *Margaret's Ghost* (of which David Mallet claimed to be the author) we read :

> 'Twas at the silent solemn hour,
>   When night and morning meet ;
> In glided Margaret's grimly ghost,
>   And stood at William's feet.
>
> Her face was like an April morn,
>   Clad in a wintry cloud :
> And clay-cold was her lily hand,
>   That held her sable shrowd.
>
> * * * *
>
> " This is the dark and dreary hour
>   When injur'd ghosts complain ;
> Now yawning graves give up their dead,
>   To haunt the faithless swain."

PLATE VIII

THE SPECTRE OF THE SLAIN

(From an engraving by Corbould)

[*face p. 244*

She comes to redeem her maiden vow and rebuke William for not keeping his word. William's limbs tremble and he rushes raving from his bed—

> And thrice he call'd on Margaret's name,
>   And thrice he wept full sore :
> Then laid his cheek to her cold grave,
>   And word spake never more.

Special attention is merited by *Sweet William's Ghost*, which is one of the poems on which the new ghost-ballad was founded. The poem relates how

> There came a ghost to Margaret's door,
>   With many a grievous grone,
> And aye he tirled at the pin,
>   But answer made she none—

and how William's ghost comes to demand of Margaret a like faithfulness to his own. But Margaret answers :

> Thy faith and troth thou'se nevir get,
>   ' Of me shalt nevir win,'
> Till thou take me to yon kirk yard
>   And wed me with a ring.

Margaret then follows her swain " the live-lang winter night " and dies when at cock-crow the ghost vanishes :

> O stay, my only true love, stay,
>   The constant Margret cried :
> Wan grew her cheeks, she clos'd her een,
>   Stretch'd her saft limbs, and died.

The freshness and unaffectedness of Percy's ballads had the same rejuvenating effect on ghost-romanticism as it had on chivalresque romance. The bravery of *Chevy Chase* showed the authors of the period how to deal with lusty bouts between knights ; its example influenced the descriptions of the knightly encounters and battles beloved of Scott, and even those of Southey. In like manner the ghost-ballads in Percy's collection made ghost-poetry more natural and showed that the *métier* could successfully be used to play upon the strings of romantic love and terror. The predominant theme, the appearance of the ghost of a (betrayed) lover or beloved to the object of its passion (or betrayer), became the framework of an extensive series of ghost-ballads, of which many have become famous and formed in turn the starting-point for interesting series of literary developments.

For long, however, Percy's initiative did not inspire any follower in his own country capable of leaving anything memorable behind him.[250] *Sweet William's Ghost* had to be reborn in Germany, where it inspired Gottfried August Bürger to create *Lenore's* grisly ride, from the popular conception of Death riding in the moonlight with its bride.[251] Lewis obviously made the acquaintance of this famous poem while in Germany, giving form to the impressions awakened by it in his own *Alonzo the Brave and Fair Imogene*, which he published as a poetical interlude in *The Monk*.

2

Alonzo is compelled to depart " to fight in a far distant land," and Imogene vows by the Holy Virgin that none other shall espouse her ; should she break her word, may God send the ghost of Alonzo to her wedding to rebuke her and to carry her off with him to the grave. Imogene forgets her vow ; a wedding takes place and Alonzo's ghost appears and carries off its bride. A glance at the history of the various lines that compose the poem is not without interest.

In writing the opening :

> A warrior so bold and a virgin so bright
> Conversed, as they sat on the green,

Lewis may have been unaware that he was repeating echoes of the opening lines of *Margaret and William* :

> As it fell out on a long summer's day
> Two lovers they sat on a hill.[252]

Alonzo is to depart to the wars " to-morrow," and William, too, speaks of " to-morrow." Margaret's ghost tells us how dark her death-closed eyes are and calls the " hungry worm " her sister ; the worms reappear in Lewis's ballad in the scene where Alonzo's ghost appears at the wedding of his faithless betrothed :

> The worms they crept in, and the worms they crept out,
> And sported his eyes and his temples about.[253]

Soon two of Bürger's ballads, *Lenardo und Blandine* and *Lenore*, join in. When we read in *Lenore* :

> *Zum Schädel ohne Zopf und Schopf,*
> *Zum nackten Schädel ward sein Kopf,*

we are reminded first of the hermit's skull in *The Castle of Otranto*, and then of those lines of Lewis's which depict the aspect of Alonzo's ghost and the bride's terror :

> What words can express her dismay and surprise,
> When a sceleton's head was exposed *!*

When Lewis writes regarding his lovers :

> They gazed on each other with tender delight,

we are reminded of the following lines from *Lenardo und Blandine :*

> *Blandine sah her, Lenardo sah hin,*
> *Mit Augen, erleuchtet vom zärtlichsten Sinn,*

and similarly it is not impossible that Lewis's great wooer of Imogene :

> A Baron all covered with jewels and gold,

hails from the same poem :

> *Weit her, von Hispanien's reichster Provinz*
> *War kommen ein hochstolzierender Prinz*
> *Mit Perlen, Gold, Ringen und Edelgestein,*
> *Die schönste der schönen Prinzessen zu frein.*

In the following lines, which depict the phantom dance of Alonzo and Imogene :

> While they drink out of skulls newly torn from the grave,
>   Dancing round them pale spectres are seen :
> Their liquor is blood, and this horrible stave
> They howl : " To the health of Alonzo the Brave,
>   And his consort, the False Imogene ! "

Lenore is represented with the lines :

> *Nun tanzten wohl bei Mondenglanz*
> *Rundum herum in Kreise*
> *Die Geister einen Kettentanz*
> *Und heulten diese Weise—.*

As regards the situation involved in the ballad as a whole and the appearance of Alonzo's ghost, the similarity between it and the wedding scene in Schiller's *Der Geisterseher*, in which the ghost of Jeronymo appears, is striking. " The sun sank and in the brightly-lit wedding-hall an excellent repast awaited the guests, loud music accompanying the boisterous merriment. In

this medley my attention was drawn by my neighbour to a
Franciscan friar, tall and lean, with ashen-grey countenance,
who stood immovable as a statue, looking with grave and
sorrowful eyes at the bridal pair. Curiosity and a sensation of
strangeness descended upon the whole company, conversation
ceased and a general silence prevailed. The monk stood
moveless as before, still gazing sorrowfully at the happy pair.
Midnight had passed, the music began gradually to die away,
the flames of the candles grew dimmer, until they burned only
here and there, and the mournfully-lit hall grew more and
more desolate, while the monk still stood moveless, always in
the same attitude, his quiet and sorrowful glance directed
towards the newly-wed. . . . " The strange monk goes
finally to the table and proposes, lifting his glass : " To the
memory of our dear Jeronymo. Let the one who loved the
dead do as I do." The fratricidal Lorenzo takes the glass
from the monk and says trembling : " To my dearly-beloved
brother Jeronymo." At that a dreadful being who has
suddenly appeared, with dripping garments and a body covered
with frightful wounds, cries " It is my murderer's voice ! "
Now in his ballad Lewis tells how the marriage had been blest
by the priest and how the wedding feast began. When the
castle clock strikes one, the fair Imogene discovers to her
surprise that a strange man, hitherto unnoticed, is sitting by
her side. He is described by the ballad as follows :

> His air was terrific ; he uttered no sound ;
> He spoke not, he moved not, he looked not around,
> But earnestly gazed on the bride.

His vizor is closed and he is of gigantic stature ; his armour is
black. His presence casts a gloom on all merriment and
laughter ; the dogs howl in terror and the lights turn a bluish
colour. Fear seizes everybody, the guests sit in silence,
paralyzed by fear. Finally, the bride entreats the stranger to
lift his vizor, which he does, revealing a picture of death, the
worm-infested skull already mentioned. Alonzo's ghost, for he
it is, chides Imogene for her faithlessness and pride, and

> Then sank with his prey through the wide-yawning ground :
> Nor ever again was Fair Imogene found,
> Or the spectre who bore her away.

> At midnight four times in each year does her sprite,
> When mortals in slumber are bound,
> Arrayed in her bridal apparel of white,
> Appear in the hall with the sceleton knight
> And shriek as he whirls her around.

If we were to adjudge what part of this poem is likely to evoke the deepest sense of fear, we should choose the lines in which the silence and immovability of the ghost is insisted upon, and which describe how he " earnestly gazed on the bride." This ghostly glance, the development of which we have followed in other connections, is an important addition to the arsenal of effects of terror and was much used later. It crops up in Shakespeare, in the arrival of Banquo's ghost at the feast, a phantom which terrifies its murderer by its glance, regarding which Macbeth says :

> Thou hast no speculation in those eyes
> Which thou dost glare with.

Comparing *Alonzo* with the nightmarish horror of *Lenore*, we note how feeble and ineffectual Lewis's realistic treatment is beside the other, despite his worms and draughts of blood from skulls. Nevertheless *Alonzo the Brave* became famous and was translated into several languages, even into Swedish and, as a hawker's ballad, into Finnish.[254] Proof of the favour it enjoyed are the parodies published on it, one of which, though hardly a good one, was written by Lewis himself.

Still keeping to the pages of *The Monk* I shall now present the ghost of the Bleeding Nun, to which we have so often had occasion to refer. Lewis acquired it from German sources (where it appears in the part of a protective ancestress) and used it only in the subsidiary episode of Raymond and Agnes ; this economy enhanced the effect of the ghost, which familiarity might have dissipated. The ghost, a former nun called Beatrice, is unable to find peace in the grave because of a crime she committed and because of her violent end. Heedless of her vows, she eloped with the Baron Lindenberg ; an atheist, she mocked at her obligations and regarded the most sacred matters as food for laughter. Soon her passion had been transferred to the Baron's younger brother, whose " strong-marked features, gigantic stature, and herculean limbs," caught her fancy. But before he would yield to Beatrice's enticements, the elder brother had to be murdered. A night was agreed upon for the deed ; at one o'clock the young baron was to await Beatrice in a cave. When the castle clock struck the first hour of morning, Beatrice thrust a dagger into her erstwhile lover's heart and went to the cave, the blood-stained dagger still in her hand, a lantern in the other. There, however, she was murdered by the young baron, who wished to conceal his share in the crime. To crown all, her body was interred in unblessed earth ; so her soul could find no peace, and began to haunt the castle. Attired as a nun and carrying a dagger and a lamp, she appears at the baron's bedside each night ; unable to bear the sight he dies, but the nun is still dissatisfied with her revenge and continues her nightly visits. Attempts to lay the ghost have only succeeded in limiting her visits to intervals of five years, on the same night and at the moment at which the murder had occurred. On these occasions she visits the cave where her bones lie and returns to the castle on the stroke of two. This was to be her task throughout a century.

Now Don Raymond's beloved, Agnes de Medina, has become a prisoner in the castle of Lindenberg, and when Raymond hears of the nun and sees how implicitly the phantom is believed in, he decides to employ it as a means to rescue his beloved. On the night when the ghost is timed to walk, Agnes is to attire herself as a nun, take a dagger and a lamp, and using the route taken by the ghost, to join Raymond outside. He sees her emerge from the opening door of the castle ; on her arm is a rosary, her face is draped in a long white veil, her dress is stained with blood and she carries a dagger and a lamp. Don Raymond seizes her in his arms and lifts her into the waiting carriage. Immediately the horses break into swift gallop, the postillions are shaken off, dark clouds cover the sky, the wind begins to howl, lightning flashes and thunder rolls. The horses fly on without pausing, dragging the carriage over the most dangerous country until at last it collapses and Don Raymond is thrown senseless to the ground. Awakening, he sees no trace of Agnes, and the district to which he has come is so far from Lindenberg that it seems impossible that he could have travelled there in a single night.

On the following night, as he lies delirious in an adjacent inn, Raymond hears the clock strike one. Listening to its mournful clang he suddenly feels the cold sweat break out upon his body and his hair bristle with terror. Slow and heavy footsteps ascend the stairs, the door opens and the Bleeding Nun, his fellow-traveller of the preceding day, enters. Slowly she lifts her veil, and Raymond sees the livid countenance of a corpse, the bloodless lips and hollow, lifeless eyes. In sepulchral tones she repeats Raymond's words at the castle door and sits down at the foot of the bed. Her eyes seem to exert the fascination of the snake, for Raymond is compelled to stare into them. When the clock strikes two the ghost seizes Raymond's hand, pressing her lips to it, repeats the same words as before, and then she slowly leaves the room. This happens each night until the Wandering Jew teaches Raymond how to make an end of the nun's visits.

The legend of the Bleeding Nun is based on the same fundamental theme as *Alonzo*: the coming of a betrayed sweetheart to demand satisfaction. There too the climax of terror is reached in the scene where the ghost sits on the edge of the bed and begins to stare at its victim with hypnotic, terror-awakening eyes.

The Monk provides yet a third ghost, that of Antonia's mother, who comes to warn her child of approaching death. With Lewis's scenic ghosts we dealt when speaking of his life, one of them, " The Castle Spectre," becoming famous through the play of that name. Lewis specialized in ghost-romanticism in his romances, ballads and plays, and succeeded in making this particular field well-known and well-despised.

It must be said of these ghosts that much more space is devoted to discussing them than to the ghosts themselves. We know how economical Walpole, Clara Reeve and Mrs. Radcliffe were in the actual introduction of ghosts ; much is said about them, in other words, their appearance is ever imminent, but that is about all, barring one exception in Walpole and certain dream-like visions and subsidiary episodes in Reeve and Radcliffe.[255] If we compare Lewis's phantoms with the threatened ghosts of his predecessors, we must admit that a much more effective method than the actual introduction of a ghost, which robs it of a good deal of its mystery, is to hint at the possibility of one appearing, or, to put the matter differently, to create an atmosphere of waiting filled with the dread of unknown supernatural agencies. Lewis's part in the development of ghost-romanticism was to take this ulti-mate step ; to bring his ghosts on the scene. At first this method succeeded in attracting the attention of the public, but owing to the lack of mystery in Lewis's " material " ghosts, this interest soon flagged. Yet the most awesome of them, the Bleeding Nun, proved of sufficient value to warrant its borrowing by Grillparzer for his *Die Ahnfrau*.

3

Traces of Lewis's ghosts are discernible in English literature either as ghosts, or transformed into other beings. Scott read *The Monk* with care, and the legend of the Bleeding Nun seems to have impressed itself deeply on his mind. If we examine the history of Constance de Beverley in *Marmion*, we cannot miss the obvious relationship with the nun of Lindenberg. Constance, like her predecessor, has fled from a convent, becoming the mistress and accomplice in crime of Marmion. When Marmion's love cools and he sets out to win Clara, the betrothed of de Wilton, Constance, like Matilda, is ready to assist him. But when, driven by her passion, she tries to destroy Clara, Marmion delivers her up to the convent, where she is sentenced to die in the dungeon described earlier—quite in the manner of Agnes in *The Monk*. In the passage, too, where Clara walks alone in Tantallon Castle, the influence of the nun of Lindenberg is evident in the lines :

> In such a place, so lone, so grim,
> At dawning pale, or twilight dim,
> It fearful would have been
> To meet a form so richly dress'd,
> With book in hand, and cross on breast,
> And such a woeful mien.

When Marmion establishes himself with his company at the inn and begins to while away the evening, his unknown guide, a pilgrim who leans on a staff and whose lean dark features are only partly visible beneath his cowl, seats himself opposite to him :

> Still fix'd on Marmion was his look,
> Which he, who ill such gaze could brook,
> Strove by a frown to quell.

The bursts of laughter become rarer, for as they look on the dark countenance of the pilgrim, the squires and archers feel their merriment die away. Finally all stare at him, while he stares fixedly at Marmion. After Fitz-Eustace's ballad of love has moved Marmion's heart to repentance and pain, as though he had heard the death-chimes rung for the nun, he asks what this feeling might portend ; and the pilgrim answers : " The death of a dear friend." Obviously we have here an attempt to imitate the power of the ghost's glance in *Alonzo*. The flash of a like influence is caught in *The Lay of the Last Minstrel*. While the feast to celebrate the outcome of the duel and the liberation of the young lord is in progress at Branksome Castle, the hall suddenly begins to grow dark. A strange mist, neither fog nor twilight, enshrouds everything, and a secret terror seizes those present, freezing their hearts to ice. All at once a flash of lightning is seen and an evil spirit (in the guise of a dwarf that has worked much evil) vanishes; Michael Scott himself has come like a ghost to the feast to carry him away with his "Mighty Book." The scene in *The Bride of Lammermoor* where Lucy Ashton signs her marriage contract recalls to mind the wedding of Imogene, which was so gruesomely interrupted at its height.

Scott, however, keeps his ghosts at a greater distance than Lewis. He uses them occasionally in Lewis's manner, as for instance in *The Tapestried Chamber*, in which a vicious ancestress appears in all her dreadful evilness, or as in *The Betrothed*, when a "red-fingered" family ghost appears. But the White Lady of Avenel (*The Monastery* and *The Abbot*), in whom the ancestress-theme is reflected, is more in the nature of a vision than a ghost of the popular Lewis style; in its being and method of materializing it resembles somewhat an elemental spirit. In his ghost-romanticism Scott comes nearer to Mrs. Radcliffe's ghostly atmosphere than to Lewis's realistic treatment of phantoms. He was much more interested in investigating popular beliefs regarding ghosts than in exploiting them in works of fiction.[256]

Byron, who ridiculed Lewis's ghosts and graveyard orgies, did not, himself, altogether despise such aids, as is shown by his poem *Oscar of Alva*. The poem is noteworthy also in the respect that it is directly based on the scene of terror in Schiller's *Geisterseher*, in which the ghost appears in the midst of a wedding feast, and on *Alonzo the Brave*. This is proved, to my mind, by the following similarities:

The first line takes us at once to the romantic moonlight which lights up the hoary turrets of Alva. Often has that "lamp of heaven" set its beams dancing on Alva's silver casques and seen the chiefs arrayed in gleaming mail; it has witnessed bloody battles and death. No longer the footsteps of men echo in Alva's towers, only storms, during which a deep vibrating sound booms from the castle hall over the mouldering wall. After this Ossian-like introduction we come to the

ballad of Oscar and Allan, the beautiful and brave sons of
Angus :

> Dark was the flow of Oscar's hair,
> Wildly it stream'd along the gale ;
> But Allan's locks were bright and fair,
> And pensive seem'd his cheek, and pale.
>
> But Oscar own'd a hero's soul,
> His dark eyes shone through beams of truth ;
> Allan had early learn'd control,
> And smooth his words had been from youth.

Oscar prepares for his wedding and the guests gather at Alva
Castle. Everything is ready, but the bridegroom cannot be
found. All search for him proves vain. Time passes and Allan
wins the love of Oscar's bride. Again preparations are made
for a wedding ; the feast begins in Alva's halls, for this time
the bridegroom is present :

> But who is he, whose darken'd brow
> Glooms in the midst of general mirth ?
> Before his eyes' far fiercer glow
> The blue flames curdle o'er the hearth.
>
> Dark is the robe which wraps his form,
> And tall his plume of gory red ;
> His voice is like the rising storm,
> But light and trackless is his tread.
>
> 'Tis noon of night, the pledge goes round,
> The bridegroom's health is deeply quaff'd ;
> With shouts the vaulted roofs resound,
> And all combine to hail the draught.
>
> Sudden the stranger-chief arose,
> And all the clamorous crowd are hush'd ;
>
> .   .   .   .   .
>
> " Old man ! " he cried, " this pledge is done ;
>
> .   .   .   .
>
> " Say, why should Oscar be forgot ? "

Upon hearing that Oscar is dead, the stranger proposes a
toast to Oscar and invites Allan to drink it. When the latter
adds, as he drinks, that he wishes Oscar were present to share
the goblet, the gloomy stranger cries : " 'Tis he ! I hear my
murderer's voice ! " Allan has murdered his brother and the
crime is revealed in this supernatural manner. The poem
ends in Ossian-like melancholy, in lines which repeat terms
such as " lonely tomb " which " glimmers through the

254

twilight gloom," the harp which must stand " unstrung, un-touch'd," " a dying father's bitter curse," and the " brother's death-groan." As we see, the climax is borrowed word for word from Schiller.

Once more we find an echo from the same scene in Byron's *Lara*. While a magnificent festival is in progress at Otho's castle, Lara observes a stranger, who ceaselessly regards him ; they stare at each other until the stranger cries out : " It is he ! " He then accuses Lara of some mysterious deed, a deed constituting the secret of Lara's life, of which we are purposely left in ignorance. Although there is no question here of ghosts, the scene is in full accordance with its older model.

Ghosts played an important part in the works of Shelley's youth. *Ghasta* has already been mentioned ; the ballad is obviously the fruit of moods of terror evoked by a perusal of *The Monk*, the writer seeing in imagination how " the dark monk now wraps the cowl round his brow, as he sits in his lonely cell." At the stroke of one he goes to a chapel and in his despair breaks open Rosa's coffin. The dead nun raises her skeleton body, " which dripped with the chill dew of hell " ; from her half-rotted eyes shines a pale flame as she stares exultantly at the gloomy monk, etc. *The Spectral Horseman*, written in Ossian's sombre style, is a rare example of the accumulation of terms of ghostly terrors, and is descriptive of the dim and nameless forebodings beloved by the romanticists.

4

Proceeding to the Lake Poets, I venture an opinion that the most " unnatural " part of *The Ancient Mariner* is its opening, the appearance of the mariner in the vicinity of a *wedding*-feast, to accost a *wedding*-guest. What connection has the wedding with the rest of the poem ? We can hardly explain the matter otherwise than by assuming the poet to have been unconsciously influenced by the ghosts at the weddings in *Der Geisterseher* and *Alonzo*, although his poem subsequently takes a totally different turn. It helps to reveal the fundamental similarity of ghost-themes, even though they can be stretched and made to serve purposes originally alien to them.[257]

Upon me *The Ancient Mariner* has the effect of a dream coherent and clearly-illumined in all its details. A dreamer sees nothing illogical in his dream, but lives actively through all its scenes and emotions. No doubts as to the " naturalness " of his experiences assail him, nor upon awakening does he bother himself to seek a " natural " explanation for them. He is fully aware of their lack of logic ; none the less they produce their effect. In similar fashion the poet has succeeded in effacing the reader's natural inclination to view with doubt the adventures described to him, and in so doing has shown, to my mind, the right way to use supernatural material.

The Ancient Mariner is like one of its author's later opium dreams. Although one is loath to class it with the despised terror-romantic literature, it bears, nevertheless, the stamp of that school. Its metre echoes the rhythm of Percy's ballads, and even its diction, in the original form of the poem, was archaic. The hermit, who clashes somewhat with the nautical atmosphere of the poem, owes his existence to Gothic influences.

Other favourite themes of terror-romance are reflected in *The Ancient Mariner :* the voyage of the phantom ship and the idea of navigation by the dead are based on the story of that nautical counterpart of the Wandering Jew, the Flying Dutchman, while the old seafarer's glittering, fascinating glance should by now be familiar to readers of these pages. But the delirium-like, visionary contents of the poem sprang from the brain which was later to conceive *Kubla Khan*, a vision that, like *The Ancient Mariner*, incites comparison with the marvellous rainbow-coloured opium dreams of de Quincey. In origin and quality these are all related phenomena, and form together a special little group in romantic literature.[258]

Nor are ghosts lacking in Southey's work. Reading his ballads and poems one cannot help feeling the influence of Lewis's realistic paintings of ghosts and skeletons. They reveal, as we have seen, an obvious desire to evoke sensations of terror by the realistic description of material horrors, a method hardly possible before Lewis had prepared the way with *The Monk*. Proof of a relationship between the two is Southey's participation in Lewis's *Tales of Terror* with a ballad called *St. Patrick's Purgatory*, written in 1798 and accepted by Lewis for his collection before he knew who had written it. The rhythm of *Lenore* that appears so frequently in Southey's poems, the rhythm used by Scott in his translation, is further proof that he was well acquainted with the ghost-poetry of his period. And consequently we find him writing in *Thalaba* :

> The moon is bright, the sea is calm—
> Wilt thou go on with me ?
> Deliverer ! yes ! thou dost not fear—

which is a fair transcription of lines from *Lenore*.

5

The part played by ghosts in terror-romantic literature is confined by tradition ; the ghost has not proved capable either of development or of unrestricted use. If we pass in review the examples dealt with above, we find that the demoniac glance has become an important weapon for the ghost, something they all possess, and that the romantic imagination was specially impressed by the appearance of a ghost (usually as an avenger) at the height of some feast. Poe, who penetrated deepest into the essence and saw most clearly the purpose of terror-romance, practically confines his attention to these two features in making use of ghosts. In *The Masque of the Red Death* he raises to a high symbolism the theme of the supernatural visitor at a feast. A merry masquerade is in progress in Prince Prospero's castle and " it was a voluptuous scene, that masquerade." The solemn chimes of midnight ring out, the music dies down and a mysterious silence ensues. Before the last stroke a weird stranger is seen, a masked figure whose apparel awakens terror, for the winding-sheet that enwraps him and the mask portraying a plague-stricken corpse cannot denote other than an impersonation of that dread guest. Slowly and with stately steps the mask moves amid the throng, from room to room, from the blue room to the red, from the red to the green, from the green to the orange, then to the white, the purple, and finally to the black. There it halts before the strange timepiece, and when the dancers snatch away its mask, they see behind it—nothing. Red Death has come to Prince Prospero's court like a thief in the night to do its fell duty. " And the life of the ebony clock went out with that of the last of the gay. . . . And Darkness and Decay and the Red Death held illimitable dominion over all."

In this story the traditional theme is used to portray the inexorability of death, with an agitating power that transforms the narrative into a gruesome vision of that stranger who, undeterred by all precautions, will surely come to snatch mankind from all joys and delightful dwellings, from the midst of culture to eternal, timeless darkness. Here the ghost of the wedding-feast becomes a mouthpiece for that poetical pessimism which leaves nothing undestroyed, but stays in its course even the solemn and dreadful march of Time.

Poe returns to the theme in a wonderful vision entitled *Shadow: A Parable*.[259] At the time of the Black Death a company is celebrating in frivolous fashion the funeral of a young man of their circle ; the setting breathes the typical nightmare atmosphere of terror-romance ; the eyes of the dead rest with a bitter expression on the guests. The company make merry and sing, but gradually the note of merriment fades away into the black hangings of the room, which open to emit a " dark and undefined shadow," which was not that of a " man nor God." This shadow remains standing in the doorway, " and moved not, nor spoke any word, but there became stationary and remained." When it finally speaks, it reveals itself as the Spirit of the Catacombs, and in its tone the guests sense the familiar ring of thousands of dead voices. Farther on, we shall see how potent was this new being of terror introduced into literature by Poe.

It is impossible to deal with all the variety of phantoms in the enormous mass of ghost-literature. As one of the most suggestive and forceful attempts in the field I might mention Emily Brontë's *Wuthering Heights* (1847).

6

Tracing the development of terror-romantic literature, one observes that the ghosts who infest the haunted castle are soon joined by other supernatural entities, demoniac beings, and how, in seeking more and more powerful effects of terror, new finds are constantly being made. In his search for supernatural effects Lewis had recourse to demoniac beings, even to the chief of all demons, Lucifer.[260] As the theme thus inaugurated proved a fertile find for the terror-romanticists, we should glance briefly at the chief results in this field.

Lucifer plays an important part in Lewis's romance, being presented in a popular, visible, tangible form. Lewis was consequently led to describe his outward appearance in a manner revealing, by its wealth of detail, his special bent for painting material horrors and his inability to interpret the psychological side of such subjects. At the present day it would be impossible to conceive of a writer seriously attempting to present Lucifer as this kind of concrete monster, but most of Lewis's contemporaries were so much susceptible to terror-romance that the experiment was conceivable and could also be taken seriously.

On her first visit to the monastery church where she hears Ambrosio's sermon, the fair Antonia has a vision of Lucifer, who seems to be foretelling some unhappy fate. The Devil appears in the form of a gigantic, dark-skinned monster; his glance is fierce and terrible, tongues of flame dart from his mouth. From a later description we learn that his scorched limbs show marks of the Almighty's thunderbolts. His enormous body is blackish in hue and long nails grow from his fingers and toes. From his shoulders rise two mighty black wings, living serpents writhe in his hair. He addresses Ambrosio in a voice made hoarse by sulphuric fumes—a detail that even Lewis can hardly have written seriously.[261] To avoid frightening Ambrosio too much, the next time Lucifer appears it is as a youth of scarcely eighteen, irresistibly beautiful of face and form. He is perfectly naked; a bright star gleams on his brow and two scarlet wings grow from his shoulders. His silken locks are held together by a ribbon of fire, the flames of which dance in ever-changing patterns around his head, emitting brighter beams than any jewel. Diamond bands encircle his wrists and ankles, and in his hand he holds a silver branch like to a branch of myrtle. His whole being glows with a dazzling brightness, a clouded rosy illumination seems to proceed from him, and at the moment of his appearance a refreshing current sweeps through the room. Ambrosio notes the wild glance of the demon and the mysterious melancholy reflected in its countenance, telling of the angel's fall and awakening dread in the beholder.[262]

In the former coarse form we recognize the devil of melodrama, a monster presented in so crassly visible and tangible a form that the stage creaks beneath him, who comes to seize the villain of the play at the right moment and to carry him away. We are still far from Stevenson's *Bottle Imp*. In Lewis's description of Lucifer's " mysterious melancholy " and the drawing of his expression, there is a hint, not only of Milton, but of Beckford's Eblis in *Vathek*. There, too, we find a young man whose noble, regular features seem as though bitten by poisonous fumes. His great eyes reflect both pride and despair; his waving locks recall to some extent the Angel of Light. His voice penetrates to the depths of the soul, filling it with deepest melancholy.

The interest taken in the Devil by the romanticists was great, but because of a too materialistic treatment and too much physical detail, their versions of the Prince of Darkness are neither specially fear-inspiring nor possessed of suggestive power. Such effects can only be produced by the Devil when his power for evil, his fell task of destroying human bliss, is suggested in the form of a will to evil acting in the background. Melmoth has the latter method to thank for a great deal of his impressiveness, for the reader senses behind him another being, from whom the deepest tragedy of human existence emanates. This tempting of mankind from the path to bliss finds its highest expression in Mephistopheles, in whom the Devil is raised in genial manner to the most penetrative and suggestive plane of the philosophy of evil. But Mephistopheles was powerless to purify the lower stages of romanticism of the many popular variants of his own high person, which appear either modelled on *The Monk*, as for instance in Rose Matilda's *Zofloya*, or in still more folkloristic form, as in James Hogg's *The Wool-gatherer* and *Confessions of a Justified Sinner*. An example of satire connected with the use of the Devil is the famous *Devil's Drive*, attributed under this title to Byron, as *The Devil's Thoughts* to Coleridge and as *The Devil's Walk* to Shelley and Southey.[263]

7

Lucifer's assistant, the weapon used by him to encompass Ambrosio's fall, is a woman. The works of Mrs. Radcliffe reveal the dim conception of a scheming and vicious woman of this type, and in German sources she is the constant ally of wicked monks. Lewis makes her a demon pure and simple, thus endowing her with a certain awesome quality and majesty. The idea was probably suggested to him by Jacques Cazotte's little romance *Le Diable Amoureux* (1772) and by the character in that book called Biondetta, for she too is sent by the Devil to tempt one of his victims. This book was translated into English in 1791 and appeared a second time in 1810 as *Biondetta, or the Enamoured Spirit*. The translator, who has perceived the likeness between Matilda and Biondetta, dedicates his book to Lewis, with the remark : " I was surprised at a resemblance between the characters of Biondetta and Matilda, too remark-

able to have escaped your recollection if the work of Mons.
Cazotte had ever fallen in your hands." Lewis denied having
read the book, but it is difficult to account otherwise for certain
passages that coincide almost word for word. Thus Cazotte
relates how Biondetta's " dress discovered part of her bosom,
and the moonbeams darting full upon it, enabled me to observe
its dazzling whiteness "; Lewis uses the same picture as
follows : " The moonbeams darting full upon it enabled the
monk to observe its dazzling whiteness." This proof as to
sources does not, however, do away with the fact that Matilda
is much more impressive in her demoniac beauty and power
than the childish and delightful Biondetta ; she achieves
something of the dimensions of Vathek's mother, Carathis,
while Biondetta resembles more his beloved Nouronihar.
In knowledge and skill Carathis is like Matilda. She is the
ally of Eblis and a master of the black arts. Foreseeing that
she would some day attain to close acquaintance with the
powers of the underworld, she had gathered together in secret
hiding-places mummies from the Catacombs, oil made from
poisonous snakes, rhinoceros horns, intoxicating and strongly-
perfumed woods, skulls and skeletons and thousands of other
horrible rarities. Her camel Alboufaki is on a par with its
mistress, for its greatest delight is to inhale poisonous vapours,
while it has an extraordinary passion for old graveyards. There
were thus models in plenty for the demoniac qualities of
Matilda and her great cabbalistic learning.

Following her fortunes more closely, we come almost at
once to a picture of the Madonna admired and worshipped by
Ambrosio. He has received it from an unknown well-wisher,
and so great is its fascination that he sinks every day into a
rapt contemplation of its beauty, thus unknowingly exposing
himself to the first stage of his temptation—for the picture is
that of Matilda. We are aware of the touch of romance such
portraits can be used to induce. The idea was not despised
even by Schiller, who uses it in his own romance, *Der Geisterseher*, which contains a description of a picture of the Madonna
greatly admired by the hero, the picture portraying a super-
naturally beautiful young woman. " Her long fair hair, tied
in two thick plaits, flowed in delightful disorder down her
back ; one hand rested on a crucifix, and sinking gently forward,
she rested on the other (. . . *sanft hinsinkend ruhte sie auf der
andern*)." Gazing on his picture of the Madonna, Ambrosio
admires its beauty. " What beauty in that countenance ;
how graceful is the turn of that head ! What sweetness, yet

what majesty in her divine eyes ! How softly her cheek reclines upon her hand."

If we take into account that the chief characters in these books show the same kind of love for their pictures, and the similarities in the descriptions of these, we cannot be far wrong in assuming that in this particular Schiller's romance had influenced that of Lewis.

Such is the assistant-demon of Lewis's Lucifer. We have already seen how, in addition to these beings, he uses in his ballads and plays all kinds of spirits of water, air and fire, the vampires of popular legend, forest-sprites, witches, etc. These are all obviously theatrical demons, materializations of folklore beliefs, and as such not particularly original. Some significance attaches to their use, however, as they attracted the attention of other romanticists and induced them, Southey, for instance, to build up whole fantastical poems on the existence of such demoniac beings. A feature common to all is their indefiniteness, their lack of individuality ; the poets seem as little able to obtain a firm hold of them as of ghosts, and they flutter through the poems as misty and vaporous spirits, representing now the spirit of good, now that of evil, acting as mouthpieces for the opinions of the authors. In the literature of the period the part assigned to them is an important one and characterizes the nature of this literature.

8

In my opinion Lewis's Matilda proves to be the only one of these demon-types capable, by reason of her vitality and human propensity for passion, of further development. Her beauty, her terrible task and the manner, in itself arousing terror, in which her supernatural qualities are gradually revealed, leave a lasting impression on the mind. As a matter of fact, this female demon boasts a famous descendant.

It is difficult to deny her sistership with the mysterious, dread Geraldine of Coleridge's fragment *Christabel*, even though the circumstance that the poem was never completed prevents us from knowing the part ultimately assigned to her. Nevertheless, the date of its creation, a couple of years after the publication of *The Monk* (1797-1800), its typically terror-romantic contents and the suddenness and mystery of Geraldine's appearance on the stage, the purely " Gothic " atmosphere of the poem, connect it irrevocably with the very centre of terror-romanticism and justify us in drawing parallels between Matilda and Geraldine.[264]

What the poet intended by his poem it is impossible for us to say ; he himself gave no explanation. Judging from the fact that he kept the poem a long time without publishing it, only to leave it after all unfinished, he was not clear as to its continuation. He seems to have caught a glimpse of some being symbolizing forces injurious to natural man, a kind of Undine-theme, but its development to a logical conclusion was apparently beyond him.[265] Even as a fragment, *Christabel* is a masterpiece of the poetry of terror, and has enriched literature with an extremely effectual female demon, one endowed, moreover, with a terror-romantic feature of special interest, namely, the evil eye, the fascinating glance of the snake. The first time Shelley heard the scene where Geraldine disrobes, the enigmatical element of terror affected him to such a degree that he had a clear vision of two eyes in Geraldine's breast.[266] This evil and mischievous glance denotes a development of the demon-theme. Lewis's material devil becomes gradually transformed into the principle of evil, losing its concreteness ; for the later romanticist is fully aware, in searching for a suitable form of demoniac being capable of acting as a source of mysterious and inexplicable terror, that no coarsely material-istic daylit devil of Lewis's type will do. On the contrary, a personification of evil must remain indeterminate in outline and vague in feature before it can provide the necessary scope to the much more suggestive artistry of the imagination. This was the path along which the most gruesome demon of terror-romance, Lytton's " Dweller of the Threshold " in *Zanoni* was to be evolved, its earliest model being apparently Poe's *Shadow*, and an earlier ancestress, perhaps Milton's loath-some Sin.[267]

Before the student of occult wisdom, prepared by long exercises of soul and body, can achieve contact with the " Beyond," he has to endure a struggle with the said " Dweller," which is evil and horror personified. As there are beings of light, so are there also beings of darkness, the prince of the latter being just this dread " Dweller of the Threshold," to withstand whom superhuman fearlessness, combined with absolute purity of mind and body, is necessary. " She is surpassing in malignity and hatred all her tribe—one whose eyes have paralysed the bravest, and whose power increases over the spirit precisely in proportion to its fear." In the case of young Glyndon, whose ancestors include an advanced student of secret knowledge, and who has thus an inherited instinct to take up the attempt to reach the " Beyond," it is his sensuality which prevents him from rising to the high and pure state of mind essential to success. On the occasion when he intrudes into his master's laboratory, lights the lamps and inhales the mysterious elixir, he succeeds in conjuring up a series of dim spirits and hears " a low sound, but musical," but only for a moment. The beings of mist vanish through the window and are replaced by another being, who in some strange fashion transforms the bliss recently experienced by Glyndon into horror : " By degrees, this object shaped itself to his sight. It was as that of a human head, covered with a dark veil, through which glared with livid and demoniac fire eyes that froze the marrow of his bones. Nothing else of the face was distinguishable—nothing but those intolerable eyes ; but his terror, that even at the first seemed beyond nature to endure, was increased a thousandfold, when, after a pause, the phantom glided slowly into the chamber. The cloud re-treated from it as it advanced ; the bright lamps grew wan, and flickered restlessly as at the breath of its presence. Its form was veiled as the face, but the outline was that of a female ; yet it moved not as move even the ghosts that simulate the living. It seemed rather to crawl as some vast misshapen reptile ; and pausing at length it cowered beside the table which held the mystic volume, and again fixed its eyes through the filmy veil on the rash invoker. All fancies, the most grotesque, of Monk or Painter in the early North, would have failed to give to the visage of imp or fiend that aspect of deadly malignity which spoke to the shuddering nature in those eyes alone. All else so dark—shrouded—veiled and larva-like. But the burning glare so intense, so livid, yet so living, had in it something that was almost *human*, in its passion of hate and mockery—something that served to show that the shadowy Horror was not all a spirit, but partook of matter enough, at least, to make it more deadly and fearful an enemy, to material forms. As, clinging with the grasp of agony to the wall—his hair erect—his eyeballs staring, he still gazed back upon that appalling gaze—the Image spoke to him—his soul rather than his ear comprehended the words it said. . . ." Glyndon is unable to withstand the power of this being and is overpowered by it, whereafter its hypnotic eyes follow him everywhere. They seem satisfied and retreat only when he commits some immoral deed, but reappear immediately to cow him whenever he tries to rise morally. Salvation from his degradation is possible only if he can collect sufficient strength to combat those eyes. With this detail the symbolical nature of the story becomes evident.

The conception of a demoniac being clothed with the suggestivity of mysticism and endowed with staring eyes had taken deep hold of Lytton. We find it in the tale of terror mentioned earlier, in which his fancy of vampire-eyes rises to gruesome impressivity. The experiences of the narrator, who spends a night in the haunted house, are given a special character by the circumstance that he encounters there, not only ordinary ghosts, but a deathless being of evil. As he walks in the yard the footprints of a child suddenly appear before him in the dust, as though a ghost-child were preceding him. He hears whispers, a dog shows unmistakable signs of terror, an arm-chair moves of its own volition, and he seems to descry a light-blue misty being of undefined shape sitting in it ; on attempting to replace the chair, the person moving it feels a painful shock in his arm. Doors mysteriously lock themselves ; an invisible hand tries to snatch away letters in which vague hints are made of the murder of a child in the same building long ago ; a pale light of the dimensions of a human body sways before the watchers, becoming finally transformed into a dazzling ball of fire and disappearing again ; the candles flicker as though in a wind and invisible force removes a watch from the table ; the dog stands as though turned to stone in its corner, its hair bristling, a wild light in its eyes, and then tries to escape, dashing itself against the wall ; it is hypnotized by terror, like a rabbit attacked by a snake. Finally, the supreme being of terror appears, in shape and power exactly like " The Dweller of the Threshold " ; here too the eyes of the demon are a special object of the writer's attention and imagination. The story is too well known to quote it here. It shows to what an extent could be developed this weird conception of eyes as a source of irresistible terror.

9

It was the study of Geraldine that led me to follow this motive of the evil eye, and to investigate the pictures of terror to which it gave rise. Returning once more to the sisterhood of Matilda, attention is attracted by Scott's *Lay of the Last Minstrel*, whose mistress of Branksome Castle was clearly born under demoniac influences of the above nature.[268] Her secret bower is guarded " by word and by spell, deadly to hear, and deadly to tell " ; except for the mistress herself no living being has ever crossed its threshold. She is depicted however, with something of the cool restraint of Scott's poetry and her mission as a mother defending the rights of her children places her in a category of her own. In Southey's poetry demoniac witch-women play an important part ; on the whole, the idea of such beings was common amongst the terror-romanticists, who often depicted them in the strongest colours. One is reminded of some such being, slightly reminiscent of Matilda, in certain of Poe's works. *Ligeia* in particular, to the description of whose beauty the author has brought all his skill, imaginative power and command of language, recalls the mysterious women of terror-romance, for in addition to her demoniac beauty she possesses an unusual depth of learning, which extends even to the remotest fields of occult wisdom. In consequence we find Ligeia awakening from the dead by will-power, in a strange and fear-inspiring manner. A similar woman is *Morella*, who is extremely beautiful and a perfect miracle of learning. Occult wisdom is her special province ; she initiates her husband, opening out to him vistas of forbidden knowledge, until the terror that is ultimately encountered in these regions falls like a shadow over his heart and estranges him from his mysterious wife. In this story Poe returns to his romantic idea of a physical life extending beyond the grave.

The French writer Villiers de L'Isle-Adam, who wrote under the influence of Poe, seems to have attempted the outline of a demoniac woman on the lines of Poe's *Ligeia* and *Morella* ; of such nature are Tullia in the fragment *Isis* and Any Sowana in *L'Ève Future*.[269]

Hawthorne's *Marble Faun* would seem to be far from the ghost-romances of the terror-romanticists, but on closer investigation it is found to have been written partly under the influence of such literature. The mysterious artist Miriam, whose gestures and demeanour frequently create an atmosphere of enigma, is in reality none other than Matilda, though purified from the influence of evil and become a woman of fine ideals. The way in which the strange plot is developed, its recourse to the old machinery of terror-romance and many traits in Miriam herself bear witness to how close the story of Ambrosio clung to the author while the poetical history of Donatello, the human faun, was being written. The modernity, however, of this version of the old female type of terror-romance carries us right into the midst of the vampire women of present-day literature, who have a bewitching and mysterious power of attracting ever new victims into their nets.[270]

VIII

INCEST AND ROMANTIC EROTICISM

I

THE first word of the heading to this chapter takes us into the midst of the most horrifying and abnormal material used by the romanticists. It evokes memories of a series of dreadful scenes and inspires the timid question, what can have induced so many authors to return again and again to the treatment of such horrors.

The theme makes its appearance in literature extremely early, in the wake of other social and moral problems. Life itself has repeatedly permitted the crime to occur, thus forcing it upon the attention of society, and literature has perpetuated it in stories since the beginnings of civilization. In the ninth song of the *Iliad*, Phœnix relates how, at his mother's request, he cohabited with his father's mistress, in order to provoke his father into dismissing her. Such was the birth of the theme of father and son as rivals. Sophocles introduced the *Œdipus*-theme, in which a son kills his father and weds his mother; in *Hippolytus* Euripides creates the theme of the mother who persecutes her son (stepson) with offers of love. The incest-motive then passed from Greek to Roman literature, where it is continued, for example, in Seneca's *Phædra* and *Œdipus*. From classical literature it is constantly spreading to other literatures, even to that of the present day, giving rise in every country to numerous variations, imitations and new combinations of the theme. Even in its historical literature, antiquity guarded against this theme of terror becoming lost; Herodotus (III, 31) relates that Cambyses killed his sister, whom he had taken to wife although she was his sister by both parents; the historian Marcus Justinus relates that Semiramis killed her own son, whom she had importuned with invitations to guilty love; the story of the Ptolemies discloses that they habitually married their sisters, following in this the inbreeding traditions of the

267

Pharaoh-dynasties; and Suetonius reveals in his history terrible pictures of the relations between Agrippina and her son Nero—to mention only a few from the abundance of examples. Reflecting contemporary views of life, even the myths of antiquity have preserved to posterity antique ideas of inbreeding: Chronos castrated his father Uranus and drove him from the throne, marrying his sister Rhea; his son Zeus overcame him in turn and married his own sister Hera; thus the perpetration of incest in the Olympian family was continued. Briefly, incest appears so frequently in the literature, mythology and history of antiquity, that one is compelled to assume sexual intercourse between members of a family to have been both more common and less feared than in later times. In the beginnings of human life, when the family and the clan were the only social communities, inbreeding within a relatively confined circle must have been an unavoidable and natural means of continuing the species, until the desire for alien blood, originally satisfied by captives, male and female, secured in war, and by rape, gradually began to develop into a moral barrier to incest.

In addition to the above, we might take up yet another ancient literary source, which deals with incest in an unforgettable manner, namely, the Old Testament. It is the source which, spreading from race to race, has dealt most openly with and most openly condemned incest. The picture of the first human beings and their children inevitably brings up the idea of marriage between brother and sister. The episode of Lot's daughters, that of Sarah and Abraham, in which Abraham declares to Abimelech: "and moreover she is indeed my sister, the daughter of my father, but not the daughter of my mother; and she became my wife"; Judah and Tamar; these are all mentioned without the slightest reference to punishment or reproof. Not until we reach the eighteenth chapter of Leviticus, do we come to a specification of the degrees of near kin and of forbidden intercourse, a passage that proves by its existence that such intercourse was common in Egypt and Canaan and that there was need for its condemnation among the Israelites. In the twentieth chapter of the same book such intercourse is specified in still greater detail and forbidden as an abomination. Incest is forbidden in the Mosaic Laws in stricter terms than anywhere else; the words employed in condemning it are so stern and noble that one can well regard them as having considerably accentuated the horrified aversion now felt against the crime.

Perpetuated in literature and deriving new vitality from actual misfortunes and crimes of this nature, the dismal theme of incest has thus come down from ancient times, and is as far from extinction as ever. Even before the birth of literature, it had become one of the most prolific themes of folklore, setting its dark tragic stamp on tales and poems, of which an example is the Kullervo-group incorporated with the *Kalevala*.

2

Shakespeare sometimes approaches the incest-theme. In *Pericles* it is presented in all its nakedness, for there the king Antiochus has seduced his daughter and keeps her as his mistress. Likewise in those plays in which, as in *The Winter's Tale*, a girl-child is abandoned, the danger of incest is near to hand, as both in folklore and mythology an abandoned child is frequently the victim, in accordance with the example provided by the Œdipus-legend, of a fate of this nature. Finally it should be noted that among the numerous theories that profess to solve the enigma of Hamlet, an argument built on our present theme has been advanced. According to this argument, Hamlet sees in the removal of his father from his mother's side the fulfilment of certain unconscious desires of his childhood : in his love for his mother there has been an unconscious erotic element joined to filial love, a side of his emotional life that has only become apparent to him in the dream-life of his manhood. Desiring the undivided love of his mother he has hoped, without being aware of it, that his father might die, and now when he sees this wish fulfilled and understands that another has usurped the place to which he himself aspired (discovering at the same time the unnatural bent of his emotions) he is overwhelmed by a loathing for himself. It is this disgust of his own being which causes him to delay revenging himself on the king, whom in the light of his childhood's desires he cannot help identifying with himself, and whose crime, measured by his own secret instincts, is therefore doubtful. The same loathing makes him rebuke his mother in words inspired by a passionate jealousy and forbid her to share the king's bed. The revelation of the direction taken by his hidden emotional life extinguishes his love for Ophelia and gives rise to his cruelty towards her, cruelty towards a beloved person being a torture and therefore satisfying to the lust for punishment self-loathing has inspired within him. Thus, while outwardly scheming to revenge the murderer of his father, Hamlet is in reality wrestling with his own soul and his terrible desires. May the argument be taken for what it is worth. It is not possible for me to go deeper into the merits of the psycho-analytical method on which the argument is based, and which attempts to explain the incestuous inclinations of the grown-up as a fulfilment of the unconscious eroticism of childhood ; I must therefore refer the reader to the literature on the subject.[271]

The other Elizabethan play-wrights made much greater use of the incest-theme. In Beaumont and Fletcher's *A King and No King* (1619), horrified suspense is evoked by the suddenly-aroused passion of the king Arbace for his sister Panthea ; the situation is solved towards the end by the information that Panthea was not after all his sister. Two other dramas by the same authors, *Women Pleased* and *The Fair Maid of the Inn*, deal with incest, which is likewise the foundation of the plot in John Ford's *'Tis Pity She is a Whore*. The Elizabethan dramatist turned willingly to painful and torturing themes, amongst which that of incest is probably the best adapted to stir the moral calm of the spectator to the point of storm.

To come to the class of literature with which we are here concerned, I would point out that the incest-theme hovers perilously near in *The Castle of Otranto* : Manfred desires to marry, after the youth had died, his son's betrothed, thereby creating a relationship not wholly free from a flavour of incest. Walpole's drama *The Mysterious Mother* shows that this horrible theme had impressed itself on his mind. He relates having heard, as a child, of a woman who had asked Bishop Tillotson's advice in the following matter : [272] she had borne her son a daughter and now, unaware that she was both his own daughter and his sister, the son wished to marry the maiden ; the bishop had advised her not to disclose the secret. This story Walpole averred was the source of his play. Be that as it may, we find in the story of the *Heptameron* for November 30th, a series of incestuous acts similar in every respect to those in Walpole's play : in the belief that he is embracing his mistress a young man embraces his mother ; she bears him a daughter, whom he subsequently marries, unconscious of her relation of sister-daughter to him. In *The Mysterious Mother* the Countess of Narbonne has secretly taken the place of her son's mistress and given birth to a daughter, whom her son later marries. When the secret is revealed, the countess commits suicide,

Adeliza enters a convent and Edmund seeks death on the battle-field.

If it were desirable to investigate this play in the spirit of the German psycho-analytical method already referred to in connection with Hamlet, we should first delve into Walpole's childhood, paying particular attention to his relations with his mother, in order to establish, if possible, what were the unconscious desires of his childhood, and, in case his attachment to his mother proved strong enough, to draw the conclusion that somewhat in the manner of an unconscious medium, he had interpreted these early desires in his play, not forgetting at the same time to mirror the deepest and most subtle currents of the psychology of his times. Not being able to discover the slightest reason for these assumptions, we refrain from the experiment. Explanations of the above type proceed in general from assumptions and not from facts, and only lead to conclusions that do violence to the literary product they seek to interpret, while a critical analysis of these conclusions shows the results obtained to be of doubtful value. To the question as to how and why Walpole came to occupy himself with the incest-theme, the answer must be sought elsewhere.

The brief reference to the time of Shakespeare and the frequency with which the incest-theme then appears were intended to show the peculiar and characteristic affection of the romanticist for this, and all other themes of terror, be the period Elizabethan or late eighteenth century. Sooner or later the romantic author seeking for melodramatic horrors was bound to come into contact with this dark phenomenon and to feel himself inspired by the tragic conflicts in which the theme is rife. Incest is the kind of motive that an author with a cool and passionless conception of beauty would avoid as violent and unnatural,[273] whereas a mind fired by romantic defiance of the limits of art and bent upon evoking horror would be secretly drawn to it. When Walpole began to create a " Gothic " literature, it was only natural that in pondering over the most suitable characters with which to people his haunted castle he should chance upon the idea of incestuous relations between them. As the motive offers good opportunities of evoking that terror and suspense-filled atmosphere of mystery which is one of the chief aims of the terror-romanticist, it is to be expected that wherever literature turns into romantic channels, the subject of incest will sooner or later emerge. Thus, while studying " Gothicism " and indulging himself in effects of terror, Walpole tried in the course of his literary experiments—

remembering perhaps the story he had heard in his childhood—the effect incest would make among the other horrors of his haunted castle. From the historical point of view it must be admitted that in making this experiment Walpole showed himself, as in his romance, a reviver of literary traditions; *The Mysterious Mother* brought the incest-theme again to light, sending it forth to play a not inconsiderable part in the romanticism of the following decades.

3

The subject is such a delicate one that the eminently respectable pens of Clara Reeve and Mrs. Radcliffe scarce dared approach it. In the case of Mrs. Radcliffe it is nigh, however, in *The Romance of the Forest*, in which the Marquis de Montalt unwittingly lusts after his niece; and as we have previously remarked, incest is imminent, owing obviously to the influence of *The Monk*, in *The Italian*, or so at least the author would have us believe. Nevertheless, the part played by the theme in the work of these two authors is small. It was left to Lewis to display it with the most lurid details in *The Monk*, in permitting Ambrosio to rape and to murder his sister, although, it is true, the monk is unaware of their consanguinity. Of all the realistic depictments of horrors provided by the book, this bestial crime in a gruesome vault of the dead is the climax, to which most of the opposition directed towards the book was undoubtedly due. As though in defiance, Lewis resuscitates the incest-motive exhumed by Walpole, flinging it, thanks to the wide circulation of his book, into the open for the public to squabble over and for graver writers to study.

Surveying in the light of this motive the subsequent romantic writers, we discover in it a kind of touchstone of literary character. The author who utilizes it is obviously permitting his intellectual life to stray in peculiar paths; in this respect that author can be said to go farthest who permits his characters to commit incest, fully aware of the nature of the deed. Scott, for example, does not directly revert to the theme,[274] and we can well understand how impossible it would have been for him to do so; his whole literary character is too clean and healthy, inclining him to love the more beautiful and natural aspects of romance. The theme was alien alike to Southey and Wordsworth, whose puritanical morality, blame-lessness and bourgeois conception of what was permissible must have made even the idea of such a subject repugnant to them. As regards Coleridge we cannot be so certain, for his nature comprised a good deal more of the defiance and love of adventure, not to say decadence, that makes it possible for an author to treat with such themes. Nevertheless he has not dealt with it. The decadence referred to is found in Walpole and Lewis, and a considerable share was possessed by both Byron and Shelley. Unnatural as it would be to find Scott working out the motive, so natural is it to find the latter two poets doing so. The reason for their apparent interest in the subject of incest has been sought in their respective natures and private life. In this respect the following argument goes farthest.

In 1905 Lord Lovelace, Byron's grandson, published for private circulation a work entitled *Astarte: A Fragment of Truth concerning G.G.B.* (new revised edition 1921), based on family documents and intended to prove the justice of the old accusations levelled at Byron, that he had lived in forbidden intercourse with his step-sister Augusta.[275] The book was a titbit for the psycho-analysts; on the strength of it Otto Rank declared Byron's guilt to be established beyond argument. Looking at the matter coolly and impartially, one is compelled to admit that in none of those letters regarded as the most deadly evidence is there a single sentence that could justify an objective reader in accusing the poet of the crime. They contain strangely heated hints regarding the relations between Byron and Augusta, but no definite, irrefutable proof for the conclusion drawn by those whose shameful curiosity led them to lay bare the poet's private life. Beyond a certain point such study no longer concerns the history of literature, but is a matter for psychiatrists. The private life of a poet does, indeed, cast some light on his work, but not to the extent assumed in this case; every aspect of a poet's production cannot and should not be projected on to his private life. For the prominence given in Byron's works to the incest-theme, no conclusions can truthfully be drawn regarding his own deeds, at least not on the basis of the material now available.

The fact that Byron obviously devoted a good deal of thought to the idea of incest may be explained by the strength of his erotic feelings and the abnormal passionateness of his emotional ego. Defiant, always on the look-out for new poses, this romanticist who waged open war on conditions, institutions, customs and established conceptions, and desired to appear worse than he actually was, affected to regard—to such lengths can affectations of this nature be carried—the usual disgust against unlawful love as a superstition, of which liberty-loving souls could, if they so desired, divest themselves. The fact that Byron never deals with incest as a misfortune occasioned by ignorance, but always as a deliberate action, shows that he meditated much over the matter, especially after the accusations against himself had begun. Then, in full accordance with his nature, he took the mystifying and defiant attitude : Well, and what then ?

He was also attracted to the theme by the nature of his romanticism. I have already pointed out that Byron bases the effect of his poetry, in much greater measure than his predecessors had done, on the dark mystery in which his hero is usually clothed; this mystery is generally evoked by hints intended to convey the existence of some terrible crime, abhorrent alike to feeling and morality. What, in such circumstances, could be better calculated to provide a background for such hints than secret incestuous relations? This desire for romantic, dreadful mystery suffices, taken together with the pose of sinfulness affected by the poet, to explain Byron's position towards the subject, making it unnecessary to delve into the secrets of his private life. It was not his theme alone, but belonged to the whole romantic school.

In the beginning of *The Bride of Abydos* the possibility of criminal love between brother and sister flashes forth, and the reader is led to expect a different ending to the poem than that actually given. Can Byron have had some other end in view when he began his poem, from which he subsequently retreated as though afraid of his own plan ? One is inclined to ask this question because the kind of subterfuge that makes Selim and Zuleika originally appear as brother and sister is alien to Byron's nature ; it does not even play a decisive part in the inevitable element of mystery that centres chiefly around Selim and his life as a pirate. It is not impossible that Byron had originally intended his poem to deal with the fateful love of brother and sister, especially as he was at the time involved in scandals of a like nature, and that he only relinquished this plan as his work progressed and his defiance cooled down.

Relations between brother and sister is the form of incest that interested Byron most. He returns to the theme in *Cain*, whose wife is his step-sister Adah, and not content with passing the matter by as an inevitable result of the scarcity of human beings, he attempts a general defence of such relations. Adah confesses to loving Cain more than she does her father, and asks Lucifer if this is a sin ; and when Lucifer answers that though not a sin in her case it will be in that of her children, Adah is bewildered, unable to grasp that conception of love can change. In dealing with this Biblical theme Byron felt himself on such distant and neutral ground that he was not afraid to deal openly with incest, tacitly accepted as it was by Christian readers whenever they troubled to think of the first family and the propagation of the human race. Subsequently, he based the almost impenetrable mystery of *Manfred* on, as far as I can see, the same criminal relationship.

Astarte, Manfred's only friend, whose mere name is sufficient to evoke an atmosphere of mystery-tinged eroticism, lives no longer, and Manfred seeks forgetfulness of their common secret. On the appearance of the " seventh " spirit in the form of a beautiful woman, Manfred cries out :

> Oh God ! if it be thus, and *thou*
> Art not a madness and a mockery,
> I yet might be most happy. I will clasp thee,
> And we again will be—

When the hunter offers him wine, he refuses it, saying that he saw blood on the rim of the goblet :

> I say 'tis blood—my blood ! the pure warm stream
> Which ran in the veins of my fathers, and in ours
> When we were in our youth, and had one heart,
> And loved each other as we should not love,
> And this was shed : but still it rises up,
> Colouring the clouds, that shut me out from heaven,
> Where thou art not—and I shall never be.

Manfred's crime has been that his " embrace was fatal " :

> I loved her, and destroy'd her !
>
> .   .   .   .   .
>
> Not with my hand, but heart, which broke her heart ;
> It gazed on mine, and wither'd.
>
> .   .   .   .   .
>
> Thou lovedst me
> Too much, as I loved thee : we were not made
> To torture thus each other, though it were
> The deadliest sin to love as we have loved,

says Manfred to the spirit of Astarte, begging her not to loathe him. Seen against the background of the usual themes of terror of those days and of Byron's own life, regarding which, as the pious abbot remarks to Manfred :

> . . . Rumours strange,
> And of unholy nature, are abroad,
> And busy with thy name ; a noble name
> For centuries,

these purposely vague passages cannot denote other than incest and the resultant pangs of conscience. In such fashion does Byron attach this theme to his hero, who in consequence becomes, as we have earlier remarked, an embodiment of the entire spiritual capital of the terror-romantic school, an individual who draws unto himself most of what had been thought and expressed in this field before his arrival, and exalts it into a symbol of suffering and atonement, of a deeply human sense of guilt.

4

In the life of Shelley we find features which make the appearance of the incest-theme in his poetry comprehensible. This poet of ethereal visions—" By solemn vision, and bright silver dream, his infancy was nurtured " (Alastor)—had felt in his soul, ever since childhood, a deep yearning to be loved, a feeling which set his imagination seeking a purified and ideal love. During his childhood it was his sisters who listened to his weird fairy-tales ; of a mother's influence we can discern no trace, and from his father's side he heard only the stern and unyielding demand for obedience. Altogether, his experiences were well adapted, particularly after the first stirrings of love had led to disappointment,[276] to awaken in him the conception that sisterly love was the purest and most lasting of all the forms of love. To support this conception came the engrained scepticism with which he regarded all mortal institutions and conventions, a state of mind that would not permit him to accept unchallenged the justice of the term " unnatural " as applied to love between blood-relations. During the whole of his life Shelley supplemented " earthly " love with a " heavenly " love ; in other words, his family comprised, besides his wife, a lady for whom he felt a Platonic love. In his poetry these parallel affections expanded a step farther into love between brother and sister that was no longer wholly Platonic. It is in similar fashion that he projects his conception of his father into his verses, where fathers usually represent the most boundless tyranny, and are raised to the dignity of symbols of that oppression and injustice against which Shelley waged his spiritual warfare. Thus, like Byron, Shelley uses the incest-theme deliberately, after due consideration to which the impulse can only have been supplied by his experiences and his erotic susceptibility.

> Till in the vale of Cashmire, far within
> Its loneliest dell, where odorous plants entwine
> Beneath the hollow rocks a natural bower,
> Beside a sparkling rivulet he stretched
> His languid limbs. A vision on his sleep
> There came, a dream of hopes that never yet
> Had flushed his cheek.   He dreamed a veilèd maid
> Sate near him, talking in low solemn tones.
> Her voice was like the voice of his own soul
> Heard in the calm of thought ; its music long,
> Like woven sounds of streams and breezes, held
> His inmost sense suspended in its web
> Of many-coloured woof and shifting hues.
> Knowledge and truth and virtue were her theme,
> And lofty hopes of divine liberty,
> Thoughts the most dear to him, and poesy,
> Herself a poet.   Soon the solemn mood
> Of her pure mind kindled through all her frame
> A permeating fire. . . .
>
>   Sudden she rose,
> As if her heart impatiently endured
> Its bursting burthen : at the sound he turned,
> And saw by the warm light of their own life
> Her glowing limbs beneath the sinuous veil
> Of woven wind, her outspread arms now bare,
> Her dark locks floating in the breath of night,
> Her beamy bending eyes, her parted lips
> Outstretched, and pale, and quivering eagerly.
> His strong heart sunk and sickened with excess
> Of love.   He reared his shuddering limbs and quelled
> His gasping breath, and spread his arms to meet
> Her panting bosom : . . . she drew back a while,
> Then, yielding to the irresistible joy,
> With frantic gesture and short breathless cry
> Folded his frame in her dissolving arms.

For this ideal being of his dream Alastor searches until death releases him. We discern in it a poetical disguise for Shelley's own unattainable ideal of transfigured love, for which he vainly sought compensation in earthly love and which he imagined might be reflected in love between brother and sister.[277] This pure sisterly love of his soul he later glorified in his *Epipsychidion*, in which he uses the words " sister " and

" bride " in a parallel sense. In his idyll of *Rosalind and Helen*, where the two women relate the tragic history of their loves, and which, in the episode of Lionel, closely mirrors the poet's own life, the shadow of incest is present in the background. The place whither Helen goes to meet her friend Rosalind is truly romantic : silence and dusk reign there ; nature slumbers, the snake sleeps in his cave and the birds dream on their boughs ; only the shadows creep forth, the glow-worms twinkle and the owls and nightingales awaken ; the owls flee however to a merrier glen, for the moon sleeps behind a cloud ; the nightingale broods on a branch, sad, for its false mate has fled. In this dismal spot a gloomier crime has been committed, for here brother and sister have surrendered themselves to each other body and soul :

> . . . The multitude,
> Tracking them to the secret wood,
> Tore limb from limb their innocent child,
> And stabbed and trampled on its mother ;
> But the youth, for God's most holy grace,
> A priest saved to burn in the market-place.

These words reflect the poet's own standpoint towards the event. In this spot, first Rosalind relates her story, the tragedy of which is deepened by the shadow of incest ; she stood already before the altar with her heart's beloved, when her father returned from distant lands in time to inform her that the bridegroom was her own brother. In my opinion, both references to incest are irrelevant to the poem ; the first is altogether gratuitous and is hardly more than an additional black stripe in the fabric of the poem ; the second is not the only rock on which Rosalind's happiness could have been shattered. In using them the poet introduces a discord into his harmony, diminishing thereby the peace of the idyll which, expressed in the melancholy resignation that follows misfortune, gives to the poem its character. The very irrelevancy of the incest-motive in this case shows how prominent a place the idea must have occupied in Shelley's mind at the time when he wrote his poem.

The idea of a brother and sister united in an idealistic love, yet in such manner that the boundary between sisterly and sensual love seems at times to vanish, is a common and special feature of Shelley's poetry. In *The Revolt of Islam* it is absent, but it was in the original plan of the work. The title intended for this poem was *Laon and Cythna*, who are expressly said to be brother and sister.[278] After being parted for long by fate they meet again and the joy of meeting grows into a passion of love, causing them to sink, oblivious of their real relationship, into an ecstasy of love that lasts for two days, a love so impetuous that the lines which depict it seem to quiver under a rosy veil with the fire and passion of a surrender that knows no bounds. After reading these lines one can understand why Shelley's publisher demanded the alteration of the sisterly element to something else ; Cythna was to be made the playmate of Laon's childhood. Shelley himself saw nothing to take offence at in their blood-relationship, as his image of the highest and purest love originated, one might say, in affection between brother and sister.[279]

As regards his famous incest-drama *The Cenci* (1819), it obviously falls without the true boundaries of Shelley's spiritual kingdom of poetry. It did not spring from the same spiritual conflicts and meditations over the problems of life as the main part of his poetry, but is the fruit of romantic interest in the picture of a beautiful woman and her tragic fate, and of a burning humanitarian sympathy. The incestuous element— the mystic and awful threat of a father towards his daughter— is not the interpretation of an ideal as, for instance, in *The Revolt of Islam*, but the verification of an abnormal crime by a person standing outside. In my opinion, *The Cenci* is chiefly the story of an individual crime, which poetical treatment has not been able to raise into the sphere of poetry and universality.[280]

5

These examples may suffice to show the importance of the part played by a love-theme of terror, such as incest, in the work of the English romanticists. Classifiable as it is with melodramatic materials in general, it appears specially developed in those times when romanticism surges nearest to its ultimate, pathological frontiers. The desire to deal with such a theme is, in itself, a pathological feature of romantic psychology.

Different shades can be distinguished in the general attitude taken by the literature of those days towards love. Love as seen by Mrs. Radcliffe is an elegant and delicate pastoral idyll, behind which quivers a sentimental, tearfully-pure and ethereal yearning ; Clara Reeve's love is similar in quality, in the little she gives beyond the mere assurance that the hero loves the heroine and wins her; Walpole, the founder of the school, gave the first impulse towards this tender melody of love with his account of the idealistic relations between Theodore and Matilda, but this was unable to tempt the two women writers into falling in with the other symphony of love which begins with Manfred's schemes against Isabella and ends in a dissonant crash of chords in *The Mysterious Mother*. This strain was taken up by Lewis, and variations upon it are found in the nobler music of Byron and Shelley, of whom the former does not neglect either the healthily sensual, unphilosophizing type of love. Scott keeps on the whole to legitimate bourgeois love, healthy, overjoyed at the prospect of a wedding, a love depicted with a humorous wink, and turns only rarely, as in *The Bride of Lammermoor*, to the darker pigments of tragedy. The scale is thus an extensive one, but thus differentiated does not give rise to further comment. It is not until we have discovered the underlying affinity in all terror-romantic depictments of love that we hold a key to the real world of that love.

One of the chief features of the plot in the works of Walpole, Clara Reeve, Ann Radcliffe and Lewis, is the persecution to which the heroine is subjected. This persecution, irrespective of the conditions in which it occurs, is at bottom an erotic feature, and reflects, no matter what the type of literature or the period may be, the active love-instinct of the male and the passivity of the female. The terror-romanticist deals with this old natural theme in the melodramatic style beloved of him: the young woman is persecuted not so much by cunning schemes for seduction, as by direct threats of violence. To give the matter a more dreadful appearance the terror-romanticist chooses the most gruesome surroundings he can invent for this persecution; the desolate passages and crypts of the haunted castle, the catacombs of monasteries, etc. To my mind, this choice of *milieu* is in general, and particularly in its application to eroticism, an abnormal trait. In the interest which Lewis displays in depicting an eroticism bordering on bestiality in circumstances of secrecy and night, it is hard not to descry the fruits of inflamed, neurasthenical, sexual visions, of a pathological psychology which betrays, unknown perhaps to the writer himself, an abnormal trait in his composition. The more lonely the spot to which he leads his victim, the more heated and lively does the imagination of this author become. It is from some such source as this that an explanation is to be sought for the orgies of horrors which infest Maturin's pages;

though these are not directly concerned with eroticism, at bottom they spring from the sexual excitement of a neurasthenic subject. Proof that romantic eroticism, when it is truly romantic, displays symptoms of abnormality, is provided, in my opinion, by the incest-motive and by such lines as the following (spoken by a madman) from *Julian and Maddalo :*

> That, like some maniac monk, I had torn out
> The nerves of manhood by their bleeding root
> With mine own quivering fingers, so that ne'er
> Our hearts had for a moment mingled there
> To disunite in horror. . . .

IX

THE YOUNG HERO AND HEROINE AND OTHER CHARACTERS

I

THE most clearly-defined character of romance is the tyrant of the haunted castle, from whom the Byronic hero and the superman are gradually evolved. With the exception of the monk and the old seneschal, who are clearly, if somewhat conventionally characterized, the rest of the cast, including the young hero and heroine, are frequently bloodless and unsubstantial shadows. Nevertheless, the outward apparition annexed later in their darker and more criminal days by the monk and the Byronic hero belonged originally to the young hero of Otranto, the brave Theodore. The vagueness of these secondary characters is due, however, to natural reasons; on account of their virtues and ideal qualities they were not specially interesting to the romanticist. The hero of *Paradise Lost* is not Jehovah, but Satan. Virtue is boring, insipid, unromantic; sin is fascinating, variegated and romantic. Romantic literature is full of the gaudy colouring of sin, but towards ethereal and celestial virtue it displays but a Platonic interest.

Despite this circumstance, the young hero and heroine of romance have an important part assigned to them, and cannot be summarily dismissed. He is the romanticist's symbol of young, pure and idealistic heroism; she, a rosy embodiment of womanly beauty and virtue. The dark side of the former finds expression in the Byronic hero, of the latter in the demon-woman; what we are now concerned with is the sunny side of the type.

Reviewing Walpole's production, we observe that his heart was with the night-side of the type, embodied in Manfred and the monk Benedict ; Theodore and Edmund retreat, pale ideal creatures, into the background. The life-story of Theodore—he is a prince abandoned in infancy—shows him to be derived, in the first instance, from that romantic world of faerie to which the lost princes of *Cymbeline* belong. Clara Reeve's young hero shows that the author was whole-heartedly on the side of the sunny type ; her criminal lord is abased to the level of the common usurper or criminal, on whose brow no cloud of tragedy rests. Mrs. Radcliffe strives valiantly to mould her young heroes into the noblest possible beings, but while succeeding theoretically she fails in an artistic sense, for a type so pure and noble as young Valancourt lacks interest just because of his too decorative and model virtuousness. The artist in the author is really, although she almost succeeds in disguising the fact from herself, attracted by the darker shades ; her true heroes are men of the Montoni type.

Lewis is whole-heartedly, as one might have expected, on the side of "wickedness." The young and noble-minded aristocrats of *The Monk* do not rise in any respect to greater individuality than any of the characters in the picaresque novels who relate their fortunes and misfortunes. Thus, up to about the time of *The Monk's* appearance, the young hero lived an extremely modest existence as a subsidiary character, revealing only, in the person of Edmund of *The Mysterious Mother*, an inherent capacity for falling victim to misfortunes so tragic that they impress his picture on the mind. In all these years no sign had appeared of that idealism in the cause of high principles, which was later to give such impetus to the type and to make him the interpreter of the positive philosophy of romanticism, in contrast to the doubting and negative views advanced by the Byronic hero. The young hero lives for the future ; the Byronic hero among the ruins of the bitter experiences of the past.

The poetical work which opened the path to idealistic greatness in the young hero is, in my view, Landor's *Gebir*. This tears him from the walking-on part assigned him by tradition, strips him of all the tinsel inherited from the affected world of pastoral idylls, and makes of him a strong, purposeful, indomitable hero-type, classifiable, in spite of the austerity of his nature, with the bright beings of romance. Gebir lacks a predecessor, for it is impossible to range him with the tame and sentimental youths of early romanticism. Yet he is the typical young hero of the romantic school; both variations have their origin in the same impulse. The romanticists instinctively felt the need for a completion of their night-world by effective contrasts; they had, moreover, to create the dualistic balance characteristic of their kind, and thus they groped after a suitable embodiment of the qualities of light. They did not succeed until the virile, poetic soul of Landor, contemptuous of the night-side and brooding over mighty dreams, immortalized this striving in the person of Gebir. Although the work awakened little interest on its appearance, time was to show that it had opened out a new path for the treatment of the romantic hero.

The poet who most openly and consciously began to follow this path was Southey. We have already remarked on his "discovery" of *Gebir*;[281] actually, Southey was the first to grasp the great beauty of the poem and to make it known to his contemporaries. It evoked responsive echoes in his own soul; it corresponded to some extent with the romantic melodies he had already cultivated and was then attempting to carry farther in the great mythical poems of his dreams. Southey's poetry must be viewed in the light of a hero-type akin to Gebir: in constructing his long and laborious epics, his aim was to depict nobility of character, manliness, bravery, high aims—every ideal quality. Of such substance are *Thalaba* and *Madoc*. Southey becomes, consequently, the interpreter of a certain romantic striving of his period, and this is the fundamental cause of his survival in the history of English literature. In dealing with him, some writers on English literary history seem unable to find words strong enough to express their sense of his insignificance as a poet,[282] yet they devote considerable space to him. Why speak of him, if he is such a nonentity? He has none to defend him, now, and it is not worth while to thunder against the circles which made him Poet Laureate. His significance lies in the fact that notwithstanding his poetical mediocrity he expresses the striving of his period towards the creation of a bright hero-type that shall contrast with the dark pessimistic type, and he does so in a way that renders a picture of his time incomplete without him.

The worship of this bright ideal hero suited Southey. Not that he was himself a heroic nature; at least there is no indication of such qualities in his quiet and hard-working existence. One might call him, rather, a hero of industry and a sense of duty. He was an eminently respectable man and a good citizen,[283] just the type who would be as little able to peer into the dark caverns of the soul as he would be capable of understanding the tragedy of Sin ; which is why he can so cheerfully pronounce sentence on the sinner. He is so thorough in his service of purity that he endows his young heroes with superhuman virtues, and consequently makes them humanly impossible, so that they become monotonous and boring. In this respect he might be called a victim of the bright romantic ideal of his day : it killed him as a poet.

Southey was fully conscious of the sunny virtuousness of his ideal. When he became aware of the faint interest it awakened everywhere and saw how the parallel type, how Cain, the dark and tragic brother of the gentle shepherd Abel, Byron's black-browed and satanic hero, irresistibly took every fancy, sowing ideas of scepticism, mockery and negation, he was overwhelmed by bitterness and anger, for in all this he saw a denial of virtue and an approbation of evil. This apparent coldness towards virtue was not, however, so bad as he deemed ; it was not a superior morality that was being spurned, but only bad poetry ; it was not the triumph of a low and criminally-immoral type, it was the appeal of noble poetry. In Southey's eyes the moral purity of his ideal was identical with its poetical beauty, and the doubtfulness of the Byronic hero's morals an indication of his poetical worthlessness. Spurred on by this delusion, Southey entered the lists on behalf of his own hero-ideal against Cain, against Byron, hurling in the preface to his poem *The Vision of Judgment*, stern words against the Satanic School of poets. The answer came in Byron's mocking poem of that same name, an answer which placed Southey beyond all help, in the pillory he himself had erected. He is still sometimes exposed to the derision of that answer, but it should be remembered that he defended Abel against Cain. But who feels for the gentle Abel ? He is the tame youth of idylls, while Cain is the chief character in a mighty tragedy enacted in the bosom of all men.

3

Southey was incapable of feeling tragically ; or if he could he took care to polish out of his work anything that might have betrayed direct feeling. Scott, who in the construction of his

romantic epics, the optimism of his nature and the blame-
lessness and diligence of his life, shows points of resemblance
with Southey, is richer in poetical capacity for sympathetic
feeling. The young hero visualized by Scott was not Southey's
theoretical ideal, but a being closer related to common mankind and thus more interesting. In his epics Scott is decisively
under the influence of the dark hero, even if he does not
expend on him the wealth of sepia and other raven hues which
Byron squandered on his favourite character. Yet when he
takes up the prose romance, he rounds off his gallery of
characters with a contrasting type to the dark hero, a bright
and sunny young man, and henceforward the two appear either
separately or in combination. In his case the dark hero is
distinguishable as an offshoot of the older, criminal tyrant,
though retaining the exotic beauty of the youth and abandon-
ing criminal tendencies ; the element of romance lost thereby
is compensated by strength of passion and a tragic fate written
in the stars. A good example of this is Edgar Ravenswood, who
represents the Hamlet-type in Scott's production. It would
also seem that in Scott's imagination the Highland Gael represented the dark, tragic type, while the Lowlander or
Saxon as naturally suited the bright hero-type ; it is further
to be observed that a strong sense of reality helps him to avoid
any too schematic construction, and to give his heroes an
individuality in harmony with the period and the situations
involved.

These two types are exemplified in Waverley and Fergus
MacIvor, the chief characters of Scott's first prose romance.
Edward Waverley makes a pale, fairly mild impression. He
likes to sink into romantic dreams and is constructed somewhat on Radcliffian lines ; nevertheless, he is manly and brave,
and where necessary enters into the most daring adventures.
The romance spun around his person is tame in quality,
inclining the reader to suspect from the beginning a happy
ending in the form of a marriage. On the other hand, Fergus
MacIvor is immersed in a romantic dark cloud of fate ;
outwardly he is above the average in height, harmoniously-
developed, a Highland costume giving full scope to his physical
perfections. His beautiful countenance wears a manly and
open expression, to which the Scotch cap with its eagle's
feather lends a martial stamp ; thick, raven-black locks frame
his face. The proud curves of his eyebrows and upper lip show
that he is accustomed to command and to exact the fullest
obedience. At the faintest touch of temper lightning flashes

from his eye, no less terrifying because of the perfect control kept over it. He retains this proud carriage unbroken to the executioner's block. In this instance, also, romance in the person of a hero, which is usually tragic in nature, is connected by Scott with the dark type. Even where he succeeds in endowing the fair type with truly romantic qualities, as in the case of Ivanhoe and Quentin Durward, the fate destined for the hero is a bright one, in which the threatening clouds discharge nothing more dangerous than showers over his swift journey towards the final haven of wedlock. But when it is the dark type that interests him most, he can create such characters as Edgar Ravenswood, whose deeply tragical fate it is not easy to forget. Such, on the whole, is Scott's share in the development and his use of the young hero.

4

I need not pause over Byron, whose hero has already been dealt with in all essential points. I will only remark that in his case the boundary between the Byronic and the dark young hero often disappears. Selim, for instance, is nearer to the young hero than to the Byronic hero ; the difference between them is that the young hero of necessity lacks the chequered past which gives to the Byronic variety its mystery. Moreover, in comparing the two it becomes apparent that the former— the dark type—has very slender hopes of an independent future ; with the growth of his experiences he passes into the ranks of the Byronic heroes, and there becomes lost amongst them.

Shelley chooses the light type as unconsciously as Byron does the dark, impelled thereto by his own fundamental character. He, too, has his hero-type, though it is not as famous as the Byronic type ; its divine transparence and ethereality render it invisible against the bright background of eternity which is the essence of Shelley's poetry. As Byron is himself the dark hero of romance, so is Shelley its bright hero ; both project their own selves into their art and complete each other. Shelley's imagination creates a youth of superhuman beauty who dreams and does battle in airy romantic surroundings, frequently in the spirit of the winds of sea and heaven, for the supreme aim of mankind, liberty. He expressly says, indeed of Laon :

His eyes were dark and deep, and the clear brow
Which shadowed them was like the morning sky. . . .

. . . .

Beneath the darkness of his outspread hair
He stood thus beautiful . . .

but somehow the imagination refuses to credit him with dark
colours, and gradually evolves a picture of him with hues taken
from the morning sky and the intensive light of the glittering
ocean. This lightness of tint is supported by the purity and
clarity of spirit, the idealism of another world, which characterizes the young hero of Shelley's symbolical poems. His
idealistic construction and attitude is directed outwards
towards the spirit of evil ; he has not in his own soul that fire-
surrounded scorpion which turns its poisonous sting on itself
on finding every road to salvation closed, nor the perpetually
gnawing secret sin around which the thoughts of the Byronic
hero, feeding his agony with his own blood, constantly revolves ;
on the contrary, he is utterly free from the sense of individual
guilt and suffers only because of the misfortunes of mankind.
Although he is bitter on account of the oppression and misery
prevailing in the world outside, this bitterness is not the biting
mockery (turned into a negative pessimism) of the Byronic hero,
but rather a holy anger based on a flaming optimism, on an
invincible conviction that all misfortune, all injustice and
wrong could be swept away, if only mankind would free itself
from the illusions and prejudices into which it has been led
by the powers of evil during the course of the ages. As the
pioneer of the poet's own ideals, Shelley's young hero rises with
his art to greater heights than ever, symbolizing an idealistic
and burning faith in the future happiness of humanity,
becoming an unconquerable spirit of optimism, " liberalism "
itself in the most absolute significance of the word.

The concentration of Shelley's poetry around an idealistic
hero of this type helps, like certain outward features of his
poetry, to elucidate the much-maligned Southey. Landor and
he are, as already observed, the fathers of this idealistic young
hero—a fact of which we are made increasingly aware if we
compare the poetical works of Shelley and Southey. Southey's
hero-ideal is essentially the same as Shelley's ; from this point
of view his poems are no mere exhibitions of inventiveness and
formal skill, but are symbols of the battle between ideals and
evil. But he lacked the boldness of spirit and the inner,
proselytizing love of liberty which refuses to be chained by
the smooth verse of a Court poet, but discharges itself in the

air like the arrows of Hercules, killing without pity the dread eagles of evil ; and for this reason he failed to transmute his young hero into terms of high and lasting art. Shelley fulfilled what was lacking in Southey's poetry and thus the young hero became the symbol, poetically beautiful, often misty and fanciful, yet ever highly artistic, of the most idealistic and noble strivings of those days.[284]

5

Such are the main lines of the young hero's life ; all that might be added would take us deeper into a study of fine shades and details than is necessary. Let us now glance at the young heroine and see what was the romanticist's ideal of young womanhood.

We have already mentioned her, in connection with Walpole, Clara Reeve and Mrs. Radcliffe, that finely-virtuous and well-bred, beautiful, idealistic, constantly-persecuted young woman, whose sentimentality is something astounding. Her descent is best sought in Pamela's family-tree, in spite of her acquisition of traits from the world of pastoral idylls. Mrs. Radcliffe's heroine is often like a picture by Watteau, in which a virtuous rococo maiden retreats from the overbold advances of a lover. One would willingly enter the birth of the young heroine under Shakespeare's name in the great pedigree of literary history, but for that there is not sufficient justification. Granted that in Imogene (*Cymbeline*) there is something of the angelic virtue and charm aimed at by later romanticism, and that Shakespeare's maidens are extremely romantic, yet in spite of all a gap exists—except in a few individual cases—in every chain of evidence that seeks to link them with those of subsequent writers. The cause of this gap is the intervening period of shy rococo affectation and puritanical virtue, of which Shakespeare's damsels, with their healthy, unblushing preference for the wedding-bed, are wholly free. In this respect the Elizabethan maidens represent the realism, vigorous sensuality and joy of life of the Renascence, in vivid contrast to the unhealthier dream-world of the young heroine of romance.

Referring to what has been said earlier on the subject, I need only dwell briefly on that subdivision into types of young heroine, in outward appearance as well as in character, which is apparent in the tender self-sacrifice of Walpole's Matilda and in Isabella's sturdy purposefulness, which Mrs. Radcliffe further developed in creating her blonde, blue-eyed Emilys and dark-curled, night-eyed Julias. The first-named type breathes a fine femininity, a tender and sacrificial maternal spirit, fighting the battles of life with the weapons of resignation and tears, and bringing to love everything that is divine, passion excluded. The second type, more spiritedly poetical, is represented in the independent and oppositional beauty, who feels deeply, demands freedom of movement and choice, and is not impervious to passion. This division into two contrasting types reflects the similar development in the picture of the young hero.

Mrs. Radcliffe did not venture farther than this in the exploitation of the young heroine. The character reflects the quiet, dreamy soul of the author herself, and can rise to no greater heights of idealism than is contained in pure love and melancholy, sentimental brooding in a beautiful summer night. Lewis's actual young heroine, Antonia, is no heroine at all, but a child, a doll-like being who, totally unaware of the wickedness of the world, falls victim to a criminal. She is interesting for her childishly angelical purity and because she represents an attempt to create in words the picture of an untouched, only half-ripe girl. This in itself can be beautiful, but is not particularly romantic; Lewis expended almost the whole of his romantic colours in painting the portrait of his demon-woman Matilda, leaving, however, enough to enable him to create, towards the end of the book, a healthy and pleasant type of womanhood (corresponding to Walpole's Isabella) in the person of Virginia, who soon discovers the way to console Lorenzo.

After this, the young heroine runs parallel to the young hero. In the poems of Landor and Southey she stands beside him, sharing his struggles and his ideals, gradually withdrawing, in still greater degree in Shelley's poetry, from all reality. She becomes a poetical vision, translucent and pure, a conception of Art itself, an embodied synthesis of their dream of beauty and the life-nerve of their philosophy. As a woman she is the essence of womanly beauty with the physical element deleted, as a spiritual being she is the warring spirit of Freedom, flitting ahead of humanity towards happiness:

> She moved upon this earth a shape of brightness,
> A power, that from its objects scarcely drew
> One impulse of her being—in her lightness
> Most like some radiant cloud of morning dew,

Which wanders through the waste air's pathless blue,
To nourish some far desert : she did seem
Beside me, gathering beauty as she grew,
Like the bright shade of some immortal dream
Which walks, when tempest sleeps, the wave of life's dark stream.

In this form the young heroine is Landor's invention, upraised by Shelley to symbolic heights, and as such she was finally exalted by Rossetti in *The Blessed Damozel* into a Dante-like heavenly being, a Beatrice, an ethereal symbol of beauty :

The blessed damozel leaned out
From the gold bar of Heaven ;
Her eyes were deeper than the depth
Of waters stilled at even ;
She had three lilies in her hand,
And the stars in her hair were seven.

6

Scott leans towards the Radcliffe-types in his descriptions of the young heroine, especially as regards outward appearance. A recurrent feature of his prose romances is a division of his maidens into fair and dark types, a division perhaps more obvious than in the case of the young hero. Rose Bradwardine in *Waverley* gives the keynote in the sharps, and Flora MacIvor in the dark and tragical flats, if one may be allowed the simile, of this melody of young womanhood. Rose, the " Rose of Tully-Veolan," was " a very pretty girl of the Scotch cast of beauty, that is, with a profusion of hair of paley gold, and a skin like the snow of her own mountains in whiteness. Yet she had not a pallid or pensive cast of countenance ; her features, as well as her temper, had a lively expression ; her complexion, though not florid, was so pure as to seem transparent, and the slightest emotion sent her whole blood at once to her face and neck. Her form, though under the common size, was remarkably elegant, and her motions light, easy, and unembarrassed." Flora MacIvor is introduced to us in the following romantic fashion : " Here, like one of those lovely forms which decorate the landscapes of Poussin, Waverley found Flora gazing on the waterfall. Two paces farther back stood Cathleen, holding a small Scottish harp, the use of which had been taught to Flora by Rory Dall, one of the last harpers of the Western Highlands. The sun, now stooping in the west, gave a rich and varied tint to all the objects which surrounded Waverley, and seemed to add more than human brilliancy to the full expressive darkness of Flora's eye, exalted the richness and purity of her complexion, and enhanced the dignity and grace of her beautiful form. Edward thought he had never, even in his wildest dreams, imagined a figure of such exquisite and interesting loveliness. The wild beauty of the retreat, bursting upon him as if by magic, augmented the mingled feeling of delight and awe with which he approached her, like a fair enchantress of Boiardo or Ariosto, by whose nod the scenery around seemed to have been created, an Eden in the wilderness." As the spot in which this vision confronts Waverley is one to which the roar of a mountain torrent, a crystalline backwater and dark rocks with the trees and bushes growing between them, lent both a stern and a gentle romanticism, one can understand with what joy the author has described the scene. If we now take into consideration that both Rose and Flora are musical natures, both playing the harp and singing old ballads and folk-songs, as well as being skilful in all other dainty feminine arts, it becomes fairly obvious to us that the ground-plan of these heroines of Scott's was an inheritance from Mrs. Radcliffe.

As I have observed, Scott is, on the whole, fairly consistent in this division into fair and dark types. Other examples justifying this view are the tragic heroine Rebecca and the fair, noble, regal, Saxon beauty Rowena of *Ivanhoe*. Romance seems most inclined to linger around Rebecca, leaving the calmer and cooler Rowena to await her more natural and happier fate. This division affects, however, only the outward aspects of Scott's heroine-ideal, and does not reveal the whole truth.

Full-blooded a romanticist as was Scott, he was notwithstanding a rarely sane and sharp-eyed dweller in realities. In his romances we find a series of characters depicted with so much truth to nature, down to the finest turns of speech, that their creation must have demanded much observation and an unusual memory. His Scotch hags, beggars, Highlanders, farmers and officials, are no products of imagination, but persons who had come within the range of his own experiences ; this side of his work provides one of the first examples of the realistic treatment of scenes from the life of the people. Scott's " realism " merits the attribute much better than the naturalism of the picaresque novels, which is, in reality, based on those romantic tales of artful rascals which form one of the elements of folk-lore. A special depth and a touch of modernity is given to Scott's descriptions of popular life by the strong sympathy, upborne by a wise humour, with which he regards his characters, a sympathy which reveals to us a worthy soul beneath rags or an otherwise modest exterior.[285] This feeling for reality, this sympathy and love for his people, is extended to the heroines, and as his own manly, chivalrous character inclined him to dreams of ideal young womanhood, the outcome of these two influences was a type of maiden no longer to be classed with Mrs. Radcliffe's Emilys and Julias, with the damsels of castles or the dark-curled beauties of tradition, but a vigorous, healthy, natural Scotch girl of the type of Jeanie Deans in *The Heart of Midlothian*. Scott does not equip her with any of the outward marks of romance—Jeanie is small and unassuming, with a pleasant expression on her freckled, sunburnt, slightly irregular features—but describes her objectively as she is : the daughter of a poor, sternly puritanical farmer, a maiden whose numerous duties and habit of helping others leave her little time for dreaming. Yet to her is given the opportunity of realizing a very romantic dream ; when sentence of death is about to be passed on her stepsister Effie, accused of infanticide, Jeanie resolves to do what becomes a sister, a daughter and a Christian woman ; alone and in the teeth of much advice and opposition she sets out to walk to London, to implore mercy from the King and Queen for her sister. Breaking off her own engagement, for she thinks that her sister's shame renders her unfit to be anyone's wife, Jeanie accomplishes her adventurous journey, and with her clear common sense, her childish trustfulness, naïve charm and Scotch accent, achieves what had been deemed impossible. Jeanie is throughout reflected in her actions as a girl of deep humanity, purity and goodness, whose chief characteristic is a true heroism in overcoming the misfortunes and difficulties of life. In such characters Scott was, in my view, at his highest as an artist, raising an originally bloodless and conventionally romantic lay-figure to a stage of individuality upon which Dickens was later to base his own characters. Thus through Scott, the young heroine becomes a living being, treading paths totally dissimilar to those trodden by her sister, the ethereal idealist of Southey and Shelley.

7

Byron's young heroine differs from these in having no spiritual mission; her only principle is that of love, a truly romantic, suddenly-flaring burning passion, for which she lives and dies. Especially in his Oriental poems does he present us with a series of these objects of his passionate dreams and experiences, young women who leave an impression, thanks to the profligacy with which attributes are squandered on their beauty, and no less to the romanticism of their surroundings, and their mournful fate, of glittering starlit southern nights, of the spell of harems, the delights of forbidden love, mourning cypresses and the white marble of graves. Byron is the young heroine's troubadour, whose lute and song are devoted to the service of a southern passion, of a dreaming beauty whose burning glance flashes forth from the ravishing shelter of a veil, a harem or a balcony.

> Her eye's dark charm 't were vain to tell,
> But gaze on that of the Gazelle,
> It will assist thy fancy well;
> As large, as languishingly dark,
> But Soul beam'd forth in every spark
> That darted from beneath the lid,
> Bright as the jewel of Giamschid.

In these words the Giaour describes his Leila, a daughter of Circassia, who moved on earth " as rears her crest the ruffled swan." The bride of Abydos is

> Fair, as the first that fell of womankind,
> When on that dread yet lovely serpent smiling,
> Whose image then was stamp'd upon her mind—
> But once beguiled—and ever more beguiling.

She is

> Dazzling, as that, oh ! too transcendent vision,
> .   .   .   .   .
> Soft as the memory of buried love ;
> Pure, as the prayer which Childhood wafts above.

Such is Zuleika, of whom the poet is moved to say,

> Who hath not proved how feebly words essay
> To fix one spark of Beauty's heavenly ray ?

Inspired by this conception, the poet sings her fate—death for the sake of love—in lines whose contents, bordering on sentimentality, must have moved his own heart and those of the romantically-inclined of his followers. They display, as symbols of poetical sorrow, such images as " the sad but living cypress that glooms and withers not, though branch and leaf are stamped with an eternal grief " ; " a single rose which is shedding its lonely lustre, meek and pale, and looks as planted by despair ", and blooms ever ; " the nightingale that sings the livelong night his long entrancing note, as soft as harp that Houri strings, and whom they who listen cannot leave, but linger there and grieve, as if they loved in vain " ; " the white marmor by which flourishes the mourning flower :

> Hath flourish'd ; flourisheth this hour,
> Alone and dewy, coldly pure and pale,
> As weeping Beauty's cheek at Sorrow's tale !

In similar fashion, Conrad's beloved Medora lives for him alone, and when he is compelled to depart immediately after his arrival,

> The tender blue of that large loving eye
> Grew frozen with its gaze on vacancy.

Medora's eyes are deep-blue, her eyelashes long and dark, her tresses fair. Gulnare, Seyd-Pasha's favourite wife, is a dark-eyed, chestnut-haired beauty, highly-inflammable, who to liberate Conrad murders the pasha. While using alternately dark and light colours in describing the appearance of his heroines, Byron endows them all with a capacity for the most devouring passion which demands all and is prepared to sacrifice life if need be. In this respect Byron is original, even as a romanticist ; he is the Court Poet of romantic love, a poet who makes the young heroine the central motive of highly-coloured paintings of passion, feeling neither the necessity nor the desire for any other ideal. The picture of the young heroine thus becomes a fundamental fruitful element of Byron's poetry, the inevitable parallel to his heroes. All the romantic promise contained in Mrs Radcliffe's visions of maidenhood, Byron, following his own paths, brought to fulfilment.

8

The fact thus emerges that notwithstanding a certain tendency to recede into the background, the young hero and heroine represent an important side of the romantic author's imaginary world. As regards the other secondary characters only a few brief remarks need be added. The old seneschal of Mrs. Radcliffe's castles, and in general the old faithful family servant, was a successful invention possessing great vitality. This ancient upholder of traditions was urgently needed by many authors not only for clearing up their plots, but as a suitable channel for the infusion of humour into their pages. An excellent example of this is found in Scott; the old butler Caleb, at the ruined castle of the Ravenswoods, with his tragi-comical behaviour is the sole source of melancholy humour in the otherwise sombre pages of the book. Even *Ivanhoe* would be poorer by one brilliant character if the swineherd Gurth, who awakens memories reaching back to the Odyssey, were not there with his robust and unkempt person, his faithfulness towards his young master and his equally faithful dog. Possibly it was the romantic idea of an old family servant that led Scott to understand so well the inherent possibilities of the humble characters mentioned a page or two earlier. Proof of the great vitality of the old-servant theme is provided by Saveljitsh in Pushkin's *The Captain's Daughter*. The example is pertinent since the Russian literature of those days was an offshoot of European romanticism, though it is, of course, possible that the old-servant theme was indigenous to Russia.

With regard to Walpole's loquacious Bianca, I would point out that although the talkative chambermaid was no original invention of the romanticists, yet she became a useful and important personage who could be used to represent naïve and merry womanhood and be capable of yielding, as circumstances demanded, a great number of variations in a harmlessly innocent style. Compared with the highly romantic heroine and her high-flown ideals the Bianca-type appears in healthy contrast as a pleasantly unself-conscious and natural damsel, who compensates for her lack of great ideas by a human capacity for innocent flirtations, which seldom affect the reader un-pleasantly. One aspect of her may possibly have provided the first sketch for the country maiden who abashes her polished listeners by an unrestrained and bold naturalness.

The romantic gallery naturally contains a great number of other characters, but as these are mostly the personal property of their respective creators and show no inclination to become public property, they call for no mention. From what has already been said it is clear that romanticism created its own characters, in whose psychology, actions and fate it tried to interpret dimly envisaged ideals of beauty, fantastic dreams and strange conceptions of life.

THE HAUNTED CASTLE

The mass of material presented in these chapters provides, it is to be hoped, adequate grounds for the conclusion expressed earlier that the central themes and chief imagery of what has here been termed the terror-romantic school unconsciously passed, as products of their age and of the contemporary atmosphere, into the hands of those authors who created the great English romantic school. Freed from its fetters and refined in the fire of superior poetical skill, material that had once been raw and primitive develops into a world of imagery and ideas that proceeds, as though conscious of its liberty, to throw off a wealth of new forms.

X

OTHER THEMES

I

I HAVE already remarked that from Walpole onward a common and important feature of terror-romantic literature is its preoccupation with an atmosphere of oppression and innocence in danger, the development of situations based on persecution and a constant fleeing from pursuit. The basis on which the whole plot rests is usually some form of usurpation, an old crime, or the like; but the actual impulse is derived from this state of danger and persecution; it furnishes the suspense necessary to keep up the reader's interest. The creation of a state of suspense is not altogether a literary invention of the romanticists, as it played an important part (see I, 15 and Note 75) not only in Shakespeare, but in the works of such writers as Fielding and Smollett. Nevertheless it must be admitted that romantic authors of Mrs. Radcliffe's type made it an aim in itself, devoting hundreds of pages to the creation of situations whose sole purpose was to expose the most likeable characters to danger and in this manner evoke the greatest possible fright and suspense on their behalf, a suspense kept up to the very last moment.

Another general feature descriptive of terror-romantic literature is that it invariably deals in one form or another, either in the past or present, with crime and with criminals who prey on innocence. The next stage, after such materials and situations have been developed to their fullest extent, is to carry out what has probably been the underlying idea from the beginning, namely, to make the criminal himself the object of pursuit for purposes of vengeance. This had already formed the concluding scene in most of Mrs. Radcliffe's works; all that was now necessary was to make this pursuit the main theme of the book, *i.e.*, its source of suspense. From this turning of the tables the present-day detective or criminal story was, in all essentials, practically evolved. An appreciable advance in this direction was made by Godwin in *Caleb Williams*.

Caleb Williams begins to suspect that his master and benefactor, the noble-minded and aristocratic Falkland, has committed murder. Although it is none of his business, he is seized by a curiosity so overwhelming, almost abnormal, that he decides to spy upon his master. " The instant I had chosen this employment for myself, I found a strange sort of pleasure in it. To do what is forbidden always has its charms, because we have an indistinct apprehension of something arbitrary and tyrannical in the prohibition. To be a spy upon Mr. Falkland ! That there was danger in the employment served to give an alluring pungency to the choice. I remembered the stern reprimand I had received, his terrible looks ; and the recollection gave a kind of tingling sensation, not altogether unallied to enjoyment. The further I advanced, the more the sensation was irresistible. I seemed to myself perpetually upon the brink of being countermined, and perpetually roused to guard my designs. The more impenetrable Mr. Falkland was determined to be, the more uncontrollable was my curiosity." In this manner Williams keeps Falkland under a tireless espionage, noting his most trifling actions, expressions and words, ultimately to discover his secret. The criminal's nervous behaviour, the secret burden on his mind and his eagerness to hide it from the eyes of the world, in combination with the unresting, treacherous and calculating curiosity with which Williams preys upon his victim, already build up in a fashion the framework of a kind of detective story.[286]

In this field of criminality, in which the question is no longer of traditional Gothicism as such, but of psychological analysis, with criticism of social justice as a background, Godwin was succeeded by the founder of American fiction, Charles Brockden Brown (1771-1810), who was a pupil of Godwin in his ideas of social philosophy and received from him the first impulse for his literary work.[287] Parallel with Godwin, Mrs. Radcliffe seems to have influenced Brown, for besides utilizing her terror-romantic artifices, he annexes her gloomy hero ; German terror-romanticism, too, does not appear to have been wholly unknown to him.[288] The secret societies of Europe— the Rosicrucians and Illuminates—apparently interested him. The general impression derived from his work is that both in character and style he was a realistic describer of actual life who, unaware of his own powers, fell victim to the literary fashions of his day, in which it was impossible to achieve any noteworthy success.

A constructional inheritance from Godwin is the recurrence of a relationship between pursuer and pursued similar to that in *Caleb Williams* ; on one side a master, on the other a protégé occupying a humbler position, usually a young and gifted person from the country. The patron (sometimes a woman), is an echo of Falkland, expanded and made gloomier in the style of Mrs. Radcliffe's sombre tyrant, and forms the most signal and important expression of English " Gothic " influences on American literature. Terror is aimed at by such means as ventriloquism, which is practised by a mysterious person, capable in other respects of inspiring terror, by crimes, by realistic descriptions of yellow fever epidemics, the sufferings incidental to deserts, Indian cruelties, crimes committed in a state of somnambulism, etc. Thus, in addition to the old tyrant of " Gothicism ", criminal, yet capable of inspiring respect, fear-inspiring settings, etc., Brown uses new themes of terror, thereby opening the path along which Poe was subsequently to advance so far.[289]

On the score of his *Edgar Huntly or Memoir of a Sleep-Walker* (1799), Brown is usually credited with a certain influence on the development of the detective novel. The chief character in this story is the usual gifted country youth, in the present case an Irishman called Clithero, whose patron is a woman. Clithero is seized by insanity and in a fit of madness murders his benefactress, afterwards fleeing to America. He finds employment on a farm, but here he begins to walk in his sleep. Edgar Huntly, his master, finds his behaviour strange and suspects him of having killed Waldegrave, a friend of Huntly's, who has been found murdered, at the foot of a tree ; and as he is not known to have possessed an enemy and as no tracks or clues are found, it is impossible to know whom to suspect of having perpetrated the crime. So Huntly begins to keep an eye on Clithero and by detective-like supervision establishes the fact that Clithero has murdered Waldegrave in a sleep-walking fit. In his pursuit of Clithero, which ends in the suicide of the latter, Huntly becomes involved in adventures in which the desert and Indians play a part, his salvation being invariably left to the last moment. Finally he, too, begins to walk in his sleep.

In this romance the establishment of Clithero's guilt is assumed to point to the detective novel of the future. Nevertheless the genesis of the detective story was still distant.

Like the rest of "Gothic" romance, this book and *Caleb Williams* form the basis of detective fiction only in respect of their general setting of terror and element of pursuit, which had necessarily to precede the real detective story and without which Poe might never have made that invention which forms the actual model for the modern detective story. Poe, that strangely-equipped nature, delighted, as he himself tells us in *The Gold Bug*,[290] in the elucidation of ciphers, mysterious signs, puzzles and other such matters. His powers of observation and of combining facts were early developed, enabling him to evolve a kind of deductive method which, used in combination with his keen power of observation, frequently enabled him to draw from quite insignificant-looking details conclusions that seemed to comprise the main truth of the case in question. All that was necessary therefore, was for Poe, whose imagination enabled him to inject new life into so many aspects of terror-romance, to apply this deductive method to the relations between criminal and pursuer, and the detective story stood complete. The book in which this idea was realized, *The Murders in the Rue Morgue* (1841), exercised a quite decisive effect on detective fiction. One might draw up from it the following list of features familiar to all readers of modern detective fiction, especially of the adventures of Sherlock Holmes : the narrator's friend, Auguste Dupin, who shares his dwelling, is a singular and isolated nature, with a special gift for razor-keen logic and analysis, the application of which delights him, not so much for reasons of vanity, but because it shows him to what depths thought can penetrate. "He boasted to me, with a low chuckling laugh, that most men, in respect to himself, wore windows in their bosoms, and was wont to follow up such assertions by direct and very startling proofs of his intimate knowledge of my own." He astonishes his friend by suddenly formulating, after a long spell of silence, the conclusions at which the latter was on the point of arriving, and then by explaining in the most natural and commonplace manner how he had read his friend's thoughts. Dupin has made a thorough study of his method, which is based on exact observation of facts and the deduction of logical conclusions from these. The terrible double murder in the Rue Morgue (related by Poe in the witness-box and notebook style used by Conan Doyle) awakens Dupin's interest. Regarding police methods as inadequate, because of their lack of logical method, he studies the case in its smallest details, and lays bare the whole course of events by a kind of philosophical logic in which practical deduction follows inevitably on deduction until they lead to the only correct conclusion. Here we have the origin of the detective story in its modern form, a model so like the Sherlock Holmes stories, that I have no hesitation in terming Conan Doyle a direct imitator of Poe.[291] All the features that give to Conan Doyle's stories their special character, namely, the two chief characters Holmes and Watson, their friendship, character and secluded bachelor quarters, crime and its detection by quasi-scientific methods, even the general method and style of narration, are found ready to hand in the Rue Morgue story and appear unchanged, except for the names, in Conan Doyle's works.

Such in its main features was the development of the detective story. In seeking its sources, it is my opinion that all attempts to draw aside from the channels suggested above can only lead to generalizations and vagueness, especially if the part played by Poe is ignored.

2

Reference has already been made to the share of terror-romanticism in the birth of the historical novel and to such matters as, for instance, the influence exerted by Southey's poems on products of the type of Rider Haggard's exotic novels of adventure. This last deserves greater attention.

We have noted the existence, parallel with the narrower type of haunted-castle "Gothicism," of another, exotic, Orientally-attired, more liberal "Gothicism," and seen how at one time the traditional romance-form began to break up, to become in great measure poetry in the form of fantastical heroic epics, in which local and Oriental "Gothicism" unite. Materials were introduced at this point which I am inclined to regard, with their nautical flavour and colonizing spirit, as typically English. Robinson Crusoe has altogether, and Gulliver in part, this fact of nationality to thank for their respective journeys; such books could only be produced by a nation which had for centuries gazed from their island home beyond the mysterious ocean. In *Robinson Crusoe* and *The Adventures of Captain Singleton* English literature, long before the time of the romanticists, had stored away a treasure of exotic adventures, presented in a form so realistic that they could seem familiar and plausible even in much later times. Smollett further enriched this treasure with his novels, which contain much valuable description of nautical life.[292]

As soon, therefore, as "Gothicism" began to draw apart from the haunted castle in its narrower aspects, it was only necessary for attention to be drawn to this old national treasure of nautical romance for a new and fertile species of literature to be born. The discovery was made, as we have seen, by Coleridge in *The Ancient Mariner*. In a peculiar helpless fashion the introduction to this poem exposes, as I have shown, its dependence on the central setting of terror-romanticism, the haunted castle, and the stranger who arrives at the height of a feast. The story told by this stranger then takes the reader to entirely new scenes, but returns again to "Gothicism" in the form of the old chapel and the hermit. *The Ancient Mariner* becomes the sesame for exotic tales of adventure and suffering at sea of a terror-romantic nature. Wordsworth enters into the adventure in *The Borderers*, Scott in *Rokeby*, Byron in *Don Juan*, depicting in a manner faithful to tradition famine and cannibalism amongst sailors; Poe, who greatly respected Coleridge, takes direct advantage of the opportunity offered and moulds the stuff of *The Ancient Mariner* into his weird story of suffering at sea *The Narrative of Arthur Gordon Pym* (1838). The ground thus opened proved exceptionally fruitful, and gradually assimilated several other themes of exotic romance. Among these the romance of piracy, already exploited by Scott and Byron, may be mentioned, to which Poe imparted a mighty new impulse with *The Gold Bug*. R. L. Stevenson's *Treasure Island* (1883), a direct descendant of the last-mentioned, carries the line to its ultimate perfection. Without multiplying these examples,[293] I will content myself with remarking that sea-stories, irrespective of whether they deal with sufferings arising out of shipwreck, piracy, treasure islands, coral-reefs or savages—with any subject, in short, connected with exotic seas and colonies— are still popular in this country (especially amongst the young) and that the revival of this branch of literature inaugurated by Defoe was helped to a great extent by terror-romanticism.

3

We can now recall to memory the romantic portrait. This has appeared in *Hamlet ;* it has an important part assigned to it in *The Castle of Otranto ;* in Mrs. Radcliffe's works it becomes a miniature invested with tender memories ; it displays in every castle hall the features of ancestors ; and finally proves effectual in transmitting a sombre impression of that mysterious wanderer on the face of the earth, Melmoth. From the very beginnings of terror-romanticism it exercised a special fascination on authors; it is to them not merely an inanimate object, but in some enigmatical way an animated being, like the picture in *The Castle of Otranto.*

In the beginning, this view of the romantic picture was hazy; in the style of his other naïve miracles, Walpole endows it with life and the power of stepping down from its frame, while Mrs. Radcliffe sees in it only something to revive tender memories. But Lewis, consciously or unconsciously, uses the picture in a manner capable of deep interpretations. Matilda's portrait, admired and worshipped by Ambrosio, is alive with the inexplicable power of beauty, with a fascination that prepares the monk's soul for the coming temptation. In the picture of Melmoth this power becomes demoniac : by virtue of the traditions attached to it and the expression of the eyes, the picture exercises a terrifying effect on members of the family and even on outsiders, awakening an indefinite suspicion of some hidden, dreadful crime in the family.

Melmoth's picture, with its mystery and blazing eyes, usually a source of personal magnetic terror with the romanticists, was peculiarly adapted to awaken speculation as to the reasons for this strange power. Ever inclined to strange processes of thought, the romanticists saw in it a new supernatural theme, and thus we find Poe setting out to explain the origin of a picture of this nature. With characteristic thoroughness he pondered over the relation between the picture and its maker, and gave expression to his theory in *The Oval Portrait.* In this an artist paints the portrait of a beloved model and surrendering himself wholly to his task seems to transfer with each stroke of the brush something of the soul and life of the sitter. As the picture gains in life, so does the model pine away, until with its completion she dies, her life continuing in the picture. Art is therefore entirely egoistic : it will not permit its worshipper to love any other than itself, and jealously drains the life of its rivals. Thus a picture is born that might with truth be called " living," a term already applicable to Melmoth's portrait. The romantic power of Poe's story springs from the fact that although it contains nothing unacceptable to the intelligence or of a supernatural nature— for in the neglect of his love for art's sake by an artist, even to the point of allowing it to wither away and die, there is nothing unnatural—yet its suggestive power is such that the reader cannot refrain from attributing to some supernatural agency the transference of the model's vitality to canvas. Here we have one method of accounting for the origin of the mysterious portrait : it may contain the whole personality, transferred to it by mysterious powers, by love and sorrow, of the person depicted, so that it is now as though " charged " with this personality.

The same fundamental idea is behind Rossetti's *Hand and Soul*, which relates how, in a moment of doubt, the soul of his art appears to a painter in the guise of an enchanting woman, a vision immediately transferred to canvas in a burst of inspiration. The result is no ordinary painting, but a picture with a mystic influence, a soul depicted by an inspired hand, *manus animam pinxit*, as an admirer who fell under its spell some centuries later deciphers in one corner of the canvas. Then, in *Saint Agnes of Intercession*, Rossetti comes very near to Poe's story. An artist paints the portrait of his beloved and seems to be transferring the whole of her being to canvas ; here, too, the model dies. With the story is connected the idea of re-incarnation, as the artist subsequently finds a portrait, painted some centuries earlier, of himself and his model, a love-story similar to his own attaching to the originals of this portrait. As *The Portrait* indicates, Rossetti's imagination saw in the picture of a beloved being, when painted by a lover, some mystic life invisible to others.

Lytton takes much the same view of the power inherent in a portrait. As in primitive magic an image charged with the inextinguishable power of a potent curse can be introduced into the dwelling of an enemy, so we find Lytton adding to the various magnetic appliances and batteries of his haunted house a vengeful curse embodied in a miniature portrait of the original central character of the story, which, to judge from the baleful expression of the eyes, plays a leading part in the magic with which the house is impregnated. The portrait is obviously loaded with the will to evil and exerts its influence until overcome by a stronger will. In this case, also, we find the romantic idea that the whole personality of a being can be transferred to a portrait. Whether in this there is some echo of magical conceptions—studied and consciously exploited— I am not prepared to judge.

Poe's story ends with the completion of the portrait, and provides no hint as to the future existence of this picture-personality. To this question we find an answer in Oscar Wilde's *The Portrait of Dorian Gray* (1891), which seems to have borrowed from Rossetti's short stories for its portrait-theme, though it then develops with great boldness the idea of the picture's independent existence to further lengths. Dorian Gray's portrait is created in the manner suggested by Poe and Rossetti; in the grip of an inspiration inspired by a rarely passionate interest in the model, in his unusual beauty, that is, the artist transfers to canvas, as by magic, the entire personality of his sitter, thus creating the latter's double. When Gray begins to sink deeper into the mire of life, he observes to his horror how the portrait undergoes a change : like a mirror reflecting his most secret deeds, bearing in form, colour, expression and glance, incorruptible witness to what Dorian Gray has become. The portrait thus represents the evil half of his being as Mr. Hyde does the evil in Dr. Jekyll. In this manner Wilde brings to light an idea that had probably always lain behind the portrait-theme—that the picture constituted in some mysterious way the sitter's double, living a parallel life and reflecting his personality. The strength of Wilde's story lies in its power of inducing the reader to believe in the altering portrait. What the author is actually arguing is simply that a vicious life leaves its own marks, visibly as in a mirror, on its man, or in this case, on his portrait. The romantic portrait interprets therefore the most common and most unendurable experience of mankind.

Such is but the simplest outline of the portrait-theme's genealogy ; space prevents me from entering into all the different and weird conceptions that form offshoots of this main branch.[294] Even in the form given above it has tender memories of the past, whole commandments of moral warnings and terrible visions of the powers for good and evil that dwell in the human breast.

4

The word " solitude " crops up with some frequency in the preceding chapters of this book. It reflects a mood and a propensity characteristic of both the Byronic and the young hero.

The young hero's love for solitude springs from the sensitivity of his emotional life. Cultivating melancholy as a pleasure, he seeks, especially when in love, solitude, wild and romantic scenery or the shady groves beside forest brooks, so that he may peer undisturbed into the gently throbbing spot in his breast whence proceeds his melancholy, with which is mingled a bitter-sweet pleasure of ultimately erotic origin. Walpole's Theodore felt the spell of such solitude ; most of Mrs. Radcliffe's young heroes follow suit ; it was felt by Southey's Joan of Arc and continues to be represented in Scott's *Rokeby*. The desire of the young hero (or heroine) for solitude was not based on any deep passion (with the exception, perhaps, of Wilfrid in *Rokeby*), but was rather a harmless emotional dalliance with nature, well in accordance with the general sentimental tendencies of the authors, which for its finest and highest flights demanded solitude.

The solitude of the Byronic hero is of a different quality. His sense of loneliness springs from the realization that he has overstepped the moral and emotional laws recognized by society. While the young hero's loneliness is the most refined pleasure that melancholy is capable of yielding, a strangely-fascinating mood evoked by the superabundance of the spiritual forces set into movement, the Byronic hero gazes into his own soul as at the smouldering embers of some conflagration, as at a deserted and dreary world whence life has fled. He has lost the power to catch fire and to become fruitful, and his soul is lit by a graveyard moonlight, cold, dismal and despairing. Such is the solitude of the Giaour, Conrad and Lara—moral isolation beyond good and evil.

The loneliness of the Byronic hero approaches that state of mind so tempting to the terror-romanticist with all its potential horrors—insanity. While writing *The Mysterious Mother* Walpole pondered over the possibility of introducing insanity on to the stage and wrote in his epilogue : " When madness has taken possession of the person, such character ceases to be fit for the stage, or at least should appear there but for a short time ; it being the business of the theatre to exhibit passions not distempers. The finest picture ever drawn of a head distempered by misfortune is that of King Lear. His thoughts dwell on the ingratitude of his daughters, and every sentence that falls from his wildness excites reflection and pity. Had frenzy entirely seized him, our compassion would abate, as we should conclude that he no longer felt unhappiness."

Nevertheless, the terror-romanticists did not always follow this wise advice. Signora Laurentini's madness is of the pleasant variety that is satisfied with playing the guitar in the moonlight, but Lewis's *The Captive* reflects, as remarked earlier, the strait-waist atmosphere of a madhouse. The maniac in *Julian and Maddalo* is really mad, while from the pages of *Melmoth* we can almost hear the dreadful screechings of the raving. Scott is the first to achieve balance in this respect, bringing to literature, amongst his many humble types, such gently insane characters as Davie Gellatley in *Waverley*, which, adopted by later writers, form a class of their own much in favour. A grotesque descendant of Davie, a distorted example of what terror-romanticism was capable of in this field, is Quasimodo, in whom is also discernible the influence of Scott's numerous dwarfs.

5

In *The Monk* we came across the " Black Art," cabbalism, used by Matilda to provide Ambrosio with opportunities for his crimes. The idea was known to the romanticists of Shakespeare's days, but Walpole made no use of it; his romanticism, like that of Clara Reeve and Mrs. Radcliffe, turns elsewhere for nourishment. Lewis got the idea from Germany; Godwin took it for his *St. Leon* from the general information available on alchemy; Shelley from Rosicrucian traditions and Byron from *Faust*. This cabbalism is a puerile type of magic that has no romantic effect at all when its materials—the curious will find fuller information on this subject elsewhere than in romantic literature—are catalogued with their various uses; it does not become romantic until used by the romantic author to create mystery.

It becomes most interesting when, according to the example set in *Faust*, it begins to form the mantle of mystery around the tyrant and the Byronic hero. It may even happen, as in *Manfred*, that the tyrant actually becomes a kind of Faust, in which case the most inaccessible chamber of the haunted castle, hitherto the haunted room, becomes a cabbalistic laboratory, where the bounds of knowledge are shattered and the spirit solves the basic problems of existence. Manfred's Alpine home is a typical haunted castle and he himself a tyrant of Byronic hue, but his tower room is a stage for mystical powers, Faust's chamber, the former laboratory of alchemists and sorcerers. The cabbalism of earlier romanticism is the forerunner of the " science " of a later generation, and leads gradually to the use of scientific-looking methods and the kind of mysteries to which the method lends itself. Thus, Mary Shelley, in beginning *Frankenstein*, breaks away from the traditional haunted castle and chooses as her chief character a young scientist who succeeds, in the course of his lonely nocturnal laboratory work, in extending the bounds of human knowledge to the point where the problem of the creation of organic life can be solved. The idea of using science to support a romantic plot, has proved exceedingly fertile in later romanticism.

The science brought in to help romanticism bears the stamp of the period. Cagliostro, to whom we have already referred, may be said to represent the cabbalistic and Rosicrucian stage, while Mesmer, who denotes an advance, represents magnetism and hypnotism, or in other words, a modern species of occultism. In the first half of the nineteenth century a school of mystical-philosophical knowledge developed in Germany, its theoretical expositor being the physician Jung-Stilling. According to his system, the human being comprises three elements : the physical body, an ether body or soul, which is the determining factor in life, and an everlasting spirit. This system was appropriated by Poe, who in his *Mesmeric Revelation* confesses to a belief in two bodies, one primitive, the other perfect—a larval and a butterfly stage ; death is simply the painful transition from one state to the other ; under mesmeric influence the primitive body comes under the control of the ether body and a person is therefore liberated in that state from the fetters of the primitive body, in other words, acquires the gift of clairvoyance (telepathy). This train of ideas proceeds to the study of the threshold that is death and to the question as to whether mesmeric influence could keep the soul in the body even after organic life had ceased. By allowing this experiment to succeed, Poe achieves an effect of terror in *The Case of Mr. Waldemar*.

With this motive the romanticists arrived along paths of their own at the old idea, found in Slavonic myths, of the existence of vampires. A vampire is a person whose spirit does not depart from his body when organic life has ceased, but remains there, preventing it from decaying and making the body return at night to the living to suck their blood. The first English author to take up the idea was Byron : when Mary Shelley began *Frankenstein*, Byron simultaneously began a story called *The Vampire*, which was never finished. It is my belief that he had reflected upon the theme earlier, and that the vampire of his imagination is partly responsible for the staring eyes, pallor and general nocturnal aspect of his sombre hero, and also that Lara's being and in particular the enigmatical scene of terror in the night, are closely related to some nebulous fancy of the visit of a vampire. In later romanticism we find the vampire idea attached to a pallid chief character as a token of sombre, mysterious inhuman qualities. The actual vampire-theme of folk-lore has not been much cultivated in romantic literature—it has been dealt with most powerfully, to my belief, by Nikolai Gogol—interest being usually confined to the idea built upon it of blood-sucking in general, especially in a spiritual significance.[295]

The idea of a material and astral body led naturally to that of a double existence in a new sense : themes relating to somnambulism and hypnotism and deeds committed under such influences now emerge on the romantic horizon.[296] Similarly, the idea awakens of depicting the visions and visionary life of a person in a trance as actual fact, and finally of depicting the continued life of the astral body in ever-new physical bodies, or the idea of the transmigration of souls. In *A Tale of the Ragged Mountains* (1844) Poe joins the mesmeric state to the idea of the transmigration of souls and thus invents one more method of dealing with never-ending life : Bedloe " certainly seemed young—and he made a point of speaking about his youth—yet there were moments when I should have had little trouble in imagining him a hundred years of age." Poe is the romanticist who really enlisted " science " in the service of effects of terror and opened the eyes of later writers to the inherent possibilities of the method.

6

From the point where Frankenstein has created his monster, the book takes on more the character of a social study than of terror-romance. The murders committed by the monster and the pursuit through inhospitable landscapes to the death-setting in the Arctic Ocean are certainly the wildest possible terror-romance, and the inseparability of Franken-stein and his monster is not without a flavour of the double-existence idea. Yet the final impression left upon the reader is that the author has sought to air her opinions on the duties of society towards the poor, particularly as regards sympathy and education.[297] The monster was brought into the world in irresponsible fashion and lacked from the beginning human sympathy, love and education. He feels his poverty in this respect and looks with envy on those scenes of human love and happiness in which participation is denied him. Spurned with horror by mankind, he is seized by hatred and a lust for revenge, directed above all against his creator, Frankenstein, because the latter refuses to supply him with a similarly-created female counterpart. And one cannot deny a certain justification for the demon's claims ; his wrath and bitterness are to some extent well-founded, although the horror of his being is such that it is easy to take sides with Frankenstein and society. Mary Shelley's romance falls, as might have been expected, within the sphere of social philosophy represented by her father, William Godwin. His own works, *Caleb Williams* and *St. Leon*, are, notwithstanding their terror-romantic features, the fruits of social study, light cast in the form of fiction on his study of *Political Justice*. In a general sense, therefore, they brought to romanticism an idealistic side directed against social injustices, oppression and tyranny, and demanding the realization of the principle of liberty in all human relations.[298]

The earlier terror-romanticists, Walpole, Reeve and Radcliffe, display a tendentious spirit only in their efforts to shake off the fetters of traditional literary material and form, and either in the attribution of a spirit of revolt to their chief character, the tyrant, or in encompassing his fall. Lewis, however, is not altogether innocent in this respect ; *The Monk* is undeniably imbued with a conscious spirit of opposition. In spite of its incoherence it was well adapted to dispose the reader critically towards the Bible, as regards, for instance, its suitability as reading for the young. It is impossible to mistake the spirit of freethinking breathed by the book. We have seen that Lewis was capable of grasping the demands of liberty and humanity, and that he attempted to realize these as far as could be practicably done in the circumstances then prevailing. Yet one cannot but admit that from the appearance of *The Castle of Otranto* to the French Revolution, romanticism lacked, so to speak, roots ; it laboured only for the achievement of " romance." It was the French Revolution that gave to English romanticism its positive tendentious stamp. After it had passed, one might have divided the romantic authors into the following two groups :

Setting out as friends of the Revolution, Coleridge, Wordsworth and Southey, discontented with its many mistakes, ended with opinions chiefly conservative in nature. Not that they became opponents to reform ; they merely refused to sanction their realization by revolutionary methods. Southey, who was an active journalist to the end, was unyielding and even in his riper years convinced of the justice of his demands for reforms that were frequently of a far-reaching nature. At the present day one would be inclined to call him a calm and intelligent, cautious worker for " conservative " reforms, who did not lose his grasp of reality.[299] They were joined by Scott, although he arrived at their standpoint along roads of his own, from the " past," in a romantic-historical sense of the word ; the attribute of conservatism, taken literally, describes his position well.

The opposite camp, a group revolutionary in every respect and opposed to the Lake Poets, was formed by Byron and Shelley and their satellites ; with epicurean cynicism the former mocked at everything, hated tyrants and longed for a liberty, the actual extent of which he never made definitely clear ; the latter, a disciple of Godwin, expressed, as the deeper thinker of the two and in obedience to his own logic, his demands for liberty in theoretical conclusions, regarding his right to think for himself and to be himself and no less regarding his position towards society. The principles of both wear a certain poetical and abstract air, indifferent to real life. Quite apart from these two schools stand such poets as Keats, who, raised above all earthly considerations, sought only beauty, and Landor, who refused to countenance " Gothicism," although he too sometimes succumbed to its blandishments.

The relations between the two camps were in general inimical, though points of connection were not lacking. Scott and Byron were friends, and respected each other ; similarly Southey and Landor. Shelley appreciated *Thalaba* and *The Curse of Kehama*, to which *The Revolt of Islam* owes a debt of gratitude, and even visited Southey at his home.[300] Landor and Byron could not endure each other, but the last-named wrote : " He (Landor) really is a man whose brilliant talents and profound erudition I cannot help admiring as much as I respect his character ; " and Landor : " Say what you will . . . there are things in him (meaning Byron) strong as poison, and original as sin." [301] Byron's part in the Greek War of Independence was in Landor's eyes a deed that would make his name for ever famous.

Posterity, with its wider perspective, is inclined to regard the differences between the two camps as superficial. All these authors proceed from the romantic, emotional and intellectual currents of the end of the eighteenth century, each absorbing his portion, which he then cultivates according to his individuality, but always to the same end, that is, for the benefit

of human ideals. Thus, Wordsworth points out the close
relationship between mankind and nature, and creates the
conception of a new pantheistic brotherhood dominating the
whole of nature. Southey provides an accompaniment to
this music, raising aloft fabulous ideals of virtue and heroism,
justice and liberty. Coleridge gives depth to the intellectual
life of his period by interpreting to it the spiritual achievements
of German philosophy. Scott displays the past in a romantic
light, awakening love for it and thus indirectly for the people
and the nation as a whole; he gave consequently a powerful
impetus to the national spirit and the dawning strivings for
liberty. Byron stirs up the stagnant pools in the spiritual life
of his mother-country with all the stormy, convention-
hating brilliance of his writings and his personality, inspiring
everywhere in the world a poetical enthusiasm for ideals.
Shelley's spirit flies prophetically to the future, in rosy visions
showing the path to the true happiness of his dreams. Landor
upholds the Roman ideals of Brutus: tyrants he hates with a
hate more deadly than that of Byron, but demands at the same
time beauty, nobility and real manliness not only in thoughts
and words, but also in life and deeds. Not one of these programmes is in conflict with the others; all are but facets of the
spiritual lighthouse these men had built.

7

A special feature of English terror-romanticism is its
love for a southern setting. The Castle of Otranto is in Italy,
whither also Mrs. Radcliffe places her Udolpho and *The Italian*
and her *Sicilian Romance*. The action of *The Romance of the
Forest* takes place in France, and that of *The Monk* in Spain.
St. Leon is a Frenchman, Schemoli an Italian. The romantic
longing of these writers apparently derived satisfaction from
this exoticism, from the colours and luxuriance of the south,
to which is joined a correspondingly greater majesty of
mountain scenery, and from the fieriness and passionateness of
the southerner. The transference of the setting to these
countries, or in general as far from their own surroundings
as possible, either geographically or historically, was no mere
affectation, but formed a kind of primary condition for the
achievement of a truly romantic effect as they understood it.
It is to be observed that in the south the Roman Catholic

religion still prevailed, with the same spiritual atmosphere of which the romanticists dreamed while reviewing in fancy in their own old churches the poetically-illumined Middle Ages ; there monasteries were still to be found and the reign of the Inquisition was no very distant matter. Amongst all the romantic horrors of the south, the latter was particularly adapted to awaken in Protestant countries a series of pleasing and excitingly torturing visions, that it is not surprising, there-fore, that so many romanticists, among them Mrs. Radcliffe, Lewis, Godwin, Maturin and Coleridge, had recourse to it.

This longing for the south, for any alien and distant setting, is typical of romanticism, and reflects the effort of their imagination to break away from the fetters of homely ex-perience. Byron obeys this call throughout his work. But on acquaintance with the south, his realistic feeling for colour disclosed to him a new scale—the Orientalism which had encroached upon the antique world—and finding in this a suitable background for the working of his imagination, he kept to it for a great part of his work. His nature was not as deep as Landor's or Shelley's, who found in the south the true spirit of the antique and were spiritually reborn in the crystal-line brightness of Hellenic art. The classicism which flourished in the English Universities was more in the nature of philology than a true investigation of the antique spirit ; romanticism with its susceptible soul found the Hellenic spirit, rescued it, and rendered a great service to the world, not least to science, in so doing.

At the present day we are inclined to wonder what strange processes of thought led Southey to choose as settings the marvellous lands of *Thalaba* and *Kehama*, fabulous Araby and India,[302] whence he drew the boldness to write in all earnest-ness a poem on the last king of the Visigoths, and how the vigorous and fiery Landor came to create a great play around another character of the same nation—somehow it all seems to us far-fetched and affected. But to them it denoted entrance to a territory and an atmosphere where, freed from the narrow confines of their surroundings, their visions, passions and the characters with whom they dealt, could develop to dimensions that in any other connection would have been both impossible and unendurable.

The Castle of Otranto is a short, lively and spirited story. The conversations are swift interludes in the narrative, which never pauses for a deep analysis of situation or mood. One recognizes throughout the animated, cursory, rapidly-flitting epistolary style of its author. The works of Clara Reeve and Mrs. Radcliffe are ponderous and slow in style ; the latter frequently pauses in the midst of her descriptions and attempts to lighten her style with somewhat pointless conversations— merely notes to accompany the description. Lewis is very modern in his narrative style ; his sentences are short, the *tempo* brisk and the dialogue animated. In this respect his book is incomparably more readable than Godwin's or Maturin's works, where elaborate explanations in long strung-out sentences call for energy and effort on the part of the reader. Godwin is particularly weak in dialogue, nor does he greatly cultivate this style of writing ; Maturin is better, but his conversations have constantly to give way before the overflowing, torrential flood of descriptive matter. These books developed the technical side of the romance by showing how best to divulge and apportion the plot so that interest shall be kept alive to the end. Scott undeniably learned a good deal as regards the technique of plots from Mrs. Radcliffe.

Gebir revived a technical form that had long been forgotten and was in so far new—the fantastical epic form. The reader who has struggled through this poem and renewed his sufferings beside Southey's hopelessly long and fatiguing epics, cannot but think with respect of the belief in the value of poetry, the diligence and energy, and the inextinguishable enthusiasm to which they bear witness. When to this voluminous series we add Scott's brisker verse, Shelley's extremely abstruse visionary epics, Byron's tempestuous and cynical poems, Campbell's epics and Wordsworth's excursionary works, not to mention the many others, the wealth of poetry that poured forth during this quarter of a century strikes one with astonishment. It seems as though the epic form became the special field of the romanticists. The interest of these epics is now more or less historical in nature ; they have become phenomena descriptive of a past epoch and former tastes, and have little chance of ever being resuscitated. Nevertheless, if any writer of our own day were to embody his conception of life in some such epic and accomplish his work with all the energy and skill, all the fertility of invention typical of English poets a hundred years ago, even our own times, lacking as they are in literary ideals and strict literary schooling, would hardly withhold its respect from the fruits of his work.

A third literary form which romanticism attempted to cultivate was the drama, though with poor results. Not one of the authors I have mentioned created a dramatic work of permanent value capable of being acted. To my belief, the reason lies in the unsuitability of the romantic mechanism for the stage. In action, romanticism, with its lurid effects, was inclined to become melodramatic, which is ever a bar to artistic success. Melodramas in Lewis's and Maturin's style are the only romantic plays that created a sensation in their day; yet they, too, have entirely disappeared, to lie on the dustiest shelves of libraries in silent witness to the interests and failures of the period in this field.

In lyrical poetry the form most favoured by the romanticists was Bishop Percy's gift to the world, the ballad, which in spirit approaches closest to the epic. If the worthy bishop could have foreseen the flood of ballads that was soon to inundate all Europe, he might have paused before publishing his collection. In the ballad the romanticists found a miniature harp, on which they could strum some fragment of an emotion based on a short tragic tale of the past. One cannot aver that the romantic ballad shows much variation in its themes, but the popular style in which its horrors are presented, coupled with the tearful sadness of its contents, made it the literary form most beloved by the people. Sung " to a well-known air," ballads spread even to the illiterate, introducing and fostering a love for romance much more effectively than products of a more exacting literary standard could have done. Owing to its popular foundation the ballad became once more— as it had already been in Elizabethan days—a favourite of the great public and the special field of uneducated poetasters; broadsheet poetry in its later forms is, indeed, closely affiliated with the romantic ballad.

The main and most important part of this flood of romantic literature poured so swiftly into the literary world of England, and with such an effect of novelty and surprise, that its effect on contemporaries was, one is inclined to believe, petrifying. It seemed as though the whole preceding century had been wiped out, as though Doctor Johnson and his ideals had been left on the farther side of an impassable abyss,[303] somewhere in distance whence his voice no longer carried. Criticism, which had worked contentedly at niceties of scansion and purity of rhyme, and had conscientiously registered the various stages of morality, suddenly perceived that its weapons were too blunt to deal with these new products. It could, indeed, discern faults in Byron's versification and rhymes, in his choice of words and metaphor, yet to its horror it discovered that the enumeration of these blemishes in no way seemed to shake the prestige of this Titan. And above all, it discovered that the question was no longer one of anything specifically English, of deftness of versification and canonical, High Church morality, but of a sudden liberation of the intellect and its enlistment in the service of the happiness and prosperity of all mankind, a movement that carried all Europe forward into a century of new thoughts and new strivings.

XI

SUSPENSE AND TERROR

I

THE species of literature which has been my main theme in the preceding chapters is known in literary history as "the romanticism of terror" (*Schauer-romantik*). The name is apt. As the reader will have observed, the evocation of an atmosphere of suspense and of terror forms the goal at which these writers aimed. They did so consciously, having their own conception of a "fear-inspiring beauty," as Lytton later formulated it in *Zanoni*. Terror, horror, thrilling fear, all are emotions obviously not without their pleasing and satisfying side to these writers. Lytton's words show that he did not mean fear only, but fear with an accompanying sense of beauty. The same applies to the other terror-romanticists. This "terror" and the accompanying "beauty" call for closer attention and explanation.

We can regard suspense as the preliminary and preparatory stage of terror; this in itself is a cumulative and continuous state of mind that becomes transformed, when a certain stage of intensification is reached, into a state of petrified terror, a paralysis that also manifests itself physically. Withdrawal from it is only possible by a change of conditions caused by physical movement, in which moreover the outward contact with the cause of terror is broken. One notices accordingly that the means used by terror-writers to lead the reader by degrees to an ultimate state of terror are the creation of suspense, and its subsequent maintenance and intensification.[304]

2

In *The Castle of Otranto* and the works of Mrs. Radcliffe, the general supporting atmosphere of suspense is furnished by the danger constantly threatening the chief characters. The suspense in *The Monk* is created by the question, will Ambrosio err, and what will the consequences be ; that of *Caleb Williams* by the uncertainty as to whether the person who gives his name to the book will discover Falkland's secret, whether and how he will escape the latter's revenge ; that of *St. Leon* by curiosity as to what St. Leon will accomplish by his alchemy and how he will emerge from the difficulties this art of his exposes him to ; that of Byron's Oriental poems by the mystery attaching to the heroes ; that of *Melmoth the Wanderer* by his search for a suitable successor ; that of *Frankenstein* by uncertainty as to whether the scientist will succeed or not in his mystical experiments and whether he will be able to destroy the being he has created, etc. Side by side with the general suspense created by the main plot, the authors make extensive use of suspense created by the situations in which the characters find themselves ; examples of this are Isabella's flight in the crypt of Otranto, Emily creeping through the gloomy passages of Udolpho and pondering over the mysteries of the curtained picture ; the flashing of mysterious lights in the deserted tower of a castle ; the light turning blue in the room where ghost-stories are being related ; the tyrant attacking the heroine with evil intent ; battle scenes ; the disclosure of secrets ; the interruption of the reading of an old manuscript at a critical point ; a night in a gloomy inn situated in a dark forest, etc.,—all those innumerable situations, in short, in the invention of which the writers of " romances " were past masters. With all these artifices the terror-romanticists did their utmost to prepare the reader's mind for the final shock which was to hypnotize him into a state of terror.

In this preparatory work of keying the reader's mood to receptivity by means of suspense, one can discern different elements on which success ultimately depends. Isabella's flight is thrilling, but the thrill is of the superficial variety, which is easily ended and is accompanied the whole way, so to speak, by the reader's doubts, ready at the first occasion to dash the effect already achieved. Battle scenes are in general exciting, but without result as regards the development of the disposition to terror. Mere outward suspense, which can be evoked, for instance, by spirited action, danger, flight, battles, etc., is obviously not adapted to tauten the reader's soul to a susceptibility to terror ; for this end an additional factor is needed.

The suspense evoked by *The Castle of Otranto* is superficial and furnishes no light in this respect, but *The Mysteries of*

Udolpho reveal what this additional factor is. As we have seen, the author creates a great part of her suspense by gradually exciting the reader's curiosity to its highest pitch by enigmatical hints, half-sentences, inexplicable and weird phenomena, until he begins dimly to discern and to fear something, the nature of which is hidden from him, and to which he himself gives the form most terrifying to him. Suspense of the kind that leads up to a state of terror is thus to be evoked by suggestion, in other words, the reader's imagination is to be excited into seeing in events, words and hints, more than they need actually convey, and, if possible, into working independently, imagining, suspecting and fearing, as though outside of the book, in spiritual worlds of its own. If the author succeeds in providing a *dénouement* in which the duly prepared soul of the reader can be held without the neutralizing effect of awakening doubt and sanity, in other words, so completely that intellectual control ceases, the literary experiment, which had as its aim the creation of terror, has succeeded in this part of its aim.

The greatest hindrance to success lies in brain-control, in the unflagging suspicion of the reader ; this must first be eliminated and prevented from creating an inauspicious state of mind. The only effectual weapon for this purpose is suggestion. Action can be either natural or unnatural, credible or incredible ; success does not depend on such factors. This is decided solely by the author's power of transferring the reader, by means of suggestion, into the world in which the action takes place, into an atmosphere where even the most incredible events seem credible.

3

Keeping to this view of the power of suggestion as an essential condition for evoking a genuine state of terror, let us see in what measure the terror-romantic writers fulfil this condition and how far they succeed in creating a culminating effect of terror.

The reader is already aware that *The Castle of Otranto* lacks in suggestive power. True, the poet Gray wrote to Walpole that he was afraid to go to bed after reading it in the evening, but this is to be taken either as politeness towards his friend Walpole, or as being due to weak nerves ; it may also be assumed that the period in question was more susceptible than our own. In any case, the present-day reader finds in the book not a trace of anything liable to key his soul to such a pitch as would expose him either to insidious or open attack by terror. He is thus incapable of accepting as gospel truth the gigantic objects and events which Walpole obviously intended as climaxes of effect. From the point of view of true suspense and terror, the story has overstepped the mark.

Clara Reeve's book is too lucidly explanatory to possess much suggestive power ; an inkling of it is, nevertheless, to be found in her sudden gusts of wind, her phenomena in haunted rooms, the broken, mysterious hints of the old seneschal, and similar features, but as the end of the book fails to come up to the expectations awakened by these suggestions, even the small measure of suspense achieved dissolves in disappointment. So this book, too, fails to achieve its purpose.

Mrs. Radcliffe's works are, as frequently remarked, fairly rich in suggestive power. Their only fault is that the author fears to make full use of her means, does not dare, notwithstanding her power of carrying the reader off his feet, to bear him away bodily, but, as though alarmed at the result already achieved, eliminates it by common-sense explanations. Taken as a whole, therefore, her romances do not yield a perfectly harmonious effect of terror. Yet it is to be noted that in numerous details she succeeds in working upon the suggestibility of the reader to a degree capable, in favourable circumstances, of culminating in a state of undiluted terror. Her works thus deserve to be called terror-romanticism, even though they destroy, by their explanations, the effects created by the way.

Returning to a point further away in time, let us take up *Vathek*. Although its author probably never gave the matter a thought, this little romance is extremely suggestive. The reader feels its fundamental theme—uncontrollable surrender to the lust for pleasure, which proves insatiable and demands ever new food—grip his own uneasy conscience in a quite individual way and compel him to follow with a sense of personal guilt the fortunes of the Caliph and Nouronihar right to the castle of Eblis. The author then leads this troubled conscience, by outward description of situation and the final turn taken by the plot, to the catastrophe which has throughout been feared, and succeeds in evoking a state of terror.

The terror evoked by *Vathek* is similar in quality to that of *The Monk*. In writing his book Lewis does not seem to have consciously aimed at suggestion, but to have related what he had to say in a straightforward manner. But the matter is of a nature to inspire a feeling in which interest, suspense and disgust are mingled, a sensation rising at the climax of the work, the murder of Antonia, to downright terror. Maturin's stories possess a stronger suggestivity and more ultimate logically-reached terror than any work of his predecessors, and he shares with Lewis the honour of having best succeeded as an inspirer of terror. In *The Ancient Mariner* and *Christabel*, Coleridge succeeds both in suggestivity and in the logical exploitation of it. The mystery of Byron's Oriental poems is closely-calculated suggestion, which leads occasionally to typical states of terror, as in *Lara*. In *Werner* an effect of terror is achieved by a sudden and totally-unexpected murder, and by the gradual disclosure of a picture of the chief character totally unlike that already formed by the reader.

On the basis of all that has transpired above and earlier regarding these writers, I arrive, therefore, at the conclusion that they were not fully conscious of the decisive importance of suggestion in the creation of terror. They used it, indeed, occasionally, in some cases (Mrs. Radcliffe for example) bounteously, but blind to all its bearings, they forsook it again and allowed the brain to regain control and destroy the effect already made. On the other hand, *The Monk* shows that the preliminary conditions for terror were obtainable by other means of suggestion than those used by Mrs. Radcliffe, or by the automatically working suggestivity of a realistic depictment of horrors, a method characteristic of Lewis's romance and those of Maturin. As soon, therefore, as an author succeeds, irrespective of the means employed, in evoking by suggestion a state of receptivity to terror—a peculiar susceptibility to terror—and logically completes this state by his culminating horrors, keeping the whole time the critical faculties in check, he can be said from the point of view of perfection of effect, to have succeeded—a conclusion reached by other means in an earlier section of this chapter and now shown to be correct by a detailed consideration of the literature which aimed at such effects.

4

What then are the means by which the mind keyed up by suggestion can be immersed in its final bath of terror? The various chapters of this book have already provided an answer.

A glance at their contents—the Haunted Castle, with its horrors of solitude and night, the monk with his dreadful crimes, the idea of a double existence, ghosts and demoniac beings, Ahasuerus and the problem of never-ending life, the Byronic hero, incest and all the gruesome matters that have emerged as we have studied these—all show clearly that terror was aimed at by means of the supernatural and the unnatural. Even where the question is of a romantic fatalism that irresistibly bears its victims to a previously determined end, the deepest effects are secured by recourse to supernatural agency ; the romantic " scientist " using his science to solve problems insoluble by ordinary science, works in reality hand in hand with supernatural powers. When Shelley imagines he sees eyes in Geraldine's breast, when Cenci persecutes his daughter with his lust, Ambrosio rapes his sister, sailors in distress feed on their companions, goldsmiths fall unnaturally in love with ornaments they have created ; in pictures of insanity, of landscape, of a situation in nature—as Poe does [305]—in which all else is natural but the absolute silence and immovability that prevails, the question is of things unnatural intended to inspire terror. This is in full accordance with the aims of romanticism, for it strives in everything to pass beyond the ordinary and everyday, to ignore the boundaries within which lies logical, daylit naturalness.

The terror-romantic authors sought thus to evoke terror by the following means :

1. By dealing with supernatural events as such, *i.e.,* without argument or explanation. In this class we can include *The Castle of Otranto*, *Vathek*, *The Monk*, *Melmoth the Wanderer* and Shelley's romances.

2. By dealing with them in such manner that they only appear to be supernatural and are capable of being satisfactorily explained. Such works include *The Old English Baron* and the works of Mrs. Radcliffe.

3. By dealing with them in a manner that permits of " scientific " explanation. Such are, for instance, *St. Leon* and *Frankenstein*.

4. By dealing realistically with horrors, of which the worst reach into abnormality. This class includes *Zeluco*, *The Mysterious Mother* and *Caleb Williams ;* also, in part,

Vathek, *The Monk* and *Melmoth the Wanderer*; similarly, *Manfred*, *Werner*, and *The Cenci*.

Provided attention is paid to suggestion, success is possible in the first, third and fourth classes, the methods of the first and fourth being capable of being used simultaneously in the same work, as in *The Monk*.[306]

If we keep in mind the condition of suggestion and the neutralization of intellectual control, and examine in this light the work of the later romanticists, such as Poe, Hawthorne, Lytton and Stevenson, it is easy to observe that it falls into classes one and three, written with the realism of class four. Suggestivity is in this case consciously exploited, carefully thought-out and used to its smallest details. Poe devotes himself so whole-heartedly to suspense and terror that the other emotional values of romanticism, colour, etc., are neglected, so that his work possesses a great terror-romantic value, but in other respects only restricted romance. Hawthorne uses his themes of terror with caution and skill, causing the reader to believe in and imagine the presence of supernatural powers which need not exist in verity, but at the same time retains a poetically romantic atmosphere of age, which enriches his scale of colour. Lytton is inspired by a powerful interest in the supernatural, invidiously transmitted to the reader through many channels, with the aid of every emotional and colouristic resource of romanticism. Stevenson induces the reader to believe in all he relates by the gravity and directness of his style, and makes particular use of the " scientific " method—in this resembling Poe—with fine success. Before the method of suggestion, which now seems so obvious and forms the basis of every terror-romantic work, had been evolved, much experimenting had thus been needed.

5

With the above methods and materials the romantic author aimed at an effect of terror. This suspense and terror obviously denoted something else to the romanticist than the naked terror of the arena ; watching two strong wrestlers we can feel suspense, which becomes transformed into unmixed terror if one were to attempt to strangle the other. This was not the terror at which the romantic author aimed ; in his case it comprised a dominant colour and secondary colours placed so that they resulted in what one might call harmony. This word "harmony" covers all that Lytton meant by his words regarding " beauty " related to " terror." [307]

These secondary colours have been dealt with in the foregoing in connection with the prime materials of terror. The first of them has a special right to be called " romantic " atmosphere, and consists of the depictment of events and objects belonging to the past and apt to awaken a sensation of yearning—dear to the yearner. The thought and recollection of an object of yearning always sets afoot a series of visions that awaken tender feelings, and lead to a sentimental state of mind. These visions are capable of being strengthened and rendered clearer by subsidiary influences in harmony with them, one such being the silence and peace of nature seen at night, which, by its dimness and effects of light, is inclined to increase the susceptibility of the soul. The object of yearning can also give rise to a series of visions of a different kind, depending on the nature of the object and the individual quality of the yearner's soul, but all these moods I am inclined to class together as " romantic."

The counterpart of peaceful and soothing nocturnal nature in romanticism is a harmonious, daylit nature, which is usually the typically English, luxuriant brook-landscape described earlier, with its distant signs of human culture expressive of happiness. The sight of this landscape awakens an atmosphere of idyllism, in which the romanticist can rest from the sentimentality of the night. The contrast to the peaceful nocturnal scene is the stormy night, howling winds and torn clouds, between which the moon occasionally peeps forth, casting a mournful illumination over raging seas or a dismal landscape. The daylight counterpart to this is the wild and savage mountainous scene with deep chasms, roaring rapids and eagles soaring high in the air. These materials the romanticist uses to evoke an atmosphere of nobility and sublimity. A condition, though not an essential one, for the creation of all these moods is solitude—the " solitude of the forests " so often met by the reader of such literature.

We have seen that the romanticist uses a variety of smaller materials to keep alive an emotional rippling of the reader's soul. Disregarding these, let us pass from the sublime to that emotional mood which accompanies the sufferings, crimes and mighty passions that prepare the mind for the reception of terror. Suffering may have in it something sublime, and when joined to crime, great passion and catastrophes, it leads to what approaches tragedy. In the vicinity of terror-romanticism frequently hovers, as the fate of the Byronic hero shows, the spirit of tragedy, which ultimately leads (although its emergence is neither entire nor wholly legitimate) to a purification and exaltation of the emotions. Ambrosio's end is an example of this ; the reader feels that he has been the spectator of a deeply human play that extends to eternal matters, and in spite of Ambrosio's crimes, he is prepared in the end to extend a pitying sympathy, compelled thereto by his own secret sense of guilt.[308]

Accompanied by these emotional colours the romanticist proceeds on his road to terror, and thus is born ultimately the " beauty that inspires fear."

NOTES

(1) A portrait of Walpole accompanies the 1907 edition (Chatto & Windus) which I have used. He was refined to the point of effeminacy. " He always entered a room in a style of affected delicacy, *chapeau bras* between his hands, knees bent and feet on tiptoe. He usually dressed in lavender, with partridge silk stockings and gold buckles, and with lace ruffles and frill." R. Garnett and E. Gosse : *English Literature*, III, p. 367 (1903). A fine edition de luxe (containing also *The Mysterious Mother*), with a preface by Montague Summers, was issued by Constable in 1924 (*vide* article by E. Gosse in *The Sunday Times*, Nov. 2). The above description of Walpole hails originally from Letitia Matilda Hawkins's *Anecdotes, Biographical Sketches, and Memoirs*, where pp. 87–117 and 307-312 are devoted to Walpole. The father of this author, Sir John Hawkins, was a friend and neighbour of Walpole and wrote the biography of Doctor Johnson which was so severely handled by Boswell. She gives the further information regarding Walpole's personal appearance : " His figure was . . . not merely tall, but more properly long, and slender to excess ; his complexion, and particularly his hands, of a most unhealthy paleness." Quoted from De Quincey's article *Anecdotage*.

(2) The cause of the quarrel was Walpole's inability to refrain from boasting of his position as the son of the omnipotent minister. In any case they were not well-matched travelling companions ; Walpole danced and amused himself, while Gray studied Art and Music. Later they were reconciled and Walpole acknowledged himself to have been at fault. E. Gosse : *Gray*, pp. 43–44.

(3) " Gothic, a term of reproach, synonymous with barbarous, lawless and tawdry." W. L. Phelps : *The Beginnings of the English Romantic Movement*, p. 15 (1893).

(4) Scott makes good-natured fun of this description in *The Antiquary*. Mr. Oldbuck's find, a stone with what he takes to be an important ancient inscription, appears in much the same way as that of " Bil Stumps His Mark " in *Pickwick Papers*.

(5) *A Description of the Villa of Mr. Horace Walpole at Strawberry Hill*, 1768. I have not had the opportunity of reading this work. Descriptions of Walpole's villa are included in all works written about him, amongst which I would mention Austin Dobson : *Eighteenth Century Vignettes* (undated), "A Day at Strawberry Hill," pp. 206–217, 2nd ed. A picture of Strawberry Hill is given by Garnett and Gosse. The most exhaustive source is Paul Yvon's book *La Vie d'un Dilettante*, Book IV, pp. 487–646 ; " Walpole ' gothicisant ' " ; p. 551 : " *Strawberry Hill et le Château d'Otranto, le roman de Walpole, sont donc, selon la volonté de leur créateur, indissolublement liés.*"

(6) " Gray and Horace Walpole exceeded all their English contemporaries in the composition of charmingly picturesque familiar letters." (Garnett and Gosse, *op. cit.*, III, p. 363.) Information regarding Walpole : the work by Dobson mentioned in the preceding note ; Sir Walter Scott : *The Lives of the*

Novelists (1821), originally published as an introduction to Ballantyne's edition of *The Castle of Otranto* (1811) and included with the latter in *Ballantyne's Novelists' Library*, Part V; my own copy is from the *Everyman's Library* Series, London, pp. 188–203; Henry A. Beers: *A History of English Romanticism in the Eighteenth Century*, pp. 229–243 and 249–255 (1906); Oliver Elton: *A Survey of English Literature, 1780–1830*, I, p. 203; Wilbur L. Cross: *Development of the English Novel*, pp. 101–103 (1911); Fr. Hovey Stoddard: *The Evolution of the English Novel*, p. 95 (1913); Helene Richter: *Geschichte der Englischen Romantik*, I, pp. 172–191 (1911); Austin Dobson: *Eighteenth Century Studies*, pp. 166–177; *Dictionary of English Biography*; Macaulay: *Critical and Historical Essays*, in which is a murderous criticism of Walpole as a politician and an author; *Chambers's Cyclopædia of English Literature* (1901); Henrik Schück: *Allmän litteraturhistoria*, V, pp. 372–376; P. v. Tieghem: *Le mouvement romantique*, 2nd ed., Paris (1923).

The most noteworthy and exhaustive sources of information regarding Walpole are Paul Yvon's *La Vie d'un Dilettante; Horace Walpole, 1717–1797; Essai de Biographie psychologique et littéraire* (XV + 872 pages, large 8vo); and his *Horace Walpole as a Poet* (XV + 217) (1924), both of which I have utilized. The passage relating to Hurd has been compiled from the text-books mentioned and the preface written by Montague Summers. Schück declares Walpole to have been ignorant of medievalism.

(7) Biographies of Clara Reeve and Mrs. Radcliffe are included in Scott's *Lives of the Novelists;* as a rule they are mentioned in the same text-books as Walpole; in Richter's history much space has been devoted to them (pp. 191–197 and 219–239). The versions of their works used by me are included in Ballantyne's Library (this does not include *Gaston de Blondeville*). Amongst the critical essays dealing with Mrs. Radcliffe, I wish specially to mention those contained in George Saintsbury's works, *The English Novel*, pp. 161 and 172 (1913), and *A History of Nineteenth Century Literature, 1780–1900* (1910), and in Sir Walter Raleigh's *The English Novel*, pp. 227–234, 5th ed. (1907). Other sources are Mrs. Oliphant: *The Literary History of England in the End of the Eighteenth and Beginning of the Nineteenth Century*, II, pp. 277–285 (1882); Allan Cunningham: *Biographical and Critical History of the Last Fifty Years*, pp. 122–125 (1834); William Hazlitt: *Lectures on the English Comic Writers*, pp. 125–127 (Everyman's Library); A. A. S. Wieten: *Mrs Radcliffe. Her Relation towards Romanticism* (1926).

(8) March 9th, 1765, to William Cole. Quoted also by Beers, p. 236.

(9) Walpole founded his printing-press, *Officina arbuteana*, as he called it, at Strawberry Hill, in the summer of 1757; its first publication was Gray's *Odes*. He had been so severely criticized for his earlier literary production that he had become timid. *The Castle of Otranto* was at first ascribed to Gray, which made Walpole remark that people must be fools indeed to think such a trifle worthy of a genius like Gray. Gosse: *Gray*, p. 169. Doctor Johnson admitted that " Horry Walpole . . . got together a great many curious little things, and told them in an elegant manner." By this the Doctor did not however intend *The Castle of Otranto*, which it is hardly likely that he had read, as Boswell is silent on the matter. Walpole did not belong to the admirers of the " Great Bear," or even to his circle of acquaintance, for the Doctor had made acquaintance difficult by his Parliamentary Reports in *The Gentleman's Magazine*, in which he invariably made out a poor case for Sir Robert Walpole. Moreover, Walpole was a Whig, and thus in the Doctor's eyes a " dog " and a " rascal." The only

question on which Walpole and Johnson were of the same opinion was in regard to Ossian. Phelps, *op. cit.*, p. 110.

(10) Both Beers, p. 253, and Dibelius : *Englische Romankunst*, I, pp. 290–293, 2nd ed. (1922), and other investigators of terror-romanticism take into account the central position of the Haunted Castle, but they have not arrived at the synthesis of the material, at its decisive significance, to which my own studies have led. Yvon, *op. cit.*, p. 490 : " Comment cet Anglais du milieu du XVIIIᵉ siècle (Walpole), grand seigneur, homme en place et homme à la mode, s'était-il ainsi épris du charme du passé ? Pour le comprendre, il suffit de garder sans cesse, présente à l'esprit, l'image du petit château gothique de Strawberry Hill à travers toutes ses transformations, et de rappeler que ce château est moins une tentative de reconstitution archéologique, que l'expression d'un état d'âme."

(11) The account given in the paragraph can be compared with pp. 18, 19, 21, 62 and 72 of *The Castle of Otranto.*

(12) *The Old English Baron*, pp. 618, 622 and 651. It might be brought forward against my argument that in *The Castle of Otranto* there is a ghost and a gigantic vision ; an enormous mailed hand and foot. Dorothy Scarborough is building on these when she says in *The Supernatural in Modern English Fiction*, pp. 17 and 19 (1917), " The Ghost is the real hero or heroine of the Gothic novel," and, " The genealogical founder of the family of Gothic ghosts is the giant apparition in *The Castle of Otranto.*" This view is not, however, fully in accordance with the facts. The only true ghost in *The Castle of Otranto* is that of the hermit, in a bye-episode ; the remaining supernatural matter must be understood as being of a visionary nature, and distinguishable from ghost-tradition ; neither have been located in a part of the castle with the reputation of old of being haunted. This point was added later by Clara Reeve, who thus introduced a popular ghost-tradition into the new species of literature and discovered in a new sense the empty haunted suite.

(13) *The Castles of Athlin and Dunbayne*, pp. 721, 725. *The Mysteries of Udolpho*, pp. 233, 325.

(14) *The Sicilian Romance*, pp. 36 and 43. *The Mysteries of Udolpho*, p. 325.

(15) *The Castles of Athlin and Dunbayne*, p. 759 ; *The Sicilian Romance*, pp. 45, 60. The passage dealing with the thistle is in *The Romance of the Forest*, p. 82. The thistle is common in Ossian, *e.g.*, pp. 3, 4, 44, 53 and 57 ; the phrase used by Mrs. Radcliffe is on p. 61 (Carthon), the only difference being in the tense. *Poems of Ossian*, Walter Scott Publishing Company, London.

(16) *The Mysteries of Udolpho*, p. 326 ; *The Sicilian Romance*, pp. 19 and 44 ; *The Castles of Athlin and Dunbayne*, pp. 738–740. " Holy calm " appears in James Thomson's *The Seasons*, Summer, line 550.

(17) *The Mysteries of Udolpho*, pp. 368, 415, 434 ; *The Castles of Athlin and Dunbayne*, p. 730 ; *The Sicilian Romance*, p. 24. *The Mysteries of Udolpho* bear on p. 368 as motto the following lines by Mason, which depict extremely well the fateful romance represented by the clock, or bell :

> The midnight clock has toll'd ; and hark the bell
> Of death beats slow, heard ye the note profound ?
> It pauses now, and now with rising knell
> Flings to the hollow gale its sullen sound.

Edward Young in his *Night Thoughts* (First Night) has the following :
>   The bell strikes one.
>   As if an angel spoke,
>   I feel the solemn sound . . .
>   It is the knell of my departed hours.

(18) *The Castles of Athlin and Dunbayne*, pp. 726, 728, 730, 739, 747 ; *The Sicilian Romance*, pp. 27, 31, 61, 63 ; *The Romance of the Forest*, pp. 86, 98, 121.

(19) *The Castle of Otranto*, pp. 15, 22, 148 and 154.

(20) *Ibid.*, pp. 42, 93, 154–155.

(21) *Ibid.*, pp. 93–95 ; *The Old English Baron*, pp. 618, 650.

(22) *The Castles of Athlin and Dunbayne*, pp. 722, 727, 735 ; *The Sicilian Romance*, pp. 33, 36, 38 ; *The Mysteries of Udolpho*, pp. 226, 242 ; *The Romance of the Forest*, pp. 85–86. On the last-mentioned page we find the sentence : " The environs were sweetly romantic."

(23) *The Castles of Athlin and Dunbayne*, pp. 726, 742, 749, 759 ; *The Sicilian Romance*, pp. 24, 33, 35, 57 ; *The Romance of the Forest*, p. 141.

(24) Scott : *Lives of the Novelists*, p. 197.

(25) *Faerie Queene*, Canto IV, verse 4 ; VIII, 2–3, 29–40 ; IX, 33.

(26) Phelps, *op. cit.*, p. 47 : " Spenser was the poet of Romanticism as Pope was of Classicism " ; p. 48 : " Very few men took him seriously ; they read him for amusement, and they practised his versification for amusement."

(27) Northam Castle—*King John ;* The Tower and Pomfret Castle—*King Richard II ;* Elsinore Castle—*Hamlet*.

(28) By this I mean the conception usually derived from reading or witnessing *Hamlet*, which, allowing for individual taste, is pretty much the same for every one. The indications regarding the Castle of Elsinore given by Shakespeare himself are extremely vague. From Horatio's words one might conclude it to be situated on a lofty height, one slope of which falls steeply to the sea. Brinus Köhler : *Die Schilderung des Milieus in Shakespeare's Hamlet, Macbeth und King Lear* (1911).

(29)   For now hath time made me his numbering clock :
>   My thoughts are minutes, and with sighs they yar
>   Their watches on unto mine eyes. . . .

(30) *Faerie Queene*, Canto I, verse 34.

(31) The chapters in Beers's book entitled " The Spenserians," " The Landscape Poets " and " The Miltonians," contain, *inter alia*, the quotations given by me. Beers does not however lay stress on the ruined tower as a special feature ; my own view of the significance of the motive finds support in A. Brandl's *Life of Coleridge*, in which he says : " Der hohe einsame Thurm des Penseroso zerbröckelt bei Dyer und Collins zu einer melancholischen Ruine, wird bei Mallet zu einem Grabdenkmal, bei Gray vollends zu einem Gottesacker." *Samuel Taylor Coleridge und die englische Romantik*, p. 34 (1886). The fifth chapter of Phelps's work : *The Influence of Milton in the Romantic Movement ;* Mathilde Müller : *William Shenstone* (1911) ; Otto Bundt : *Akensides Leben und Werke* (1897) ; Alfred Biese : *Die Entwickelung des Naturgefühls im Mittelalter und in der Neuzeit*, 2nd ed. (1892) ; Palgrave, *The Golden Treasury of Songs and Lyrics*. Thomson's romantic feeling for nature

deserves more space than I have given to it; see Winter, 5–6, 109, 143–144, 192–194; Autumn, 711, 970–973, 1030–32; "The lonely tower," Summer, 1670–81. D. C. Tovey: *The Poetical Works of James Thomson* (1897); Edmund Gosse: *The Works of Thomas Gray in Prose and Verse* (1902); *The Pageant of English Poetry*, Oxford University Press (1916).

(32) Richard Lange: *Edward Young's Natursinn* (1911). I am indebted for the comparison with an owl to Lange. Carl Müller: *Robert Blair's " Grave " und die Grabes-und Nachtdichtung* (1909), a noteworthy and lucid study which shows, *inter alia*, that contrary to the general belief, Blair is not indebted to Young, although their poetry is contemporary; he draws attention to the Book of Job, Milton and Shakespeare. The quotation given is from the beginning of the poem, p. 2. Mikko Erich's study *Ugo Foscolo come uomo e come poeta lirico* (1912) contains an account of grave-poetry. Tieghem, P. v., *La poésie de la nuit et des tombeaux en Europe au XVIIIe siècle* (1921).

(33) Joseph Brey: *Die Naturschilderungen in den Romanen und Gedichten der Mrs. Ann Radcliffe, nebst einem Rückblick auf die Entwicklung der Natur- schilderung im englischen Romane des* 18. *Jahrhunderts* (1911). This shows a few similarities between the descriptions of nature in *La Nouvelle Héloïse* and *The Romance of the Forest*. *The New Heloise* appeared in English in February, 1761; by May there were already two editions. *Emile* appeared in 1762, and was likewise published in several editions. In 1767 a selection of Rousseau's works in five volumes appeared in London, this in addition to *The New Heloise* and *Emile*. G. Adolph Frisch: *Der Revolutionäre Roman in England. Seine Beeinflussung durch Rousseau*, p. 9 (1914); Gray: *Journal in France*, 1739, Gosse Edition, I, pp. 244; *Journal in the Lakes*, 1769, Gosse Edition, p. 281; Rousseau: *La Nouvelle Héloïse*, Manz ed., *e.g.*, I, pp. 90, 92, 93, 94, 99. Rousseau depicts the beauty of the Alps in his *Confessions*. Daniel Mornet: *Le Romantisme en France au XVIIIe siècle*, pp. 94–95 (1912). The chapter entitled " Le lyrisme romantique " is illuminating in this respect. Equally so, in its study of the birth in England and France of the feeling for sublimity in nature, is Yrjö Hirn's *Eremiter och pilgrimer* (1924); see chapter: " Lands- kapsromantiken och La Grande Chartreuse," pp. 91–110.

(34) Edition used: Edinburgh, 1797. It appears from Boswell's *Life of Dr. Johnson* that Beattie was greatly in favour with the Doctor's circle and that his poem was known there. Gosse points out (*Gray*, p. 176) that *The Minstrel* has to thank for its special character a poem, " Psyche," by Gloucester Ridley, which appeared in 1754. Mrs. Radcliffe was fond of using Beattie for her mottoes. Kurt Püschel: *James Beattie's Minstrel* (1904).

(35) In constructing the *Poems of Ossian* from Gaelic fragments, Mac- pherson modelled his diction from the language of the Old Testament's prophets. It is not impossible that in doing so he added to Gaelic inconsolability something of the sense of sorrow and desolation of the Lamentations of Jeremiah and Isaiah. In the Lamentations " ways mourn," " gates are desolate," " the rampart and the wall lament." The picture of desolation painted by Isaiah includes details such as the overrunning of a city by wild beasts: "And wolves shall cry in their castles and jackals in the pleasant palaces." Bailey Saunders: *The Life and Letters of James Macpherson*, p. 82 (1895): " The likeness between Mac- pherson's measured prose and the style of the psalms and prophetical works of the Old Testament is sufficiently obvious."

(36) *The English Novel*, p. 228.

(37) Salvator Rosa attracted the attention of the romanticists; he is the

chief character in E. T. A. Hoffmann's story *Signor Formica* ; Mrs. Radcliffe
mentions his name in *The Mysteries of Udolpho*, p. 236. The view seems general
that his influence on the formation of Mrs. Radcliffe's conception of romantic
landscape was considerable. In so far as it is needful to regard Mrs. Radcliffe's
landscapes as descriptions of romantic pictures, another painter exists who was
probably much better known to her than Salvator Rosa, namely, Richard Wilson
(1714–1782). Wilson studied in Italy, whence he returned in 1755 ; characteristic of his landscapes are mountainous scenes, waterfalls, idyllic lakes and ruins.
Myra Reynolds : *The Treatment of Nature in English Poetry between Pope and
Wordsworth*, pp. 296–304 (1909). Regarding Mrs. Radcliffe the author remarks
(p. 221) : " But thought of as in her own day, Mrs. Radcliffe must always rank
as a discoverer, so new and fresh was this element she brought into fiction."
She has also had some acquaintance with the work of Claude Lorrain. See
Cl. Fr. McIntyre, *Ann Radcliffe in Relation to her Times* (1920).

(38) *Vathek*, p. 222, Greening & Co., London (1905).
The Oriental story had its beginnings in France in a collection by Petis de la
Croix (1620–75), entitled *Contes Turcs,* a translation dealing with the Sultana
of Persia and forty viziers. The legend of Santon Barsisa, to which we shall
return, is contained in this collection, which appeared in English in 1708.
As translators of Oriental stories mention must be made of Galland and Claude
Comte de Caylus (1692–1765). Such collections of tales became very fashionable
in the seventeenth and eighteenth centuries, and include the *Contes Tartares* and
Contes Chinoises ; contemporary writers soon found in these a good weapon
and a masquerade dress for their own aims, their *double entendres* and audacities.
Crebillon Jeune's romance *Tanzai et Neadarné* pretends to have been translated
originally from the Chinese, ten centuries before Confucius ; the Chinese was in
turn a translation from the Japanese, and so on, until finally it was rendered into
Latin by " the famous German scholar Crocovius Putridus " who had achieved
world-fame by his investigations into whether Diana kept only male or also
female hounds. This Oriental line leads both to Voltaire and to such authors
as Jacques Cazotte (1720–1792), whose work *Le Diable Amoureux* is to be
understood as a fabulous story written under Oriental influences, spirits, enchantments and love being its chief ingredients. Rudolf Fürst : *Die Vorläufer der
Modernen Novelle im achtzehnten Jahrhundert* (1897).
In England Oriental literature began with the translation of the *Thousand
and One Nights* (1704–1712). In 1708 came the *Turkish Tales* and in 1714 the
Persian Tales. In 1722 was published *The Travels and Adventures of the
Three Princes of Serendip*—the work which may have influenced *Zadig*.
Thomas Simon Gueullette (1683–1766) published the *Chinese Tales* (1725),
Mogul Tales (1736), *Tartar Tales* (1759) and *Peruvian Tales* (1764). The
burning hearts in *Vathek* are derived from the *Mogul Tales ;* in addition, it has been
appreciably influenced by a work published in 1729, *The Adventures of Abdalla,
Son of Hanif*, as regards, for example, the scene where Vathek comes before
Eblis and the picture of Eblis. Martha Pike Conant : *The Oriental Tale in
England in the Eighteenth Century*, pp. 4, 27, 30, 36–49 (1908). Sir William
Jones (1746–1794), one of the first scientific Orientalists in England, translated
Oriental literature, his work being used by Southey, Moore, Byron and Shelley.
Marie E. de Meester : *Oriental Influences in the English Literature of the Early
Nineteenth Century*, pp. 6–11 (1915). William Raleigh Price : *The Symbolism
of Voltaire's Novels with Special Reference to Zadig* (1911), is a study of Voltaire's
Oriental sources.
There is a tendency to distinguish between Oriental and " actual "

romanticism. The distinction is none the less arbitrary, particularly as regards terror-romanticism. Orientalism is essentially terror-romantic in nature, as the central setting of the fabulous world on which it rests is a kind of enchanted Bluebeard's Castle with hundreds of mysterious rooms, all of which the captive maiden may enter with the exception of one, which though it does not indeed harbour a ghost, nevertheless contains a tub filled with blood or some other horror. W. A. Clouston: *Popular Tales and Fictions*, I, pp. 199–204 (1887).

To come to Beckford, his own life and short novel provide a good example of the peculiar fashion in which Oriental and English romance could become merged, like any other related phenomena. The *Arabian Nights* read in child-hood took so exclusive a hold on his imagination that his bent for magnificence and grandeur can be said to have been formed at that time. Soon, however, these Oriental dreams of splendour and greatness were enhanced by the lofty and noble imaginative world of Ossian. The letters of Beckford's youth, many of which are written with a typical Ossian feeling for majestic nature, show clearly how easily this Biblically-inspired rhythmical prose could be made Oriental in colour and subject-matter.

Beckford was in everything a romantic child of his period. Thus, Fonthill Abbey, like Strawberry Hill, is a realization of its owner's romantic dreams. Having returned to England in 1796, he entrusted James Wyatt with the task of drawing up the plans for a building which was to resemble an abbey and to be partly ruined. The result was the famous building with its central tower 300 feet in height. When this collapsed, Beckford merely deplored that he had not seen the crash. A new tower, 276 feet high, likewise collapsed, but by then Beckford was no longer the owner ; its new proprietor, likewise an inordin-ately rich man, but of a more modest nature, calmly remarked that now the building was not too big for him. A tower was an essential feature of Beckford's ideal building, and one had to be added to the building erected for his old age at Bath.

Both Fonthill Abbey and Strawberry Hill, in common with Abbotsford and Landor's building activities on his estate in Wales, show the Haunted Castle to have been the central idea of the romanticism of those days, the focus of all its interests and a general source of emanation.

Lewis Melville: *The Life and Letters of William Beckford of Fonthill*, pp. 20–21, 29–58, 60–66, 93, 220 (1910). A picture of Fonthill Abbey will be found in this book. Allan Cunningham, *op. cit.*, *The Effect of the Cultivation of Oriental Literature on the General Literature of Great Britain*, pp. 326–348. Compare Note 298. Stéphane Mallarmé: *Divagations*, pp. 61–63 and 95–109 (1897) ; this reflects the reawakened admiration for *Vathek* and claims proprietary rights and the honour of having inspired the book for France.

(39) *The Castle of Otranto*, p. 2.

(40) *Ibid.*, pp. 27 and 67.

(41) *The Castles of Athlin and Dunbayne*, pp. 726–727 ; *The Sicilian Romance*, p. 23 ; *The Mysteries of Udolpho*, p. 233 : " Montoni was a man about forty, of an uncommonly handsome person, with features manly and expressive, but whose countenance exhibited more of the haughtiness of command and the quickness of discernment than of any other character."

(42) My opinion is upheld by Sir Walter Raleigh, *op. cit.*, p. 222 : " The defence of Shakespeare that Walpole interpolates in his preface is highly significant. A revival of romance in England must have meant a revival of Shakespeare, but here he is definitely and closely associated with the first stirring of the new

spirit." Saintsbury is more doubtful, *The English Novel*, p. 157: "Après coup, the author talked about Shakespeare (of whom, by the way, he was anything but a fervent or thorough admirer) and the like." Yvon shows, however, that Shakespeare was Walpole's idol, whom he placed above all other authors; next came Milton. ("Walpole as a Poet," p. 153.) After writing the above I note that Bernhard Fehr has come to the same conclusion in his *Die englische Literatur des 19–20 Jahrhunderts*, pp. 30–31 (1923). The theory regarding the historical Manfred of Otranto was propounded by Alice M. Killen in a work to which I shall frequently have occasion to refer, pp. 10, 14–15.

(43) Dibelius expresses his opinion that the romances of Walpole, Clara Reeve and Mrs. Radcliffe were influenced in their most essential points by Fielding and Richardson (*op. cit.*, I, p. 289) and that their basic construction was generally borrowed from Fielding. As the reader will observe, I have reached a different conclusion, one more natural from the romantic point of view. The production of Richardson and Fielding (Smollett's perhaps after all the most) did not contain the romantic materials necessary decisively to attract the romanticists, and even those which the romanticists did make use of, *e.g.*, the finding of Tom Jones as an abandoned infant and the travel-motive, were already known from Shakespeare. To the part played by Richardson, Fielding and Smollett I shall return later.

(44) An exhaustive account is given of *Zeluco* in the work by Helen Richter previously referred to; I regret that I have not had the opportunity of reading it, owing to its being such a literary rarity nowadays. Raleigh says of it (*op. cit.*, p. 193): "*Zeluco*, owing to the praise bestowed on it by Mrs. Barbould, has been far too generally accepted as one of the most notable of eighteenth-century novels. Zeluco, the Byronic villain, and Laura, his amiable and suffering wife, are highly conventional types of evil and of good." Saintsbury remarks (*The English Novel*, p. 172): "But it is not quite certain that its villain-hero (*Zeluco*) had not something, and perhaps a good deal, to do with those of Mrs. Radcliffe who were soon to follow, and, through these, with Byron." These statements bear out my view of the significance of Zeluco for the development of the romantic tyrant-type.

(45) *The Castle of Otranto*, pp. 40, 62, 65, 66, 94 and 159. Can Walpole, in describing his young hero, have been painting a kind of idealized portrait of himself in youth? Austin Dobson describes Walpole as, "High, pallid forehead, dark brilliant eyes under drooping lids, and a friendly, but forced and rather unprepossessing smile."

(46) *The Castles of Athlin and Dunbayne*, p. 763. In the young hero and to some extent also in the young heroine I am rather inclined to discern something of what Dibelius (though he generalizes his argument too much) calls the influence of the old "heroic-gallant" romance. The adventures of the young hero and heroine, stamped in both cases by refinement and dignity, form an essential part of such works as Sir Philip Sidney's *Arcadia*, in which the division into two contrasting types of beauty (of which more anon) already appears, together with names like Pamela, and Madeleine de Scudery's romances. It is reasonable to assume these works to have been known to Mrs. Radcliffe, of whose refined spirit they display a good deal. Compared with Fielding's young men, Valancourt is quite different; Smollett occasionally approaches the type, as for instance in Rinaldo (*Ferdinand Count Fathom*); I cannot connect Richardson with the young hero. An exhaustive account of the novel of gallantry is given in John Dunlop's *The History of Fiction* (1845).

(47) *The Castle of Otranto*, pp. 19–21, 96–97. The young hero answers the question put to him in the following words : " Beauteous and all-perfect as your form is, and though my wishes are not guiltless of aspiring, know, my soul is dedicated to another. . . ."

(48) *Ibid.*, pp. 1, 5, 50, 63, 89 and 91.

(49) *The Castles of Athlin and Dunbayne*, pp. 740, 745 ; *The Sicilian Romance*, pp. 4, 5, 61 ; *The Romance of the Forest*, pp. 79, 88 ; *The Mysteries of Udolpho*, pp. 225, 270.

(50) Quoted from E. Gosse : *A History of Eighteenth Century Literature*, 1660–1780, p. 248 (1906). I am not prepared unconditionally to grant a share in the young heroine to Fielding ; Smollett's Monimia (*Ferdinand Count Fathom*) comes nearer. Mrs. Radcliffe's works display so much originality that one is as a rule loath to search for her sources. The plot of *The Italian* hails from France, as I shall later show. The fate of the Pastor Le Luc and his children (*The Romance of the Forest*) recalls *The Vicar of Wakefield*. (Hans Möbius : *The Gothic Romance*, p. 91 (1902).) Dunlop observes that as regards the crime, the plot of *The Romance of the Forest* could have been taken from Gayot de Pitaval's *Causes célèbres et intéressantes* (1734).

(51) *The Castle of Otranto*, pp. 89–94.

(52) *The Castles of Athlin and Dunbayne*, pp. 732, 739, 841 ; *The Sicilian Romance*, pp. 18, 21 ; *The Mysteries of Udolpho*, pp. 271–272.

(53) *The Castles of Athlin and Dunbayne*, p. 737 ; *The Mysteries of Udolpho*, p. 225 ; *The Sicilian Romance*, p. 18. The poem quoted contains images such as a " sadly pleasing tear " from Gray's *Ode on Adversity* : "And Pity, dropping soft the sadly pleasing tear." " Evening's dying gale " appears in Collins's *Ode to Evening* : " Thy springs and dying gales."

(54) The omission of any mention of Werther and Wertherism as a source of tearful sentimentality might seem a mistake on my part. Werther was published in English, as a translation from the French, in 1779, under the title *The Sorrows of Werter ; a German Story, founded on Fact*. In criticizing it, in 1785, the *Monthly Review* remarks on its harmful tendency and denies all artistic value to it ; the critic regards it as a work of Wieland. (Ernst Margraf : *Einfluss der deutschen Litteratur auf die englische am Ende des achtzehnten und in ersten Drittel des neunzehnten Jahrhunderts*, p. 74 (1901).) If we now recollect, with an eye on Gray's " sadly pleasing tear," that English literature had discovered the sentimental possibilities of nature extremely early, developing it in *The Seasons*, graveyard and night poetry, odes, *Pamela* and *Clarissa Harlowe*, Ossian and other similar products to a stage of strength and fine sensitivity long before Werther had appeared, and that Werther himself feeds his soul on the hopelessness of Ossian, and further, how even at that time, English literature kept itself apart and independent of the rest of Europe, it becomes apparent that Werther is an offshoot of English sentimentality and that of Rousseau, in nowise necessary to these or to their development, although it can have influenced them in the manner of a wave cast back by an opposite shore. For this reason I have not been able to connect Werther any closer with Mrs. Radcliffe, for her sentimentality can be explained otherwise, and her young heroes lack the despairing decision of Werther. In a work called *Episoder. Några kapitel om liv och litteratur under sjuttonhundratalet* (1918), Yrjö Hirn shows Wertherism to have appeared in England, where it accounted for the murder of Miss Ray, the friend of Mrs. Frances Lewis, who was shot in a fit of Werther-like despair

by a parson named Hackman who was unhappily in love with her. This is an instance of Wertherism in real life—in English literature it never achieved any noteworthy position owing to the disinclination of the Byronic hero to make way for it. The line *Saint-Preux, Werther, René, Obermann* and *Adolphe* is a continental one. Sources: Joachim Merlant: *Le roman personnel de Rousseau à Fromentin* (1905); René Canat: *Du sentiment de la solitude morale chez les romantiques et les parnassiens* (1904). (Werther was translated into French by George Deyverdun, in 1776.) Louis Morel: *Les principales traductions de Werther et les jugements de la critique, 1776-1782 ; Archiv für das Studium der neueren Sprachen und Litteraturen,* 119, pp. 139-159.

(55) I am unable to connect Schiller's *Die Räuber* (1781) with these robbers. Nowhere have I seen any indication that Mrs. Radcliffe was acquainted with the German language ; her journey on the Rhine was made later, after she had written her work. *Die Räuber* was translated into English in 1792 by Scott's friend, Alexander Fraser Tytler (Lord Woodhouselee). Mrs. Radcliffe's chief robbers, her tyrants, would form the closest link with Schiller, but as we have seen, the derivation of the type is purely English. The robber-bands who form, as it were, a chorus for Mrs. Radcliffe's settings hail from the picaresque novels, in which scenes of this nature are common.

(56) *The Romance of the Forest,* pp. 138, 140, 179 ; *The Mysteries of Udolpho,* p. 226 ; *The Sicilian Romance,* pp. 9, 24. The æolian harp, which is the favourite instrument of the sentimental evening poets, I do not recollect seeing in Mrs. Radcliffe's works. See Beers, *op. cit.,* p. 165, footnote.

(57) *The Castles of Athlin and Dunbayne,* p. 750 ; *The Sicilian Romance,* p. 60 ; *The Romance of the Forest,* pp. 200, 213 ; *The Mysteries of Udolpho,* pp. 227, 235.

(58) The basing of a story on a mysterious document is an artifice with which authors have amused themselves for centuries. Cervantes pretended that *Don Quixote* had originally been written by the Arabian historian Cid Hamed ben Engeli. All the 17th and 18th century " Tartar " and " Chinese " tales were alleged to be copied from mysterious manuscripts, and the same fashion was adopted, as witness the previously-mentioned work of Crebillon Jeune, when authors began to use the materials of such stories for original work. *Gulliver's Travels* were supposed to be based on the discovery of the traveller's notes. Samuel Johnson published, in 1749, *The Vision of Theodore,* which professed to be the work of the hermit himself and was said to have been found in his cell. The romanticists accepted the artifice with delight, as it furnished them with an excellent means of bringing contemporary readers face to face, as it were, with some figure from the past.

Yet this " discovered manuscript " could have serious enough results. In practice, the romanticists generally used the artifice in a fashion that made it easy for the reader to see that only a literary trick was intended, so that people became accustomed to regard the practice as a harmless pleasantry. Consequently, when an author, as in Macpherson's case, could in the main truthfully assert that his work was based either on an old manuscript or other knowledge preserved from ancient days, he was not believed, for one reason, because the public had become used to regarding such assertions as literary tricks. In these cases an author could be greatly wronged, as happened precisely to Macpherson. A fondness for the method could on the other hand lead an author to such lengths that he would attempt in all seriousness, as Thomas Chatterton did, to awaken belief in an actual, momentous find of old papers. He too met with scepticism, and the old manuscript idea led in this case to a tragedy. One cannot help thinking that the doubt cast upon Ossian was partly the result of an over-great use of the method, and that Chatterton's attempt arose out of a morbid desire to make one real " find " of marvellous and valuable contents, which would cover the finder with honour.

(59) *The Castles of Athlin and Dunbayne*, pp. 730, 757 ; *The Sicilian Romance*, p. 17 ; *The Romance of the Forest*, p. 97 ; *The Mysteries of Udolpho*, p. 330.

(60) *The Castle of Otranto*, pp. 4, 15–16, 24, 31, 69, 78–79, 80, 106, 130, 141, 155.

(61) *The Old English Baron*, pp. 608, 616, 622, 623, 631, 632, 650. Walpole was obviously displeased at this competing enterprise, as he remarked apropos Clara Reeve's book, " It is so probable, that any trial for murder at the Old Bailey would make a more interesting story " (than *The Old English Baron*). Raleigh, *op cit.*, p. 227.

(62) *Lives of the Novelists*, p. 215.

(63) *The Sicilian Romance*, pp. 5, 6, 15, 16, 19, 22, 25, 30, 38, 39.

(64) *The Romance of the Forest*, pp. 84, 104, 129.

(65) The term was first used by Theodore Watts-Dunton. See *Chambers's Cyclopædia of Engl. Lit.*, III, Foreword.

(66) Shakespeare knew even such a man of might as a Lapland wizard, of whom a glimpse is caught in *The Comedy of Errors*.

(67) The witticism is from Beers.

(68) *Pamela*, p. 92. Hogg's *New Novelist's Magazine* (1792).

(69) *Tom Jones* (Everyman's ed.), pp. 8, 294, 301–307, 336, 378. *The Man of the Hill* is pure romanticism.

(70) *The Adventures of Roderick Random*, p. 29 ; *Peregrine Pickle*, p. 14 (Routledge editions) ; *Ferdinand Count Fathom*, I, pp. 115–116 ; II, pp. 202–203 (Gibbins & Co., 1906).

(71) Daniel Defoe was fully convinced of the truth of ghosts and visions. He remarks : " I must tell you, good people, he that is not able to see the Devil, in whatever shape he is pleased to appear in, is not really qualified to live in this world, no, not in the quality of a common inhabitant." His attitude towards ghosts is the same as that of his contemporary Joseph Glanvill, of whom more in another connection. (Defoe quotation from Raleigh, *op. cit.*, p. 135.) Defoe even published books dealing with the supernatural, *viz.*, *True Relation of the Apparition of one Mrs. Veal* (1705) ; *The Political History of the Devil* (1726) ; and *Essay on the History and Reality of Apparitions* (1727). In Thomson's *The Seasons*, in " Winter," there is so much ghost-belief that the whole poem becomes " the goblin-story told to a ring of pale faces round the farmhouse fire." (Gosse : *A History of Eighteenth Century Literature*, pp. 220–223.) Even in his undergraduate days, Thomson was so afraid of ghosts that if left alone in a dark room he would dash out in panic. It was generally believed that his father's death was due to some evil design of the Devil, owing to his over-bold defiance of the famous " Woolie Ghost." (Garnett and Gosse, *op. cit.*, III, p. 273.) The graveyard and night poetry of Blair and Young is full of ghostly atmosphere and was well adapted to key up minds to receptivity to such material. David Mallet lays claim (although unjustifiably, as Phelps has proved) to the ballad of *Margaret's Ghost* (1724), which was subsequently included in

Percy's collection and was of great significance for the development of the ghost-ballad. A well-known poem is Richard Glover's *Admiral Hosier's Ghost*. *The Minstrel*, by Beattie, to which I have referred, gives a good deal of ghostly atmosphere in the form of graveyard poetry :

> And ghosts, that to the charnel-dungeon throng,
> And drag a length of clanking chain and wail,
> Till silenced by the owl's terrific song,
> Or blast that shrieks by fits the shuddering isles along.

One is compelled on the whole to say that the ghost of Otranto, which is regarded as having inaugurated ghost-romance, was no novelty in English literature ; it had merely never been presented in the same form or with the same intention as by Walpole and his followers. Sources for the study of the romanticism of ghosts and superstitions are the work by Dorothy Scarborough (which does not go farther back in time than Gothic romanticism) ; C. Thürnau : *Geister in der englischen Litteratur des* 18. *Jahrhunderts* (1906) ; Wilhelm Ad. Paterna : *Das übersinnliche im englischen Roman von Horace Walpole bis Walter Scott* (1915). My remarks regarding the opinions of Addison and Steele are based chiefly on Thürnau's work.

(72) One gathers from Boswell that Johnson believed in the existence of ghosts, which would harmonize well with his unusually great fear of death. Johnson also believed that swallows spend their winters in a state of unconsciousness under water, and that gold could be manufactured.

(73) Georges Gendarme de Bevotte : *La Légende de Don Juan*, pp. 18–19 (1906). The animated statue (picture) has been a theme for tales since Pygmalion. Charles Godfrey Leland's *Legends of Florence* (1895) contains the mass of such material connected with Florence. A long account of the Don Juan legends is given in the third part of J. Scheible's compilation *Das Kloster* (1845–49).

(74) King Arthur's sword, Ex Calibur, Excalibore, is derived from the Scandinavian Volsung legend, whence it has been taken into Beowulf (Clouston, *op. cit.*, I, 43–44). Walpole was, however, unacquainted with mediæval literature, so that we can probably regard Spenser as the nearest source that could have led his thoughts to the enormous sword. The dripping of blood from the nose of Alfonso's statue was not an invention of Walpole's. Phelps points out (*op. cit.*, p. 108) that Dryden referred to such bleeding as an omen in popular superstition of an impending catastrophe. The drops of blood appear also in a play by John Banks, a dramatist of the Restoration :

> Last night no sooner was I laid to rest
> Than just three drops of blood fell from my nose.

(Scarborough, *op. cit.*, p. 42, footnote.)

(75) I must complete my account by remarking that suspense is plentiful in Fielding's, and especially in Smollett's works ; an example of such suspense being transformed into terror, owing to the realism with which the scene is depicted, is the famous nocturnal forest and murder scene in *Ferdinand Count Fathom*. In the above works it is seldom as romantic as in Mrs. Radcliffe's works, nor as concentrated and intense as in the scene referred to earlier in *Macbeth*, which adheres more closely to the methods adopted by the romanticists. This latter scene has always had an agitating effect. Thomas de Quincey wrote an article in *The London Magazine* for 1823 entitled " On the Knocking at the Gate in Macbeth." " The effect was that it reflected back upon the murderer

a peculiar awfulness and a depth of solemnity." (David Masson : *The Collected Writings of Thomas de Quincey*, Part X, pp. 389–394 (1897).)

(76) In this respect one often meets with exaggeration. Up to and including *The Italian* Mrs. Radcliffe used ghosts sparingly ; she is not a typical portrayer of ghostly horrors. Not until in the posthumously published *Gaston de Blonde-ville* does Mrs. Radcliffe make copious use of ghosts, which she then does in Walpole's style ; in this work she makes them appear and take part in the action, even in a tournament, quite like living characters. But the book forms an excep-tion amongst her production. (Möbius, *op. cit.*, p. 132.)

(77) Walpole's letter to Madame du Deffand, quoted in Scott's *Lives of the Novelists*, p. 192.

(78) *The Mysteries of Udolpho*, pp. 229 and 243.

(79) Mrs. Radcliffe was well paid for her books, *e.g*, £500 for *The Mysteries of Udolpho* and £800 for *The Italian*. Her books were enormously popular. Scott remarks, regarding *The Mysteries of Udolpho* (*Lives of the Novelists*, p. 216) : " The very name was fascinating ; and the public, who rushed upon it with all the eagerness of curiosity, rose from it with unsated appetite. When a family was numerous, the volumes always flew, and were sometimes torn, from hand to hand." In spite of, or better, thanks to Mrs. Radcliffe's undeniable refinement as an author, which the French, among others, have fully acknowledged, she found on the Continent a number of imitators who published either in her name or their own a great mass of the lowest kind of pedlar romance. The work of Brey's already referred to contains a catalogue of these, but in all probability many have remained unmentioned. A spacious account of the fortunes and significance of the works of Walpole, Clara Reeve and Mrs. Radcliffe in France, and the imitations they gave rise to, is contained in Alice M. Killen's study *Le roman " terrifiant " ou roman " noir " de Walpole à Ann Radcliffe et son influence sur la littérature française jusqu'en* 1840 (1915), which has a careful bibliography.

(80) Mrs. Oliphant, *op. cit.*, III, pp. 221–236 ; Raleigh, *op. cit.*, pp. 260–266 ; Garnett and Gosse, *op. cit.*, IV, p. 92 ; Léonie Villard : *Jane Austen, Sa vie et son oeuvre* (1914). The satirists had also their own periodical, the *Anti-Jacobin or the Weekly Examiner* founded by William Gifford, in which George Canning published, in 1797–98, his parody of *Die Räuber* entitled *The Rovers, or the Double Entertainment*. A parody was likewise published of Goethe's *Stella*. Pitt himself was a patron of the paper. In 1811 a mocking burlesque on Teutonism and the then fashionable equestrian plays, directed particularly towards Lewis's *Timur the Tartar* (of which more later), was presented at the Haymarket Theatre in the title of *The Quadrupeds of Quedlinburgh ; or, the Rovers of Weimar. Tragico-Comico-Anglo-Germanico-Hippo-Ono-Dramatico Romance*. Walter Sellier : *Kotzebue in England*, p. 77 (1901). In his edition of Byron (see Note 108), *Letters and Journals*, II, p. 157, Prothero relates that Colman, Junior, wrote a prologue for this burlesque, in the course of which he says :

> Your taste, recover'd half from foreign quacks,
> Takes airings, now, on English horses' backs ;
> While every modern bard may raise his name,
> If not on lasting praise, on stable fame.

During the 1811–12 season, the Lyceum presented a burlesque entitled *Quadrupeds, or the Manager's Last Kick,* in which tailors appear riding on donkeys and mules. For the work of Jane Austen and Miss Edgeworth I have used the Everyman's Library edition. A new edition of Barrett's work was published in 1909 and has been at my disposal.

(81) In 1839 a two-volume work appeared in London entitled *The Life and Correspondence of M. G. Lewis, Author of " The Monk," " Castle Spectre," etc., with many pieces in prose and verse never before published.* Byron's words " Hail, wonder-working Lewis " had been taken as a motto, and a portrait of Lewis was appended. The author's name is not given, but according to the Brit. Mus. catalogue the book was written by Mrs. Margaret Baron-Wilson. The major part of the work comprises Lewis's letters to his mother, certain other documents concerning him, fragments of prose and verse from unpublished works, etc., so that the biographical element provided by the author herself is inevitably scanty, and as regards Lewis's literary sources, extremely inadequate. As a matter of fact the chief interest of the work lies in the publication of the correspondence and the said fragments. The author's own standpoint towards the object of her work is wholly admiring, so that her book is neither critical nor objective. Its purpose has been to " point public attention to the strong good sense, good feeling, and honourable principle which marked the whole course of his general conduct in life, his exemplary duty and affection as a son and his unblemished integrity as a man and a gentleman." All subsequent biographies of Lewis are based on this work ; for additions and corrections, literary sources and an understanding of Lewis's position and significance as an author, recourse must be had to other sources. Amongst these I would draw attention to Max Rentsch's thesis *Matthew Gregory Lewis. Mit besonderer Berücksichtigung seines Romans "Ambrosio or The Monk,"* Leipzig (1902), in which all the biographical data is taken from Mrs. Baron-Wilson's book. As regards literary history, the unreliability displayed here and there by the author is apt to awaken suspicion towards the rest. Thus (on p. 12) he informs us that while at the Hague, Lewis translated Schiller's *Die Räuber,* and (p. 58) that Southey participated in Lewis's collection of ballads with the poems *Madoc* and *Roderick* from the poem *Mary, the Maid of the Inn,* further, with *Donica, Rudiger, The Old Woman of Berkeley* and *Lord William.* Lewis has not translated *Die Räuber,* nor did Southey participate in Lewis's collection with more than one poem, which is not mentioned in Rentsch's list ; I am unacquainted with any ballads by Southey called *Madoc* and *Roderick,* but I have read his long epic poems of those names.

(82) The following is Lewis's opinion of his father after the latter's death (*Journal of the Residence among the Negroes in the West Indies,* p. 60 (1861)) : " My father was one of the most humane and generous persons that ever existed ; there was no indulgence which he ever denied his negroes, and his letters were filled with the most positive injunctions for their good treatment."

(83) *Saducismus Triumphatus, or Full and Plain Evidence concerning Witches and Apparitions ;* the copy seen by me was published in 1681 (Glanvill lived 1636–80). His writings appear to have carried weight—he is regarded, for one thing, as a skilful stylist of his period—as even Poe could borrow from him the motto for *Ligeia ;* the narrative of " The Scholar Gipsy " in *The Vanity of Dogmatizing* (1661) is the theme of Matthew Arnold's poem of that name.

(84) The work mentioned in Note 82 shows the Lewises and the Sewells to be old colonial families in Jamaica. On Lewis's farm called Cornwall there was a family mausoleum, the appearance of which Lewis describes minutely (p. 53). He relates that his grandfather had ordered that wherever he should

die, his body was to be brought to the family grave at Jamaica; the family affection for this place must therefore have been great. The Spanish Town church in the capital, said by Lewis to have been extremely fine (p. 82), contained the graves of kinsfolk from both sides of the family, including that of his maternal grandfather. One of his relations on his father's side was judge in the town. The Lewis arms were checquy azure and argent, with three quarterings. (*Notes and Queries*, 2nd Series, X, p. 349.) The Beckford family also owned estates in Jamaica, this distant island being thus closely connected with the most eccentric figures in English romanticism. Beckford's enormous wealth had been accumulated in Jamaica by slave labour; on his death, in 1735, William Beckford's grandfather, Peter Beckford, left property valued at £300,000. Peter's father had been Governor of Jamaica and owned 24 farms, which employed 1200 slaves. Unlike the Lewises, Senior and Junior, William Beckford was entirely indifferent to the status and conditions of his slaves. I have not been able to discover any information regarding the relations between Lewis and Beckford, not even as to whether they were acquainted, as it seems natural they should have been. The fact that Lewis took over Beckford's seat in Parliament points to acquaintanceship and a mutual agreement, without being conclusive proof of such a state.

(85) As he was not a King's Scholar, but only a Town Boy, he could not take part in the big Anniversary play. He is said to have taken the part of Falconbridge in *King John* (probably a burlesque of the play) and that of " My Lord Duke " in *High Life below Stairs* (written in 1759 by James Townley).

(86) *Life*, I, p. 29. A similar experience befell Edward Bulwer in childhood in the old " haunted castle " of Knebworth, which consisted of two tall square towers and two wings, both of which boasted their traditional haunted rooms. The experiences undergone in this castle in childhood influenced Lytton considerably, and as an author he liked to deal with the supernatural. (*The Life, Letters and Literary Remains of Edward Bulwer, Lord Lytton. By his Son*, I, pp. 32, 34 (1883).) May it be observed however that the terror inspired by empty rooms is a common memory of childhood, and too much importance need not be attached to it.

(87) *Life*, I, p. 58. Reported to have been written at Oxford, dated 8th, without month. As mention is made, however, of a forthcoming Easter visit to Chatham at the end of the month, and this visit took place in April, 1792, the letter appears to have been written on April 8th. The dating is often deficient in Lewis's letters, although he chides his mother for this very fault.

(88) Quotations published in the first volume of Mrs. Baron-Wilson's *Life*.

(89) *Life*, I, p. 52. The only surviving letter from Lewis's stay at Paris, dated Sept. 7th, 1791 (the *Life* gives the year as 1792, which must be an error). Marsollier's play *Camille, ou le Souterrain* is more recent than *The Sicilian Romance* (1791). (See Alice M. Killen : *Le roman " terrifiant,"* p. 78), and was influenced by the latter. *Les Victimes Cloîtrées* is by Boutet de Monvel, and both in substance and significance is an important play, to which we shall have occasion to return. The French " anti-clerical revolutionary romanticism " apparent in these titles had its beginning partly in such works as *Intrigues monastiques ou l'amour encapuchonné*, published at The Hague in 1739, and Diderot's *La Religieuse* (1760) and *Les deux amis de Bourbonne* (1773). These and the drama of terror of the Revolution prepared the way for tales of terror in Mrs. Radcliffe's and Lewis's style, which were enormously popular in France in the seventeen-nineties, and until 1802, when a halt was called. The appear-

ance of *Melmoth* in 1820 made terror again fashionable. A popular manufacturer of romances in the English and German styles was Nicolas-Edme Restif de la Bretonne (1734–1806), who became a father at the early age of eleven and wrote 42 works in several volumes. German literature was the fashion in Paris about 1760–70, thanks to Grimm. Baour-Lormian depicted the Parnassus of the French romanticists in 1825 in the following lines (*Le Classique et le Romantique*) :

> L'amas incohérent de spectres et de charmes,
> D'amantes et de croix, de baisers et de larmes,
> De vierges, de bourreaux, de vampires hurlants,
> De tombes, de bandits, de cadavres sanglants,
> De morgues, de charniers, de gibets, de tortures,
> Et toutes ces horreurs, ces hideuses peintures,
> Que, sous le cauchemar dont il est oppressé
> Un malade entrevoit, d'épouvante glacé. . . .

(*Killen, op. cit.*, p. 192.) L. Reynaud : *L'influence allemande en France au XVIII° et au XIX° siècle*, p. 196 (1922) ; Yrjö Hirn : *Diderot* (1917) ; Rudolph Fürst, *op. cit.*, p. 164 ; Edmond Estève : *Etudes de littérature préromantique* (1924).

Lewis's letter provides no hint as to whether and to what extent he associated with the other Englishmen in Paris. Beckford stayed there during those years, but kept wholly apart from society. The author Helen Maria Williams lived from 1789 almost without a break at Paris, holding a radical salon where the revolutionaries and liberals of all Europe met, amongst the English being Fox and Lord Holland, both of whom belonged to Lewis's circle. In November, 1792, at a dinner held in Paris to celebrate the taking of Belgium, a British revolutionary club was founded. Lilly Baschó : *Englische Schriftstellerinnen in ihren Beziehungen zur französischen Revolution*, pp. 21–24 (1917).

(90) The second of the chief characters in Diderot's *Les deux amis de Bourbonne* is called Felix.

(91) Weimar was a fashionable resort for the English, whither the friends of German literature made pilgrimages. One of the earliest of these visitors was the friend and translator of German literature, William Taylor, who travelled there in 1782 and was granted an interview with Goethe. At the time of Lewis's visit the British Ambassador at Weimar was Sir Brooke Boothby, who formed a taste for German literature and continued to favour it afterwards. Paul Girardin : *Robert Pearse Gillies and the Propagation of German Literature in England at the end of the XVIIIth and the beginning of the XIXth Century* (1916).

(92) Letter from Weimar dated Dec. 24th, *Life* I, p.78.

(93) Thomas Moore : *Life of Byron*, III, p. 375 (letter to Mr. Rogers, April 4th, 1817). Byron knew no German whatever. During his childhood in Scotland he had " read " with a tutor the Swiss poet Gessner's *Death of Abel*, but there his study of the language ended ; later he declared that the only German he knew was a few swear-words learned from postillions while travelling through Germany. Siegfried Sinzheimer : *Goethe und Byron. Eine Darstellung des persönlichen und litterarischen Verhältnisses mit besonderer Berücksichtigung des " Faust " und " Manfred*," p. 15 (1894). To judge from *The Death of Abel*, Byron's tutor must have been a certain Doctor Willich, who is known to have admired Gessner and to have used his idylls as the gate through which he guided young Scotchmen to the secrets of the German language. His pupils in German included Walter Scott. At the exhortation of Henry Mackenzie, who favoured

everything German, Scott and seven other young Edinburgh men took up the study of German. Paul Girardin, *op. cit.*, p. 13.

(94) The information given by Lewis that he had worked while at The Hague on a book in the style of *The Castle of Otranto* has led many biographers to assume that he meant *The Monk ;* this is however a mistake. Probably he did include some of the material thus accumulated in *The Monk*, but the greatest part of this romance in Otranto-style seems to have gone to the making of *The Castle Spectre*.

(95) English authors work rapidly ; Gosse mentions that Richardson wrote *Pamela* in three months, which, taking into account the size of the book is incredible ; it is much easier to believe that Johnson wrote *Rasselas* in a week. Southey is said to have written the first of his epics, *Joan of Arc*, in six weeks, again an astonishing performance in view of the length of the poem. These statements need not be taken too seriously ; what we are here concerned with is a form of boasting beloved of authors. In the same way, when accused of being influenced by the work of some other author, a writer will hasten to aver that he has never read the works in question.

(96) In 1797 at the actor Bannister's benefit performance.

(97) Study of the sources of *The Monk* has passed through the following stages : in 1903 Georg Herzfeld published (in *Archiv für das Studium der neueren Sprachen und Litteraturen*, Part 104, pp. 310–312) an article " Eine neue Quelle für Lewis's ' Monk,' " in which he showed that Lewis had obtained the Legend of the Bleeding Nun, Lindenberg Castle and the proposed abduction of Agnes, together with the episode in which Raymond appears, from Musaeus' tale " Die Entführung " (published in the collection *Volksmärchen der Deutschen*, Part V, pp. 247–276, Gotha, 1787). In this he was perfectly right. This line of investigation was carried to a conclusion by Otto Ritter in his article " Studien zu M. G. Lewis' Roman ' Ambrosio or the Monk ' " (*Archiv*, Part 111, pp. 106–121), in which he reveals the influence of Walpole's and Mrs. Radcliffe's works in smaller details ; also that Ambrosio's death-scene was taken almost word for word from Veit Weber's story " Teufelbeschwörung " (*Sagen der Vorzeit*, IV, 1791, p. 135) ; that the nightly forest scene was adapted from Smollett's *Ferdinand Count Fathom*, Chap. 20 ; that Matilda's task was the same as Bianca's in Cazotte's *Le Diable Amoureux ;* that the Wandering Jew was an echo of Schiller's *Der Geisterseher ;* that the ballad *Alonzo the Brave* was based on Bürger's ballads ; and that the conjuring up of the Devil and the bargain with him was a Faust-theme. In the meantime, however, Herzfeld had made the acquaintance of L. Wyplel's article on " Ein Schauerroman als Quelle der Ahnfrau," in the *Euphorion* (VII, 725) in which the writer compares Grillparzer's *Die Ahnfrau* with a certain terror-romance from Prague entitled *Die blutende Gestalt mit Dolch und Lampe oder die Beschwörung im Schlosse Stern bei Prag* (*Wien und Prag bey Franz Haas*, 262 pages), and shows Grillparzer to be indebted for the theme of his play to this romance. Comparing this book with *The Monk* and finding that it corresponded almost word for word with certain chapters of Lewis's work, Herzfeld published, believing Lewis to be a plagiarist, an article " Die eigentliche Quelle von Lewis' ' Monk ' " (*Archiv*, Part 111, pp. 316–323) in which he describes his observations, regards the chief source of *The Monk* as definitely established and remarks on de Monvel's play and its influence. Otto Ritter declined, however, to assent to these views, and tried, in an article " Die angebliche Quelle von M. G. Lewis' ' Monk ' " (*Archiv*, Part 113, pp. 56–65), to prove that the Prague romance, which bore no date,

must be of later date than *The Monk*. Herzfeld retorted with an article " Noch einmal die Quelle des ' Monk ' " (*Archiv*, 115, pp. 70–73), adhering to his standpoint, but expressing the hope that a new find might settle the question. Neither of these writers had the idea of comparing the book from Prague with the German translation of *The Monk*. By doing so, August Sauer, who subjected F. von Oertel's version of *The Monk* to a comparison with the Prague romance, settled the controversy; he succeeded in establishing that the latter was for the most part borrowed word for word from the former. Consequently, in the introduction to the first volume of his edition of Grillparzer (*Grillparzers Werke*, 1909), he was able to state : " Der deutsche Roman ist nichts weiter als die Bearbeitung einiger Kapitel aus dem englischen Schauerroman Ambrosio . . . und diese Übersetzung (Oertel) liegt auch der Blutenden Gestalt zu Grunde." This assertion Sauer supported in greater detail in his annotation by giving parallel passages from the Prague book and Oertel's translation. Sauer's introduction is also illuminating both to the seeker for Lewis's sources and to those interested in seeing how motives which have originally appeared in debased surroundings can subsequently become refined by the imagination of a great author. Herzfeld's false conclusion had nevertheless already had its effect. Thus, Helen Richter accepted it and gave in consequence a misleading picture of Lewis. The mistake has also, as one can well understand, crept into many other works. I do not remember seeing it in the works of any English investigator.

From the work by Rudolf Fürst previously mentioned, I observe (pp. 88–99) that the collection *Die neuen Volksmärchen der Deutschen*, published 1789–1792 by Christiane Benedicte Naubert (1756–1819), contains a tale " Die weisse Frau," the setting of which is Neuhaus Castle in Bohemia, and which tells of the ghost of the mistress of Rosenberg. According to Fürst (p. 188), a tale similar to the legend of the Bleeding Nun is contained in a work by Kajetan Tschink (1763–1813), entitled *Wundergeschichten samt dem Schlüssel zu ihrer Erklärung* (1792). Sauer regards that the basic source of all these is *Der höllische Proteus* (Nüremburg, 1695) " mit weitläufigen Abhandlungen über die weisse Frau," written by a certain Erasmus Franciscus.

The writer of the Prague romance subsequently published a sequel entitled *Der Geist Lurian im Silbergewand oder das Gericht über Ambrosio* (238 pages, undated).

(98) Part XIX, 1796, pp. 194–200.

(99) Part XXIV, 1796, p. 403.

(100) Part XXIII, 1797, p. 451.

(101) Part XXXI, 1797, pp. 111–114.

(102) Part V, 1798, pp. 157–158.

(103) Part LIV, 1802, p. 548.

(104) Thomas James Mathias (1754–1835) was a noteworthy satirical writer and translator, greatly skilled in the Italian language, who translated from Italian into English and *vice versa*. He published a fine and careful edition of Gray's poems. The work mentioned in the text of this book was published in 1794 and met with so much favour that no less than 16 editions were published; to these Mathias made additions and corrections as authors deserving such attentions emerged into view. His book is the closest forerunner to Byron's literary satire *English Bards and Scotch Reviewers*.

NOTES

(105) The immoral subject-matter of *The Monk* became widely known, as the branding of the book as such was in itself a fine means of awakening an interested curiosity and thus of furthering its sale. " When ' Monk ' Lewis's sensational romance was in universal request, a Mrs. Lord, who kept a circulating library in Dublin, enriched it with sufficient copies for her customers old and young. . . . A highly correct *pater familias* having reproved her for imperilling the morality of the metropolis by admitting such a book in her catalogue, she naively replied : 'A shocking bad book to be sure, sir ; but I have carefully looked through every copy, and *underscored* all the naughty passages, and cautioned my young ladies what they are to skip without reading it." "Anecdote from Ireland," *Notes and Queries*, 4th Series, IV, p. 271.

(106) The first edition of *The Monk* appeared in 1795 ; I have not been able to find a copy bearing this date in the British Museum Library, but one of the year 1796. Publishers frequently dated their books, if issued towards the end of the year—*The Monk* was issued, it is true, in the summer—with the following year's date, and this is perhaps what happened in the present case. Lewis's publisher, J. Bell, issued two editions of *The Monk* as for 1796, an octavo and a quarto. In the same year a third edition, with a portrait of the author, was published at Waterford. The fourth edition was published by Bell, in 1798, and from this the author deleted the most offensive passages. In 1820 (the exact date of publication is uncertain) a new edition was published at Aberdeen. The latest are, to my knowledge, E. A. Baker's edition (1904) (George Routledge & Sons) ; Gibbins & Co (1906) ; and Brentano's Ltd. (1924). Dean & Monday published (1820 ?) a part of it as *Raymond and Agnes, or the Bleeding Nun of the Castle of Lindenberg*, of which a second edition was issued in 1841 in the series by W. Hazlitt the Younger : *The Romancist's and Novelist's Library*. A certain *Mr. Forley* formed from the part relating to Raymond and Agnes " a grand and interesting ballet," see *Memoirs of Mrs. Crouch, including a Retrospect of the Stage*, Vol. II, p. 257 (1806) ; the music was supplied by a Mr. Reeve. Another scenic adaptation in two acts of the Raymond and Agnes episode was published as No. 38 of *Cumberland's British Theatre* under the title " Raymond and Agnes, the Travellers benighted, or the Bleeding Nun of Lindenberg." J. Boaden's drama *Aurelio and Miranda* is based on *The Monk*. In America two editions of *The Monk* have appeared, in 1877 and 1884. In Germany *The Monk* was published at Leipzig (1797–98) (transl. F. v. Oertel) ; as *Mathilde von Villanegas oder der weibliche Faust*, at Berlin in 1799 ; as *Der Mönch oder die siegende Tugend*, at Magdeburg in 1806 ; and as *Der Mönch Eine schauerlich abentheuerliche Geschichte*, at Hamburg in 1810. In France it was published in 1797, as the work of four translators—Deschamps, Despréz, Benoît and Lamare. The British Museum catalogue mentions another translation from the same year, and new editions of 1803, 1807, 1819, 1834, 1838 and 1849 (Léon de Wailly's new translation, illustrated). In the series *Nouvelles et contes extraits des meilleurs écrivains du XVIIIᵉ siècle* (1883), an abridged version by E. Ploërt was published entitled " Le moine incestueux." In 1798 it was formed by M. C. Cammaille-Saint-Aubin and C. Ribié into a play called *Le Moine*. Scribe and Germain Delavigne wrote in 1852–53 the libretto for a five-act opera *La nonne sanglante*, on the legend of the Bleeding Nun to which Gounod composed the music ; it was performed on Oct. 18th, 1854. Before Gounod undertook the work, several other composers, amongst them Berlioz, had refused on the grounds of impossibility. Prosper Mérimée has formed his work *Une femme est un diable* on *The Monk*. Fernand Baldensperger : " Le Moine de Lewis dans la littérature francaise," *Journal of Comparative Literature*,

I, p. 210, New York (1903). For *The Monk* in France, see the work mentioned by Killen. In Spain a free version of *The Monk* appeared in 1822 entitled *El Fraile, o historica del padre Ambrosio y de la bella Antonia*. In Swedish it appeared in 1800–1804 and 1874. It was translated from the French by Anders Karlsson af Kullberg and Madame Ulrika Carolina Widström, mostly in all probability by the last-named.

These bibliographical remarks on *The Monk* are only intended as an indication of the great attention it attracted, and have no pretensions to completeness. I refer to the work of Killen.

(107) J. G. Lockhart : *The Life of Sir Walter Scott*, Vol. X., p. 98.

(108) Byron's diary, Dec. 6th, 1813. Thomas Moore : *The Works of Lord Byron*, II, pp. 295–296 (1835). *Ibid.* VII, p. 241, footnote on Lewis. Byron kept up a large correspondence, and his letters contain much information about his friends. The information I have given as to the relations between him and Lewis can be controlled not only from Moore's work, but also from Rowland E. Prothero's great edition of Byron : *The Works of Lord Byron. A new, revised and enlarged edition, with illustrations. Letters and Journals*, I–VI (1898–1901), which is furnished with explanatory footnotes. Latest publication : John Murray : *Lord Byron's Correspondence chiefly with Lady Melbourne, Mr. Hobhouse, the Hon. Douglas Kinnaird and P. B. Shelley* (1922).

(109) Feb. 23rd, 1798. *Life*, I, pp. 155–158.

(110) *Lockhart*, II, pp. 7–12.

(111) Byron's diary, p. 285 (Moore).

(112) Byron : *Detached Thoughts*.

(113) *Life*, I., p. 196. *Monthly Mirror*, Sept. 1798.

(114) Genest : *Some Account of the English Stage*, VII, pp. 332–333.

(115) *Sheridan and His Times*, by an Octogenarian (William Earle), Vol. II, p. 242 (1859) ; *Sheridaniana*, p. 169 (1826). *Bon-Mots of Sydney Smith and R. Br. Sheridan*, by Walter Jerrold (1904). *Over the Hills and Far Away*, written by George Farquhar (1678–1707) ; Gosse : *The History of Eighteenth Century Literature*, p. 72.

(116) *Memoirs of the Life of John Philip Kemble, Esq., including a History of the Stage, from the time of Garrick to the present period. By James Boaden, Esq.* . . . II, p. 206, London (1825). *The Kembles, an Account of the Kemble Family, including the lives of Mrs. Siddons, and her Brother John Philip Kemble*, by Percy Fitzgerald, Vol. I, p. 345. *The Journal of Sir Walter Scott*, p. 95 (1890). I can find no mention of *The Castle Spectre* and of Lewis's part in general in the Drury Lane repertoire either in Mrs. Oliphant's biography of *Sheridan* (1883), though to be sure this is a little work (published in the series *English Men of Letters*), or in Walter Sichel's large two-volume work on *Sheridan* (1909). In the second volume, pp. 275–276, the author relates how William Ireland, a literary forger in Chatterton's style, in the spring of 1796 succeeded in convincing Sheridan that he had discovered a hitherto unknown play by Shakespeare called *Vortigern and Rowena* ; the play was performed, but the public proved to be a better Shakespearean expert than Sheridan and hissed both the play and its maker off the stage. From this play (April, 1796) the author goes on to deal with Sheridan's awakened interest for Kotzebue and describes Mrs. Siddons's performance in *The Stranger* in 1798. Of *The Castle*

Spectre, which had been produced in the meantime with a success unanimously witnessed to on all hands, and which was well adapted to turn Sheridan's attention to the new taste prevailing among the public, he says not a word, which must be accounted a deficiency in his work.

(117) *Reminiscences of Michael Kelly, of the King's Theatre, and Theatre Royal, Drury Lane, including a Period of nearly Half a Century ; With Original Anecdotes of Many Distinguished Persons, Political, Literary, and Musical,* Vol. II, p. 140, London, (1826).

(118) Quoted by Helene Richter.

(119) Genest, *op. cit.*

(120) Note to a certain edition of *Ivanhoe*, found also in the Everyman Edition.

(121) *The Monthly Mirror*, Vol. V, p. 106 (1798).

(122) The part played by Kotzebue on the English stage shows to what a level the great theatre of Garrick had sunk. The honour of having introduced him to the English public rests with Sheridan, who, as I have remarked, included *The Stranger (Menschenhass und Reue)* in the Drury Lane repertoire for 1798. Altogether three translations appeared, of which that by Benjamin Thompson was approved. The other plays of any importance by Kotzebue which were translated and performed on the English stage were :

> *Kind der Liebe, oder der Strassenräuber aus kindlicher Liebe* which appeared as *Lover's Vows* (1799). Translated by Mrs. Inchbald.
> *Der Witwe und das Reitpferd (Horse and Widow).*
> *Der Graf von Burgund (Count of Burgundy).*
> *Spanier in Peru oder Rolla's Tod (Pizarro).*
> *Der Opfertod (Family Distress).*
> *Armut und Edelsinn (Poverty and Nobleness of Mind).*
> *Das Schreibepult, oder die Gefahren der Jugend (The Wise Man of the East).*
> *Johanna von Montfaucon (Johanna of M.).*
> *Der Wildfang (Of Age to-morrow).*
> *La Peyrouse (La Pérouse).*
> *Eduard in Schottland oder die Nacht eines Flüchtlings (The Wanderer ; or the Rights of Hospitality).*
> *Epigramm (The Blind Boy).*
> *Graf Benjowsky oder die Verschwörung auf Kamtschatka (Kamtschatka, or, the Slave's Tribute).*
> *Die Sonnenjungfrau (The Virgin of the Sun).*
> *Blind geladen (How to Die for Love).*
> *Rehbock, oder die schuldlosen Schuldbewussten (The Poachers).*

Sheridan's *Pizarro*, which he had adapted extremely freely from the original, was a patriotic play, whose point and high-flown tirades on liberty were directed against France and Napoleon. The public, enlivened by the recent naval victory of Aboukir, received the play with frantic enthusiasm. Nevertheless, it was not performed as often as *The Castle Spectre*. *Pizarro* remained for long in the repertoire of the London theatres—it was performed as recently as 1856. Germanophiles like William Taylor regarded Kotzebue as one of the greatest dramatic authors of Germany, and until fairly late in the past century, his fame was greater in England than in his own country. On the other hand, Goethe had to be content with less fame both in Germany and especially in England.

Walter Sellier: *Kotzebue in England* (1901). Thackeray's *Pendennis* helps one to understand theatrical conditions in England during those decades.

(123) " Sheridan, among other appropriations, had been supposed to take the idea of Sir Oliver's return from his own mother's novel of Sidney Biddulph. He might for that matter have taken it from a hundred novels." (Mrs. Oliphant: *Sheridan*, p. 99.) The " uncle from America " was too ancient a theatrical artifice for there to be any necessity for Sheridan to borrow it. This information invariably crops up in connection with *The School for Scandal* and is an example of the many stereotyped judgments in literary history which have sprung up by accident, and lack all foundations.

(124) The title can be explained to some extent by the existence of a play by Richard Cumberland called *The West Indian*. The element of bourgeois tragedy and sentimentality is derived from his German travels and a study of Kotzebue.

(125) Lockhart, *op. cit.*, II, pp. 7–12.

(126) *Diary of Thomas Moore*, IV, p. 333.

(127) Walter Scott: *Essay on Imitations of the Ancient Ballad* (1830); *Poetical Works*, Vol. IV, pp. 80–83 (1833). The letters from Lewis show that he gave Scott a thorough tuition in the use of rhymes. Lockhart relates (II, pp. 7–12) that in the printed copies hardly anything is left of the faulty rhymes and Scotticisms, etc., pointed out by Lewis, so that Scott appears to have made good use of the guidance provided.

(128) Fruits of Scott's German interests were the following translations: Bürger: *William and Helen*, an adaptation of Taylor's translation of *Lenore*, which he had heard recited; *Der Wilde Jäger;* Iffland: *Mündel;* Baho: *Otto von Wittelsbach;* Meier: *Fürst von Stromberg;* Schubart: *Abschiedstag;* Goethe: *Klaggesang von der edlen Frauen des Asan Aga; Frederick and Alice (Der untreue Knabe); Götz von Berlichingen;* Tschudi: *Schlacht von Sempach;* Veit Weber: *Die heilige Vehme (The House of Aspen);* Uhland: *The Noble Moringer*. (Ludwig Karl Roesel: *Die litterarischen und persönlichen Beziehungen Sir Walter Scott's zu Goethe* (1901).)

(129) The information regarding the earliest editions of the *Tales of Wonder* is from the preface to Henry Morley's edition of *Tales of Terror and Wonder* (1887). This is based on the copy in the British Museum, which lacks four leaves; as it proved impossible to find a faultless copy, Morley's edition is without one of the poems in the original. What this missing poem was might have been seen from Robert Southey's *Poetical Works* (1847), in which he has appended to the poem *St. Patrick's Purgatory* the note: " Published (1801) in the *Tales of Wonder*." Southey says he wrote the poem in 1798; Lewis was unaware that it was his. The rest of the contents are given below:

The ballad *The Stranger*, which Lewis describes as a " Norman Tale," is an adaptation of his, for one discerns in it the influence of *The Castle of Otranto*, in that Manfred, here become St. Aubin, the stern father of Adela (the names St. Aubert and Adeline appear in *The Mysteries of Udolpho*), declines to give his daughter to young Theodore, whom he finally poisons. As in *Romeo and Juliet*, the heroine expires on her lover's breast. *Hrim Tor, or the Winter King* is related to Scandinavian mythology, though Lewis tells the story in his own way; it is an account, gratifying to a romantic soul, of a maiden who falls into the power of a goblin in disguise; the rhythm is the galloping one of *Lenore* and the ending a naive exhortation to young women not to believe a chance stranger's fine words. The theme of *The Wanderer of the Wold*, which Lewis calls an " Old

English Tale," is the infatuation of two brothers for the same maiden, and her treachery towards them both. *Gonzalvo* is summarily described as a " Spanish Ballad," and *Albert of Werdendorff or the Midnight Embrace* as a " German Tale," though both bear too obvious marks of Lewis's peculiar style to be mere translations. *The Maid of Donalblayne* is a " Scotch," *The Pilgrim of Valencia* a " Spanish," and *The Grey Friar of Winton* an " English " ballad. Thus choosing and freely recounting in flowing anapæsts, Lewis compiled his *Tales of Terror*, leaving the reader in ignorance of the actual sources whence he had taken his ballads, and of how much of them was the work of others and how much his own. In the second part of his collection he is more careful and frequently reveals his sources, and how much of a ballad was his own work. These latter include : *Bothwell's Bonny Jane ; Osric the Lion* (which contains a note to the effect that after it had been written the author had seen a certain French ballad somewhat resembling it) ; *Alonzo the Brave* (from *The Monk*) and a parody of it *Giles Jollup the Grave and Brown Sally Green*, regarding which he admits to having been influenced by a parody published in a newspaper ; *The Cloud King ; The Sailor's Tale ; The Princess and the Slave ; The Gay Gold Ring* (not *The Gray Gold King* as Richter has it) ; and *The Grim White Woman*. A close examination of these reveals that even the *Gay Gold Ring* (in a footnote Lewis admits to having taken the theme from some Greek author whose name he pretends to have forgotten) is simply a variation, influenced by the Bleeding Nun, of Goethe's poem *Die Braut von Korinth ;* Lewis's " Greek Author " was suggested to him by the name Korinth, an extremely circumspect hint at his actual source. In addition, his collection included many translations from J. G. v. Herder's *Stimmen der Völker in Liedern*. Such is " Elver's Hoh " (Elvershöhe, the original, is a story in the first person of a delightful dream on an enchanted mountain) which Lewis makes a description by the knight Algamore ; where the spirit in the original exhorts the youth : " Steh' auf du muntrer Jüngling, auf ! " Lewis says theatrically : "Arise, thou gallant young warrior, arise ! " Even in his translations Lewis cannot free himself from the arrogant and affected style of the ballad of chivalry, but alters the easy, four-line, folk-song-like verse of the original to a heavy eight-line verse, from which the care-free quality, the mistiness of the merry youth's beautiful dream has wholly vanished. Further, the poems from Herder's collection include : " The Sword of Angantyr " (Zaubergespräche Angantyrs und Hervors), which Lewis has freely moulded to conform with his own taste, thereby losing the majestic ring of the ancient Scandinavian rune; " King Hakon's Deathsong " (König Hako's Todesgesang) ; " The Erl-Kings Daughter " (Erlkönigs Tochter) and " The Water-King " (Der Wassermann), translated with great freedom, or merely adapted. Lewis paid, as a rule, little attention to preserving the spirit and colour of the originals, but tried by fair means or foul to compel them into conformity with his own conception of a romantic ballad. The translations also include Goethe's " The Erl-King " (Erlkönig) and " The Fisherman " (Der Fischer), more carefully executed and therefore better. Scott furnished the original poems " The Fire King," " Glenfilas " and " Eve of St. John," and his translations of G. A. Bürger's " Der Wilde Jäger " (The Wild Huntsman) and of the ballad " Frederick and Alice " from Goethe's *Claudine von Villabella*. Scott's friend, J. Leyden, and the dramatic author G. Colman, Jr., furnished one poem each. A number of parodies and old, well-known ballads complete this extraordinary collection, which cannot be said to have any poetical value.

As I have remarked, Lewis is exceedingly careless as to his sources. Although, in the case of the ballads on Scandinavian themes, it was Herder's collection, he refrains from naming this and gives instead the sources used by Herder. Thus, he states that he obtained his " Sword of Angantyr," from " Hick's " collection *Thesaurus Linguarum Septentrionalium*, which was also Herder's source. The author of this collection was not, however, as Lewis in his ignorance hastily states, " Hick," but " Hickes." He states further that several of his ballads are from a Danish collection *Kaempe-viser*, but here, too, Herder, who made use of the collection, was the medium. By this *Kaempe-viser* is intended Peder Syv's *Et Hundrede udvalde Danske viser, förögede med det andet Hundrede*, published in Copenhagen in 1695, which is again based on Anders Sörensen Vedel's publication 100 *udvalgte Danske viser*. (Frank Edgar Farley : *Scandinavian Influences in the English Romantic Movement*, Boston, 1903, pp. 57–58, 86–88, 177–178 ; on page 238 is the information : " M. G. Lewis published both of Gray's Norwegian odes in his *Tales of Wonder*." These would thus be "The Fatal Sisters" and "The Descent of Odin," but neither is to be found in Morley's edition.) See also J. Viktor Johansson's study " Den förromantiska balladen in Sverge," *Göteborgs högskolas Årsskrift* (1912).

(130) *The Edinburgh Review*, I, pp. 314–315 (1803). The writer is the famous wit, Sydney Smith.

(131) *Life*, I, p. 228.

(132) *Ibid.*, I, p. 223.

(133) *Ibid.*, I, p. 229 (letter of Jan. 13th, 1803).

(134) *Ibid.*, I, p. 234.

(135) *Ibid.*, I, p. 358.

(136) *The Journal of Sir Walter Scott* (Nov. 22nd, 1825), I, p. 7 (1890).

(137) John Russell : *Memoirs, Journal and Correspondence of Thomas Moore*, III, pp. 43–46 (1853).

(138) *Ibid.*, II, pp. 55–56 (letter to E. F. Dalton, Nov. 23, 1814).

(139) *Ibid.*, VIII, pp. 43–50. To judge from Lewis's words—the question was of the printing of one of Moore's works ; it is difficult however to determine which it can have been, as *Anacreon* had appeared in 1800 and *Poems by Thomas Little* in 1801 ; in 1803 Moore went to the Bermudas, and his next work was not published until 1806. Lewis's term " poetical romance " fits *Lalla Rookh*, which was not published, however, until 1817.

(140) Moore : *Byron*, IV, p. 47 (letter to Mr. Murray).

(141) Edward Dowden : *The Life of Percy Bysshe Shelley*, II, pp. 37–38. J. A. Symonds : *Shelley*, p. 90 (1922).

(142) *Ibid.*, pp. 18–19 : " His favourite poets . . . were Monk Lewis and Southey ; his favourite books in prose where romances by Mrs. Radcliffe and Godwin." Dowden, *op. cit.*, I, p. 72 points out Lewis as the poet of Shelley's youth.

(143) The book they read was *Fantasmorgiana, ou recueil d'histoires d'apparitions, de spectres, revenans, etc. Traduit de l'Allemand par un amateur*, Paris (1812). (Maria Vohl : *Die Romane und Novellen der Mary Shelley*, 1913.)

(144) Lewis's two sisters.

(145) This information is from the frequently-mentioned *Life* by Mrs. Baron-Wilson.

(146) Russell, *op. cit.*, VIII, pp. 43–50. (Lewis's letters to Moore, Nov. 19th, 1802 and Nov. 9th, 1803.)

NOTES

(147) The British Museum catalogue gives under Lewis's name the following work : *Koenigsmark the Robber, or the Terror of Bohemia, in which is included the affecting history of Rosenberg and Adelaide and their orphan daughter*. Lewis, however, had no part in this book, which was rendered into English from one of the German robber romances by a certain Mr. Sarrat, " a man of very great abilities ; he is known in the literary world as the author of a *New Survey of London, Koenigsmark the Robber*, a romance, in one volume, *The Life of Buonaparte ;* and he has also translated a novel from the French, called *The Three Monks*, dedicated to M. G. Lewis, Esq. (*Memoirs of Mrs. Crouch*, II, p. 311).

(148) An idea of the extent of German robber romanticism is given by the following selection of authors from Müller-Fraureuth's work *Die Ritter und Räuberromane* (1894) :

One " author " called G. H. Heinse published at Gera, between 1786–93; altogether 23 romances, in 46 volumes ; in the same town another writer, Bornschein, published 39 romances ; Karl Gottlob Cramer (1758–1817) wrote 68 romances, or over 100 volumes, and was in his day the best-read German author, a man who looked down with condescending pity on such " authors " as Goethe, Schiller, etc ; another extremely prolific writer—one of whose specialities was the writing of biographies of suicides—was Chr. H. Spiess (1755–99) ; D. Th. Wangenheim published more than 30 " historical " romances ; Goethe's brother-in-law Chr. A. Vulpius, author of *Rinaldo Rinaldini*, published 61 romances, 35 plays and 5 other works, displaying a special affection for such sounding Italian names as Fernando Fernandini, Lionardo Montebello, Orlando Orlandini and Armidoro ; the priest A. H. J. Lafontaine outdid all his competitors by publishing over 150 romances. To this class of author belong *Naubert* and *Veit Weber* (Georg Leonhard Wächter (1762–1837), Ludvig Franz Josef von Baczko (1756–1823), and Kajetan Tschink (1763–1813). A good idea of the contents of these works is provided by their titles (here given in a rough translation). Romances dealing with mediævalism and the days of chivalry include : *Tales of the Past ; Ernst von Wartburg*, a family tale of the days of chivalry and papal power ; *Reinek von Waldburg*, a tale in the style of *Reynold the Fox* of the days when might was right ; *The Black Knight ; The God-fearing Vehm-Court ; Scenes from the Days of Chivalry ; Friedrich von Haustein, or monkish cunning and papal treachery ; Barthold von Urach, a true German story of chivalry from the Middle Ages*, etc. ; robber and murder romances include : *Lorenzo, the Wild Man of the Forest, or the Robber-maid ; Coronato the Terrible, or Abällino among the Calabrians ; The Heroine of La Vendée, or the Female Abällino ; Lutardo, or the Robber Chief ; Karl Strahlheim or the Grateful Robber ; Angelica, Daughter of the Great Robber Odoardo, Prince of Pechia ; A Tale of Murderer Martin the Peasant*, etc. ; ghost stories include : *A Collection of Fearful Events and Terrifying Tales ; Vitold, Grand Duke of Lithuania ; A Ghost Story ; The Ruins of Geisterburg, or the Warning Voice of Midnight ; the Spirit-seer Countess von Hohenacker ; History of a Spirit-seer ; Bilin's Nine Twins, a Tale of Ghosts and Chivalry ; Matilda von Villanegas, or the Female Faust* (an adaptation of *The Monk*) ; *The Ghost of Erich von Sickingen and its Deliverance*, etc. ; the following deal with the sea and exotic romance : *Äylo and Dshadina, or the Pyramids ; Antonia della Roccini, the Pirate Queen ; the Pirate Queen Hariad, or the Terror of Africa ; William Lancelot, The English Pirate*, etc.

Examples of the English counterparts to this type of literature, which in quality approach Lewis's work, are Rosa Matilda's (Charlotta Dacre) works, *e.g.*, her romance in three volumes *The Confessions of the Nun of St. Omer* and

Zofloya or the Mor (1812); T. J. Horsley-Curties' five-volume romance *St. Botolf's Priory or the Sable Mask*, his four-volume romance *The Monk of the Udolpho* and *The Ancient Records of the Abbey of St. Oswyth* ; Miss M. Hamilton's romance in four volumes *The Forest of St. Bernardo ;* Miss Davies's *The Monk and his Daughter*, in three vols. ; and Miss Grant's four-volume romance *Adelaide*. These and countless similar works, such as Charlotte Smith's (1749–1806) *The Old Manor House* (1793) ; Mrs. Bonhote's *Bungay Castle ;* Charles Lucas's *The History of Jack Smith, or the Castle of Saint Donat ;* F. H. P.'s *The Castle of Caithness* and *Count Roderick's Castle or Gothic Times ;* W. C. Proby's *The Spirit of the Castle ;* Maria Regina Roche's *Clermont* and *The Children of the Abbey* (10th edition in 1798); Mrs. Pearson's *Mysterious Warnings ;* Francis Latham's *The Midnight Bell ;* Marquis Grosse's *Horrid Mysteries ;* Miss Wilkinson's *The Convent of Grey Penitents ;* Miss Henrietta Mosse's *A Peep at our Ancestors* (1807); Lady Morgan's (Miss Sydney Owenson) *Ida of Athens* and *The Wild Irish Girl* (1806); and A. M. Bennett's *Anna, or The Memoirs of a Welsh Heiress, Interspersed with Anecdotes of a Nabob* (1785), and *Vicissitudes Abroad, or The Ghost of My Father* (1806), six vols. This catalogue, which I have drawn up from the works referred to earlier by Scarborough, Saintsbury and Raleigh and from J. Bell's list on the end-pages of Lewis's *Adelgitha* and *The East Indian*, and which is by no means complete, contains many of the " horrid " books mentioned by Jane Austen. In the literary advertisements of those days, printed by publishers on the backs of their books, innumerable names flash by such as *Rodolphus of Werdenberg, The Forest of Friedwald, The Mysterious Sisters, The Spanish Robber*, etc., which are probably translations from the German. I am unaware of the existence of any study in which these romances are catalogued and classed according to theme, even in the manner adopted by Müller-Fraureuth ; Dorothy Scarborough's book is deficient in this respect, nor was it the author's chief aim. A source worth mentioning in this connection is Einar Nylén's work *Skräck-romantik. Studier i tysk och engelsk förromantik*, Gothenberg (1924), and, so far as French literature of this class is concerned, the book by Alice M. Killen mentioned earlier.

In England, France and Germany, but particularly in the first two countries, a great part of such literature was produced by women, thanks apparently to Mrs. Radcliffe. The titles " Miss " and " Madame," so apt to awaken doubt of the work on whose title-page they appear, recur with astonishing frequency before the authors' names. Amongst them, however, are two " Misses " whose work has escaped the oblivion to which that of most of their sisterhood was doomed. I refer to the sisters Sophia (1750–1824) and Harriet (1757–1851) Lee. Of their rich production (Richter, *op. cit.*, I, pp. 271–277) I would draw attention to the *Canterbury Tales*, 1797–1805 in which they collaborated, and in this to the tale called *Kruitzner*, on which Byron based his play *Werner*. Richter's account of the contents of this story—I myself have not read it—proves the fact beyond all doubt ; yet this type of weak and criminal father was in all essentials ready to hand in Mrs. Radcliffe's *Romance of the Forest. Kruitzner* is further interesting owing to its being constructed on the lines of Schiller's *Robbers*. Byron said : " This tale made a deep impression upon me, and may indeed be said to contain the germ of much that I have since written " ; he read it for the first time in 1802. (Heinrich Kraeger : *Der byronsche Heldentypus*, Munich, 1898.)

(149) This notwithstanding, he gives his sources at the end of his preface. According to this statement, *Mistrust or Blanche and Osbright*, a fairly long story of the Middle Ages dealing with a family feud and the tragic love of two children, *My Uncle's Garret Window*, a longish, but natural and pleasant story on a modern

theme, *Anaconda* and *Amorassan* were all borrowed or adapted from the German ; *Amorassan* is indeed, as Conant points out in the work of her referred to, partly a translation of F. M. Klinger's tale *Der Faust der Morgenländer ; Admiral Guarino* and *King Rodrigo's Fall* are said to be ballads translated from the Spanish ; and *Bertrand and Mary-Belle, The Lord of Falkenstein* and *The Dying Bride* the same from the German (the two latter from Herder's collection) ; his own would thus be the ballad *Sir Guy the Seeker*, based on a folk-tale of a maid imprisoned for ever in a castle, whom a brave and determined knight could liberate ; *The Four Facardins*, second part, which Lewis declares he wrote as a sequel to Count A. v. Hamilton's unfinished Oriental story of the same name ; *Bill Jones, a Tale of Wonder*, a ballad of murder and ghosts in the style of *The Ancient Mariner* on a theme obtained from Sir Walter Scott; and the narrative poem in 800 lines *Oberon's Henchman, or the Legend of the Three Sisters*, begun by Lewis in the autumn of 1800, while staying at Bothwell Castle. Knowing well his own propensity to exploit the works of others, he informs us in footnotes whence an idea or line was borrowed. The poem deals with the quarrel of Oberon and Titania over the son of the King of India, but in Lewis's hands these delicate poetical spirits of nature's lyricism become unpoetical beings of power and might, better suited to the setting of vampire-tales than to rule over fairies.

(150) Lewis's own note at the beginning of the printed work.

(151) I cannot refrain from connecting this play of de Monvel's with Mrs. Radcliffe's *The Italian ;* the similarity of plot is so striking, expressly in the use of a wicked priest to prevent two young people from winning each other, in other words, in its essence, that one cannot but conclude that Mrs. Radcliffe made use of the play in building up her romance. See Edmond Estève : *Études de littérature préromantique* (1923). In the chapter " Le théâtre ' Monacal ' sous la révolution " the author elucidates (pp. 107–109) the plot of *Les Victimes Cloîtrées*. The noble-born Madame de Saint-Alban wishes to prevent her daughter Eugenie from marrying the poor, but honourable Dorval, and to crush her entrusts her into the care of her confessor, the monk Laurent, in a convent. Rumours are spread that she is dead, whereupon Dorval enters in his despair the monastery adjoining Laurent's convent. The play is in four acts, and was first performed on March 29th, 1791.

(152) *Cumberland's British Theatre*, Part 29, p. 9.

(153) *Genest, op. cit.*, VIII, pp. 235–237. See Note 80.

(154) At the end of the list of Lewis's works in Mrs. Baron-Wilson's *Life* mention is made of a work called *Village Virtues*, of which nothing is said in the text. This book is not in the British Museum Library, nor have I succeeded in tracing a copy elsewhere. Lewis never wrote such a book.

(155) Lewis was a constant visitor at Holland House, whose mistress, Lady Holland, was an extremely intelligent and witty woman. Once, when Lewis complained that he had been set to writing burlesque, which was quite out of his line, Lady Holland remarked that he did not know his own power. (*The Holland House Circle*, by Lloyd Sanders, 1908.)

(156) Boswell : *Life of Dr. Johnson*, II, pp. 146 and 148 (Everyman's Library ed.). The remarks in the following paragraph of my text regarding the influence of the slave question on Johnson's standpoint towards America, are based on Yrjö Hirn's work *Dr Johnson och James Boswell*, pp. 192–193 (1922).

(157) *William Wilberforce, his Friends and his Times*, by John Campbell Colguhamn, pp. 172–174 (1867). *The Life of William Wilberforce, by his sons*, IV, p. 292.

(158) S. T. Coleridge : *Table Talk*, 1835 (March 20th).

(159) Mrs. Baron-Wilson's *Life*.

(160) On July 10th, 1817, Byron wrote to Moore from La Mira, Venice, informing him that Lewis was there and expressing his satisfaction over the visit : " How pleasant ! He is a very good fellow." He relates that he lent Lewis " extracts from Lalla Rookh and Manuel, and, out of contradiction, it may be, he likes the last, and is not much taken with the first of these performances." Lewis stayed in Venice until the beginning of August, and left for England somewhere between the 7th and the 12th. (Moore : *The Works of Lord Byron*. Letters to Mr. Murray of July 15th and Aug. 12th, 1817. IV, pp. 47 and 53.)

(161) A certain Miss F., who was a fellow-traveller on Lewis's outward and homeward journeys, wrote a careful account of his last moments ; it is reproduced in Mrs. Baron-Wilson's *Life*.

(162) Russell : *Moore*, II, pp. 183–185, 301.

(163) *The Monk*, Vol. II, pp. 36–37 (1924 ed.).

(164) *Ibid.*, Vol. III, Chap. X.

(165) What I mean is that it was new then ; it had of course appeared in earlier English romanticism, for instance, in the Elizabethan melodrama, the realism of which is strongly reflected in Shakespeare's plays. Thus, in the Second Part of *Henry VI*, the body of Gloucester is described :

> But see, his face is black and full of blood,
> His eyeballs further out than when he liv'd,
> Staring full ghastly like a strangled man ;
> His hair uprear'd, his nostrils stretch'd with struggling :
> His hands abroad display'd, as one that grasp'd
> And tugg'd for life, and was by strength subdu'd.

The death of Cardinal Beaufort, the murder scene on the seashore and Queen Margaret's mourning beside Suffolk's head are all examples of the same species of realism ; similarly the piercing of Gloucester's eyes in *King Lear*. The scenes of terror in *Titus Andronicus* are depicted with agitating realism. Tamora says :

> Here never shines the sun ; here nothing breeds,
> Unless the nightly owl or fatal raven :
> And when they show'd me this abhorred pit,
> They told me, here, at dead time of the night,
> A thousand fiends, a thousand hissing snakes,
> Ten thousand swelling toads, as many urchins,
> Would make such fearful and confused cries,
> As any mortal body hearing it
> Should straight fall mad, or else die suddenly.

—an imaginary picture like to Bunyan's Valley of the Shadow of Death or the Castle of Despair. In *King John*, Constance calls on death in the following words :

Death, death : O, amiable lovely death !
Thou odoriferous stench ! sound rottenness !
Arise forth from the couch of lasting night,
Thou hate and terror to prosperity,
And I will kiss thy detestable bones,
And put my eyeballs in thy vaulty brows,
And ring these fingers with thy household worms,
And stop this gap of breath with fulsome dust,
And be a carrion monster like thyself :
Come, grin on me ; and I will think thou smil'st
And buss thee as thy wife ! Misery's love,
O ! come to me !

Romeo and Juliet contains the whole gamut of the romanticism of graveyards and death. The romantic worms used so frequently by Lewis (and Southey) had thus been used already by Shakespeare. The word " *Burgverliess* " was elucidated by Müller-Fraureuth.

(166) Description of the site of Ambrosio's death at the end of *The Monk*.

(167) *The Poetical Works of Scott*, Oxford Complete Edition, edited by J. Logie Robertson (1910).

(168) The subterranean dungeon in *The Castle Spectre* is, of course, the German " *Burgverliess*," taken, to judge from Reginald's fate, in the first instance from Schiller's *Robbers*. The siege scene is probably derived from *Götz von Berlichingen*. That I do not connect *Ivanhoe* with these works, which were no less well known to Scott, is because the monk and the fool in *The Castle Spectre* bring this work specially near to *Ivanhoe*, in which they have important parts assigned to them ; they prove that *The Castle Spectre*, which was in the Abbotsford library, was Scott's chief source as regards the Castle of Torquilstone.

(169) Earlier phenomena on the family tree of the historical novel than the Gothic romance (see Dora Binkert : *Historische Romane vor Walter Scott*, Berlin, 1915) were such works as Defoe's *Memoirs of a Cavalier* (1724) and Leland's *Longsword* (1762), which the author himself terms a " historical romance." The first-mentioned of these is historical in that the memoirs deal with the Thirty Years' War and with Cromwell's times, of which he gives a lively and realistic picture ; in general, however, the style is that of the picaresque writers, a consecutive depictment of events and accidents without a circumscribed and concentrated plan. Romantic colouring is lacking. *Longsword* tells a tale of the past in the style of Shakespeare's historical plays, and contains (Cross : *The Development of the English Novel*, p. 101) " nearly all the element's of Scott's historical romances," but without romantic colouring. Before the historical novel as we now know it could come into being it was necessary for two lines to merge into each other, viz., historical accuracy and " Gothic " romance. The merging was accomplished by Sir Walter Scott. From his preface to *Waverley* (1829) we learn that it was " Gothicism " which set him on the track on which he was to transmute his knowledge and understanding of history into romance ; he says : " I had nourished the ambitious desire of composing a tale of chivalry, which was to be in the style of the *Castle of Otranto*, with plenty of Border characters, and supernatural incident." The beginning of this tale (subsequently published as a supplement to *Waverley*,

also in the Everyman edition) shows clearly the importance of the historical side to Scott.

Regarding Scott's position towards " Gothicism " Walter Freye has written a study entitled *The Influence of "Gothic" Literature on Sir Walter Scott,* Rostock (1902). Amongst " Gothic " literature he enumerates *The Castle of Otranto, The Old English Baron, The Mysteries of Udolpho, The Romance of the Forest,* and *Christabel, Zastrozzi* and *St. Irvyne,* quoting side by side the passages from the above works and the poems of Scott, chiefly from *The Lay of the Last Minstrel,* which he has found to resemble each other verbally. Of Lewis's works he mentions only *The Monk,* and as regards Scott's share in *The Tales of Wonder* he is wholly silent; he has also neglected to deal with Scott's prose romances. This author has no real grasp of the underlying motives of "Gothicism" and his work is only a series of haphazard parallels. An unusual number of printer's errors disfigure his pages : Clara Reeve is presented as "Anna " Reeve and E. T. A. Hoffmann as " Theodore William " Hoffmann; *St. Irvyne* has become " *St. Iroyne.*" The sources of *Ivanhoe* are dealt with by Roland Abramczyk in his work *Über die Quellen zu Walter Scotts Roman " Ivanhoe,"* Halle a S. (1903). Amongst these sources (a great part of which Scott himself enumerates in the preface to *Ivanhoe* written in 1830) he mentions *The Castle Spectre* (which, as shown by the catalogue published in 1838, was in the Abbotsford Library) without however ascribing to it the decisive influence he should have done. On the contrary, he says (p. 141) : " So ist das Castle of Otranto sicher das Urbild des Torquilstone Castle," which is true, though only via Conway Castle. He declares (p. 138) that Manfred, Ambrosio, etc., should be derivated from the Lovelace-type, to which I cannot agree. George Hofmann's work : *Entstehungsgeschichte von Sir Walter Scotts " Marmion,"* Königsberg (1913), suffers from the same lack of a general comprehensive view of the fundamental motives of the " Gothic " movement, and consequently fails to see *Marmion* as a link in a chain of development set going much earlier. As a study of great importance I would finally mention Louis Maigron's work *Le roman historique a l'époque romantique. Essai sur l'influence de Walter Scott* (1898) in which the author says (pp. 77–78) :

" Depuis plus d'un demi-siècle, un irresistible courant poussait la littérature anglaise vers les choses du moyen âge. Horace Walpole, Clara Reeve, Anne Radcliffe, bien d'autres encore avaient mis le gothique en honneur. Tous ces prédécesseurs de l'auteur d'*Ivanhoe,* il n'est pas de notre sujet de les étudier. Ce qu'il faut dire cependant, c'est que tout ce grand mouvement vient aboutir à Walter Scott. . . . qu'il a eu le mérite . . . de tirer parti mieux que les autres des matériaux qu'ils avaient préparés."

(170) *The Poetical Works of Samuel Taylor Coleridge including his Dramatic Writings. Introduction by William Michael Rossetti* (1912). Christabel was written and widely-known from the MS. long before its appearance in print.

(171) *The Poetical Works of Lord Byron. Introduction by W. M. Rossetti.* Undated.

(172) *Elegy on Newstead Abbey :* "And sable Horror guards the massy door." Lewis (*The House upon the Heath*): "And brooding Horror on its site reposed." In his study *Lewis' Monk und Ossian in ihrem Verhältnisse zu Lord Byron* (1905) Joseph Weigang has shown Byron to have been influenced by *The Monk.* This is discernible, according to him, in such passages as the following lines (945–950) from *The Giaour :*

NOTES

It is as if the dead could feel
The icy form around them steal
And shudder, as the reptiles creep,
To revel o'er their rotting sleep
Without the power to scare away
The cold consumers of their clay—

and from *Lara* (Canto II, 660–662):

But creeping things shall revel in their spoil,
And fit thy clay to fertilise the soil—

which are regarded as denoting the presence of the terror-realistic worms of *The Monk*. Further, the pictures of the Wandering Jew and the Devil in *The Monk* are said to be present in Manfred and Cain, an assertion to which I shall return later. Finally Weigang shows, on good grounds, that the poem in *The Monk* called *The Exile* is in part responsible for the famous farewell song in *Childe Harold* "Adieu, adieu, my native shore. . . ."

(173) Harry Buxton Forman: *The Works of Percy Bysshe Shelley* (1880).

(174) Forman: notes attached to the works of Shelley's youth.

(175) Lachin y Gair.

(176) Of Maturin's works I have read only *The Fatal Revenge* and *Melmoth the Wanderer*. In all other respects my knowledge concerning him is based on textbooks such as those of Beers, Richter and Elton, and on Niilo Idman's study *Charles Robert Maturin, His Life and Works*, Helsinki (1923), in which Idman deals exhaustively with the subject-matter of Maturin's works, thus opening up these books to investigators; it must be remembered that Maturin's works are now greatly rare and are to be found only in the great English libraries. I have further had at my disposal Oscar F. W. Fernsemer's *Die Dramatischen Werke Charles Robert Maturin's, mit einer kurzen Lebensbeschreibung* (1913) and Willy Müller's work *Charles Robert Maturin's Romane " The Fatal Revenge " und " Melmoth the Wanderer "* (1908).

(177) This the above investigators have failed to take into account. In my opinion, *Adelgitha* should, however, have been mentioned, for seeing that Maturin's first work shows him to have copiously borrowed from the contemporary Gothic works, it seems only natural that they should have served him in dramatic literature; his sources are to be sought in his own surroundings. Bertram would thus be Michael Ducas; Imogine, Adelgitha; Aldobrand, Guiscard; the abbot of Anselmo, the abbess of the Convent of St. Hilda. Imogine is a similar " wretched, but spotless wife " as Adelgitha. After comparing the play with a certain play of Hannah More's and coming to a negative conclusion Idman states (p. 122) that: "A heroine of Hannah More was the least likely of any to suggest the character of the Lady Imogine "—but that is just what Adelgitha was most likely to do.

(178) Maturin's *Manuel* should be compared with Coleridge's play *Remorse*, as to my mind it was in all essentials suggested by the latter. The investigators named above have not done so, although in general construction, colour of setting and period, even in plot, Coleridge's play is very like *Manuel*. Even the names of the characters point to the same conclusion: Manuel, Count of Valdi, Marquis Valdez; Zimena, Zulimez. Don Alonzo would accordingly be Don Alvar; De Zelos, Ordonis; Zimena, Teresa. The Marquis Valdez is a similar unhappy old

father to Manuel, so that the chief motive of both, the sufferings of a father occasioned by crime and misfortune, is fundamentally the same.

(179) William Godwin: *The Adventures of Caleb Williams* (1838); by the same author: *St. Leon, A Tale of the Sixteenth Century*, in 4 vols. (1816). (The original title of the first-named was *C.W. or Things as they are*, and the date of publication 1793–94.)

(180) The first amongst the English writers of social fiction to attract wider attention was Thomas Holcroft (1745–1809), whose play *The Road to Ruin* (1792) is mentioned as the first modern melodrama in England. He was a supporter of Rousseau's principles and a revolutionary, and tried to interpret these principles in his romances *Anna St. Ives* (1792), an epistolary romance, and *Hugh Trevor* (1794–97). He was a member of Godwin's circle; the latter's philosophical treatise *Enquiry concerning Political Justice* (1793–94) is a reflection of the principles of Rousseau in England, the romances mentioned earlier being merely elucidations of the same principles in the guise of fiction. As, however, the "Gothic" romance was the prevailing favourite form of fiction, Godwin could not, and did not indeed wish to, refrain from using a Gothic mechanism. Nevertheless, this element is only scantily represented in *Caleb Williams*, and the book is actually, in point of realism and narrative style, closer to Fielding's style than to "Gothicism," which is more apparent in *St. Leon*. The third of the social writers of those days was Robert Page who wrote *Man as He Is* (1792), and *Hermsprong or Man as He Is Not* (1796). It is well-known that Shelley derived his social philosophy in decisive degree from Godwin. The influence of this philosophical school of fiction on romantic literature is altogether great. G. Adolph Frisch: *Der revolutionäre Roman in England. Seine Beeinflussung durch Rousseau*, pp. 9, 13, 16, 22, 25, 32–34 (1914); Johannes Meyer: *William Godwins Romane* (1906). A long account is given of Godwin in the work by Richter. Compare Note 298.

(181) What I mean is the element of pursuit that existed between Falkland and Caleb Williams and between Javert and Jean Valjean, which provides in both cases the opportunity for painting gripping pictures of misery and orphanage. Hugo was acquainted with *The Monk* (Alice M. Killen, *op. cit.*, p. 184) and the ballad of Alonzo, as will be seen from Madame Thénardier's song:

> Il le faut, disait un guerrier
> A la belle et tendre Imogine,
> Il le faut, je suis chevalier,
> Et je pars pour Palestine.

(The poem is quoted in its entirety in the supplements to Killen's work.) When Jean Valjean goes to work in the convent as a gardener, he is using the same method as Raymond in *The Monk*; Wieland was perhaps the first to use this motive in *Oberon*. Otto Hoffmann: *Studien zum englischen Schauerroman*, p. 38 (1915). Victor Hugo's *Les Misérables* and *Les Travailleurs de la Mer* are graphic examples of the power which the romantic realism inaugurated by Lewis subsequently acquired. A bloody terror-romanticism of like type appears with descriptive force in Hugo's *Han d'Islande* (1823), whose hero of that name inevitably recalls to mind the demon in Mary Shelley's *Frankenstein*. Both are depicted as unnatural monsters, both authors using, in speaking of them, such words as "demon" and "monster"; a boundless hate for mankind characterizes them both, likewise cruelty and hideous deeds. Frankenstein's monster is closer to Han than, for instance, Melmoth, whom I find difficult to compare with the former. If *Han d'Islande* had not been written in 1821, the playful executioners might easily have been derived from *Quentin Durward*; both appeared in the same year, 1823. Belonging to this same terror-realistic group in Hugo's production are further *Bug Jargal* and *Notre-Dame de Paris*. The relation of Hugo to English romanticism is dealt with by Gottlieb Wüscher: *Der Einfluss der englischen Balladenpoesie auf die französische Litteratur von Percy's Reliques of Ancient English Poetry bis zu De la Villemarque's Barzaz-Breiz*, 1765–1840 (1891); Killen, *op. cit.*, pp. 184–186, 204, 209, 213, 215; Gunnar Castrén: *Norden i den franska litteraturen*, pp. 217–226 (1910). Amongst the French writers of " terror " books there are yet to be mentioned Charles Nodier, whose works *Tribly, nouvelle écossaise, La Fée aux miettes, Smarra ou les démons de la nuit*, and *Histoire du roi de Bôheme et de ses sept châteaux* have been written under English influences; Gerald de Nerval and Villiers de L'Isle-Adam. (Alexis von Kraemer: *Villiers de L'Isle-Adam*, 1900.) Besides the work by Killen, see also J.-H. Retinger: *Le conte fantastique dans le romantique françois* (1909).

(182) Robert Southey: *Poetical Works*, Foreword (1847).

(183) In his school-days Southey " would glean among the fallen leaves and twigs, inhaling the penetrating fragrance which ever after called up a vision of the brook, the hillside, and its trees." " The streams were his special delight : he never tired of their deep retirement, their shy loveliness and their melody." (Edward Dowden : *Southey*, pp. 9 and 86, 1909 ed.).

(184) Southey, 1793 : " We returned by Bowdley ; there is an old mansion —now mouldering away, in so romantic a situation that I soon lost myself in dreams of days of yore—the tapestried room—the listed fight—the vassal-filled hall—the hospitable fire—the old baron and his young daughter—these formed a most delightful day-dream." (Dowden, *op. cit.*, p. 30.)

As regards Southey's Oriental sources, in Note 38 I have mentioned the works of Jones ; may it be added that a collective work, the *New Arabian Nights*, of which an English version appeared in 1792, contained a story " The History of Maugraby the Magician," from which Southey obtained the idea for *Thalaba* and the famous caves of Domdaniel. (Conant, *op. cit.*, p. 42. Albert Wächter : *Über Robert Southey's orientalische Epen*, 1890.) Thalaba might have been formed from the Portuguese name Batalha, a place visited by Southey. The name Maugraby may have suggested the name of the gipsy in *Quentin Durward*—" Hayraddin Maygrabin."

(185) " I sought for a subject, that should give equal room and freedom for description, incident and impassioned reflections on men, nature and society, yet supply in itself a natural connection to the parts, and unity to the whole." " With my pencil and memorandum-book I was making studies, as the artists call them, and often moulding my thoughts into verse, with the objects and imagery immediately before my senses. Many circumstances, evil and good, intervened to prevent the completion of the poem, which was to have been entitled *The Brook*." (*Biographia Literaria*, pp. 100–101, Everyman Ed.). The poet who exerted a special influence over Coleridge's youth and awakened his feeling for nature was Bowles—" Er fing an für Leslie Bowles zu schwärmen." (Brandl: *Coleridge*, p. 33.) Georg Bersch: *S. T. Coleridges Naturschilderungen in seinen Gedichten* (1909).

(186) Coleridge's youthful love, Mary Evans.

(187) Paul Sanftleben : *Wordsworth's " Borderers " und die Entwicklung der nationalen Tragödie in England im 18. Jahrhundert* (1907). *The Borderers* was written 1795–96 and published in 1842. This author compares Oswald

with Robespierre and declares him to be derived from Iago and Franz Moor, which is an error, as he is a descendant of Mrs. Radcliffe's tyrant; Sanftleben is unacquainted with the works of Mrs. Radcliffe. According to him, Marmaduke is Karl Moor; Herbert, Old Moor; Idonea, Amelia. In respect of Herbert and Idonea, however, *King Lear* comes closer.

(188) *A Poet's Epitaph*. In his famous *Tintern Abbey* (*Lines composed a few miles above Tintern Abbey*, 1798), which is frequently, although erroneously, mentioned in connection with romanticism, Wordsworth depicts the development of his feeling for nature. He relates how, only a little while ago, " the sounding cataract, the tall rock, the mountain, and the deep and gloomy wood " had " haunted him like a passion," but that he has since learned to hear in nature " the still, sad music of humanity." He feels the presence in nature of something which, by awakening the noble thoughts within him, renders him restless with the joy of these.

(189) *The Idle Shepherd-boys*.

(190) Wordsworth desired, as we know, to abolish special " poetical " diction and to use only the ordinary language of everyday life. Despite this wish of his, the diction of W. is more choice and noble than everyday speech, as can easily be seen by altering his poetry to prose, for which hardly more is needed than to write his lines consecutively instead of vertically. F. W. H. Myers: *Wordsworth*, pp. 106–107 (1919).

(191) John Russell: *The Poetical Works of Thomas Moore* (1850). Oscar Thiergen: *Byron's und Moore's orientalische Gedichte* (1880). The author's assertion that " beide haben ihre orientalische Werke vollständig unabhängig von einander verfasst " is incorrect.

(192) Hawthorne's works can be studied in the Everyman Edition.

(193) As an example of the extent to which Hawthorne was under the influence of this inherited "Gothic " image, *The House of Seven Gables* can be mentioned. Although the period dealt with is the end of the eighteenth century, the central setting, even the dominant element, is in typical terror-romantic fashion the ancient dwelling, darkened by hideous crimes and the curse of selfishness, of the Pyncheons'. The whole book is an illuminating example of the significance to romanticism of that most central and all-pervading factor of romance, the Haunted Castle.

(194) One of the chief works for the study of Poe is Emile Lauvrière's *Edgar Poe. Sa vie et son oeuvre* (1904), in which the vicissitudes of his life, his literary character and activities and his failing for alcohol are depicted and analyzed *in extenso*. Amongst other works I would mention Palmer Cobb's work *The Influence of E. T. A. Hoffmann on the Tales of Edgar Allan Poe* (1908); Louis Betz: " Edgar Poe in der französischen Litteratur " (*Studien zur vergleichenden Litteraturgeschichte der neueren Zeit*, pp. 16–82 (1902)), Paul Wächtler: *Edgar Allan Poe und die deutsche Romantik* (1911), and Gunnar Bjurman's work *Edgar Allan Poe. En literaturhistorisk studie*, Lund (1916), an academical thesis, which follows closely in plan and critical results the work of Lauvrière. It gives a detailed account of Poe's imaginary world, but is weaker in its history of his literary themes. In my opinion, the weakness of this side of his work is clearly revealed in the fifth chapter, which is devoted to terror-romanticism. Such sentences as the following (p. 65, given here in translation): " Mrs. Radcliffe's *Italian*, which appeared in the same year as *The Monk* (1797) ";

" Mrs. Radcliffe had however already six years earlier (1791) created the best, in an artistic sense, of her characters . . . the broken Merchant Pierre de la Motte in *The Romance of the Forest* "; and (p. 66, referring to Falkland) "From motives to which one must admit a certain moral justice, he has committed a murder and is then transformed . . . into a fiend in human shape, who heaps crime on crime to hide his original crime "—show that the author was not as familiar with English terror-romanticism as the close relationship of Poe to the school would demand. Bjurman's book shows that later romanticism cannot be correctly adjudged without knowledge of its history and the wefts emanating thence into the present.

(195) Published in 1839 in a periodical called *The Gift*. Cobb shows (*op. cit.*, pp. 31–48) that Poe obtained the theme of this story from E. T. A. Hoffmann's romance *Die Elixiere des Teufels*, translated into English in 1824. Poe knew German. I shall return later to the romance in question and to Poe's story in another connection.

(196) Published in a periodical called *American Museum* in 1838. The strange tower-chamber in *Ligeia* recurs to mind while reading Scott's preface to *Quentin Durward*. In this (pp. 32–33, Everyman Ed.) mention is made of an octagonal room which could easily have suggested an image of a room resembling Ligeia's.

(197) Appeared in *The Southern Literary Messenger* (1835). Cobb shows the basic idea to be derived from Hoffmann's story *Doge und Dogaressa*.

(198) Printed in *Graham's Magazine* (1841). Cobb shows (*op. cit.*, pp. 71–80) this to be based on Hoffmann's story *Die Jesuitenkirche in G*. The earliest English translation of this is John Oxenford's of 1844.

(199) Cobb shows (*op. cit.*, pp. 93–94) by means of stylistic examples that Poe must have known Mrs. Radcliffe's production. In this story Poe himself admits the fact, so that no better proof is necessary.

(200) Printed 1841 in *Graham's Magazine*.

(201) I cannot help connecting Prince Prospero's castle with Scott's Castle of the Seven Proud Shields in *Harold the Dauntless*, Canto VI. The latter, too, is especially luxuriously furnished and has seven rooms like Prospero's castle. The picture is, in all essentials, the same ; Poe merely recreated it in the light of his own imagination. I have not seen the circumstance mentioned in the literature dealing with Poe I have read. The idea of a masquerade hails obviously from de Quincey's romance *Klosterheim or the Masque* (1832), which resembles in several features certain episodes in *The Monk* and *Aballino*, and is one of the last typically old-fashioned terror-romantic romances written in England.

(202) "The Fall of the House of Usher " appeared in *The Gentleman's Magazine* in 1839. Cobb and other investigators regard as its source Hoffmann's story *Das Majorat* (Wächtler in addition, with good reason, Achim v. Arnim's story *Die Majoratsherren*), which was rendered into English by Robert Pearse Gillies as early as 1826. The atmosphere is the same in both, with the sole exception that *Das Majorat* is a book of ordinary length and lacks the concentration which characterizes Poe's short story. The abnormal senses, including that of hearing, in the Ushers, is obviously derived from Arnim's story. I take the liberty of quoting from the poem of Lewis's mentioned, which is also, to my mind, fairly closely related to Poe's story.

The poem relates how an unknown horseman bore off by force someone to help in a case of child-birth, and describes the deserted and cheerless aspect of the place at which they arrive :

> Fast by the moor a lonely mansion stood ;
> Cheerless it stood ! a melancholy shade
> Its mouldering front, and rifted walls arrayed ;
> Barred were the gates, the shattered casements closed
> And brooding horror on its site reposed ;
> No tree o'erhung the uncultivated ground,
> No trace of labour, nor of life around.

When the narrator in Poe's story comes on horseback " to the melancholy House of Usher," the same sensation seizes him at the sight of it : " I looked upon the scene before me—upon the mere house, and the simple landscape features of the domain—upon the bleak walls—upon the vacant, eye-like windows—upon a few rank sedges—and upon a few white trunks of decayed trees—with an utter depression of soul. . . ."

While the character in Lewis's poem is climbing the narrow staircase in the dark :

> No lamp its hospitable guidance lent ;
> Speechless he leads through chambers dark and drear—
> When a deep dying *groan* appals the ear !
> Now with increasing haste he hurries on,
> Where, through a rent, the sickly moonbeams shone.
> The light directs—his trembling hands explore,
> Sunk in the panelled wall, a secret door.
> " Within this sad retreat," he faltering said,
> " A hapless female asks thy instant aid."

This rent, as " a barely perceptible fissure," reaching from the roof to the ground, is also seen in the House of Usher ; its owner receives his visitor as a physician, and here, too, there is a sick young woman who dies. The sighing, too, which is mentioned in Lewis's poem, is heard in the House of Usher : " the noise of the dry and hollow-sounding wood." Here, also, behind a stout door, is a dreadful crypt where lies the body of the apparently dead young woman. Lewis's poem goes on :

> Now breathless silence reigns the mansion o'er,
> Save where a faint step treads the distant floor—
> Anon it pauses—ceased the short delay,
> It slowly stalks with measured pace away . . . .

The same sensation hold's Poe's narrator and Usher in its grip as they hear in the crypt the struggles of the young woman as she emerges from her trance. " Have I not heard her footsteps on the stair ? Do I not distinguish that heavy and horrible beating of her heart ? "

Lewis's poem ends :

> Lo ! angry lightnings fire the troubled skies ;
> The sun, obscured, draws back its rising ray,
> And volleyed thunders usher in the day.
>
> .   .   .   .   .
>
> Struck by the bolt of Heaven, in heaps around,
> A prostrate ruin strews the blasted ground !
>
> .   .   .   .   .

> The yawning earth pours forth a stream of blood,
> And groans re-echo, where the mansion stood.
> Pale at the sound, with oft reverted eyes,
> Far, far aloof, the starting traveller flies.

The story of Poe's ends similarly : ". . . from that mansion I fled aghast. The storm was still abroad . . . Suddenly there shot along the path a wild light . . . blood-red moon, which now shone vividly through that once barely discernible fissure (as in the beginning of Lewis's poem) . . . the fissure rapidly widened . . . I saw the might walls rushing asunder."

| The similarities are so obvious and the whole setting so alike that one might well assume Poe to have taken the theme of his famous story from the poem. The assumption would be supported by the circumstance that the other aids to atmosphere in *The Fall of the House of Usher*, particularly the furnishings of the house, display the spirit of Mrs. Radcliffe. This would denote that in his story, within a framework supplied by Lewis, Poe has carried the hollow, enigmatical sighings of Mrs. Radcliffe to their supreme limit of effectivity, thus definitely rounding-off the tale of the dreadful romantic sigh. Nevertheless, the admitted similarity of theme in the German stories mentioned is a warning against attaching unconditional belief to this assumption. |

(203) According to the works previously mentioned by Müller-Fraureuth and Nylén.

(204) "He was a man of noble port and commanding presence. His stature was lofty, and his features uncommonly handsome. His nose was aquiline, his eyes large, black and sparkling, and his dark brows joined almost together. His complexion was of deep but clear brown ; study and watching had entirely deprived his cheek of colour. Tranquillity reigned upon his smooth, unwrinkled forehead." (*The Monk*, p. 14.)

In the work referred to earlier, Edmond Estève (pp. 109–110) has the following to say of de Monvel's play : " Mais l'intérêt véritable de la pièce et son originalité ne sont pas là. Ils sont dans la création de ce personnage dont je ne crois pas qu'il, y eût encore de spécimen aussi achevé dans la littérature francaise, le moine avide, sensuel, hypocrite, dominateur et féroce, qui, du fond d'un ténébreux couvent, porte la désolation dans les familles et le trouble dans la société, pour satisfaire des ambitions inavouables et de honteux instincts." This calls for the remark that de Monvel's type has indeed exercised an inspiring effect, but chiefly on Lewis and Mrs Radcliffe, both of whom, by reason of their greater fame at a time when terror-romanticism had reached its climax in France owing expressly to these two, annexed the honour that should have been de Monvel's as the creator of the criminal monk. Whether de Monvel had read *The Mysterious Mother* or whether he found his type by following Diderot's *La Religieuse* (written in 1760, but not published until 1796) and other revolutionary anti-clerical literature, whose desire to lay bare hypocrisy is as old as *Tartuffe*, is unknown to me.

(205) Sydney Colvin : *Landor*, 1909 (1881). Landor was a man of Hellenic intelligence, a translucent strong nature, who disapproved of all turgid Gothicism. Nevertheless, *Gebir* originated in Gothicism in such measure that it is founded on an oriental story by Clara Reeve called *The History of Charoba, Queen of Egypt*, published in her work *The Progress of Romance* (1785), as a supplement to the second volume (Colvin, *op. cit.*, p. 24). *Charoba* was derived from M. Vattier's translation *The History of Ancient Egypt* (1666), written by an Arabian called Murtadi, about the year 1250. Southey wrote a very friendly

review of *Gebir* in *The Critical Review* for Sept. 1799. This Arabian tale appears to belong—in it a giant succumbs beneath the treachery of a woman—to the Samson-group. There was something in " Gothicism " that suited Landor's literary temperament, his undying hatred of tyranny, namely its type of strong character, especially its tyrant and the equivalent of this amongst the clergy ; thus Count Julian, the chief character in the play of that name, belongs to the family of vengeful Gothic barons. There is thus nothing surprising in Landor's return in his old age to a conception that had been so strongly to the fore in the literature of his youth. Gustav F. Beckh : *Walter Savage Landor und die englische Litteratur von* 1798–1836 (1911). He refuses to call Landor a romanticist ; Robert Schlaak : *Entstehungs und Textgeschichte von Landors Gebir* (1909).

(206) Appeared in 1815–16. Georg Ellinger : *E. T. A. Hoffmann. Sein Leben und seine Werke* (1894).

(207) Ellinger, who gives an account of the parallels between *The Monk* and *Die Elixiere des Teufels* in his Life of Hoffmann, leaves this verbal parallel unmentioned. The image hails from Cazotte. (See p. 261.)

(208) Giuseppe Bortone : *Fra il voto e l'amore. Note critiche sul Monaco del Lewis, sul Templaro dello Scott, sull' Arcidiacono dell' Hugo, sull' Abate dello Zola, sullo Scorpione del Prévost ece.*, Naples (1908). In addition to my own account and Bortone's work, there is still to be mentioned the parson in Hawthorne's *The Scarlet Letter*, who is obviously a member of the family, though cleansed of criminal tendencies. The work in question is one of the most mournful in literature. Estève has traced literary descendants of the criminal monk in, *inter alia*, George Sand's romances, *Lélia* (the Irish priest Magnus) and in *Mademoiselle de la Quintinie* (the Abbot Fervet). The priest Rodin in Eugène Sue's great romance of the Wandering Jew is also one of the type.

(209) Appeared in *Graham's Magazine*, in 1841.

(210) I mean that Hoffmann has obtained Medardus' journey to Rome from the legend of Tannhäuser, which otherwise contains the same sin of love as *The Monk*. The Tannhäuser-legend and its variants have been dealt with by J. G. Th. Grässe, among others, in his work *Der Tannhäuser und Ewige Jude*, Dresden, 2nd ed. (1861). Nothing is said in these books of its influence on fiction.

(211) I have dealt with the legend of the Wandering Jew chiefly as a literary tradition ; what the true symbolical foundation of the legend is, or whether it has one, I have not attempted to deal with. So far as is known to me, folk-lore has not yet succeeded in finding a satisfactory answer to the question.

(212) My information regarding the legendary material connected with the Wandering Jew is based chiefly on the 2nd ed. of L. Neubaur's *Die Sage vom Ewigen Juden* (1893), which takes into account all the previous literature on the subject, including *Le Juif Errant* (1880) of Gaston Paris, and is, so far as I am competent to judge, an accurate and exhaustive work. The work by Grässe mentioned earlier, and Friedrich Helbig's *Die Sage vom " Ewigen Juden "* (1874) show various deficiencies. This is the case also with the account given of the theme (pp. 175–182) in the work by Dorothy Scarborough mentioned in previous notes. In his *Histoire des livres populaires ou de la littérature du colportage*, I–II (2nd ed. 1864), Vol I, pp. 478–494, Charles Nisard enumerates the French literature on the subject. J. Scheible does the same in the work *Das Kloster* referred to earlier, Vol. 12, pp. 428–452. Kr. Nyrop's work *Den*

evige jøde (*Fortids sagn og sange*, II, 1907) has likewise been at my disposal. A study of great merit, *L'évolution de la légende du Juif errant*, has recently been published (*Revue de littérature comparée*, Jan.–March, 1925, pp. 5–36) by Alice M. Killen. For the part relating to the influence of the Wandering Jew on literature of art I have had at hand Albert Soergel's *Ahasver-Dichtungen seit Goethe* (1905), which provides a rich material, and Theodor Kappstein's work *Ahasver in der Weltpoesie* (1906), which has nothing new to add to the former. Soergel is unacquainted with *The Monk* and from the literature dealt with in these pages cites only Wordsworth's ballad and Shelley's part in the development of the theme. Soergel neither deals with the theme of unending life, nor pays attention to the stereotyped repetition of the picture given by Schubart. The information regarding the Indian origin of the theme is from Alice M. Killen's study.

(213) The Jews describe the mark of Cain as a kind of inscription, depicting the sins of mankind, or a horn on the forehead. According to the so-called *Book of Adam*, of Christian origin, it was a trembling of the body, *gemens et tremens*, as Hieronymos says, or his character of a wanderer, *vagus et profugus*. Ancient Jewish and Christian legends gave note to the mysterious judgment of God and attempted to elucidate the mark, without however arriving at any unanimous decision. The Lord's command that no one was to slay the accursed Cain has been the means of drawing the legendary material dealing with Cain into the circle of the similar material dealing with the Wandering Jew. As those individuals in the Bible who had seen the face of the Lord, such as Moses, bore on their brows the reflection of His glory, it can well be that the origin of the gradually forming belief in a burning light on the forehead as the mark of God is to be sought in this detail.

Mediæval mystery plays show that the fate of Cain was conceived as resembling that of the Wandering Jew. At the beginning of the fifteenth century was created in France *Le Mystère de la Passion*, which consists simply of extracts from the Bible, expanded here and there by the insertion of a legend, and *Le Mistère de Vieil Testament*, which goes more deeply into the fate of Cain. The Lord sets His mark on Cain's brow, after which Cain embarks on his endless wandering, from which there is no release until the Lord sets him free. He must suffer for the sins of the whole world and consequently longs for death to end his torment. This legend resembles that of the Wandering Jew. Cain appears also in English legend, *e.g.*, in the old versified epic of Genesis called *Cursor Mundi*, which depicts the curse of Cain as a compulsory wandering, and in which the Lord sets His mark on Cain's brow. Likewise in the so-called Coventry plays (*Ludus Coventriae*) Cain appears, as a person unable to look another in the eyes, and who, aware of his dismal fate, flees into the desert to hide from the sight of mankind. As will be seen from the above, the legend of the Wandering Jew must be studied in connection with those dealing with Cain, as they are obviously mutually indebted and—dare one assume—have a common origin. In none of the works mentioned in the previous Note has this matter been taken into account. Hans Dürrschmidt: *Die Sage von Kain in der mittelalterlichen Litteratur Englands*, pp. 11, 27, 51, 53, 54, 72, 75, 93, 101 (1919). He does not connect the two legends.

(214) Nisard (*op. cit.*) explains the name Ahasuerus as a popular corruption of Cartaphilus, that is, the lower classes took a name known to them from the Bible in place of the unknown and difficult word Cartaphilus, perhaps owing to some slight phonetical affinity. So far as can be proved, however, the name Ahasuerus crops up for the first time in connection with the eternal wanderer

in the German book referred to earlier, and is obviously an invention of its author's; he had probably chosen it because of the frequency with which it occurs in the Jewish *purim* festival-plays. Attempts have also been made to connect the name Buttadeus with the original Buddha-legend, which seems far-fetched.—Eino Salokas (*Maallinen arkkiveisurunous Ruotsin vallan aikana*, Helsinki, Finland, pp. 23–24, 1923—"The Wordly [Finnish] Broadsheet Poems in Finland under the Swedish Time") reports the existence in Finland of a broadsheet ballad of Ahasuerus; it is similar in contents to the book published in 1602 and was, according to Salokas, printed at the end of the seventeenth century, somewhere about 1695. Other Finnish popular variants are derived from the same source. A broadsheet ballad called *Jerusalemin suutari* (The Jerusalem Shoemaker) was printed at the J. C. Frenckell & Sons' Press at Turku, Finland, in 1822. The same rubbishy work, which has little to do with Ahasuerus, was published at Oulu, Finland, by Chr. Ew. Barck in 1828.

(215) *The Monk*, Vol. II, pp. 52–65.

(216) Regarding mesmerism and other matters of occult nature referred to further on in this book, the most practical source of information is Lewis Spence's *Encyclopædia of Occultism. A Compendium of Information on the Occult Sciences, Occult Personalities, Psychic Science, Magic, Demonology, Spiritism and Mysticism*, Routledge, London (1920); Nisard, *op. cit.*, I, pp. 124–186: *Magie noire, magie blanche, cabale*; J. Scheible: *Das Kloster*, Vol. II. A French work exists, published at Paris by M. Collin de Plancy in 1826, called *Dictionnaire infernal*. In the work by Pitaval referred to earlier much space is devoted to magic, *e.g.*, in connection with the terrible history of Urban Grandier published in Vol. III of Scheible's work.

(217) E. Cobham Brewer: *A Dictionary of Miracles Imitative, Realistic, and Dogmatic* (1901). *Sub voce* The Theophilus-legend.

"In A.D. 538 Theophilus was treasurer at the Church of Adana, in Cilicia, and discharged his duties so honourably that he was elected bishop, but declined to accept the office. Now came a great change. He was accused to the new bishop, deprived of his office as treasurer, and retired into private life, boiling with anger and longing for vengeance. A certain Jew, who lived by sorcery, happened to reside in the neighbourhood, and, working on the evil spirit of the man, induced him to make a compact with the devil. To this end he had to abjure the Christian faith, deny Christ and the Virgin, and sign the compact with his blood."

J. Scheible: *Das Kloster*, Vol. II (poem on Theophilus in the Latin). In Vol. III (p. 876) is a facsimile of the deed of sale between Grandier and the Devil.

(218) Dr John Campbell: *Hermippus Redivivus, or the Sage's Triumph over Old Age and the Grave*, London (1749). The book is a translation of the Latin work *Hermippus Redivivus* by Dr J. H. Cohausen, published at Frankfort-on-Main (1742). Johannes Meyer: *William Godwins Romane*, p. 46 (1906).

(219) The name Queen Mab appears in Ch. Br. Brown's *Edgar Huntly* (1799).

(220) The French popular legend, which is dealt with in Neubaur's work, is at bottom the same as the Irish fairy-tale of the shoemaker Schiane and the Finnish tales of the blacksmith and the devil. The methods of *Bonhomme Misèr* resemble so greatly those of Melmoth, that one cannot avoid drawing parallels. Peter O'Leary: *Schiane*. Nisard reports (*op. cit.*, I, pp. 405–415) the existence of a popular French booklet *Histoire nouvelle et divertissante du Bonhomme Misère, où elle a pris son origine, comme elle a trompé la mort, et quand elle*

finira dans le monde, par M. Court-d'Argent (1824). Maturin's idea of setting Melmoth, who had made a bargain covering a term of years with the Devil, to wander in search of a substitute who would set him free, is too much like the popular legend to be his own invention. Writers on Maturin fail to point out this.

(221) Mentioned by Cross, *op. cit.*, p. 159. The period was one of arresting eyes—it seems almost as though the hypnotic-glance motive had its counterpart in reality. Goethe was famous for his dark, glowing eyes, as was also Robert Burns—a flaming, entreating, burning glance was the common weapon used by both to captivate female hearts. Byron was known for his large burning eyes and penetrating glance, against which the defences of womankind were powerless. Shelley's large, light eyes reflected the ethereal blue of his ideals. Coleridge was s well-known for his dark, dreaming gaze as for his gift for talking.

(222) Saintsbury describes the complicated construction of the book as follows : "A considerable part of the book consists of a story told to a certain person, who is a character in a longer story, found in a manuscript which is delivered to a third person, who narrates the greater part of the novel to a fourth person, who is the namesake and descendant of the title-hero." (*The English Novel*, p. 185.)

(223) David Masson : *De Quincey*, pp. 73 and 161 (1911). The part relating to the Rosicrucians in Spence's work would seem to be incomplete, as it makes no mention of De Quincey's article, which is published in Masson's edition of the collected works of De Quincey, Vol. XIII, pp. 384–448. De Quincey's article is based on a German work dealing with the Rosicrucians and Freemasons by Johann Gottlieb Buhle (1763–1821), which had appeared in 1804. However, De Quincey's article cannot have been more than a reminder to Lytton, for it hardly deals at all with the Rosicrucian theurgy which is the chief element in *Zanoni*. This was probably taken from the writings on Platonic, Plotinean and cabbalistic matters attributed to *Hermes Trismegistus*. There was likewise in existence a work by a certain Solomon Semler entitled *Impartial Collections for the History of Rosicrucians* (1786–88).

(224) Isaac D'Israeli (1766–1848), had published a story entitled *Mejnour and Leila*. Lytton was on terms of great intimacy with Lord Beaconsfield.

(225) I cannot refrain from connecting this old, uninhabited house, which the narrator leases in order to establish whether there is anything supernatural attached to it, with the London building depicted in De Quincey's *Confessions of an English Opium-Eater*, in which he passed his wretched student days in London and which, with its desolation and gloom, awakens an image greatly similar to that described in Lytton's story. In both (in the latter as a ghost) a little girl living in misery appears, without having any definite part assigned to her, so that her insertion seems obviously to rest on the effectivity of De Quincey's account. *Confessions of an English Opium-Eater*, pp. 152–3, Everyman's Ed. The theme of unnaturally-prolonged life is again dealt with by Lytton in *A Strange Story* (1862). Dorothy Scarborough points out in the work of hers mentioned (p. 60), that these stories display the influence of Balzac. The prolonged youth of *Dorian Gray* is likewise to be viewed in the light of this theme. The idea of immortality interested also Hawthorne (*A Virtuoso's Collection*) and flashes by in Poe's *Tale of the Ragged Mountains*.

(226) Here my account is based on Soergel's work, which provides an extensive bibliography. Of the works cited in the following notes, I have read only a few. Dorothy Scarborough's study of the Wandering Jew is incomplete,

but she enumerates a great mass of English literature dealing with this theme and that of unending life, a list I have made use of below.

(227) The romanticists' worship of death proceeds from this fundamental idea ; the spacious accounts, intended to inspire terror, of the emblems of death already touched upon in this work are, like Melmoth's conception of the burden of life and liberation by death, manifestations of the same glorification of death. Among the German romanticists the worship of death was cultivated especially by Novalis and Zacharias Werner. It is hardly necessary to point out that we see here renewed Blair's and Young's worship of night and death. In its most extreme form this worship leads to necrophilism, love of the body of the beloved even after death. Examples are Poe's *Berenice* and Werner's *Lied der Liebe*. Here the theme joins on to the popular beliefs expressed in werewolf and vampire legends. It is from this standpoint that we must understand the theme of a destructive instinct in love ; what one loves, one wishes to destroy.

(228) For example : M. Heller : *Briefe des ewigen Juden* (1791) ; Pasero de Corneliano : *Histoire du Juif Errant, écrite par lui même*, (1820) ; Eubule-Evans : *The Curse of the Wandering Jew, a Christmas Carol ;* Charles Granville : *The Plaint of the Wandering Jew ;* George Croly : *Salathiel the Immortal, or Tarry Thou Till I Come ;* Lewis Wallace : *The Prince of India ;* etc.

In a poem *Prometheus och Ahasverus* the Swedish poet Viktor Rydberg conceives the Wandering Jew as the representative of power, egoism and pitiless imperialism, with Prometheus as an emblem of justice, humanity and liberalism. Anton Blanck (*Handelstidningens* Christmas Number, 1924, article "Ahasverus—Disraeli ") has shown that Rydberg depicts the struggle between Gladstone and Disraeli as to whether England was to obey the dictates of humanity and in spite of all selfish considerations of profit declare war as the ally of Russia on Turkey. The views of Disraeli prevailed. Features from the life and opinions of Disraeli are apparent in the picture of Ahasuerus.

(229) For example : A. W. Schlegel : *Die Warnung* (1801) ; A. v. Arnim : *Halle und Jerusalem* (1807) ; H. Chr. Andersen : *Ahasverus* (1848) ; Fr. Paludan-Müller : *Ahasverus* (1854–62) ; Z. Topelius : " Den evige studenten " (*Vinterkvällar*, 2nd coll.). The attributes used by the author and the contents of the story prove that the question is of an imaginary picture of Ahasuerus. The student Peregrinus Müller is an alien, who speaks every language and is dressed in strange half-oriental attire ; he is in the flower of his manhood, his features are noble and regular, but of an arresting pallor ; his eyes are large and dark, his glance deep, absent, sorrowful and weary. He had been alive in 1699 and seeks a famous manuscript by the aid of which he can prove himself to have been in the wrong. He is—so the story suggests—identical with the " Italian Johannes Matheus Caryophilus," who lived about 1625. Peregrinus Müller dies as soon as he has discovered the manuscript. (Pointed out to me by Prof. Gunnar Castrén of Helsinki, Finland.)

(230) Berthold Auerbach : *Spinoza* (1837) ; A. v. Chamisso : *Der neue Ahasverus* (1831) ; B. S. Ingemann : *Blade af Jerusalems Skomagers Lommebog* (1833). This conception is also behind the Swedish poet Oskar Levertin's "Ahasverus " (*Legender och visor*), in which an ultimate scene of reconciliation between Jesus and Ahasuerus is envisaged.

(231) Edgar Quinet : *Les tablettes du Juif errant* (1822) ; Karl Beck : *Fantasien am Grabe Poniatowskys* (1838).

(232) Béranger : *Le Juif errant* (1831) ; C. E. S. Norton : *The Undying One* (1830) ; Nic. Lenau : *Ahasver* (1832).

NOTES

(233) Soergel's Ahasuerus bibliography comprises 210 works, of which only a small number are English; it must be remembered that he was perhaps less acquainted with English than with German and French sources.

(234) Attempts have been made to trace Milton's solemn image of Satan back into early English Christian poetry, in other words to the Biblical verse of Caedmon. The Venerable Bede has told of Caedmon, the unlearned shepherd, who was given the gift of poetry in his sleep; he lived at the Convent of St. Hilda at Streanaeshalch (Whitby) in the seventh century (fl. 670) and according to Bede turned sacred history into poetry. The only relic known with certainty to be his is a hymn of nine lines. A manuscript containing " Caedmon-poetry " has come down however from the year 1000, and was published in 1655, by Francis Junius; as its contents corresponded well with the description of Caedmon's poetry given by Bede, Junius assumed the MS. to be the work of Caedmon. Modern investigation has shown however that the poems cannot all be the work of the same person; and as, according to Bede, Caedmon was imitated in his lifetime, it is impossible to judge to what extent Junius's publication consists of such, and equally as to the form in which Caedmon's original poetry may be contained in it. The MS. published by Junius contains a lengthy account of the Genesis, a poem on the fall of the angels and the temptation of the first man, which has been shown to be the work of the poet of Heliand. As in this and in *Paradise Lost* there are certain parallels, particularly in the defiance and pride of Lucifer, the assumption has been brought forward that Milton had in some way had access to Junius's Caedmon-poetry and been influenced by it. Nevertheless, Henry Bradley says : " The parallels, however, though very interesting, are only such as might be expected to occur between two poets of kindred genius working on what was essentially the same body of traditional material." (*Encyclopædia Britannica Sub voce* " Caedmon.") Nevertheless, the similarities must be considerable, as the Swedish critic Urban von Feilitzen (who wrote under the *nom-de-plume* of "Robinson"), who was specially interested in English literature and was one of the literary celebrities of Sweden in the 'eighties, made the same observation. In a work published in 1924 (*Urban von Feilitzen*, " Robinson ") Axel Forsström mentions the fact (p. 232, here translated from the Swedish) : " In his study of English literature Robinson was led back to the first English poet, the ancient Caedmon. It struck him while reading the latter as a ' miracle of literary history ' that Caedmon could have created in the person of his ' titanically soulful ' Satan in his Paradise-poem a mighty prototype to Milton's Satan already in the beginning of the seventh century." In a letter dated in 1900, Feilitzen mentions as a deficiency in Raleigh's book on Milton that he makes no remark on this earlier conception of Satan. Prof. Uno Lindelöf of Helsinki has kindly supplied me with information regarding Caedmon. Forsström's phrase " in the beginning of the seventh century " is inexact, as Caedmon's poetry could have been written at the earliest in the middle of the century ?

(235) I have not forgotten Scott's relation to German literature. The argument that Götz comes closer to Scott's knights than the English prototypes, rises easily in the mind when we remember that Scott translated Götz. Nevertheless the assertion is unfounded. The influence of German literature on Scott is in the main exceedingly small; he was delighted with it for the reason that he found there the same ideals and images that he himself had formed while reading Percy and the border ballads and studying the history of Scotland and chronicles of Froissart. Acquaintance with the German literature of chivalry

could, therefore, give him nothing specially new, but it could embolden him to attempt the interpretation of his own visions.

(236) Hugo Hertel: *Die Naturschilderungen in Walter Scott's Versdichtungen* (1900).

(237) To be compared with Note 148; with Byron's observation at the end regarding *Kruitzner*.

(238) This mocking and at the same time tragic laughter was a clever invention—whether it was Scott's own, I cannot say—of which the romanticists made good use. Maturin makes it a special feature of Melmoth, who heightens the bitterness that springs from suffering to its utmost limit by his terrible laughter. Laughter is also the Devil's means of expressing triumph. It is further one of the little tricks of technique that commonly denote the gradual passing over of the tragic hero's agony of mind to insanity.

(239) Karl Hoffmann: *Über Lord Byrons " The Giaour "* (1898). Deals at greater length with the personal part Byron had possibly played in the adventure of the Giaour than with the Byronic hero-type, whose derivation is not sufficiently founded.

(240) Byron's famous simile of the scorpion was perhaps derived from Boswell's *Life of Dr. Johnson*, Vol. I, pp. 346–347 (Everyman ed.).

(241) The poem is intentionally made to resemble a fragment, a trick of construction doubtlessly derived from the MS. artifice of the romanticists.

(242) *Rokeby* appeared in 1813; in December the same year Byron completed *The Corsair*. Conrad is obviously an expanded and more mysterious version of the Mortham-type. The romance of exotic seas interested Byron already from the point of view of his family history, for his grandfather, Captain John Byron (1723–86) was a madcap sailor, who found rest neither on land nor sea, and whose sufferings from shipwreck and hunger the poet Byron transformed into the scenes of terror in *Don Juan*. During the course of 1764–66, John Byron sailed round the world. He was so well-known for his bad-weather luck, that sailors called him " foul-weather Jack." John Nichol: *Byron*, pp. 7–9 (1919).

(243) Curt Lotze: *Quellenstudie über Lord Byrons " The Island "* (1902). The first idea for this poem of the sea seems to have sprung from a wish to depict the terror-romance to which a mutiny could give rise. In a nautical nation events of this nature were common and well-known and specially provocative of terror; mutinies had been described in literature ever since *Robinson Crusoe*. Such accounts included a description of the mutiny of *The Bounty* in 1789 and the subsequent fate of the mutineers; it contains many features which resemble Byron's poem. Other sources included W. Bligh's *Voyage to the South Sea* (1792) and J. Martin's *Account of the Natives of the Tonga Islands* (1814). Byron was also inspired to deal with the subject by Trelawney, who had spent years in distant lands and could relate many exciting adventures.

(244) Regarding the relation of Byron to Mrs. Radcliffe, Sir Walter Raleigh says : "And it is a testimony to the power of her art that her fancy first conceived a type of character that subsequently passed from art into life. The man that Lord Byron tried to be was the invention of Mrs. Radcliffe." (*The English Novel*, p. 228.) Saintsbury says : " The influence on Scott is not the least of these : but there is even a more unquestionable asset of the same kind in the fact that the Byronic villain-hero, if not Byron himself, is Mrs. Radcliffe's work.

Schedoni did much more than beget or pattern Lara: he is Lara." (*The English Novel*, p. 161.)

(245) Hans Maier: *Entstehungsgeschichte von Byrons "Childe Harold's Pilgrimage"* (1911). He shows on pp. 30–31 the influence of Zeluco, and includes Harold among the heroes of "*Weltschmerz*," descending from Timon, Hamlet and Werther.

(246) A slight indication of how older romanticism with its familiar features invariably creeps at the heels of the Byronic hero is the fact that to the creation of the picture of Manfred, the legend of the Wandering Jew has obviously contributed its share. This is apparent from Manfred's words:

> I have affronted death—but in the war
> Of elements the waters shrunk for me,
> And fatal things pass'd harmless. . . .

which are as an echo of the lament of Ahasuerus that originated in Schubart's poem. The following lines, too, hint at the same influence:

> Nor to slumber, nor to die,
> Shall be in thy destiny;
> Though thy death shall still seem near
> To thy wish, but as a fear;
> Lo! the spell now works around thee,
> And the clankless chain hath bound thee.

The images in this are an echo of the Ahasuerus legend, as are also those in the following:

> There is a power upon me which withholds,
> And makes it my fatality to live,—
>
> .   .   .   .   .
>
> I tell thee, man! I have lived many years,
> Many long years, but they are nothing now
> To those which I must number: ages, ages,
> Space and eternity—and consciousness,
> With the fierce thirst of death—and still unslaked.

See note 172.

(247) Heinrich Kraeger: *Der byronsche Heldentypus* (1898). This work is to show that the derivation of the Byronic hero is most closely to be sought in Karl Moor, thus, in the German romantic misanthropist-type. As will be observed from my text, my own opinion is that the Byronic hero is a national, English product. In support of this I would further point out that in Byron's youth German literature was still practically unknown in England; attention was not drawn to it until Taylor, Scott and Coleridge began to translate, and even then interest was confined to a narrow circle. Byron read Harriet Lee's *Kruitzner* in 1802, and in the preface to *Werner* admitted to having been influenced by it, but *Kruitzner* could at the most have revived a type that was already in his mind and have helped him towards the final expression of the de la Motte-character he had obtained from Mrs. Radcliffe. Byron did not read *The Robbers* until 1814. It is obvious and natural that Byron's literary images are on the whole English, as his reading consisted practically of English literature only, with merely an occasional side-glance at things German. In the preface by Caroline F. E. Spurgeon to *The Castle of Otranto* (1907 edition) it is said: "Professor Raleigh says that what the man Byron tried to be was the

invention of Mrs. Radcliffe, but surely we must go back a little further, and give Walpole credit for the first sketch of the dark, handsome, melancholy, passionate, mysterious hero of the Byronic poems." In my opinion this is correct, only we must go farther back than to Walpole, right to Shakespeare. I am unaware of the existence of any study by an English writer devoted to the Byronic hero ; yet a work of this description would be well worth the labour involved, for it would deal with the most interesting central personage of English romanticism, now claimed, wrongly, by the Germans as theirs. As I have remarked, Chateaubriand's *René* (1802), Senancour's *Obermann* and Constant's *Adolphe* are the French counterparts to this type, showing that in France, led by the same strivings as in England and Germany, dreams had arisen of a superman-type. In his *Mémoires*, Chateaubriand regards Childe Harold as his own type, which Byron had borrowed ; the line I have followed shows this view to be incorrect. Finally I would point out that Scott borrowed the type from Byron, for George Staunton in *The Heart of Midlothian* is obviously modelled on the Byronic hero, or rather, perhaps, on Byron himself and his evil reputation.

(248) The Byronic hero denotes the share of England in the evolution of the superman. The idea of a superman, of a being exceeding in dimensions all others, one who justifies his actions on grounds incomprehensible to ordinary beings, in contrast even to the latter's ideas of morality, is an invention of the romanticists, the fruit of a striving to create mighty, ruling characters of a demonic fascination. The superman of the Renascence is Prospero, passionless, nobly resigned, a being rising in his superhuman wisdom above others, in particular above the ordinary animal-man, Caliban. Another superman-type is Satan, in whom Milton embodies a superhuman spirit of revolt and defiance against the immutability of divine law. With the suffocation of the Renascence beneath the formal ideals of the Classic Age, the search for the superman ceases, until re-awakened by romanticism. A series of supermen-types now arises, a common characteristic of which is an attitude of superiority to all else, of revolt and defiance. The English world accepts from the hands of Shakespeare the inheritance of the past, pours into it the defiance and bitterness of the revolutionary years, and evolves the Byronic hero, who as Shelley's Prometheus rises ultimately to a Titan warring against Zeus. Germany creates Götz, the lonely hero, a full-fledged superman who achieves his highest expression in *Wallenstein*. The Faust-Merlin of mediævalism becomes Goethe's Faust, a ruler and a great creator of culture, who leads straight to Zarathustra. Leo Berg in *Der Übermensch in der modernen Litteratur* (1897) makes no mention of the Byronic hero.

(249) Literature on ghosts : the work mentioned by Wilh. Ad. Paterna deals with Walpole, Reeve, Radcliffe, Lewis, Godwin, Beckford, Sophia and Harriet Lee, Shelley, Mary Shelley, Maturin and Scott. It regards the Bleeding Nun and the ghost of Alonzo as the weakest of Lewis's inventions. The work mentioned by Scarborough, pp. 81--129, is mostly an enumeration of modern ghost-literature. In neither of these is there any classification of ghosts according to their chief properties of terror. C. Thürnau's *Geister in der englischen Litteratur* (1906) contains a careful list of older ghost-literature in England.

(250) I am hardly inclined to regard Burns's *Tam O' Shanter* (written in 1790) as a true ghost-ballad, for the reason that it is more in the nature of a drunkard's vision than a seriously intended story of a " real " ghost-scene. The author's own standpoint is " unromantic."

(251) A selection of Percy's ballads, altogether only eleven, amongst which was " Margaret's Ghost," appeared in German in 1767 at Gothingen.

Roesel, op. cit., p. 33. H. F. Wagener : *Das Eindringen von Percys Reliques in Deutschland* (1897). Bürger made the acquaintance of Percy's ballads in the autumn of 1771, when Hölty borrowed them from the Gothingen University Library. Wagener, *op. cit.*, p. 27. H. Lohre : *Von Percy zum Wunderhorn, Palaestra XXII*, pp. 6–7 (1902). "The Ghost of William" was published by Herder in 1773.

The theme of Death riding in the moonlight has been investigated by Eliel Aspelin, who cites in his articles "Murheen voima" (The Power of Sorrow) in the periodical *Valvoja* published at Helsinki (1882 and 1883) the lines Bürger had heard the servant-girl sing. See also W. v. Wurzbach : *Gottfried August Bürger*, pp. 88–96 (1900) :

> Der Mond scheint hell,
> Der Tod reit't schnell,
> Feins Liebchen, grauet's dir ?
> " Und warum sollt' mir's grauen ?
> Ist doch Feinslieb mit mir."

The writer then shows that the song has been sung in Spain, Italy, Greece, England, Denmark and Sweden, and demonstrates that its fundamental idea, the conception that the sorrow of the living afflicts the dead in their dwellings, appears in ancient Greek tales, in Edda, in the rune of Helge Hundingbane. Aspelin sought for the motive in Finland and established that it had been known there both in the form of a folk-tale and a poem of three lines.

Since the publication of these articles, an abundance of variants on the theme has accumulated in the archives of the Finnish Literary Society. Aspelin's investigations were completed by an article by Prof. J. Sieber in the *Valvoja* for 1900, likewise entitled " Murheen voima." According to this article the poem contains an idea common to all the Aryan peoples, mentioned already in the Hindu poem *Raghuvansa :* " For the perpetual weeping of relatives burns the deceased, we all do know." Regarding the theme of *Lenore* he says that in its prose form it was generally known both in Germany and eastward of the Germanic race, from the Inari River in North Finland to the Black and Mediterranean Seas ; " it is known to the Finn and Slav peoples. . . . Special attention is undoubtedly merited by the Polish ancient myths." The writer shows that a poem similar to *Lenore* was known in Poland before the publication of the latter.

(252) Percy's ballads frequently begin with lines such as : "As it fell out on a Pentecost day," "As it fell out on a highe holye day," "And as it befelle on a high holiday."—" Brave Alonzo " is the hero of a poem " Gentle Rover " on a Spanish theme.

(253) It has been pointed out that such worms appear in Shakespeare, and are freely used in realistic depictments of decay of a terror-romantic nature.

(254) The ghost-ballad entered into Sweden by two different paths. *The Ghost of Sweet William* was translated into Danish by Baggesen as *Ludvigs Gjenfaerd* with the addition of features from *Lenore ;* this Danish ballad was adapted into Swedish by Kellgren as *Fredrics Wålnad* (1793), and inaugurated the ghost-ballads of early romanticism in Sweden. Another powerful impulse was given to the ghost-ballad by the publication of Kullberg's translation of *Alonzo the Brave*. This was published for the first time in a periodical called *Läsning i blandade ämnen*, in 1799 (No. 25, p. 116), and has later been included in Arvid Ahnfelt's work *Verldslitteraturens Historia*, II, pp. 125–126 (1886).

Kullberg did not publish his poem as a translation, but submitted it to the Swedish Academy as an original work in a prize competition. In 1800 he received the Lundblad Prize " on the grounds of this ballad, which was declared to be ' of unexcelled merit,' ay, amongst those who championed this ghost-ballad was Leopold himself, the sworn enemy of ghost and superstition-poetry." Gustaf Ljungren, who relates the above (*Svenska vitterhetens häfder*, III, pp. 292–305), was himself at first unaware that the poem was a translation. The idea even gained credence that while translating *The Monk* from the French in collaboration with Madame Ulrika Carolina Widström, Kullberg had inserted his own ballad in it. Ljungren mentions that Alonzo " spread in copies over the country and was for long an essential item of all songbooks." In his treatise " Den förromantiska balladen i Sverige " (*Göteborgs högskolas årsskrift*, 1912) J. Viktor Johansson shows the first Swedish ghost-ballads to be based on *Sweet William's Ghost*. An account of ballads of terror is given in Martin Lamm's work *Upplysningstidens romantik*, II, pp. 596–597 (1918–20). As an indication of the wide circulation of the Swedish version of Alonzo, I may mention that at Oulu (a town in the north of Finland) a sea-captain (died in 1912) still knew the whole poem by heart ; he had learned it in his youth at Tornio, the Finnish town on the Swedish border. I have heard him recite it as an example of a dreadful song of ghosts and love. The translation was Kullberg's.

As regards the circulation of the poem in the Finnish language, the first trace I was able to discover of it in broadsheet poetry is of the year 1878, when it was published by Chr. Ew. Barck at Oulu as a song by J. Ranginen, a " poet " with a great quantity of broadsheet verse to his name, under the title " Selma, sotilaan morsian " (Selma, the Bride of the Soldier). Selma is heartsick for her Wilhelm, who has gone to the wars ; he returns however in good health and everything ends well. Then, in 1880, four " new and sweet songs of love " were printed by Emil Hagelberg at Tampere, amongst which is " Hjalmari ja Hulda," signed " G. W. G." Hjalmari goes to the wars and returns to find Hulda the bride of another. He goes to Hulda's wedding and snatches the crown from her head, at which she turns pale. A duel ensues between the bridegroom and Hjalmari in which both are killed ; Hulda too dies of the pangs of conscience. The proximity of Alonzo is thus more noticeable. The same song was published at Barck's press in 1881, but in a slightly altered form, and again in 1885 by J. Simelius' press at Helsinki as the work of Johan Kauranen.

Finally, in 1884, a direct translation of the ballad of Alonzo appeared. In that year D. Nironen published at Jyväskylä " Three beautiful love-songs " written by G. A. H. . . . nen. These include the ballad "Aalonksi ja Emueli."

The following year, published by J. Eriksson at the Suomi Press at Tampere, four songs appeared written by E. K. Saarinen, of which the first was called " Petetyn sotilaan kosto pettäjämorsiamellensa (Aalonksi ja Emueli) "—(The Revenge of the betrayed soldier to his Bride [Aalonksi and Emueli].) This is a better version than the former and in this form the ballad became widely-known and favoured in Finland. It was known in the North Ostrobothnian province of Finland as " The Young Soldier's Song." In it the " beautiful young soldier " takes leave of his sweetheart and departs to the wars. The maiden forgets her vow, with the result that the young soldier's ghost comes to fetch her from her wedding, just as " the musician's horns were sounding and the wedding company dancing." Even the worms were not forgotten, for it is expressly said of the ghost that " the worms crept in and out of his skull." Sung to a mournful valse-melody it was well calculated to provoke a shudder of fear in the hearts of the maids and farmer's lads who sang it. It circulated either as a printed broadsheet or a handwritten copy. This slight addition to the more familiar fortunes of Alonzo shows well how widely Lewis's ballad had spread ; the collections of folk-songs and broadsheet poetry in various countries would certainly provide the material for a study of its circulation, which went deeper perhaps into the masses than even *Lenore*.

A clumsy Finnish translation in a collection of broadsheet and folk-songs, " Laululipas " (" The Chest of Songs "), published by the Helsinki bookseller Joh. K. Lindstedt, is designated " an old song from the days of the Bishop Agricola " (!) Bishop Agricola died 1557.

In the ballad of Alonzo, as in *Lenore*, one might remark on the existence of a certain misogynist tendency, for the reader's opinion is that the fates of both Imogene and Lenore are too cruel compared with their crime. The fact that Imogene consents so readily to the new bridegroom connects the ballad with the ancient tale of the matron of Ephesus—a theme treated by Lewis in his poem *The Soldier's Grave* (printed in Mrs. Baron-Wilson's *Life*, I, p. 251). See Yrjö Hirn's article " Hjalmar Crohns : Den trolösa hustrun in två medeltida sagosamlingar " (Argus, Helsinki, 1912, No. 24, *Korta anmälningar*).

Sweet William's Ghost too is known in Finland as a broadsheet ballad that begins with the ghost knocking and sighing, and Marianna opening the door and inviting her Wilhelmi to enter. I have not succeeded in tracing the original copy of this even as late as the year of "Aalonksi," so that it is probably of still later date.

The work by Salokas mentioned earlier is not sufficiently up-to-date to provide an account of the spreading of the terror-romantic ballad in Finland, either in broadsheet form or otherwise.

Older than the ghost-ballad in Finnish literature would seem to be the ballad of the seducer, the origin of which is Bürger's poem *Des Pfarrers Tochter von Taubenhain*. The poems written under its influence include Franzén's *Förföraren* (1809) while distant traces of the same poem are discernible in his *Den gamle knekten* (1793). Bürger's poem was translated by Kullberg in 1795. Echoes of such poetry are poems like *Risti Idan haudalla eli Ida ja Frans Alfred* (The Cross on Ida's Grave, or Ida and Frans Alfred), printed in 1835 by Frenckell & Son at Helsinki and subsequently widely circulated by Barck at Oulu and Londicer at Vaasa. This is a Finnish version of Charlotte Berger's (*née* Cronhjelm) sentimental ballad " Korset på Idas graf " (also published in the songbook *Svenska sångstycken*, edited by Axel Ivar Ståhl, new ed. edited by Birger Schöldström, 1892). A verse of it has strayed into Aleksis Kivi's famous Finnish romance *Seitsemän veljestä* (Seven Brothers). It was based originally on *Den gamle knekten*.

On the whole, romantic broadsheet poetry in the Finnish language is of much later date than elsewhere in Europe and scanty both as regards number and themes. If we mention, in addition to the above, the broadsheet ballads *Wilhelmi ja Emma*, *Pista ja Ilona*, *Albert ja Maria*, and *Merimiehen eli Stralsburgin laulu*, the most important items are enumerated. The ballads written to commemorate murders and catastrophes and the numerous conscript songs hindered its creation and prevented it from spreading.

(255) I have not taken into account *Gaston de Blondeville* in which the ghost appears in such material form and so devoid of special features that it is as commonplace as any other of the characters ; at the tournament it kills its opponent like any knight in armour.

(256) In addition, Scott uses ghosts in the following works : *The Antiquary*, *Anne of Geierstein*, *The Fortunes of Nigel*, *Waverley* and *The Bride of Lammer-*

moor. The White Lady of Avenel is reflected in the story *Ljungars Saga* by Topelius.

(257) Brandl, who deals widely with the origins of *The Ancient Mariner* in his life of Coleridge (pp. 209–217), notes this circumstance, which links the poem in characteristic fashion with contemporary terror-romanticism.

(258) Coleridge and De Quincey indulged in opium, Poe in gin and Hoffmann in wine. In the production of all four one discerns an artificial stimulation of the imagination.

(259) Appeared in the *Southern Literary Messenger* in 1835; Lauvrière regards it as one of the most important of Poe's works—*un chef-d'œuvre* (*op. cit.*, p. 80).

(260) Lucifer entered into literature by way of the Bible and Christian superstitions, achieving a special significance in the originally Jewish cabbalism and the occult sciences, and the various branches of magic, alchemy and astrology that flourished in its connection. Milton's conception of Satan's kingdom and the various degrees of devils, of whom there are so many that they form a great army, is based on mediæval demonology, an extensive and detailed "science" based in turn on old magical ideas inherited from Platonic-Gnostic sources. Lucifer is thus an ancient spirit come down to the Old Testament and thence to the Christian Faith from the Orient. When, as referred to earlier, collections of Oriental tales began to spread in Europe, in the 18th century, they brought in their train a number of the fabulous beings, good an evil genii, djinn, etc., grouped around the person of King Solomon, thus enriching the possibilities of romance from a new source; as a third source the romanticists had access to innumerable spirits and fairies of folk-lore. For the history of the Devil see Arturo Graf: *Naturgeschichte des Teufels* (undated, the original Italian work appeared in 1889), an elaborate depictment of the history of the Evil One; also Spence's frequently-mentioned work.

(261) The early romanticists usually treated the Devil in a very "material" spirit, keeping to the conceptions of mediæval legend. Southey was still at this stage. With him sulphur is still the characteristic odour of Hell and its ruler.

(262) According to Spence, this is the original form, inherited from his angelic days, of Lucifer. Milton describes him as follows:

And now a stripling Cherub he appears,
Not of the prime, yet such as in his face
Youth smiled celestial, and to every limb
Suitable grace diffused; so well he feigned.
Under a coronet his flowing hair
In curls on either cheek played; wings he wore
Of many a coloured plume sprinkled with gold,
His habit fit for speed succinct, and held
Before his decent steps a silver wand.

(*Paradise Lost*, Bk. III, ll. 636-643.) In this form Lewis's Lucifer was thus derived from Milton.

(263) I refer the reader to Dorothy Scarborough's work, in which an account is given of the works by Hogg and Rosa Matilda mentioned. In his collected works, in a note attached to the poem, Southey declares the Devil's excursion theme to be his own invention.

(264) Brandl compares (*op. cit.*, pp. 222–228) Geraldine with Spenser's Duessa and Christabel with Una ; Spenser's knight would thus be Christabel's father and the object of contention. The similarity is indeed striking and is further supported by the general atmosphere of faerie in which *Christabel* moves. On the other hand, as I have remarked, the terror-romantic castle element is so strongly and familiarly represented—Brandl pays too little attention to this— that Geraldine can well be coupled with the demoniac female of Coleridge's own times. Speaking of the castle in *Christabel*, Brandl says : " Der Schauplatz der zweiten Scene, das Schloss, stammt aus der Radcliffe'schen Romance des Waldes," which shows that the ubiquity and dominating status of the chief setting of terror-romance was not wholly perceived by the writer. In Heinrich von Kleist's play *Kätchen von Heilbronn*, Kunigunda's bath-scene, which Kätchen chances to witness, without being able to describe later what she had seen, resembles the disrobing of Geraldine. Kleist's play was published in 1810, while *Christabel* was written earlier but published later. Moreover, the arrival of Kunigunda at the castle and her influence over its master display points of similarity with the plot of *Christabel*.

(265) Attempts at explanation fail ; Coleridge apparently desired to avoid all tendency, "criticism of the shooting of an albatross," and set out to write a fairy-tale, which he left half-way. His " green snake " hails from *As you Like It*, in which a character dreams of a " green gilded snake " coiling around the throat. In *King Lear* the Duke of Albany calls his wife a " gilded snake." From *The Ballad of the Dark Ladie* (1799) and the introductory poem and interlude in the same (" Introduction " and " Love ") it appears in addition that Coleridge's imagination had been engaged at that time in a larger theme, of which the chief ingredient was love. The interlude " Love " shows him to have had an idea of a woman who enslaves her lover with her charms, treating him meanwhile with disdain, until he was beyond saving. The lines :

> There came and looked him in the face
> An angel beautiful and bright ;
> And that he knew it was a Fiend,
> This miserable Knight !

show to my mind the image of the demoniac woman to have hovered near. Notwithstanding, the main motive of these fragments : enslavement in the bonds of an unhappy and fatal love, in connection with its treatment, bring them nearer " Lady Holde's " world of love than to the brutal, invented demon. Another poem belonging to the same world is Keat's *La belle dame sans merci*, which is neither more nor less than Tannhäuser's story of his sojourn with Frau Holde :

> She took me to her elfin grot,
> And there she wept and sighed full sore,
> And there I shut her wild, wild eyes
> With kisses four.
>
> And there she lulled me asleep,
> And there I dreamed—ah! woe betide !
> The latest dream I ever dreamed
> On the cold hill's side.

(266) Occurred at Geneva, on the evening of July 10th, 1816. " Byron recited the lines in *Christabel* about the lady's breast, when Shelley suddenly

started up, shrieked, and fled from the room.   He had seen a vision of a woman with eyes instead of nipples." (Symonds : *Shelley*, pp. 90–91.)

(267) *Paradise Lost* (Bk. II, ll. 647–653 and 666–670) :

> . . . Before the gates there sat
> On either side a formidable Shape.
> The one seemed woman to the waist, and fair,
> But ended foul in many a scaly fold,
> Voluminous and vast—a serpent armed
> With mortal sting.
>
> . . . The other shape—
> If shape it might be called that shape had none
> Distinguishable in member, joint, or limb ;
> Or substance might be called that *shadow* seemed ;
> For each seemed either—*black it stood as Night*. . . .

These last descriptions of shadowy beings recur in Poe and Lytton.

(268) *Christabel* was not published until 1816, but had meanwhile become widely known in literary circles in MS. form.   Walter Scott read it and derived considerable impulses for his *Lay of the Last Minstrel*, including the general feature of supernatural powers determining the fates of the characters.   The lady of the castle and her chamber of magic are echoes of Matilda, Geraldine and the haunted castle.

(269) Dante Gabriel Rossetti, whose favourite reading was this early English romanticism, obtained from the Lady of Branksome Castle and her chamber of magic the idea for his poem *Rose Mary* (1871), in which, in conformity with his model, the evil spirits of the beryl-stone decide the fates of the characters.   Without the agency of Scott, he inherited Geraldine the demon-woman, direct from Coleridge, creating from her his Lilith, who, a Jewish legend tells us, was the first wife of Adam.   In the poem *Eden Bower* Lilith begs the snake for its form, in order to be able to revenge herself on Adam and Eve :

> O my love, come nearer to Lilith !
> In thy sweet folds bind me and bend me,
> And let me feel the shape thou shalt lend me.

With this woman, around whose limbs the serpent coils, Rossetti has attempted to depict the demoniac and dangerous fascination of woman.   It was from him that the German painter Stuck obtained the idea for his picture " Sin."   William M. Rossetti : *The Collected Works of Dante Gabriel Rossetti*, preface, p. 28 (1897) : "Any writing about devils, spectres, or the supernatural generally, whether in poetry or in prose, had always a fascination for him ; at one time, say 1844, his supreme delight was the blood-curdling romance of Maturin, *Melmoth the Wanderer*."   Kurt Horn : *Zur Entstehungsgeschichte Dante Gabriel Rossettis Dichtungen*, pp. 79, 83 (1909).   Rossetti's relation to terror-romance is partly explained by the fact that Byron's travelling companion and doctor in 1816, the Anglo-Italian Polidori, was his maternal uncle ; Rossetti naturally heard accounts of him in his childhood and had read his book.   See next Note. Villiers de L'Isle-Adam, see the study by A. von Kraemer mentioned in Note 181.

(270) Themes like that of the Bleeding Nun, who comes at night to torment her victim, of Matilda, who entices her victim to perdition, and Geraldine, in certain respects approach the vampire-theme.   A vampire is a human being who leaves his grave to suck the blood of living humans, and hails originally, as

the name denotes, from Slav legend. Byron became acquainted with this idea in Greece, and gives a glimpse of it in *The Giaour*. He pondered over the idea, for he began a story on it at the same time that Mary Shelley began *Frankenstein*. It was left, however, unfinished, but was completed by Doctor Polidori, who published it in 1819. In it the chief character, Lord Ruthwen, is a vampire in full accordance with popular beliefs. The pallor and peculiar glance of the Byronic hero may also, in some subtle way, be an echo of the corpse-like features of the vampire. The theme ultimately develops in the direction that mysterious persons of both sexes, who encompass the ruin of persons of the opposite sex, are given a certain vampire-stamp. Spence, *op. cit.*; Scarborough, *op. cit.*, pp. 158–166, enumerates a number of later English works in which the vampire-theme appears. An echo of the theme is reflected in Stevenson's story *The Body-Snatcher*, and in his novel *The Master of Ballantrae*, where the demoniac Ballantrae dies and is buried, but on being exhumed opens his eyes; he had been given a narcotic. Hugo's *Han d'Islande* is also a member of the vampire-family.

(271) Otto Rank: *Das Inzest-Motiv in Dichtung und Sage. Grundzüge einer Psychologie des dichterischen Schaffens*. Leipzig and Vienna (1912). In psycho-analytical method Rank sets out from Sigismund Freud's assertion that the attachment in childhood of a son to his mother and a daughter to her father signifies an unconscious manifestation of sexual selection, and that the horror experienced by adults against such relations is a repulsion of the earlier feeling. On such grounds Rank then analyses, amongst other works, *Hamlet* and *Don Carlos*; as the fundamental motive in Schiller's dramatic production he sees the impulse of a boy's hate for his father. The negative attitude against this school of thought apparent in my work is directed towards Rank's book.

(272) John Tillotson (1630–94), Archbishop of Canterbury, a religious author. Walpole gives his explanation in the concluding remarks to *The Mysterious Mother*. He denies having remembered the story in the *Heptameron*. The preface mentioned earlier by Montague Summers deals widely with the appearance of the incest-theme in English literature.

(273) Goethe does indeed touch upon the theme, but in a delicate manner and with due consideration for the reader's feelings; he inserts it in the fate of the old harp-player, in this way diminishing the coarseness of the theme by increasing the distance, and by its use achieves his purpose, which was to cast a shimmer of tragedy and sorrow over the life-story of the old musician. Chateaubriand deals with erotic feelings between brother and sister in *René*.

(274) One cannot say an author actually uses the theme if he merely permits, as Scott does in *The Antiquary*, one of his characters to persuade another that he has unwittingly entered into incestuous relations.

(275) Ralph Milbanke, Earl of Lovelace: *Astarte. A Fragment of Truth concerning George Gordon Byron, Sixth Lord Byron. New Edition with many additional Letters*, by Mary, Countess of Lovelace (1921). On page 58 he says: " So Lady Byron wrote on her own responsibility, in conformity with the urgent advice of Wilmot and Mrs. Villiers, and announced what she knew. Augusta did not attempt to deny it, and in fact admitted everything in her letters of June, July, and August 1816."

These letters are published on pp. 213–215 (June 6th), 219–220 (June 22nd), 223–225 (July 3rd), 232–235 (July 15th and 16th), 241–244 (July 20th and 23rd), and 249–251 (Aug. 5th and 9th). But the reader who is not convinced beforehand of the guilt of Byron and Mrs. Leigh cannot find that these letters admit anything of weight. On the contrary, while reading them, the idea is suggested that Mrs. Leigh draws back in horror from such a subject, the expression of which she may have regarded as a manifestation of her sister-in-law's unhealthy state. Nor is there any convincing evidence in Byron's letter to Mrs. Leigh from Venice (pp. 81–83, March 17th, 1819), as its passionate tone need not denote more than the sense of orphanhood felt by a person longing for his own country and the only person he loves. With the exception of the German psycho-analysts, writers on literary history have on the whole declined to be convinced of Byron's guilt, at least, they do not state their positive opinions, and at the utmost quote only the most delicate passages in the above letters. This, for example, is what Emmanuel Rodocanachi does in his work on Byron (1924); compare also J. V. Lehtonen's article in the July number of *Valvoja-Aika* (Helsinki, 1924), entitled " Lordi Byronin jälkimaine " (Lord Byron's After-fame), in which he shows the accusation still to lack definite grounds. Others, as for instance, the Swede Per Hallström (*Levande dikt*, 1914, " Byron-figuren," pp. 95–123), regard the matter as fully settled. As a matter of fact there are no juridical proofs and any standpoint must be subjective : some wish to believe Byron guilty, others not. The tone of Lord Lovelace's book is inimical to Byron ; he entered upon his task with the intention of vindicating his grandmother's reputation, to which attaches the enigma, inexplicable despite all attempts at explanation, that although she accused her sister-in-law of this unnatural crime she nevertheless lived on friendly relations with her. This problem is not cleared up by the Astarte-book. See also G. Åman-Nilsson : *Lord Byron och det sekelgamla förtalet* (1915). " In Swedish literature and the Press voices have recently been audible announcing the judgment that the ' Byron-mystery ' was now definitely cleared up. . . . The studies I have pursued for long in the literature that has grown up around Lord Byron's name, have meanwhile awakened in me a totally opposite conception." This is probably intended as a rejoinder to the above-mentioned article by Hallström, which with its arrogant cocksureness and pharisaic judicial tone affects one unsympathetically.

The accusation of incest must also be viewed in the light of the extraordinary narrow-mindedness of the England of those days. Byron was not the only one similarly accused ; rumours of like nature circulated regarding Beckford. Suspicion of incest was in the air as it was in literature. *René* contains the same mystery as *Manfred*. The classicism then tottering towards its grave, the be-nighted conservatism of the past century, could not understand how such themes could be dealt with in literature, unless it was bitter remorse that was driving the authors to self-confession. The darkest mystery of romanticism was pro-jected on to the private lives of the authors.

(276) Care must be taken not to permit the admiration showered on the son to colour one's judgment regarding the relations between Shelley and his father. In his life Shelley shows that he neither understood nor tried to understand his father, but even in youth held with a peculiar tenacity to his theories and to their logical fulfilment—often indeed the mark and sign of a true poet—and showed himself to be entirely lacking in the ordinary art of living. It was for this reason that he became estranged from his father, who would have been, in the opinion of his age and surroundings, an unnatural kind of man if he had been able to give his undiluted blessing to all the proceedings of his son.

(277) " Liebesglühendes Suchen nach einem vollkommenen Seelischen, das seiner Einbildungskraft als Weib erscheint, ist, dunkler oder klarer bewusst, der Grundantrieb seines Dichtens." Otto Maurer : *Shelley und die Frauen*, p. 35 (1904). Reading the quotation from *Alastor* in the text, one is reminded of Gustaf Fröding's poem *En morgondröm*.

(278) The work was printed with this title, but Ollier, the publisher, began to be afraid of the impression the brother and sister relationship might make, and did not circulate it in this form. A few copies—how many is unknown—had already been sold. Symonds: *Shelley*, p. 97.

(279) At the end of the original preface to *Laon and Cythna* the following passage occurred, which was subsequently deleted (published in full in the Forman ed., I, pp. 85–98):

" In the personal conduct of my Hero and Heroine, there is one circumstance which was intended to startle the reader from the trance of ordinary life. It was my object to break through the crust of those outworn opinions on which established institutions depend. I have appealed, therefore, to the most universal of all feelings, and have endeavoured to strengthen the moral sense, by forbidding it to waste its energies in seeking to avoid actions which are only crimes of convention. It is because there is so great a multitude of artificial vices, that there are so few real virtues. Those feelings alone which are benevolent or malevolent, are essentially good or bad. The circumstance of which I speak was introduced, however, merely to accustom men to that charity and toleration which the exhibition of a practice widely differing from their own, has a tendency to promote. Nothing indeed can be more mischievous than many actions innocent in themselves, which might bring down upon individuals the bigoted contempt and rage of the multitude." Here Shelley has added the following foot-note : " The sentiments connected with and characteristic of this circumstance have no personal reference to the writer."

(280) Ernest Sutherland Bates : *A Study of Shelley's Drama The Cenci* (1908). "*The Cenci* is a work of art ; it is not coloured by my feelings nor obscured by my metaphysics " (p. 19). Bates does not go deeper into the incest-theme in his work. Wilhelm Wagner : *Shelley's " The Cenci."* *Analyse, Quellen und innerer Zusammenhang mit des Dichters Ideen* (1903). The author says, on page 10 : " Hier begegnete Shelley seinem Lieblingsthema, einem von ihm oft bekämpften Gegner, der Tyrannei. Er fand hier die Tyrannei in ihren verschiedensten Gestaltungen, die politische, die kirchliche und die häusliche Tyrannei." Of this I am not convinced.

(281) Southey first made the acquaintance of *Gebir* on his trip to Portugal, in the spring of 1800. At that time he knew nothing of its author. He had by then already published *Wat Tyler* and *Joan of Arc* and written *Madoc*, so that his pleasure at meeting in an unknown direction with a similar heroic-myth epic to his own is readily comprehended. Edward Dowden : *Southey*, p. 67.

(282) For example, Arthur Symons : *The Romantic Movement in English Poetry*, pp. 148–160 (1909). The views I have expressed regarding Southey's share in the bright hero-ideal of romanticism have not been perceived by me anywhere in Southey literature, and are given entirely on my own responsibility.

(283) The rectitude of Southey was his misfortune, as in a way it irritated people as much as Byron's " viciousness " did ; it still seems to have the power to irritate, to judge from the remark by Symons (*op. cit.*, p. 152) : " What renders Southey so irritating as a man, for all his virtues, is his conscious rectitude." Southey's interests were directed so exclusively to literature (a material impulse being the necessity to provide for both his own and Coleridge's family), that he had no time over for matters in which the disclosure of human frailties might have made him more " sympathetic " to posterity. He was a downright, straight-forward man, who despised in argument the use of such qualifications as " to my

belief," " in my view," etc. He accepted the post of Poet Laureate, but refused the baronetcy; Scott did the opposite. The former provided an income, the latter occasioned expense.

(284) Shelley has obviously been influenced by Southey, and in *The Revolt of Islam* he ranges himself beside Southey as a cultivator of the fantastical Oriental epic. He read *Thalaba* with admiration, a fact discernible in several respects in *The Revolt of Islam*. In the preface to this poem he says : " I have avoided, as I have said before, the imitation of any contemporary style. But there must be a resemblance, which does not depend on their own will, between all the writers of any particular age. They cannot escape from subjection to a common influence which arises out of an infinite combination of circumstances belonging to the times in which they live. . . . And this is an influence which neither the meanest scribbler nor the sublimest genius of any era can escape ; and which I have not attempted to escape." Shelley was to all appearances himself aware that his poem belonged to the species represented by Southey.

(285) An example is the greatly-respected beggar Edie Ochiltree in *The Antiquary*, whose family-tree can be said to begin in the Odyssey ; he belongs to the same branch as the Finnish poet Runeberg's "den aktade tiggaren Aron " (the respected beggar Aron). Important secondary characters of this description, beggars, servants—occasionally, as in *Quentin Durward*, a gipsy— appear in all of Scott's romances.

(286) *Caleb Williams* (ed. mentioned, p. 107). It is still a long step from this to the detective novel in its present significance, in the respect that the desire of Caleb Williams to trace his master's crime springs from a morbid curiosity, and lacks any further purpose. In the persons of Falkland and Williams the author presents to us a type with an unhealthy twist to its mind, characters in whom some such spiritual property as jealousy for their good name or curiosity have become dominating traits, even to the exclusion of a moral sense of duty.

(287) Lillie Deming Loshe : *The Early American Novel*, p. 30 (1907) : " It is from Godwin that Brown received the impulse to write the first American novels that possess any real merit." P. 32 : " They sought a plan to improve and secure human happiness and looked to William Godwin as the inspired high-priest of political wisdom." Godwin was in turn influenced by Brown's *Wieland*, as shown by *Mandeville's* preface.

(288) America had its own Lewis, a certain William Dunlap, who acquainted America about this time with German literature, in one way by translating Kotzebue's plays. (Loshe, *op. cit.*, p. 32.)

(289) The works by Brown which I have not been able to read are, according to Loshe (the account in Bjurman's study of Poe mentioned earlier is incomplete) : *Wieland, or the Transformation* (1798) ; *Arthur Mervyn* (1799) ; *Edgar Huntly or Memoir of a Sleep Walker* (1799) ; *Ormond, or the Secret Witness* (1799) : *Jane Talbot* (1801) ; *Clara Howard, or the Enthusiasm of Love* (1801). *Wieland* is built on the lines of *Caleb Williams ;* the hunted person is in this case a woman, Clara, and the pursuer, a mysterious alien named Carwin, who uses a gift for ventriloquism to bring about gruesome situations and deeds. Welbeck, the tyrant in *Arthur Mervyn*, is a common criminal, whose deportment and activities nevertheless awaken a fear-tinged respect ; the element of terror is founded on descriptions of yellow fever. *Ormond* is a tyrant, who, trusting to the strength of his personality, despises all laws and commandments, and wrapping himself in a cloak of mystery, inspires with his deeds and conflicting character a fearful horror ; the great idea of his life is to

found a new Utopian community somewhere beyond the sea. *Jane Talbot* and *Clara Howard* are not romances of terror; they are written in the form of letters; Loshe remarks concerning them (p. 49): " The author's intention was to make them women of a newer type, to let them speak and act and love for themselves, relying on their own judgment," which is Godwin's doctrine. In the preface to *Edgar Huntly* (Loshe, *op. cit.*, p. 69) Brown himself says: " It is the purpose of this work . . . to exhibit a series of adventures growing out of the conditions of our country, and connected with one of the most common and wonderful diseases of the human frame. One merit the author may at least claim: that of calling forth the passions and engaging the sympathies of the reader by means hitherto unemployed by preceding authors. Puerile superstitions and exploded manners, Gothic castles and chimeras, are the materials usually employed for this end. The incidents of Indian hostility and the perils of the western wilderness are far more suitable. . . . These, therefore, are, in part, the ingredients of this tale." Brown is, indeed, the founder of the Indian romance.

(290) Appeared in *The Dollar Newspaper*, in 1843.

(291) Friedrich Depken: *Charakter und Technik der Detektivnovelle*, (1914). On page 29 he notes Conan Doyle's dependence on Poe. See also Olaf Homén's work *I marginalen* (1917), essays on *Detektivlitteraturen* (p. 142), *Fader Brown* (p. 154), and *Rymmare och fasttagare* (p. 165). Voltaire's *Zadig* should be mentioned in connection with the detective story.

(292) Arno Schneider: *Die Entwickelung des Seeromans in England im* 17. *und* 18. *Jahrhundert* (1901). Deals for the most only with Defoe and Smollett. No mention of *Robinson Crusoe* (!) The indebtedness of the sea-story to terror-romanticism is ignored.

(293) Before Poe, the sea-story was raised to fame by the American author James Fenimore Cooper (1789–1851) with the works: *The Pilot* (1823), *The Red Rover* (1828), *The Water Witch* (1830), *The Two Admirals* (1842) and *Wing and Wing* (1842). Beside him may be placed Captain Marryat (1792–1848), whose whole production, more than 30 novels, deals with life and romance at sea. With *The Phantom Ship* (1839) he brought into literature the nautical counterpart to the *Wandering Jew*, namely, the *Flying Dutchman*. During the lifetime of these writers several other workers in the same field appeared. Later writers include W. H. G. Kingston (1814–80), Charles Kingsley (1819–75), Charles Reade (1814–84), R. L. Stevenson (1850–94), etc. (Karl Richter: *Die Entwicklung des Seeromans in England im* 19. *Jahrhundert*, 1906. Mentions Defoe and Smollett, but proceeds from these straight to Cooper, ignoring the intervening romantic literature of the sea.) C. N. Robinson's work *The British Tar in Fact and Fiction* (1909) gives a careful account of the English sailor in fiction and other literature.

(294) Examples: M. R. James: *The Mezzotint;* Mrs. Nesbit: *Grim Tales;* E. F. Benson: *The Judge's House;* Le Fanu: *An Account of Some Strange Disturbances in Aungier Street.*

(295) Compare with Note 270.

(296) Compare with Note 289.

(297) Mrs Shelley: *Frankenstein or the Modern Prometheus* (1817). (The edition I have used is undated, published by George Routledge & Sons.) In the preface the author describes the German ghost-literature which they had read together in Switzerland, and which gave the impulse to write *Frankenstein*: " There was the History of the Inconstant Lover, who, when he thought to

clasp the bride to whom he had pledged his vows, found himself in the arms of the pale ghost of her whom he had deserted," which points to a tale like to that of the Bleeding Nun. (See Note 143.) The monster created by Frankenstein suffered from the loneliness, horror and persecution to which his unnaturalness exposed him (p. 190) : "There was none among the myriads of men that existed who would pity and assist me ; and should I feel kindness towards my enemies ? No : from that moment I declared everlasting war against the species. . . ."

(298) Compare with Note 180. The school dealt with further includes Charlotte Smith (1749–1806) and her romances *Desmond* (1792, in the form of letters), *The Old Manor House* (1793) and *The Banished Man* (1794), all of which are concerned with revolutionary ideas ; Elizabeth Inchbald (1753–1821), revolutionary romances, *A Simple Story* (1791) and *Nature and Art* (1796); and Amelie Opie (1769–1853), the romance *Adeline Mowbray* (1804). After this, for historical reasons, stories imbued with a revolutionary spirit cease, until revived again by the publication in 1830 of Lytton's social romance *Paul Clifford*, in witness to the still living Godwin that his humanitarian ideas had not ceased to affect men. The social-humanitarian novel rose shortly afterwards to a new great significance in the works of Charles Dickens.

(299) Southey's social programme included in his old age, according to Dowden (*op. cit.*, p. 155) the following points : State schools ; the distribution of good literature at a cheap price ; well-organized emigration ; special attention to the children of the poor in large towns ; the training of Protestant nurses and the founding of hospitals ; the founding of savings banks ; the abolition of flogging in the Army and Navy, except in extreme cases ; the renewal of the Poor Laws ; alterations in the Game Laws ; alterations in the Criminal Laws by decreasing the range of the death penalty ; alterations in favour of the workers in the Factory Laws and the abolition of child labour ; the provision of public works in times of distress ; the supply of land to labourers. To judge from these, Southey's decried " conservatism " was no more than a return from the revolutionary fancies of youth to common sense, which directed its demands for reform to the worst sores in existing conditions ; in any deeper sense he cannot be said to have sinned against those ideals of his youth which rested on any material foundation. It is impossible to know what would have become of Byron's and Shelley's radicalism, if they had lived to Southey's age.

(300) In the winter of 1811–12. Southey said of him : " Here is a man at Keswick who acts upon me as my own ghost would do. He is just what I was in 1794." (Dowden, *op. cit.*, pp. 121–124.) Three years later Shelley sent *Alastor* to Southey. Landor and Southey did not become acquainted until 1808, when a lifelong friendship was begun. Southey made the acquaintance of Byron in 1813 : " Southey finding in Byron very much more to like than he had expected, and Byron being greatly struck by Southey's ' epic appearance.' " (*Ibid.*, p. 172.)

(301) Sidney Colvin : *Landor*, p. 94 (1909). Landor admired Shelley's poetry, but cared little for Wordsworth.

(302) Compare with Note 38. Oriental romanticism continued to flourish ; after *Vathek*, works belonging wholly or in part to this school include : Coleridge's *Kubla Khan* and *Lewti* ; Southey's *Thalaba*, *The Curse of Kehama* and *Roderick* ; Landor's *Gebir* and *Count Julian* ; Scott's *The Vision of Don Roderick*, *The Betrothed*, *The Talisman*, *Ivanhoe*, *Count Robert of Paris* and *The Surgeon's Daughter* ; Byron's Oriental poems ; Shelley's *The Revolt of Islam* ;

Lytton's youthful poem *Ismael ;* Washington Irving's *Alhambra ;* Disraeli's *Alroy,* etc.

(303) In her admirable depictment of life in a small town, *Cranford* (1853), Elizabeth Gaskell draws amusing parallels between Dr Johnson and Dickens, and shows how the style of the former had become antiquated—so completely, that the author achieves a humorous effect simply by quoting Dr Johnson. This kind of sacrilege had been begun earlier by Barrett, who mocks at the Doctor's style in the Xth letter of his heroine in such passages as :

" Debarred by my secluded life from copying the polished converse of high society, I have at least endeavoured to avoid the vulgar phraseology of low ; and to discuss the very weather with a sententious association of polysyllabic ratiocination."

(304) From this point of view the romantic literature of suspense and terror is suited to cast light on the so-called complement-theory of æsthetics. According to Dubos, art is the complement of life and a compensation for a lacking reality, in such fashion that it satisfies in a general sense the need for spiritual activity, which reality does not always sufficiently or variedly enough satisfy, and thus eliminates the feeling of emptiness or boredom induced by inactivity. This need for spiritual activity art satisfies by providing the opportunity for interesting, yet fundamentally dangerless emotional experiences. The emotional experiences provided by art are dangerless because of our knowledge that the exciting and as such essentially soul-stirring events and images of life which art expresses are not real, but only imitations of real events and phenomena. If we consider which is the first and most universally understood state of mind longed for in circumstances of monotony and boredom, we find it best expressed by the word " excitement." In its most primitive form, *i.e.,* as inspired by a fight or a competition, it can be experienced by all, even by those who are still totally irresponsive to the fascination of the finer and ennobled " excitement " provided, for instance, by art. Thus the type of literature which is chiefly concerned with this primitive excitement born of danger, battle, pursuit, the supernatural, fearful events and visions, and love, appeals to the widest circle, and provides it, in compensation for reality, with the kind of excitement it desires. Here is to be found the explanation of the invariably wide circulation of this primitive type of exciting literature, and the special favour accorded to it by the great public. The reason why the higher forms of art, in this case the literature that builds on the subtler phases of psychological excitement, do not enjoy such favour, is expressly the fact that it no longer satisfies the craving for primitive excitement. K. S. Laurila : *Estetiikan peruskysymyksiä* (" The Fundamental Questions of Æsthetics "), Helsinki, p. 398 (1918).

(305) " The Silence," appeared in *The Gentleman's Magazine* (1839).

(306) Helene Richter (*op. cit.,* pp. 160–172) classifies terror-romance as follows : (1) supernatural events ; (2) exciting events and mysterious, enigmatical characters, without the supernatural element. No mention is made of suggestivity as an essential condition of terror.

(307) In this light the whole terror-romantic movement resolves itself, as it were, into an experiment with Edmund Burke's theory, according to which everything calculated to awaken mental images of agony and danger, *i.e.,* everything in any way alarming, connected with alarming matters or giving the effect of fear, is a source of the sublime. When the alarming directly threatens us, it is purely agonizing, yet becomes pleasurable if it merely awakens mental images of agony and danger without really exposing us to danger. If we cast a

glance at terror-romanticism, and note how it attempts to awaken by suggestion the emotions of suspense, fear and terror, and how fully it has apprehended the stern beauty of mountainous landscape, and cultivated all the recognized aids to " sublimity," such as storms, lightning, mountain cataracts, the eagle, moonlight, mighty natures in the toils of spiritual conflict, etc., we must admit that we are faced here with a practical demonstration of Burke's theory of fear and sublimity, based ultimately on the theory of Dubos. Burke's *Philosophical Inquiry into the Origin of our Ideas on the Sublime and Beautiful* (see John Morley : *Burke*, p. 12, 1923) appeared in 1756, and is undoubtedly a theoretical study of the two main atmospheres at which the terror-romanticists aimed, namely, fear and sublimity, or " fear-awakening beauty." His book was known in literary circles, where it interpreted the ideas, then already in the air, of the dawning romanticism, and is probably not wholly free from implication in the experiments in fear and sublimity in which Walpole and the other terror-romanticists soon engaged. (Laurila, *op. cit.*, p. 145.)

(308) It is necessary for me to remark that I have used the word " tragic " as denoting in general an agitating fate or deep sorrow, without attempting to express any definite standpoint as regards the conception of what really is " tragic."